The Same Ax, Twice

The Same Ax, Twice

꧁ ꧂

RESTORATION AND RENEWAL

IN A THROWAWAY AGE

Howard Mansfield

University Press of New England / Hanover and London

University Press of New England, Hanover, NH 03755

© 2000 by Howard Mansfield

All rights reserved

Printed in the United States of America

5 4 3 2 1

CIP data appear at the end of the book

In memory of Ken Neumeyer

Daily, as we are daily
wed, we say the world
is a wedding for which,
as we are constantly
finding, the ceremony
has not yet been found.

—PHILIP BOOTH,
"Saying it"

Contents

Preface: The Fires of 1899

"On the evening of Saturday, August 26, New Hampshire from boundary to boundary was dotted with strange fires. Flame told flame, from hill to hill and from peak to peak, that the state's first Old Home Week was on. . . . paths of light were blazed in the midsummer darkness," a road of glimmering light, from the seacoast to the White Mountains, leading homeward.

"I wish that in the ear of every son and daughter of New Hampshire, in the summer days, might be heard whispered the persuasive words: Come back, come back!" said Governor Frank Rollins. "Do you not hear the call?" Come back to the old farm where you were born, the lilacs and the orchard. Come back and restore your village. The governor had created this homecoming holiday. He was working for the recovery of his state's abandoned farms and depleted villages. Those goals were long ago fulfilled, but one hundred years later we still celebrate Old Home Day.

Old Home Day is a holiday that is Victorian in its pomp and earnestness, and modern in its contradictions and longing. Today in so many ways, which I'll explore, we are looking, sometimes daily, for our own Old Home Day ceremony. We are looking for a homecoming, a peace that is within ourselves and our surroundings. There's a hunger for the solace of restoration, return, and mending.

This book looks at the impulse to preserve and restore, an impulse we share with the farmer who keeps changing the handle and head of an old ax in an attempt to have the same ax. This impulse leads us into the contradictions of time and history (and some of the folly and silliness).

The Same Ax, Twice is about the different axes we make—it's about restoration, original spirit, accidental invention, "the dumbfoundering abyss" between object and person, and the ways we whisper *come back, come back.*

I have been looking at preserved buildings, neighborhoods, ships, airplanes, engines, artifacts, farms, and entire ecosystems for more than twenty years. In the last years I have been wondering what makes a true restoration. As I neared my forties, I realized that the best restorations are truly restorative. The object has been repaired for all to admire, but a deeper, more important renewal has also taken place, a spirit has been revived.

For years I have sought out restorations that have this dual life. I have talked with the restorers of sawmills, steam engines, antique gas engines,

Wright Brothers aeroplanes, the U.S.S. *Constitution*, furniture, art, grave-stones, paper, daguerreotypes, roadside signs, and houses. I have visited more house museums than I care to admit: the Shakers, Elvis, Robert Frost, U. S. Grant, Charles Dickens, Teddy Roosevelt, Winston Churchill's war rooms, and in the former Yugoslavia, Josip Broz Tito, to name but a few. I have visited preserved rural landscapes, towns such as Old Deerfield, and the industrial ruins of railroad yards and factories. For reasons that will be clear later, I attended auction school, a star-gazing convention, New Age rituals, hang-gliding school, and a prehistoric fossil dig. I sought out the wise women and men I call Noahs, people who have some an-swers—not big plans and policies, but a touch for mending the world.

I have lived under the identity of an eighteenth-century frontier settler on a farm where we tried, with each word spoken and each chore, to re-create that era. With a savvy driver I recreated an old-time motor trip in a 1916 Cadillac on a road that had opened in 1914 and was much the same. I marched and "fought" with the Sixth Regiment New Hampshire Volun-teer Infantry at the 135th anniversary reenactment of Antietam. Some of these experiences are discussed in the essays that follow; others served as background, providing the right questions.

When men volunteered to fight in the Civil War, they sometimes said they were eager to see the elephant. The Civil War reenactment I attended was a vast undertaking to build that elephant. These activities and mu-seums are all exercises to build the elephant, to restore the past.

This is not, I realize, the standard roster for an inquiry into preservation. I was trying to discover examples of a living restoration, trying to go be-yond discussions about correct historic colors, materials, and techniques.

I look to the past for guidance, to find the graces we need to save. I want to be an importer. This is not nostalgia; I am not nostalgic. I am *not* look-ing for a way back. "From where will a renewal come to us, to us who have devastated the whole earthly globe?" asked Simone Weil. "Only from the past if we love it."

What I am looking for is the trick of having the same ax twice, for a res-toration that renews the spirit, for work that transforms the worker. We may talk of saving antique linens, species, or languages; but whatever we are intent on saving, when a restoration succeeds, we rescue ourselves.

The Same Ax, Twice follows *In the Memory House* (1993). In that book I said that memory was a defining characteristic of New England. I ex-plored the ways we choose our ancestors, choose the stories we tell.

In the opening essay, a tour of memory houses large and small, in the Ford Museum we come upon a test tube holding what may be Thomas

Edison's last breath. Henry Ford idolized Edison. Ford had moved Edison's lab, complete with soil, to his museum; he had originally named his museum for Edison. He had this man's works; did he have his spirit? When Edison was on his deathbed, Ford asked Edison's son to catch a last breath. We want to save the dying breath of yesterday.

We can't. So how can we find renewal from the past? The sealed test tube is the old way of preservation: Stop-time. We need a new way. We are after something alive.

In the Memory House began and ended with the image of a plugged spring, a symbol of modern times. *The Same Ax, Twice* is about how we work to keep the springs open. That is the real work of restoration.

This is a book of fire, breath, and water, three of the enemies of a restored object, three of the elements of life.

Hancock, New Hampshire   H.M.

THE SAME AX, TWICE

Back when I went to school, there was an administrator, a vice-president of something or other, who was given to rough-hewn statements, the kind of homilies that were meant to show his populist stuff. He was particularly set on tearing down the wooden houses on campus. They just weren't practical.

We said: They can be repaired. There are wooden houses that have stood for hundreds of years. And all buildings, no matter the material, need repair and renewal.

He said: I know a farmer who says he has had the same ax his whole life—he only changed the handle three times and the head two times. Does he have the same ax?

I did not have a good reply then. But in the twenty years since, talking with preservationists, carpenters, and architects, I have come to realize that so many controversies about saving and rebuilding are to be found in this one old joke. The debates about the restoration of the Parthenon or about the vinyl siding your neighbor has put on his 1789 cape come down to this one question: Do we have the same ax? I would answer with two riddles.

What's the oldest unchanged house in the world?

Hint: It is made of a common material and lasts only a season. It is a house of water.

Igloos, a form unchanged for 50,000 years, are said to be the oldest shelter known. Each single igloo was a perishable item, but represented a tradition that lived until recently. One winter's igloo was a song in a performance lasting thousands of years. The Inuit wouldn't try to maintain an Inuit Colonial Williamsburg, a freezer-land world of ancient igloos. It would be like having a museum of silent pianos, instead of a music school.

Another riddle: The most rebuilt wooden structures in the world are the most unchanged.

The Ise Shrine in Japan has been rebuilt almost every twenty years since the year 690 A.D. The Outer (Geku) and Inner (Naiku) and the fourteen affiliated shrines were rebuilt for the sixty-first time in 1993.

The Shinto shrine to the goddess of the sun is made of wood. The Japanese and Chinese conserve by copying and rebuilding. This is, after all, how the body maintains itself, replacing cells. We are, and are not, the same person we were only a year ago. In the West we are used to monuments of stone, the pyramids standing against time. To the Japanese, Ise is 1,300 years old. It is the same ax, rebuilt sixty-one times. Not to the keepers of the lists: Ise is not ancient enough to be on UNESCO's list of World Heritage Sites.

Completely rebuilding a shrine was once the common practice. Ise is the only shrine to carry the tradition forward. The Imbe priests begin the rebuilding with prayers to the mountains to protect the workers who are cutting the timber for the new shrine.

Both the Outer and Inner shrines are divided into eastern and western sectors. The new shrine is built in one sector, before the old shrine, in the other sector, is disassembled. The heart pillar is left standing, dressed with a sacred evergreen tree and protected by a little house. The new shrine has as its companion an empty white-graveled space. The bright new wood of the rebuilt shrine and the crisp thatched roof begin to dull in the sun, marking the time until the next rebuilding.

There have been some changes in 1,300 years. Ise is not an exact replica. Back in 690, after the Imperial Works Bureau took over the shrine building from the Imbe priests, they added some gold-colored fittings, and enlarged the Outer shrine. In the middle ages there was war in the Japanese islands, and for more than 120 years the shrine was a neglected ruin. When the rebuilding began after this upheaval, there were changes in the location of some shrine buildings, in the alignment of the roof and doors, and in the joinery. Much later, added ornamentation, a Victorian opulence, snuck in during the Meiji era (1868–1912), and has since been removed. And over the years the craftsmen have given up many specialized tools, as the taste changed from a rougher look to a refined finish.

But for an object that has passed through thousands of hands, in a society as changed as Japan's, this is as pure as it may get. Ise, the scholars say, maintains the original "rigid distinction between sacred and profane space within the shrine precinct and the elaborately styled and refined features of each shrine sanctuary."

So, does that farmer have the same ax? Yes. His ax is an igloo, and a Shinto shrine. He possesses the same ax even more than a neighboring farmer who may have never repaired his own ax. To remake a thing correctly is to discover its essence.

A tool has a double life. It exists in the physical sense, all metal and wood, and it lives in the heart and the mind. Without these two lives, the tool dies. The farmer who restored his ax has a truer sense of that ax. He has the history of ax building in his hands. Museums are filled with cases of tools that no one knows how to use anymore. A repaired ax is a living tradition.

We have our own Ise Shrine, our igloo, a U.S. government-sized farmer's ax, the U.S.S. *Constitution,* Old Ironsides, the oldest commissioned warship afloat in the world.

The *Constitution* saw its last battle in 1815, but it is still commissioned on the active roster, a part of our national defense. A duty crew sleeps on board each night. The ship has survived some close calls with oblivion— being saved one time when a poem, "Old Ironsides" by Oliver Wendell Holmes, Sr., rallied the public, and another time with pennies collected from the nation's school children. In 1905 the Navy had recommended using the decaying hull for target practice. In the early 1920s the ship leaked so badly the hull had to be pumped out by a tug each morning.

Saving a wooden ship is a job that's never finished. The *Constitution* has been rebuilt and repaired in 1833, 1858, 1871–77, 1906, 1927–30, 1953, 1963–65, 1973–75, and the most recent and most extensive restoration, 1992–96. (At the same time that the Ise Shrine was rebuilding.)

Anywhere from 10 to 20 percent of Old Ironsides (depending on who you talk to) is original. The farther down you go, the older the wood is: dating from 1851 below the waterline. The keel is original. "Salt water is not an enemy of the ship. Fresh water is what rots the ship," says ship restorer Ralph McCutcheon. A ship is like an old house without a roof.

How could this be the same ax? Old Ironsides is more like a wooden garden. This an ancient philosophical question. But then historic preservation is old-time philosophy. Any time you open a wall, try to match a historic color, any time you stop to ask, "Now just what is it that we are looking at?," you are back there with the ancients questioning reality and its perception. The ancient Athenians also had a ship they maintained, one that was said to have belonged to the great Theseus.

Theseus, a hero whose story evolved from a wildman adventurer to a civic founder, was the "most famous and revered of all the heroes of ancient Athens," says Anne G. Ward in *The Quest for Theseus.* "To the classical Athenians he was an immediate and real figure." Theseus slew the Minotaur in the Labyrinth, defeated the Centaurs, and united Athens as one city-state. His legend was a part of daily life: Theseus was celebrated on pottery, in sculpture, painting, poetry, and in several shrines, including his ship. Each year, to commemorate Theseus's journey, the Athenians sailed his ship on a sacred mission to Delos. During that time, the city was kept pure. This was the voyage that delayed Socrates' execution.

"The ship wherein Theseus and the youth of Athens returned had thirty oars, and was preserved by the Athenians down even to the time of Deme- trius Phalereus, [280 B.C.]," Plutarch notes, "for they took away the old planks as they decayed, putting new and stronger timber in their place, in- somuch that this ship became a standing example among the philosophers . . . one side holding that the ship remained the same, and the other con- tending that it was not the same."

If another entire ship were made of the discarded planks, this debate continued, then some claimed there would be two identical, authentic ships. ("Which is absurd," said Thomas Hobbes.)

We tend to settle this question for ourselves pragmatically by having it both ways—it is and is not the same ship—and we get on with the other demands of life, such as food, shelter, and status.

Consider "the most famous basketball floor in the world—the Boston Garden Parquet" (as appraised by Red Auerbach). Like any sacred object, mythical powers have been attributed to the floor: hidden dead spots that stop other teams in mid-dribble. First set down in 1946, most of the boards have been replaced, and yet care was taken to move this floor to the Celtic's new arena. An Associated Press report is captive, in short space, to both sides of the ancient ship debate. Headline: "New house, same old parquet." Last sentence: "Although the same floor has been used for 48 years, most of the original structure has probably been replaced."

When I visit the U.S.S. *Constitution*, the ship, undefeated in battle, looks as if it has been seized by the crew of *This Old House*. Squeezed into the pinched quarters of the low-ceilinged decks is a modern construction site: metal scaffolding, yellow "caution" tape, work lights, workers in hard-hats hammering, sawing. Up toward the bow a radio is playing a wailing guitar riff from some early 1970s rock hit.

A sailor leads a tour group through the undressed decks. The sailor is wearing a Navy uniform from 1812: a short, double-breasted matador-like jacket with wide lapels, and a cowboy-like hat with a streamer behind. He is talking about shipboard life in 1800—a ship jammed with 450 men (room for only half to sleep at one time), livestock, cannons. But much is missing on his tour, such as the entire captain's quarters, and all 54 cannons, which lie bedded in a shed up the dock, like a small herd of iron cattle.

A drill whines as it bites into some dense live oak. Behind the small tour group several men are guiding a new plank in through the cargo hatch, calling and signaling to the crane high overhead.

Some visitors go away disappointed, sorry that the museum has been disrupted. But far from being an interruption, this restoration is the life of the ship. The Navy's oldest commissioned warship is kept alive with a mix of ancient skills, power tools, and materials both traditional and updated. The *Constitution* is not a ship in a bottle.

Before this restoration began, drawings of a sister ship, the *President*, were discovered in British archives. The British had captured the *President* in the War of 1812, and studied its impressive construction. The Navy learned that the *Constitution*, through its many rebuildings and near destruction, had lost some important structural bracing.

Massive braces are being replaced to fight "hogging," the natural buoyancy that pushes up the middle of the ship, threatening, over time, to break the keel. The *Constitution* had hogged more than 13 inches. To lessen the hogging, for more than fifty years the ship has been without its seven-ton rudder. The ship is receiving a rudder, new masts, new rigging, and is being reclad below the waterline with sixteen tons of copper, supplied by the original contractor, Paul Revere's old company.

"It's a very unusual opportunity," says Ralph McCutcheon, proud to be one of forty on the restoration crew, the same number that worked on the other two major restorations this century. "Within the last hundred years that's only one hundred and twenty people hired to do this work. That's a select group. You try to do the best you physically can. You try. You're creating longevity for the ship. It's going to be two hundred years old and you want to make damn well sure its going to last to three hundred years."

Inside the repair and maintenance shop, up in the rigging loft, three men are carefully tailoring 27 miles of line. This is the first new, complete rig since 1927. Thick black ropes lie all over the floor. There is the strong smell of pine tar. Frank Brackett, age seventy-three, whose father was a rigger, works at a rigging vise that can be seen in use in a photo from 1890.

"Rigging hasn't changed in five hundred years," says Dave Mullin, a rigger expert in the old ways. The tools are the same—marlin spikes and serving mallets—the lines, though, are a stronger, lighter synthetic.

Mullin works from old sources. He uses the notebooks of the *Constitution*'s designer, Joshua Humphreys, a ship survey done after the last battle in 1815, and the old rigging manuals of the era. Mullin picks up tricks where he can find them, like the technique of stacking the rigging on the mast. How do you do it? In England he found a 1905 book. Someone had devised a formula. The book was in a glass case. He found the curator and got him to open the case and turn the page. He wrote down the formula. "Like everything else in rigging, you find something like that, you write it down, you draw it up and you keep it." Other tricks he has learned from the old riggers. He used to skip school and hang out at the Navy yard. "Ever since I was a kid in school I wanted to do this," Mullin says.

He is caught up in the life of this ship. On his own time, he has made a model of an anti-boarding rifle, and a steel and leather boarding cap (topped with bear skin—in this case shoeblacked sheep skin).

"Most people will never see the work we do—it's up in the air. It doesn't matter. The guys we want to impress are the ones taking it apart twenty years from now," Mullin says, expressing the spirit of a good restoration. This is not work to fill a government contract, or even to entertain or educate the public. This is done to rebuild the ship, certainly, but much shorter routes are available. This is work for the joy of doing one thing exactly right, as it used to be done. The greatest restoration at this site is not the *Constitution*, but the art of wooden ships.

Mullin looks out the window at the ship sitting in dry dock, surrounded by scaffolding. The *Constitution* was the first ship to use this dry-dock, back in 1833. Behind him Brackett and Bobby Fall patiently rig the lines.

"Her keel was laid two hundred years ago this year, so in essence she would be building. I was thinking about it the other day," he says. "The keel was laid in 1794. She was launched in 1797. The funny thing is we are two hundred years and a quarter mile away."

Two hundred years later they are still building the same ship.

The *Constitution* had not sailed in 116 years. No ship this old, of any type, still sails. After the 1927–30 rebuilding, *Old Ironsides* made a "thank you cruise." The ship was towed, without sails, from Bar Harbor, through the Panama Canal, to Seattle. More than four million turned out to see the ship. Since then the ship has been confined to Boston Harbor. Once a year, on July 4th, the rudderless *Old Ironsides* was pulled out of the dock by a tugboat like some fabulous invalid, and turned around to weather evenly.

On the 200th anniversary of the ship's launch, July 21, 1997, a gray drizzly day, *Old Ironsides* sailed downwind for five and a half miles at almost four knots. Six new sails were set, battle configuration in its forty-four victories. (About one-third of the possible sail area.) The U.S. Navy was a little short on experience in sailing a three-masted frigate. On the first day of practice, it took three hours to set the sails. ("Brace all yards square to the wind!") By the voyage, it took ten minutes.

Four knots is not too fast, but it's fast enough to outsail those ancient philosophical questions. "The ship is alive," said Boatswain's Mate First Class John Hutchinson. "She's talking to us. She's talking," said the head of the volunteer Marine detachment, Bill Moss.

"The ship is kind of spiritual," said Boatswain's Mate Chief Joseph Wilson, captain of the deck. "Why is this ship still around? Why is the document that the ship is named after still around?"

"To sail her was what the hearts and minds of the American people wanted," said Commander Michael Beck, the ship's sixty-fourth commanding officer. "All those things that people talk about—courage, commitment, honor—they're all embodied in the ship's sailing."

The *Constitution*'s victories in the War of 1812 stunned the British, as well as the Americans. "It is not merely that an English frigate has been taken," said *The Times* of London, "but that it has been taken by a new enemy, an enemy unaccustomed to such triumphs, and likely to be rendered insolent and confident by them."

"We went into that war as Carolinians, Virginians, and Bay Staters," says Tyrone G. Martin, naval historian. "We came out of it Americans, largely because of this ship."

Nine former commanding officers were on board for the sail. When the "old man's club" meets for its annual dinners, a place is set for Captain Isaac Hull, who gave the U.S. Navy its first great victory at sea.

A descendant of the ship's designer was also on board. Joshua Humphreys created a stronger, faster hull. He had one advantage: live oak from the south, which is almost 40 percent denser than other oak and rot resistant. The live oak and white oak hull, two feet thick at mid-deck, gave the ship the "iron sides" to stop cannon balls. Lying next to the drydock where the ship was restored are a few dozen live oak tree trunks. They are being dried for the *Constitution*'s next major restoration in 2010 or 2015.

Igloos, the Ise Shrine, *Old Ironsides*—these are, admittedly, the purest examples. We don't always get the same ax. The ax is changed by joyful invention and stubborn blindness. The blade may be duller, the handle awkward. Things are changed in their use. Sometimes they are worn into a new shape; sometimes they become their opposites. Sometimes it is the same ax—a living heritage, and sometimes it is just the best ax at hand, a mix of the old and the new.

A refinement: It is not the same igloo, not the same ax, but the life of the ax, igloo, temple, or ship that continues.

Endeavors guided by the spirit have a double life. Restored tools, houses, farms, nature sanctuaries, telescopes to observe the night sky, are important in themselves, and in the acts of preservation and loving attention they call forth.

In remaking an ax, in restoring a house, we carry the fire of the original spirit. We commit anew, plant, put our hands to touch the work of a craftsman hundreds of years gone, and then once feeling that work, pick it up again. And therein lie renewal and hope.

In America we tend to the crash program—the discovery of impending disaster, the urgent fund-raising appeal, the high-tech application. The scaffolding comes down to reveal a factory-fresh, new-old building: epoxy-injected, scoured, and laced with steel.

We focus too often on the finished object, not on the craft to restore it. These things exist for us to revive. They call us back to a proper relationship with the world, to our home place. We don't have village gods, but we need ways to feel the spirit of a place. Restoration is our version of making an offering, getting closer to the animating spirits of wood, brick, mud. This the closest thing we have to a pilgrimage—the kind where you bow down and pray at each step.

Each time we renew the meetinghouse steeple, replant a forest, heal an injured animal, teach someone to read, each time we do this we are restoring the life, the best in us, as well. Mending the world, rebuilding it daily, we discover our better angels. We are on the side of life.

True living preservation is the baton passed, the handing off of skills, beliefs, and love. It is not mummification, it is not stop-time.

Good preservation is a life preserver thrown to us in a shipwreck. Good preservation keeps us in touch with the graces of this life. It's bricks and mortar, yes. It's arguments about true colors and authenticity and representation. But true preservation is like the hand that shelters a fire from the wind. It protects the spark of life.

You can't save the dying breath of yesterday. But you can keep breathing—keep the love, work, and ideas alive. People rummaging through the myths of other religions, and books on the soul, are looking for breathing lessons.

As for that college administrator, he went on bulldozing and leveling houses. He only understood the lessons of commodities in a throw-away age. He would have long ago thrown away that ax for a chainsaw. With new things at his touch always, he would have lacked renewal.

Unearthing the Mammoth

❧ ❧

I. The Buried Life

The mammoths have been opened to daylight. Exposed, they are only more mysterious. Why were there only males? How many could there be? From where we stood above the pit, they looked as if they were in a free fall. We were peering back thousands of years.

A chance encounter had brought them to view. At a construction site in the Black Hills of South Dakota, George Hanson was bulldozing a hill for a housing development when he struck some bones. His son Dan, who was taking a college geology course, visited, and stubbed his toe on a mammoth tooth. They summoned the experts: "Please come to Hot Springs. We think we have mammoths!"

If the bulldozer scrape had gone another way, the secret might have remained buried. People would be eating dinner and watching television sitcoms, while huge mammoths slept beneath them.

The houses were canceled. The land was sold at cost to a nonprofit group. After the first summer's dig, a dozen mammoths had been found, including a complete skull with tusks and teeth. After a few years, a big building sheltered the discovery. You can watch the dig as it takes place.

There may be a hundred mammoths. Less than half the site has been excavated. Hanson's bulldozer had uncovered the world's largest known "primary accumulation" of mammoth fossils, animals that lie where they died.

Some 26,000 years ago this was a pond fed by a warm spring, a natural draw for animals. Sediment at the spring's bottom built up during the course of 300 to 700 years, and like a slow-rising bread, the pit became a hill.

The pond attracted young bachelor mammoths out on their own. There are no fossils of calves, and very few old mammoths. An illustration in Mammoth Site's brochure shows rather jaunty mammoths painted in the style seen only in natural history dioramas and textbooks. (Why do artists think that the sky in the Pleistocene era was a smudgy orange?)

They died of laziness, an adolescent's liking for short cuts, theorizes Larry D. Agenbroad, director of the site. During the long winters, rather than scrape off deep, heavy snow with their tusks, they were drawn to the green plants growing at the edge of the warm spring. Easy pickings—except that when their feet hit the wet shale they lost their footing and fell in. They could not pull themselves out: The side walls were too steep or overhanging. They were doomed to be—26,000 years later—a roadside "AAA Star Attraction," "An Educational Experience for the Entire Family!" A moment's poor judgment forever on display. Hot Springs, South Dakota, was a hell for foolish mammoths.

They are primarily Colombian mammoths, relatives of the woolly mammoths usually found farther north. Some stood 12 feet tall at the shoulder and weighed eight tons. The spring also claimed a rare, extinct, giant short-faced bear, a camel, a llama, shrub oxen, and various carnivores, rodents, antelopes, raptors, amphibians, minnows, clams, and snails.

The most complete mammoth was found in the alley (the town's right-of-way) and named "Napoleon Bone-apart." The second most complete mammoth was named "Murray." (These names are a further indignity for the foolish.)

We stand and look in the manner that tourists regard canyons and memorials, wonders natural and man-made, all presented for our viewing with subtitles like a foreign film. We scan it for superlatives. Details are lost. We get the postcard, the gee whiz! wow! of it. Numbers impress: the largest, deepest, oldest, most, costliest, etc.

The mammoths resist numbers. They are as mysterious as the night sky. We want the ground to be solid, unmoving. This is why we have trouble with those National Park Service signs, which deliver 400 million years of geological history in four sentences. Seas, forests, deserts; advance, retreat, dance, do-si-do. It produces vertigo.

People read the signs, squint out at some gorge or outcropping, take a picture and leave. They have 300 miles to go. Sixty-five miles an hour—that's the distance and time we understand.

Once when my wife and I were standing at the rim of the Grand Canyon, a man next to us read the sign, looked out, and demanded of us: *What happened here? What caused this?* He sounded like an insurance claims adjuster in a hurry. Blame must be assessed and corrective measures taken.

We told him what we had learned from the park rangers—the river rose and the land fell, or the land rose and the river lay down deeper. There were two main theories. It was unconvincing in the retelling. He regarded this as crazy talk. At heart we believe in an unchanging, rock-solid earth. We want to be the actor, not the acted upon. No one likes being upstaged by the ground beneath your feet.

We might as well have told him that everything in the universe was racing away from everything else in the universe pell-mell; distances were growing, some galaxies rushing from us at hundreds of miles a second, and he'd better get driving.

Light from the center of our galaxy, the Milky Way, takes 28,000 years to reach us. Mammoths, wise and foolish, lived where we stood gawking, 26,000 years ago. At the mammoth pit, we are stargazing. We are looking back thousands of years. These mammoth bones are the constellations of a vanished world. There's the mammoth Napoleon, and there's Murray, there's a skull, and a leg and a tooth. Most have been found in a band at the edge. On the map of the dig, the pattern looks like the Milky Way.

II. Bare Bones

We are standing in Abbott Lowell Cummings' dream house. The house is stripped bare: interior walls removed, framing exposed. There is no furniture or any other niceties. This is a house opened for study, a surprising place. Outside, the house looks like a trim citizen of 1665 or 1687. Inside, these houses are cold and barn-like, a little disheveled, as if the carpenters had inexplicably dropped their work one day three hundred years ago. You are inside the whale here, standing amid the exposed posts and beams, boards, and bits of plaster.

"Some of these houses are bit raunchy. I hope you don't have to be brought back to the bus and revived," Cummings, a pioneer of study houses, tells a touring group of preservationists. In another era, he might have been described as "dapper" in his pin-striped pants with cuffs, his gray hair under a flat cap. He has spent a lifetime in these study houses. He wrote his master's thesis in 1946 on the early houses of Colonial Massachusetts, at a time when there was little published. He was hired by the Society for the Preservation of New England Antiquities in 1955, and later taught at Yale. Now retired, he teaches a course or two at Boston University. It is next to impossible to get into his classes.

Study houses are an antiquarian's ideal. The walls are always open, and the debate can continue about how the house was built and later changed. The houses avoid the restoration hazards of having to make your best guess, fixing this too much and that not enough. At houses undergoing serious restoration, the restorers are often reluctant to close the walls, ending the exploration. After a few hours in these study houses, one is disappointed by mere museum houses. They are too demure, hiding their secrets in the walls.

We are visiting three of the antiquity society's houses with Cummings, houses "so critically important we have in effect lowered a glass bell jar over them," he says.

A tour with Abbott Lowell Cummings is a bravura performance, an opera aria, a day-long song of the intricacies of First Period architecture, the first houses built in New England as the carpenters of the Old World, who had packed their tools for the journey, encountered the abundance of the New World's forests. Here the post-medieval buildings of England waded ashore and began their journey to Levittown.

Cummings is a fluid, fast talker, the freshness of discovery in his voice. He wastes few words; his attention is to the text at hand—clapboards, purlins, summer beams, paint chips. He wants you to see what he sees. He can talk for hours about one wall.

He has looked and looked at these houses for decades, written about them, searched England for antecedents, and yet he is ready to entertain any novice conjecture about how a beam was cut, or why a wall was moved. He is quick to say what he doesn't know, and how he's been wrong, misreading a house. "It's a *poozle*," he jokes.

The study house shows the house marching backward, walls off, frame revealed, marching back to the craftsman's hand, sketches, ideas, and to the trees themselves: how the tree grew, when it was felled, by which blade. Dendronchronology they call it. Proof that our houses are tree houses.

The study houses are archeological digs, mammoth sites. They share the excitement of many digs—so much mystery, so near at hand.

His texts today are "Gedney" and "Boardman," as well as the Coffin house. A bus load of us have set out from a national preservation conference. We arrive first at the Boardman house in Saugus, Massachusetts. The house was built by a successful joiner in 1687, and stayed in the same family until 1911, remaining remarkably unchanged. The land has changed. The house was built on a 300-acre farm, adjoining other large farms. Early in this century, the land was chopped into lots for small bungalows. Today the Boardman house has too much presence for its small suburban plot, like an aged leading man forced to take a small role in a bad movie. Eccentricity is the only role offered, but eccentricity is a kind of dissent.

This house tells a story of changing habits, says Cummings. When the house was nine years old, in 1696, William Boardman dramatically reordered his household. He built a "lean-to" across the back of the house, added a fireplace, and moved the cooking out of the "hall," the house's principal room. "Stop and think what that meant," Cummings says. A separate room for cooking was a break with the medieval past. William Boardman was up to date with the urbane trendsetters miles away down in Boston.

His move was well documented by "the terribly exciting thing of the 1696 inventory," Cummings says. William died at age thirty-eight, shortly after building the lean-to, and as was the practice, a room-by-room inventory was taken, a snapshot of his material world. ("2 Feather-beds and bedsteads with all the furniture belonging to them that stand *in the Parlour*. . . . 2 Iron pots. 2 Kettles. 2 tramels . . . a chafingdish & some old iron.")

Cummings leads us through the house. We look into a little room off the kitchen, near the hearth. In the nineteenth century they called rooms like this "borning rooms." The Colonial Revival fastened on to this because of half-remembered legends, he says. There is evidence that the warm chamber was used for births, but it's nonsense that the room was kept shut up exclusively. Indeed, older relatives would sleep there.

Cummings casually implodes myths. He doesn't make a big show of it. Rather, he is like a bomb squad technician who has been trained by English butlers. He quietly removes a dearly held myth, and far off, there is a muffled *thump*. (No, the average colonial settler did not build his house. "Nothing could be further from the truth." From the start there were carpenters and joiners.)

We examine the windows, which are not the original medieval-looking ones. He tells us about a letter from a man who remembered the last Boardman sisters. He played in the house as a child, and recalled a pile of iron casements with leaded glass in the attic. Everyone gasps *oh!*, involuntarily, as if they had come within one number of winning the lottery. The windows didn't survive until 1914, he concludes.

Where the old casement joined the wall, there's a bump. "But the question is: how were they tied in?" Cummings asks. "You have to do a lot of musing when you work with seventeenth-century houses." William Sumner Appleton, the founder of the antiquity society, and the country's first full-time preservationist, once pulled something out of a house, had his doubts, and rescued it from the dump that night, he tells us.

Upstairs he leads us to the hall chamber. "This is what I call the holy of holies. You are standing in 1687 and also in 1914." In more than two hundred years, no one ever got around to plastering the back wall. The room is not finished off. The back wall shows the brick and clay infill "nogging" between the timbers, as if an ancient adobe dwelling was hiding in the walls. There are seventeenth-century hinges on the door and early lead-gray paint. The floor is worn and pitted, and is patched with pieces of metal. "It's just unimaginable what Appleton must have thought when he came up here," he says as if thinking aloud. One of his students whispers to another, "Thanksgiving Day he spent *all day* in this room!"

After a tour of the attic, we're back on the bus heading toward the Gedney house in Salem. Eleazer Gedney was a shipwright who chose a half-acre lot, which in 1664, met the water on two sides. He wanted a "build-place" for his boats. The house was expertly crafted by John Turner, who also built the House of Seven Gables. (Another myth imploded: Shipwrights didn't build houses.)

The house was remodeled several times over the centuries. When the antiquity society came upon it in 1963, it was being gutted for apartments. Only one thin wall was left inside. Even the chimney had been knocked down.

The house stood with its structural secrets exposed. "We wouldn't have done it," says Cummings. But they used the destruction as an opportunity and left the house in its distressed state. Some necessary structural repairs were tagged a "Gedney green," a clue to the "modern orthopedic assistance which this house needed desperately."

He calls the Gedney a "seventeenth century vocabulary house. It has one of everything in it." It is really two study houses: a seventeenth-century front and an eighteenth-century lean-to, which has been left for the next generation to study. Others on this tour remember being here twenty years earlier, poking around with flashlights in the freezing cold.

The Gedney house survived, in part, because it was over built. The carpenters from the West of England built lavishly with the plentiful wood they found here, while the East Anglia builders in the New World continued to build conservatively, he says. The old houses are eight times stronger than they needed to be.

But look here, says Cummings standing in the hall, a beam has been cut through right at a critical point. If a wall wasn't there, it would have caved in. Why did they do this? Were they showing off? he asks.

In the next room he presents a history that is almost geological. He used to leave students in here for fifteen minutes and come back to ask them what had happened. Why did the ceiling whitewash end inches from the wall?

First the summer beam was removed to raise the ceiling. Then the wall was moved further out. The unpainted part of the ceiling was once an outside overhang.

Upstairs we come to another of Cummings' rooms for musing. "This is a room I often think people should be required to take off their shoes," he says, another holy place. "We have here some of the first color evidence that has survived from seventeenth-century New England."

The first time he went through the house, he thought the room was just whitewashed. But later he saw traces of a green that was painted on the bottom joists in 1664. It is an "optical green," a mixture of blue and yellow.

Then about 1680, the central post and summer beam were painted with lamp black to contrast with other parts of the white-painted frame. Early in the eighteenth century, the third paint job brightened the room. Red ochre on the beam; everything else in yellow. "You can imagine what a colorful room this was."

By the mid-eighteenth century the curtain came down on this color show. A lath-and-plaster ceiling was built, along with a casing for the beams and paneling, hiding it for the next 100 years.

Outside, Cummings points to the half-house cape on the same lot. "Used to be a widower who lived there. The whole hall was covered in rotogravure photos of the saints, all the way back, and then facing it was a wall of girly pictures," he says and leaves at that. Another puzzle house.

By the time we reach the Coffin house in Newbury, Massachusetts, we are dragging. Cummings has worn us down. It is like listening to good poetry; close attention is tiring after a while. Cummings is unruffled; students in their early twenties are exhausted.

The Coffin house was occupied by the family from 1650 until the antiquity society acquired it in 1929. When the front house was added in 1770, it was built on an angle to the back house. "Why? This is the big question with this house," he says. There are many questions. "Short of tearing this house down, we're just going to go on guessing about it."

We look at rooms and finishes that are miraculous survivals, and we are relieved of another myth when a student asks about a peg hole in a beam. What was it for? "There are carpenter's mistakes," Cummings says. "The American myth about seventeenth- and eighteenth-century craftsmen is that they could do no wrong."

On the lawn outside, the students gather around him. "The answers aren't all in yet," he says of a lifetime's work. "It's a poozle."

Study houses are paradoxes: preserving a house by not preserving it. The house exists in all its contradictions. No one has attempted any resolution. The house has not been dressed up as 1676 or 1870 or any one year or period. Rather, the house speaks in the mingled, confusing voices of years of habitation—changes, additions, ceilings raised, walls moved, doors nailed shut and opened again. Rooms painted green, then black, then red and yellow.

The house is more like a natural landscape. Standing before an undressed wall, one is reminded of the Grand Canyon or the Badlands. You are looking at layers of rock, by turns red, tan, and yellow, but you are really looking at time itself.

The scale is smaller in the study houses—three hundred years—but you are looking at time. Seven generations of life represented by a notch on a girt, a paint chip on a summer beam, the way the head of the adze met the wood one winter day in 1664.

This is a house that is not a memorial to a hero, a great patriot or president; it is not an interior that tells of a particular epoch of wealth and parties. Time is the hero in this house. Generations of life, children born, elderly senile parents rocked in adult cradles.

This house isn't about the beams and girts and purlins. This isn't just a house undressed until it is a barn. Life flowed through here and like a glacier left its marks upon wood and plaster.

In Levittown, where more than 17,000 houses were built starting in 1947, a landmark commission is looking for a few unchanged houses. They want to find a study house. They have not found one without some alterations. The modest houses have been remodeled, remuddled, expanded, rooms, dormers added. A few of the original "Cape Cods" are now "Contemporary Victorians."

"It's unrecognizable," the builder William J. Levitt said in 1974. "It's so beautiful. It's a collection of very distinctly individualistic homes with a great many people who are very proud."

Daphne Rus, who has lived in Levittown since 1959, has watched the arrival of many new, young homeowners. "They come in here and everywhere you look, people are still changing their houses. It never stops." All the trips to Home Depot, the new carpeting, the vinyl siding, skylights, the dumpster out front packed with crumbled sheetrock and old plumbing. It's the Gedney and Boardman houses thousands of times over. We dwell in puzzle houses.

III. Backbone

One a.m., prime time. On a hillside in Vermont, hundreds of people are looking through telescopes at Saturn, and galaxies and nebulae, like the Hercules Cluster and the Veil Nebula. A meteor shoots across the sky, followed by a rolling wave of cheers and shouts. Only then are you aware of just how many people are out there in the darkness. Even the smallest flashlight would be glaring. All flashlights are covered over with red plastic, and held close to the ground. The dim lights float up the path out of the woods to the clearing, looking like large fireflies.

As they stand in line at a telescope, people are looking up at the Milky Way. They may be talking to someone, but they can't take their eyes off the night sky. Indeed, some dislike summer because the nights are shorter. It is less than five hours to sunrise and there is the universe to see.

Stellafane, "shrine to the stars," is an enchanted place. It's as if hundreds of people and hundreds of telescopes summon the universe. One is aware, everywhere, of the night sky. The field seems to float upward. These few acres are a carpet ride, the pasture spinning through space.

This hillside in Springfield is hallowed ground for amateur astronomers. Stellafane was established by Russell Porter, a hometown boy and arctic explorer who later was called to work on the creation of Mount Palomar. Porter started a small group dedicated to making their own telescopes and grinding their own mirrors.

He was a gentle apostle for telescope making. The word spread. Twenty showed up for the first convention in 1926 and three times as many the next year. These days conventions draw more than 1,500 "TNs"—"telescope nuts" and "Stellafanatics" from all over the country and from England. (A few license plates: I Gaze [Conn.]; Nebulae [N.Y.]; Seestars [N.Y.]; and bumper stickers: "I Brake for Asteroids," and "Red Giants Aren't So Hot.")

Many make the pilgrimage yearly to Stellafane, the oldest convention of amateur astronomers in the country. Berton Willard, an optical engineer and Porter biographer, has been coming here since he was thirteen, back in 1953. Melinda Callis and Gerry Deluca met at Stellafane in 1984 and were married here in 1989. Allan Mackintosh, the oldest attendee at age eighty-five, had come from England for his twenty-eighth Stellafane. For others coming from the cities and suburbs, this is the first place they ever saw the Milky Way. The night sky at home is washed out by a flood of light. The first thing people ask each other about where they're from is: "How's the viewing there?"

The pink clubhouse stands at the center of the gathering on Breezy Hill. Incised on the gable in large letters, an inscription from Psalm 19 has presided over each convention: "The Heavens Declare the Glory of God." The small cottage, a National Historic Landmark, was designed by Porter in 1923. There are two conflicting stories about why the house is pink. One says that pink was the cheapest paint available. But Porter's daughter, Caroline Porter Kier, says that her father, a dedicated watercolorist whose work was praised by Maxfield Parrish, had fancied an off-white "spruce gum" pink. This proved far too subtle for the paint mixer. The cottage is always repainted using the same formula: It goes on hot and orangey, but tones down quickly.

Inside, the clubhouse resembles a small ship's cabin. Every available surface is crowded with memorabilia from the different generations of amateur astronomers who have inhabited the place. There are Porter's sketches of the first members, and photos of past conventions when you could line up everyone for one picture. On the fireplace mantel is a hunk of glass from the first try at the Palomar mirror. In the kitchen there is a yellowing sheet of 1934 verse dedicated to marauding mice. And on the blackboard, one of Porter's formulas for mirror making is reproduced and signed "RWP" as if he had just been by.

To be a member of the Springfield Telescope Makers, the club that runs Stellafane, you must make your own mirror. Simply put, this involves about one hundred or more hours of walking around a barrel on which you slowly grind and polish a round blank of glass into a precise shape. "Pushing the glass," as it is called, is addictive, say the telescope makers. Club member Margaret Salter made her first mirror at age seventy-five. She was recovering from a hip replacement and had to use a walker to move around the barrel. Other members like Maryann Arrien dream of their next mirrors as they slowly grind the current project. Arrien,who is working on an eight-inch mirror, wants to do a 12-inch next. And after that? "I have it planned. I want to have done one Cassegrain in my life," she says referring to a particular design.

Observing the stars through a telescope you've built, producing something precise by simple means, "there's something special knowing that you unlocked it, and not your gold card," says Arrien.

"Amateur astronomy is pure. Just in it for the love," she says. "That's why I've come to feel so at home. I want it to live on . . . It should be extolled."

Dedicated amateurs can contribute to the field, monitoring meteor showers and thousands of variable stars. Professionals can't watch the whole sky. Clyde Tombaugh discovered Pluto in 1930. David Levy has discovered twenty-one comets, some through his homemade telescope. He shared the discovery of the Shoemaker-Levy comet, which hit Jupiter in 1994. He had searched for nineteen years before finding his first comet.

Trying to convert the wary, club members set up seven drums with mirrors in different stages of finish and enticed people to push the glass. People were tentative at first, but they got used to the feel of rough grit like "black Maui beach sand" rasping on glass. It sounds like an iron lung.

A large photo of Porter grinding a mirror presided. Under the photo, in pencil, was this quote: "Nothing gives me more satisfaction than realizing that I have helped towards giving thousands of people the pleasure of creating with their own hands a tool to unlock the wonders of the heavens."

At Stellafane the homemade telescope is honored above all else. No commercial telescope makers are allowed displays, and a field of telescopes awaits judging for their mechanical fitness, the craftsmanship of their finish, and their optics. The optics are judged at night. Judges will apprentice for ten years before assessing optics.

These are not the standard-issue white tubes, or "light buckets" as Newtonian reflectors are sometimes called. Several innovations first seen here are now widespread. There are telescopes made from burnished aircraft aluminum, and boxy scopes of roughly finished plywood, and there are ten-foot tall telescopes that are open cages and look like some sort of satellite that has landed. One year there was a telescope made out of Legos.

There is a tradition of using scrounged parts. The thriftiest telescope, which was built by a Vermonter, had a mount that moved on a Teflon sheet, and an old LP of Bruce Hornsby and the Range. He also used half of an old binocular for his finder, which cost him three cents. There was a huge thirty-two-inch telescope that used a discarded gear from a CAT scan, and an entry from Canada that used hockey stick handles as part of the tripod.

Quite a few of these parts were acquired at Stellafane's famous swap tables, the Filene's bargain basement of amateur astronomy, a feeding frenzy that each year is not supposed to start until 8 a.m. but gets going at 6 with spirited trading.

After that flurry, there's a long wait until dark. By day, people at Stellafane exhibit the lethargy of nocturnal animals. An astronomy convention is an upside-down world, one that snoozes through the day and waits for midnight. People hang about their tents, or sit around talking Newtonians and *f*-sizes. A couple of hundred gather under the big tent for the technical talks, and later in the outdoor amphitheater for the twilight lectures.

One year it clouds up at 4 p.m. By the time the amphitheater lectures begin, it is spitting rain enough to suggest it's a prelude to a soaking.

But at 9 p.m. the sky clears, as a Harvard professor is talking about the search for extraterrestrial intelligence. MIR, the Russian space station, passes overhead just as the stars shine through. People cheer. (They knew exactly when the space station was due to cross this spot in Vermont.) By two and threes, they begin to slip out of the amphitheater. The speaker begins to talk faster, cut things out of his talk. Up in the field there is an unveiling: black and blue garbage bags coming off the telescopes. We're back to prime-time darkness.

"Have you seen the comet Hale-Bopp?" a voice asks us. What one remembers are the helpful voices in the dark. The man points out the comet—a smudge—a faint blur parked about two fists away, at 4 o'clock, from the Milky Way. By the fall, Hale-Bopp will be an astonishing companion, visible each night to the north, presiding over our travels.

We go from telescope to telescope: What are you looking at? Jupiter, Saturn, M11, M31, 7737, a double-double, the globular cluster, the Dumbbell Nebulae, the voices in the dark answer. At some telescopes we wait in line, at others we walk right up. We totter high on ladders, or kneel down and squint to look out years. We are "drifting along the celestial river, cruising the Milky Way," as one telescope builder said.

The chill grows on that Vermont hillside. Time passes toward morning. Jupiter slides down the sky toward the trees.

Stellafane is about the restoration of true scale. Our planet in the cosmos, light years, billions of galaxies, solar systems piled up like grains of wheat eight-feet deep over a field. There is a unity in all these orders of magnitude. Daylight is the great concealer. Night is primal; we are back to the beginnings here.

The equipment fades in the dark. The theories and mirror grinding wait for morning. It's all about this finally: seeing. Pulling in as much of that distant light as possible. Just seeing.

A few years ago, Stellafane was blessed with the Northern Lights. "Fantastic. Like a dream land," says Robert Morse, the club president. "A couple of hundred people sitting under the stars, oohing and ahhing."

Carl Breuning, the club vice-president, remembers a similar night many years ago. It was his first convention. At 2 a.m., someone knocked on his tent: "'Get out here—there's the most spectacular aurora.' Two thousand people out in the field. Now remember, they're from New York, New Jersey. They see stars in the planetarium. This guy yells out: 'Let's hear it for the projectionist!' Everyone cheered."

Stellafane looks to the stars, and carries forth an old model of amateur exploration from the grand days of natural history. Stellafane is a romance of the sky.

E. V. Flanders was a charter member of Stellafane, and the only one to have seen Halley's Comet twice—the second time with artificial lenses in both eyes. He was getting anxious about seeing it again. Flanders was ninety-one. He and his wife Fran talked about it for years. The first time they had a chance to view Halley's return, they took their binoculars and drove to the top of Elm Hill, away from the lights of town. Fran saw the comet as a fuzzy blob. He could not see it. He was disappointed. They could only stay out for a short time. "So I began to bite my fingernail and think he wouldn't be able to do it," said Fran. Then the club members gathered with some telescopes on a cold December night. Flanders saw the comet he had last seen when he was 15 years old. That visit had begun his interest in astronomy. He built a telescope. Halley's Comet was not as bright this time around, and the tail was shorter than it was seventy-six years earlier. The temperature was in the teens, and they soon went into the house. "Now I can relax, we've at least seen it," said Fran. E. V. Flanders died 9 months later. The club, as is the tradition, sent flowers, a Star of Stellafane, to his funeral.

Once upon a time, in this century, you did not have to go to Vermont or Texas or Oregon to see the night sky.

In 1910, Chicago hotels held parties in their roof gardens to see Halley's Comet. Today there are 230,000 streetlights in Chicago (and no hotel roof gardens). To see Halley's Comet on its return in 1986, a dedicated observer had to drive for hours out into the country.

When the comet rose at 7 p.m., it was washed out by the lights in most places. The much-heralded return just didn't transfix us. We are used to bigger fireworks shows, full 3-D, *Sturm und Drang* on the Disney plan.

There are 2,500 visible stars. In a city you may see a few dozen if you're lucky. In the suburbs, you may see two to three hundred stars.

Seen in a satellite photo, North America at night is lit up like the heavens—as if the stars had fallen to the ground. Towns with a population as small as 5,000 can be identified. A strange reversal is taking place. We have too much light of the wrong kind.

The skies above city centers are twenty-five to fifty times as bright as the natural sky; the typical suburban neighborhood is five to ten times as bright, says Arthur Upgren, professor of astronomy at Wesleyan University. Even a small village is washing out the night sky with light twice as bright.

"Most people will cease to see the stars in the twenty-first century if we do not change the way that power-utility companies, developers, and the general public view outdoor lighting," says Daniel W. E. Green, a Harvard-Smithsonian astronomer, and an organizer of the New England Light Pollution Advisory Group, which is fighting for the night sky like a partisan resistance, streetlight by streetlight, it seems, promoting local ordinances and state legislation.

Only one in ten Americans lives below the full dark sky. A city friend visiting us in New Hampshire looked up at the night and said, "It's like another planet." Another time, a visitor asked about the band of stars that ran through the sky. She had seen it once before and wondered what it was. It's the Milky Way, I said. "Is it always there?" she asked. The Milky Way is fading from view like some prehistoric cave painting.

This is an unprecedented change, a broken connection between us and all of human history. The Milky Way was a storied presence. To the Eskimos the Milky Way was the snowy path of the Great Raven. In Lapland it was the route of migrating birds. The Tartars of the Caucasus saw the flight of a thief, spilling part of his stolen wheat. For Muslims it marked the pilgrims' way to Mecca. For the Chinese it was a river linking earth and heaven. And for one tribe in Botswana the Milky Way was the spine of the night.

The night sky is a family album, says astronomer and physics professor Chet Raymo. There are star names from the Arabic, Greek, Latin, Chinese, and Sumerian languages. And there are different habits of seeing. In earlier times, people saw dark constellations. The aborigines in Australia saw an emu, the Quechua-speaking Indians of Peru saw a bird, fox, and baby llama. Far north, the Eskimos regarded the stars as small lakes in the dark grass of night.

New stories could be told, new things seen; but those stories could be at an end. Year by year we are burying the family album, walling ourselves off with a flood of light.

Astronomers are in retreat. Mt. Palomar, the famous 200-inch telescope, is fighting lights from San Diego 40 miles away. The observatory won a reprieve in 1984 when San Diego replaced white street lights with low-pressure sodium, a yellow light astronomers can easily filter out. But San Diego has had second thoughts and wanted brighter lights for downtown. Other observatories are now limited in their studies. Mt. Wilson's 100-inch telescope, once far off in the desert, has been blinded by Los Angeles. Astronomers who need the darkest skies, to study quasars and faint galaxies in the search for the size and age of the universe, have only a few sites in the world. Amateur astronomy, once a backyard hobby, is now a quest for the last dark skies. At Stellafane, an amateur gave a talk on building a telescope designed to be backpacked into the wilderness.

Street lights cause about three-quarters of light pollution. One-third of all outdoor lighting is sent up into the sky, two billion dollars of electricity wasted annually, says the International Dark Sky Association. The astronomers are having a new vocabulary forced on them. They speak of light trespass (a light shining beyond the property it's on), glare (brightness that interferes with vision), of uplight, overlighting, and skyglow. And they know people believe in this lighting as strongly as other cultures were tied to the constellations.

To many people bright lights are shelter and safety. Yet, the National Institute of Law Enforcement and Criminal Justice concluded a lengthy study, saying there is "no statistically significant evidence that street lighting impacts the level of crime."

To win darker skies, the astronomers argue economy and public safety.

(With less glare it is easier for older drivers to see at night.) "Don't approach them and say you're amateur astronomers," advised Mario Motta. "They'll think you're a fringe group." The astronomers have been often told that "they're just crazy astrologers."

Tucson, home to three major mountaintop observatories, is the city of light that offers hope. The Milky Way is still visible from downtown due to a 1972 lighting ordinance. Tucson has since grown tenfold, and the number of streetlights has doubled, but the light sent into sky has dropped 7 percent.

Town by town there is some good news. Boston and Cambridge have been replacing their streetlights, with hooded "cut-off" versions that keep the light on the ground. In Maine all new and replacement lighting using state money must have a full cut-off. To save money, Los Angeles has turned off some streetlights. Counties and towns in Arizona, Hawaii, and California have passed ordinances to control outdoor lighting. New Mexico has proclaimed itself, rather hopefully, a "dark sky state."

But light keeps pouring into the night. The newer kinds of lighting use about half the energy to produce the same brightness, but some power companies replace a 200-watt mercury lamp with a 200-watt metal halide or high-pressure sodium light, increasing the light on the ground and in the air by two to eight times.

In Stellafane's home state, Vermont's big ski resorts are promoting night skiing. A snow-covered mountain bounces a lot of light into the sky. "In 1970 Vermont outlawed billboards; that's why the state feels so clean when you arrive," says Brad Vietge, a Stellafane club member. "The lights on Mt. Mansfield are a four-thousand-foot tall billboard."

One survey of Vermont tourists found that 47 percent said they come to Vermont for the night sky. "This is another natural resource, just like maple trees or trout streams," Vietge says.

And there are threats that are so crazy, they sound as if they were made up. Some advertising agencies foresee a market in illuminating skyscrapers with advertising that will be visible from the ground and to captive airline passengers landing at busy airports. There is already one such sign near the Los Angeles airport.

A company called Lunix sells a lighted balloon to make nighttime day for movie sets or sports events. A larger version is being developed. Space Marketing Incorporated wants to put a billboard into orbit around the earth. The mile-wide, thin-Mylar sign would appear as large as the full moon. International protest and the $30 million cost have delayed the branding of the earth.

Radio astronomy is also being squeezed out, but by noise. Cellular telephones, paging devices, television broadcasts, and even garage door

openers are crowding the spectrum radio astronomers use to listen to the
dark, invisible matter that may make up 90 percent of the universe's mass.

The astronomers know they will be shut out one day. Paging device
businesses have petitioned the Federal Communications Commission to
take over part of the radio spectrum astronomers use to listen for hydrogen. Billions have been spent on the satellite systems. One network will
have sixty-six satellites in orbit. Customers will be able to receive or make
calls anywhere on earth, in the jungles of Borneo or the mountains of
Bhutan. Already astronomers are being asked to work during the low periods of phone use. In essence they've had to surrender their private line for
a party line.

The astronomers hope to one day put a radio telescope on the closest
quiet spot, the dark side of the moon.

On the side of Herman Heym's telescope it says:

> Baltimore's
> Street Corner
> Astronomer
> *Hav-A-Look*

For nearly a decade, Heym has taken his telescope to the streets. He loves
sharing the sky with the public. To help support himself, he puts a hat out.

It is a conjuring act, a magic trick: the universe downtown. Out of the
sky at noon, he has pulled Venus, Arcturus, and Jupiter, surprising people
by confusing the realms. It changes your concept of day and night, a
neighbor said to me when I told her about this. Day seems a veil, a short
interlude in the night. Nighttime the stronger.

People are thrilled to get a look, day or night. They ask him: Are the
phases of the moon caused by the earth's shadow? Is it really true that the
stars we're looking at died long ago? Can you see the flag on the moon?
And also, many people ask him if he is an astrologer.

Saturn provokes the greatest response. Heym takes his telescope to Fels
Point at night, where there are many restaurants and bars. "You can go
into those bars at 10 or 11 and there's a raging debate: 'It's a slide!' People
don't believe you can see it yourself."

Professor Kristine Larsen's astronomy students argue with her because she
makes them find stars with a telescope. "We won't be using this stuff, we'll
be using computers, CCD's," they say. Fine, she says, but when you go
talk to a kindergarten class, you're going to be out there in the parking lot
with a "cheesy six-inch telescope, not some CCD."

"I have trouble with professional astronomers who have never seen a nebula, eyeball to eyepiece," Larsen says. They lose the central wonder. "The fact that we can know the universe is amazing."

"You get so removed from what you actually see out there." She knows a professional astronomer who had trouble with a bright spot on his computer photos. Finally he went outside and looked up at the sky: Oh, yeah, there is a bright star there.

As we get further out in the universe, nearer to the big questions of the universe's origin, we lose the average person who just likes to look up at the sky, she says.

"We're losing the heart of the amateur astronomy. . . . Get someone to look through the scope—that's the heart of it. Show them Saturn and the moon. That's when you grab them."

Maybe. First-time observers are sometimes disappointed with how small the planets and stars appear. You can see better pictures in books, or in those planetarium talks. But, says Mel Bartels, an amateur astronomer from Eugene, Oregon, "this is the original, right here in front of you. I think if people could go out and dig for *T. rex* skeletons like we can look at the stars, you'd see enormous one-thousand-person archeological digs. Obviously they can't but anyone can get a 'scope and look at the skies."

"Seeing through a telescope is 50 percent vision and 50 percent imagination," says Chet Raymo. He describes watching the Crab Nebula, the debris of a star that exploded in the year 1054. (Bright enough to be seen in daylight, the Chinese recorded.)

"What I saw in the telescope was hardly more than a blur of light, more like a smudge of dust on the mirror of the scope than the shards of a dying star. . . . In the blur of light I could easily imagine the outrushing shock wave, the expanding envelope of high-energy radiation, the torn filaments of gas, the crushed and pulsing remnant of the skeletal star. . . . I felt a powerful sensation of energy unleashed, of an old building collapsing onto its foundation in a roar of dust at precise direction of a demolition expert. . . . But there was no sound."

"They go in awesome silence," says Raymo.

For Russell Porter the telescope was the ultimate tool for knowing where you are. "Surely the making and putting into use of a powerful astronomical telescope goes far toward properly orienting one's self in the great scheme of things," Porter wrote in 1923 of teaching a group of machinists how to build a telescope. Before long they "became seriously interested in the wonderful mechanism of our universe."

"They sense the direction of the axis of our earth and know where its north end at least pierces the celestial sphere. They had to in order to adjust their telescopes. They sense the celestial equator sweeping across the southern skies, and see upon it the dial of an immense clock whose hours come to the meridian in unfailing regularity."

One time, camping in Quebec, Porter and a friend located themselves without a map. He used maple syrup, a sextant, and some figuring, says his biographer Berton Willard.

He set out a saucer of syrup, which served as the artificial horizon. With his sextant he took sight on the north star, and the reflected image of the star in the syrup. The altitude of the north star is half the angle read from the sextant. Making the proper corrections, he converted the altitude to latitude.

Longitude was trickier, says Willard, requiring an accurate reading of universal time, which he lacked. Porter used his watch, set to local time, and a copy of *The Nautical Almanac*. He selected a star, and again using his maple syrup horizon, measured its altitude. With his almanac, and some other tables, he found their longitude. He jotted down the coordinates and handed it to his friend, saying, "That's where we are."

Our culture is "a very restricted medium . . . entirely deprived both of contact with this world and, at the same time, of any window opening onto the world beyond," Simone Weil wrote in 1943.

"A lot of people think that a little peasant boy of the present day who goes to primary school knows more than Pythagoras did, simply because he can repeat parrotwise that the earth moves round the sun. In actual fact, he no longer looks up at the heavens. This sun about which they talk to him in class hasn't, for him, the slightest connection with the one he can see. He is severed from the universe surrounding him, just as little Polynesians are severed from their past by being forced to repeat, 'Our ancestors, the Gauls, had fair hair.'"

In a television commercial for a computer, a father and son are stargazing, laying back, looking up into the night. "What are the stars made of?" the son asks. "Gases," his father says. "But what holds them together?" the son asks. The father hesitates and is silent. He does not resort to Shakespeare, Galileo, or Newton. He just looks lost. In the next scene they are inside at the computer screen, online happily after. They have turned away from the silence of the stars.

"We flee from the wild silence and the wild dark," says Raymo. We must contemplate the galaxies and light years "even at the risk of spiritual vertigo." But we are hiding out.

In big and small ways we have moved indoors. Many city buses were once open on the top, as were a few taxis. On the newer ferries, such as the ones that cross the English Channel or New York Harbor, there is little outside deck space. At sea, survivors from a shipwreck who were adrift for days in a lifeboat in a busy shipping lane watched as ships passed by them. No one was on deck. Everyone was inside tending the machinery and computers.

A friend, Elizabeth Marshall Thomas, was studying wolves out west. Denver has sprawled out, but the wolves have adapted. A wolf can walk unseen right through a suburb in early evening or at night. Everyone is inside watching television or on the computer.

Children aren't free to play and explore outdoors. Playtime has been replaced by managed activities. "Someone is teaching kids to turn on computers. Who does that for nature?" asks A. Elizabeth Watson, co-author of *Saving America's Countryside*.

A retired newscaster, Jack Borden, took a poll one day. He stopped twenty-five people on a city street, and asked them to describe, without looking, the sky that day—the sky above them at that moment. "It was a beautiful June day, the sky was a brilliant blue dotted with fluffy white cumulus clouds, and not a single one of them knew that," he said. He started For Spacious Skies, to get people to look up, to see the sky not as a weather forecaster or pollution indicator, but just for its beauty, just because "The sky is the daily bread of the eyes," as Ralph Waldo Emerson said. For Spacious Skies created a curriculum that has been used in more than 1,400 schools.

Children respond. Tests show that the artistic, musical, and literary skill of program participants markedly improved. "The sky starts at your feet!" says a sign in a third grade classroom. Or as Borden says, "The air in our lungs is part of the sky."

The ancients believed that the "edges of the earth" were quite close. Today, for all our talk of the information glut and satellite communications, we are blind. We are alive in a golden age of discovery. The bulldozer is striking bones and tusks.

In the last few years astronomers have found the first planets outside the solar system, called exoplanets or extra-solar planets. They have now identified more planets outside our solar system than within. The planets are little known, much debated, and are a part of the discoveries thrilling astronomers, leading them to call this a new golden age of their science.

"Every few weeks brings more spectacular pictures from the depths of space, pictures of the moons of Jupiter, the nurseries of newborn stars and the galaxies taking shape when the universe was young. They embolden cosmologists, the historians of the universe, in the audacious belief that many answers to questions of cosmic origin and evolution may be within their grasp," John Noble Wilford wrote in *The New York Times* in 1997.

The planets are not directly observed, but inferred from painstaking observation of the slightest wobble of a star, or a shift in the spectrum. Earth-sized planets are beyond detection thus far. There is talk of satellite missions to get a sharper look. Half of the Milky Way's 100 billion stars may be shepherding planets.

Dr. R. Paul Butler, age thirty-five, working in the Lick Observatory recalled his discovery, with another astronomer, of a planet six times the mass of Jupiter, orbiting a star 80 light years away. "I really felt the presence of Kepler standing at my shoulder," he said.

"The movements of the heavens are nothing except a certain everlasting polyphony (intelligible, not audible)," Johannes Kepler wrote. Kepler published his laws of planetary movement in 1609. Galileo first looked through his telescope in 1610, seeing stars "so numerous as to be almost beyond belief." These discoveries are contemporaries of the Gedney and Boardman houses. We have just begun our serious study. Regarding the orbit of the planets, Kepler said, "I contemplate its beauty with incredible ravishing delight."

The night sky, light millions of years old, is being buried like the mammoth bones. The world moves indoors. We bury mystery as we go along.

"You tell your students about the Milky Way and ninety-nine percent have never seen it," said Professor Larsen. "You look at the Milky Way at Stellafane and you want to cry. You realize why ancient cultures thought that the Milky Way was the backbone of the night sky." If that spine were broken, they believed, the darkness would come crashing down.

Long ago, under darker skies, in Ancient Greece, Anaxagoras was asked, "To what end are you in the world?"

"To behold, sun, moon and sky," he replied.

A childlike answer. Our neighbor, Chris Streeter, was at a party when he saw his three-year-old daughter Melissa and some other children walking out across the pasture.

"Where are you going?" he asked.

"We're going to touch the moon."

The mammoth bones in their constellation, the bones of the Boardman and Gedney houses, and the stars at night: They are here for our wonder.

Building the Elephant

❧ ❧

Reveille at dark. Four a.m. Bugles call, far off and near. There are rows and rows, acres upon acres, of small tents, ghost-white under the stars. Dark blue figures are emerging. The Union blue uniforms make us nearly invisible to one another. We fade from view in just a few feet. We stand for roll call and then huddle by a small fire crowded with tin cups holding coffee.

"Tomorrow at dawn you march into the cornfield," we had been told. At the Battle of Antietam in September 1862, 8,000 men were killed or wounded in a battle in a cornfield in an hour and a half. The soldiers walked into corn taller than they were, and by battle's end, not a stalk was left. We are here at the 135th anniversary of Antietam, the bloodiest day in American history. Twenty-three thousand men were dead, wounded or missing, and both armies marched away to fight for another three years.

In a practice drill we had advanced into a cornfield, aiming our muskets. I grew up playing in and around cornfields. They were exciting mazes. But this, even though it is only a drill for a mock battle, has a small taste of terror, looking down a rifle into the green.

We fall in and march off in the dark, four abreast, our company joining the others until there are long lines of Union blue, rifles high, marching, halting, advancing again. Up and down the line, the officers shout commands: *Orderrr! . . . Arrrms!* In the distance, the battle flashes orange-red. The battle has begun, a thunderstorm close to the ground.

We march into a bean patch adjoining the cornfield. It's smoky, misty, dark, mysterious. Cannons and muskets fire, flaring orange-red. The cannons shake the earth, smash into your ears. The cornfield can be seen in the smoke up a rise.

The Confederate gray blends into the low-lying fog and the gun smoke. Long gray lines of soldiers appear and disappear. We stand and fire, loading the black gunpowder into our musket barrels and shooting on command. The gray line across the field is lost at one moment, and then at the next is rapidly gaining definition. They are charging forward, the fog seeming to reform itself as men with rifles. Officers all about are shouting orders. Bugles are sounding orders. Officers are racing by on horseback. Preset ground explosions go off, scattering dirt. It is difficult to pick out your commanding officer's voice. We fire and fire, fall back, wheel left, fire again and again. Fifty feet from us, I can read the eyes of a Confederate captain. His sword held high, he charges his men toward us. He is screaming. If he had live ammunition he would kill me. I take a hit and fall forward. The field is full of noise—cannon and musket, shouting, cheering, screaming. The noise moves through the ground and you at once. Here is noise to fill a Sunday morning.

A small crescent of the rising sun shows through the gun smoke and fog. The battle looks like those vast nineteenth-century panoramic battle paintings. It is as atmospheric as any of the great Romantic paintings, lacking only a few allegorical figures coming through center, touched by a few rays of light: Lady Liberty, attended by, say, Clio. This is one of the strangest scenes I have ever been in the middle of, and I think, whose dream is this? A field surgeon appears to dress my "wound."

The whole scene comes at you like a dream and stays in your dreams for days afterward. The sounds and rhythms of that life linger. Not only the heat and noise of the battle, but the peace of camps. Field after field of tidy rows of white tents. The sounds of crickets at dusk, talking, horses whinnying, drums, bugles and fifes. There is always music. A haze of campfire smoke, the smell of coffee and chicken cooking. No cars or radios. There's an experience of heightened spectacle and peace.

In all my dreams I'm marching to the drums. Long lines of Union blue stretch over a hill into the morning light. Long marching rows that take a half-hour to pass a spot. To stand shoulder to shoulder in a line of forty or so men and fire in unison, as thousands fire, to wheel and move as a unit, the whole spectacle stays with you.

Going to see the elephant. That is what many Union boys called going to war. They would see for themselves.

On this fine September weekend, some 15,000 men, women and children had come together here in this Maryland field to reenact Antietam. Some had come from as far away as England to fight this battle again. More than a few were fighting their third Antietam; some had been fighting the Civil War longer than the war itself had lasted. This is a show we put on for ourselves—for each other. Believe in it, have faith, attend to the details and we can build a better elephant.

Just what were we creating here in this field and why?

I. Building the Elephant

This is war without death, just what the peace movement always wanted. Many people find reenacting the Civil War disturbing, or silly, playing trick-or-treat on the graves of the solemn dead.

I had never intended to go to Antietam. I knew nothing of reenactors until I met the Sixth Regiment New Hampshire Volunteer Infantry.

On a rainy April Saturday they were holed up inside the G.A.R. hall in Peterborough. The G.A.R., the Grand Army of the Republic, was the Civil War veterans' organization. (Other veterans have since taken their place and meet to play bingo.) The Sixth had only recently formed to portray the farm boys of Companies E and K who had marched off to the war from the small towns in sight of Mt. Monadnock. They had about two dozen members, of which only half made most of the thirty parades and events each year.

There were three or four guys in Civil War uniforms, and displays of old photos, guns, uniforms, and a recipe for making your own hardtack. They had set up some tents, duct-taped to the floor downstairs. A tripod of guns stood nearby, locked at the bayonets, the rifle butts duct-taped to the vinyl floor. A half-dozen visitors drifted around the hall.

Jim Sutherland, a shy postman from Goffstown, had joined the Sixth in the previous year. His ancestors served in the war, one as a surgeon's assistant in the Eleventh New Hampshire.

Sutherland had already been to some big battle reenactments. He drove twenty-four hours to get to Shiloh in Tennessee. There were "10,000 boys" there ready for the show. They were routed by torrential rains. Streams ran through the tents. The red Tennessee clay stained his baby blue trousers a greenish tint. When the porta-johns flooded out, a general retreat was sounded.

He also fought his way through the heat at the Battle of the Wilderness in Virginia. A freak April heat wave sent the temperature to 105 degrees, he says. There were "8,000 boys" in their Union and Confederate wool suits, and as Sutherland recalls, 149 fell to heat stroke, and 7 to heart attacks. "But no one died," he tells me. A much better result than the first battle, I think to myself.

Reenacting seemed to be gently ironic: modern life breaking in with duct tape and porta-johns. "We did the Pheasant Lane Mall," says a reenactor who is visiting from another regiment. "We've got the howitzer now; we're doing Confederate. Plus we've got three flags." He is talking shop with Mike Sebor.

Sebor had started the Sixth. He was a twelve-year veteran of reenacting and spoke with such enthusiasm that he drew a circle of listeners. With his

crew cut and short stocky build, Sebor, age thirty-three, has a military
bearing. He was standing by his tent in the basement, explaining an average soldier's equipment and food.

"My unit is hard-core," Sebor says. "We walk in with our knapsack and
set up. Some guys from New York drive cars right on the field—it looks
like hell." They have big tents and big boxes of supplies, such as were not
usually found outside the quartermaster's supply in D.C., he says. Sebor
works hard for accuracy.

He hands me a lead minié ball, the musket shot weighing more than
one ounce. The shot feels substantial in the palm. He holds the lead to his
wrist and explains, in part, the carnage of the war: lead at close range
meeting flesh and bone.

"If you look at this—this is soft lead and when it hit, it even mushrooms
out further. Picture it twice the size of that wrist. It would literally shatter
your bone. Back then doctors couldn't set that kind of fracture, so they'd
amputate your arm."

"These weapons were used in devastating company," he says, a full regiment, a thousand men firing, accompanied at times by cannons. At close
range the cannoneers could load "hell-can fire," chunks of metal and balls
in chicken wire, which would spray out like a huge shotgun shell. Men
would march, shoulder to shoulder, flags held high, into this fire.

"It was the last Napoleonic war," he says of the battle tactics, "and the
first modern war."

From a piece of lead, he draws a panorama. This is why he is standing
here, on his free time, dressed up. He knows that some people think it
foolish. Sometimes they are hostile. "We get the ignorant ones who walk
by on the sidewalk and say, 'Oh look at the little boys with their guns.'
We're not out there just because we've got guns," says Sebor, who as a po-
liceman in Peterborough sees enough guns. "If they'd come up the steps
they'd learn. The weapon—that's just a piece of equipment—that's not the
focus. We do it to preserve the history that's in each soldier, in each regiment, in each town," he says.

Most often, people ask: Is that a real gun? Aren't you hot in that uniform? If there's a chicken cooking over a campfire, they ask: Is that a real
chicken? If a reenactor has brought a baby along in period dress, they ask:
Is that a real baby? These questions are so common that the *Smoke & Fire
News*, a newspaper listing reenactments of many eras, has a regular feature, called "Tourists say. . . ."

The questions reveal people's confusion, not about history, but about
what they are seeing. What they are really asking is: What kind of make
believe is this? Is this play or history? Is this real or let's pretend?

It's both: It's let's pretend this is real. Let's make believe and we'll find our way back. It's serious play; it's work and leisure. This is war as play, war as homage, war as peace.

"Is that some kind of Hollywood, some kind of Disneyland?" a friend asks me after I return from Antietam.

"No," I say, "It's some kind of worship."

War Is Play

I am wearing a wool suit out in an open field late in August. It is like being strapped into a wool bake-oven. I am draped with equipment like a decorated Christmas tree: musket, cartridge belt, bayonet, haversack, canteen, hat. Wool is hot. Who said wool breathes? Maybe when it's got a few bullet holes in it.

Worse, I am dressed up like a soldier marching around in public. I feel so dorky. I feel as if I've just joined the dorkiest club in the school—somewhere beyond the chess nerds or the A.V. squad. It's a borrowed Union uniform and the pants are clownishly large and lacking suspenders. I'm in danger of losing my pants.

Mike Sebor drills his seven soldiers: Attention, order arms, shoulder arms, right shoulder shift, support arms, to the rear and in open order march, inspection arms, stack arms, count off, without doubling right face, left face, close ranks march, fix bayonets, charge. *Huzzah!* We shoulder the guns, cradle the guns, present the guns, rest the guns, stack the guns.

Wheeling in circles under the sun, firing black powder at nothing, wearing the uniform of a dead war, we are comrades in arms, men in the Union blue, ready to march for a war long over. We are building the elephant.

Many of my comrades were in the Army. Some still wear uniforms daily as police or postmen. I don't even play team sports. I was a Boy Scout once; helped start a fruit riot. (It was the late 1960s. Even if there was no merit badge for Civil Disobedience, we were intent on earning it.)

I'm a step behind: the guy still fiddling with his rifle while others are at the ready. The comic possibilities are great and tempting, and my tendency is toward slapstick. I suppress my inner Marx Brother.

For a summer, I follow the Sixth New Hampshire as they gain members, parade for the public, and drill for themselves. I load paper gunpowder shells at the G.A.R. hall as we listen to Civil War marching music. Given the rank of private, I hop in the van with four of them at 2 a.m. for the ten-hour drive to Antietam.

Corporal Sebor is a terrific recruiter. Each time I see him that summer he has signed up another two or three guys.

"Have you ever fired a black-powder musket?" he asked me in his quick manner.

"Ah, no."

He would teach me. I had to "fall in" for training. And soon I was shopping for reproduction eyeglasses and 1851 Jefferson brogans. He rounded up the rest of the uniform and the musket. It can cost up to $1,500 to equip yourself. Most guys buy a few pieces a time and borrow the rest. If they or their wives sew, they buy the patterns and make it themselves. To appease their wives, they tell them that their uniform will never go out of style. Or, as one member of the Sixth told his reluctant wife: I just turned forty, it could be worse—I'm not buying a sports car or taking a mistress.

Back before Sebor had a job, a wife and two young ones, he lived one whole year practically in his Civil War tent, just going from battle to battle. His family was a little concerned. He has worn out three pairs of reproduction brogans. He is in the select group of reenactors who have been called on for the battle scenes in movies like *Glory* and *Gettysburg*. On his honeymoon he visited Gettysburg and Chancellorsville. Heading home, he snuck in another Civil War site, even though his sainted wife Nancy thought they were safe in Upstate New York. ("That right there tested the strength of my marriage," he says.) He likes New Hampshire fine, and he is only, as he says, eight and a half hours by the highways from many major Civil War battlefields.

Finally we load and fire. I hold the rifle in front of me, tear open a black gunpowder paper cartridge with my teeth, tasting the powder, hurriedly spill the powder in the muzzle, place the firing cap, and on command: fire. The noise is loud and satisfying. There's smoke. We stand in two rows. The back row is shooting over the shoulder of the front row. We're guys. Blam! Blam!

We rest. We're out in the ankle-high grass of a beautiful rolling pasture, Carnival Hill in Wilton, named for the winter games that were once held here. Sitting in the grass, the men pass around dried apple and dried peach, and discuss Lincoln and his generals, and different battles. "These guys have been reading about the Civil War since they were kids," says James Hadley, who has joined the Sixth in the last year. I have seldom been among people whose discussions were so thickly footnoted with books. Many reenactors I met could quote parts of soldiers' letters and diaries, the way that people used to recite beloved poems. Standing around camp, I listened to some tough debates about the value of eyewitness letters and regimental histories versus the longer view of later scholarship.

Imagine your eight-year-old dinosaur fanatic, grown up with twenty or more years of reading, all dressed up as Triceratops standing around in a circle with other Triceratops discussing the Mesozic era, or in this case, Lincoln and his generals, and you have an idea of the intensity of the discussions.

The reading has led them to take up arms. "You've exhausted the books to read," says Sebor. "Now you want all your senses in it. You want to taste it, smell it, see it. You want to get out there and see what they felt." The day of discovery arrives when they see their first reenactment. They're excited. They ask about joining. The real question has been answered: Adults can play! They can do this.

They discuss the history of the "Bully Sixth," which fought in twenty-three major battles and numerous skirmishes, including Antietam, Second Bull Run, Vicksburg, Wilderness, Cold Harbor, Fredericksburg, Petersburg, and the Mine. They took part in amphibious assaults and were considered the best sharpshooters in the Ninth Army Corps. "The Sixth was one of the hardest-fighting regiments in the Union army," Sebor says. He picked them from the state's eighteen infantry regiments. The Sixth is overlooked, he says. The Fifth New Hampshire already has its reenactors and is celebrated. Sebor is determined to make the Sixth better known. At the Antietam battlefield, he shows us where he thinks there should be a monument to the Sixth, by Burnside's Bridge. Trying to take this narrow bridge, the men of the Sixth were turned back twice, losing one in five men, killed or injured.

Another recent recruit, Alan Gross, wants the Sixth's muster grounds memorialized. Gross teaches special education students in Keene. From his classroom window he can see the old muster grounds, now the ballfields of Wheelock Park. When he says this, he just looks off as if he were seeing the soldiers there now. He is smitten. Gross reads about thirty to forty Civil War books a year, in addition to his other reading. You don't know how exciting it is, he says, to find others who share this passion.

Each member of the Sixth takes on the identity of a real soldier of the regiment to do an "impression." They research his history, locate his grave, and, if needed, tend it. Sebor was Osgood Hadley of Peterborough, a color-bearer who was wounded seven times. Hadley was a medal of honor winner. Then at one encampment James Hadley showed up asking questions. "I'm looking for my great grandfather. I understand somebody impersonates him," Hadley said. "You're talking to him," Sebor answered. "But you are a blood relative. I hand him over to you now." One hundred thirty five years later there is a Hadley in the Sixth New Hampshire Volunteer Regiment.

A few of the fifty-four "rules and regulations for the 135th anniversary reenactment of the Battle of Antietam (Sharpsburg)": "Period footwear is

mandatory! Anyone wearing inappropriate footwear will need to find correct footwear or be asked to leave. . . . *No* anachronisms on the person.
This includes, but is not limited to: wristwatches, earrings, jewelry (except
wedding bands), cigarettes, lighters, bandannas. . . . *No* visible anachronisms in camp at any time. This includes, but is not limited to: coolers,
modern cans/bottles, cigarettes, bags of chips, bread in plastic bags,
twentieth-century clothing (shorts, T-shirts, etc.). No speciality impres-
sions (Lee, Lincoln, Longstreet, etc.) are allowed without the written ap-
proval of the host."

Each detail builds the elephant. At Antietam we drill and drill, fall in,
count off, march. How quickly this becomes the rhythm of your life. At
roll call, you feel as if you've been listening to these names linked in this
order forever. In the heat, the weight of the rifle becomes familiar. *Order
arms, shoulder arms.* . . . We do a bayonet drill to the manual, in French.
Lines of men on the drill field, choreographed, a cross between aerobics
and courtly fencing. A grisly pantomime.

We are following orders, studying the tactics that killed hundreds of
thousands. The bugle sounds advance, retreat, lie down. We stand back to
back, four soldiers, with bayonets out, a spiny cluster, defending against a
cavalry attack. Custer's last order, I'm told.

I receive much instruction from the men around me: march with your
left foot first, count off louder, snap that gun crisply, hold the rifle here
. . . and I receive far too many compliments. I am conspicuous in my gun
fumbling.

Performing poorly breaks the spell, disappoints the others. It's not
playing fair. Good soldiers "look period." When the proud cavalry officers
ride by, they are dirty and have a hungry stare that is uncanny. Poor players
are derided as "Farbs." (As in: "Far be it from me to say . . . but the buttons on your uniform are not period.") Farbs are not the real-fake thing.
Standing at parade rest, our unit watches a soldier crossing the parade
grounds with a modern cooler, and jeers: "*Nice* impression."

And Farbs please take note: "There were no chubby guys in the Army.
Anyone who marched was lean and wiry," says Doug Cooper, a lieutenant
with the First Minnesota. There are many chubby reenactors, sometimes
called, by their wives or girlfriends, TBGs, tubby bearded guys.

At the other end of the spectrum are the "hard-core." Some of the Confederate hard-core might starve themselves down to one hundred pounds,
eat berries and rancid bacon, and go without shoes.

Most campfire criticism is reserved for the rebels: They won't die. Entire companies that should fall to close-range fire continue fighting. On
the battlefield, I observe the Superman effect on both sides. Our casualty
rate is slim.

Dying is optional and also open to criticism: "If you're dead—stay dead!" one reenactor complained after Antietam. "When wounded, do not lounge on your arm, propped up to watch the battle."

At Antietam, the Sixth camps with the Fifth New Hampshire. The camp strictly follows the 1861 Army manual: neat rows of small "dog" tents. Each tent has some straw beneath the bed roll. (My head sticks out one end and feet the other.)

Facing the company "street," the tents look like a low-lying version of a nineteenth-century Main Street, the white houses of the Greek Revival only waist high. An entire pasture of tents lies before you like the graves at Arlington National Cemetery.

"We have people who come in the middle of the night who can find our camp in the whole sea of white," says Steve Workman, quartermaster for the National Regiment, an organization of about twenty regiments that strive for authenticity. "If you were a soldier and you wanted to eat, or you wanted a change of clothing, you had to carry it on your back." Each company also had a supply wagon, but frequently they marched without it. On some campaigns they went without tents and blankets.

In a few neighborhoods of the encampment, twentieth-century comfort has crept in. The tents are larger, some with canvas porches, and camp chairs, or as Sebor says, "lawn furniture." Air mattresses have replaced straw, Coleman lanterns have replaced candles. They are white canvas Levittowns. Farbvilles. (The Confederate camps are rumored to be wilder places, with large bonfires. At night on our quiet company street, we can hear the distant rebel yells. Do rebels have more fun?)

"We believe that to do the men honor that we're trying represent we have to live as closely as possible to the way they lived," says Randy Cook, a lieutenant in the Fifth New Hampshire. "What's the point of just putting on a uniform and pretending you're a soldier if you're going to go out and *not* do it correctly."

Good play is honorable. When I fall in battle and a surgeon appears, he offers me a choice of wounds: arm, leg, chest? (Wanting to live, I choose an arm wound.) He dresses my wound with a red rag, tells me not to worry, it won't stain the uniform. As he departs, in the midst of the battle noise, he says, "Thank you for playing."

War Is Homage

Americans are said to have no interest in history; last month's news fades into the same background as the Roman Empire. In the evening, walking among the fields of tents, I thought it amazing that so many—15,000 or

more, each at their own expense, each acting as their own museum curator—had traveled so far in search of so much.

And what had they come in search of? Honor, valor, truth, glory, fidel-
ity, and honesty. The men who had fought the Civil War were men of conscience and endurance, I was told. They braved much, endured hardship
and triumphed in pursuit of their ideals.

Yeah, guy after guy will tell you, the gun stuff, the uniform, the salt
pork and hardtack, is part of it. But it's all to summon forth an appreciation of those old values.

"It's a chance to do honor to the Americans of that era," says Doug
Cooper. In his day job he is a Navy commander. "The thing that fascinates
me is the Victorian ethic. The work ethic, the way they thought: It was
duty, honor, country and it really meant something. These people didn't
have the distractions of the twentieth century so they could concentrate
upon the things that are really important: bettering their minds, making
life better for the people around them, building this country. It wasn't a
'me generation.'"

This was an era when your word meant something, says Roger Joly of
the Sixth. He tells me a story of Union soldiers invited to a Confederate
dance. As the dance was ending, a Confederate officer arrived and, finding
the enemy among his men, wanted them arrested. We can't do that, his
men told him, we have given our word. Their officer honored this and
stepped aside. "Amid all the carnage," Joly says, "it's incredible the respect
these men showed for each other."

"Life was harder, but it was more true," says Mike Ryder, a recent recruit to the Sixth. Today things—call it the rat race—get in the way of
what's truly important, he says.

Tom Nixon, who has been a reenactor for a decade, says, "It's just an
honor to think about these men." He tells me how General Sherman's
men set the record for marching: twenty miles a day. And this was without
roads, off in the fields and woods. Standing by the campfire, late at night,
he says, "They were just stronger, better people than we are."

Activities that "tax our limits of endurance scratch at the surface of
what these men endured every single day," says Randy Cook of the Fifth.
Several times during the weekend, Cook talks about Pvt. John Haley of
the 17th Maine: He was a short-legged guy who would fall hours behind
his company. He was the last in to camp but he was "always present for
duty. Even when he was ten miles behind on a road, he caught up and he
saw the thing through. And that's the determination all these men had.
The ones that didn't have the determination, didn't last long."

This where the reenactors touch bedrock, or to borrow an old fable,
they reach out from our era like the blind men touching the elephant.

"What was important to them? What wasn't important to them?" says Cooper. "So that's what we try to figure out. You're hoping that you understand it based on doing what they did."

At Carnival Hill, during a break in our practice, the men of the Sixth stood around talking of loyalty and patriotism.

"You can't know how the man's emotions were," says Bob Corrette, at age fifty, one of the oldest in the Sixth, but "there are the same basic fears. We are the same."

"Don't you think loyalty or patriotism had a different emphasis?" asks Walt Sy, age forty-eight

"We went downhill—" says Corrette.

"Downhill or uphill," says Sy. "When Bob and I were kids, Memorial Day was a big deal. Loyalty, Nationalism, Jingoism—those were positive words. If you were a healthy male, there was a sentiment: Who were you to stay home?"

"It was an honor to give your life," says Corrette.

"Vietnam was the first war where those words had a different meaning," says Sy. "Loyal to what? Yourself or the government?" His children have a different view of war. "When I was fifteen I thought America was always right." I didn't know that there was another culture that also had its beliefs, he says. "So when men would line up shoulder to shoulder, marching into five cannons it was the right thing to do. Now maybe you think: well that side has a right to exist too."

It is easy enough to make a cap or musket in the fashion of 1862; understanding the beliefs of the soldier who wore that uniform is the true restoration. Why did they march straight into fire? Why didn't they run? These are the first questions asked by those who are unfamiliar with the Civil War. Cook answers by telling of the charge at the battle of Cold Harbor. "These veterans knew they were going to die. They knew they were never going to make it. What did they do? They took their coats off, wrote their names on pieces of paper and pinned it inside their coats so that they would be buried in a grave, so they wouldn't be an unknown. Grim determination, plus resignation to see their duty through no matter what."

"The ethic of that time says that bravery and example are everything," says Cooper. That's the elephant many reenactors had come to see. For them the battlefield is a meditation.

"I'm with the 18th Virginia, Company G," says Christopher W. Gowin, "and I can tell you, now I know just a little of what my ancestors went through as they arose at three a.m. to be marched into a melee of terrible firing in a cornfield on that day in eighteen sixty-two. I practically cried as I watched the artillery fire from the next hill as we waited to be rushed in as reinforcements. I cannot express the gratitude I have for all who organized, coordinated, and volunteered to work at this event. I only pray that one day my child may be able to see this as I did with my father, who is also a reenactor in the same event. . . . God Bless you all."

II. "Come, Oh Dreams"

That summer before I went to Antietam, I visited other reenactments: a French and Indian War siege of a fort; an American Revolution battle in a city park, which was like a stately waltz to fireworks. I visited the Pilgrim village of 1627 where you can chat up Miles Standish, saw one-person shows where the likes of Louisa May Alcott performed, and even attended a restaging of a political way of debate, the nineenth-century Chautauqua under the big tent. On different nights, Frederick Douglass, Elizabeth Cady Stanton, Horace Greeley, Andrew Carnegie, and Abraham Lincoln lectured from the pulpit and took questions from their timid twentieth-century audience. They were available for breakfast the next morning: You could split a bagel with Lincoln.

We are building a grand dreamtime of history. We are image consumers, connoisseurs of millions of dollars of special effects. We enjoy a good lie. And we've been at this long before we looked west to Hollywood for our dreamshows.

Entering the encampment of the Patriot militiamen who were readying to fight the Redcoats, a mother said to her daughter: "This is how they lived."

No, I wanted to say: This is how we live, how we play.

We say that this is educational, a living documentary. These claims were once made for another activity that faded from American life: historical pageants. Pageants flourished in a brief period, before and during the First World War. They were often vast undertakings attempting to portray the entire history of a town or city. St. Louis had seven thousand people on stage in 1914. They were highly stylized, and scripted to provide an Olympian, noble view of history. From the first settler to that moment on stage, all citizens past and present were joined hand in hand, in a story of a progress. In archives I have come across photos of these outdoor pageants: They seem anachronistic, arrestingly strange, as if the photos had been beamed back to us from a distant satellite. And yet to understand the pageants is to understand something about the weekend players at Antietam.

Pageants were first revived in England in 1905 by the artists of the Arts and Crafts movement. They wanted to emulate the medieval festivals and Renaissance masques. "Pageantry and display were apparently as meat and drink to our forefathers," wrote one. The entire show would be crafted by local hands, from the costumes to the acting.

One of the first pageants in America was held in Peterborough, New Hampshire, not far from where the Sixth New Hampshire meets in the G.A.R. Hall. The pageant was staged in 1910 at the MacDowell Colony, a retreat for artists, writers, and composers. An outdoor amphitheater was built in the woods with a view toward Mt. Monadnock, and a Harvard drama professor eager to stage a pageant got his chance. He brought along a few famous singers of the day, but his acting troupe consisted of two hundred locals: mill hands and farm hands, shopkeepers and school girls, hard-working people who had to leave rehearsal for milking, or had to be at the mill before the whistle.

When the pageant opened, Peterborough shut down, "as if for a national holiday." A town of "perfect New England propriety" had taken time out to play. Special trains ran from Boston. About 3,500 people in all attended the three performances, exceeding Peterborough's population at the time.

The pageant began with the muse of history, Clio, emerging from the piney woods. She was dressed in diaphanous, flowing white veils. Clio called out, "Come, Oh Dreams." Out of the woods came her sister muses: Euterpe, Melpomene, Thalia, and Terpsichore—the muses of lyric and music, tragedy, comedy, and dance. They were attended by dreams in "gleaming grey draperies which swirled as they danced."

And the dreams began. For the next three hours or so, the dreams of the composer Edward MacDowell were told in 16 scenes. "The pageant was based on the thought that, born from the dreams of men, interpreted in them, history begins and is represented," said Professor George P. Baker, the show's author and director.

MacDowell's dream was the entire epic of Peterborough's history, as set to his music, and performed by the town's people dressed for the show: a tailor as an Indian chief, an undertaker as a Puritan, a farmer as a farmer (praised by the Boston critics for this faithful portrayal).

Seen from this distance, it seems like a "dream within a dream." This dreamtime history is wrapped in the moment of August 1910, before the Great War, and before movies and autos were common.

The white Yankee faces look so serious in the Plains Indians outfits borrowed from a Canadian company. The photos are a little grainy and each face recedes a bit as you look at it, dissolving into dots and blur. The history, too, is blurry: The pageant places the Puritans in New Hampshire, shows blacks in racist caricature, and creates a new episode in Irish history. But accuracy was not the point. Farmers, merchants, the village undertaker were all celebrating something big and mythic, as in a walking daydream.

Clio and Euterpe and Thalia, and the attending dreams in grey veils, were played by Miss Bartholomew and Miss Johnson and other Misses— that's how the program lists them—no first names. After dancing outdoors, trailing ethereal veils, would the rest of the century seem like a rebuke? Would you in later years, cooking the one thousandth supper for your husband and children, regard this pageant as youthful folly? Some of these muses and dreams would live until the early 1970s. See that elderly woman in the corner, watching *Hollywood Squares*? She was a muse—in her youth—she was Clio. These muses would give birth to the children who would go off to fight the Second World War: Clio's son on the beach at Anzio.

Looking at the old photos and reading lines like "Come, Oh Dreams" they seem foolish, innocents dancing at the edge of a piney woods; they seem brave, these farmers and merchants and schoolgirls, dancing a dream in daylight, taking on all of history. This is child's play and we look on as adults, knowing what the next eighty years will bring.

The pageant at Peterborough was part of an earnest effort to create a national pageant movement. Many reformers and civic boosters had adopted pageantry. Some wanted to spread an appreciation for theatre by getting thousands of people on stage. Baseball had won the nation's heart this way, they reasoned. Give a boy a bat, a glove, and a ball, and you have a fan for life. Others wanted to bring order to raucous holidays like July 4th, and instruct recent immigrants, and the fading old families, in their patriotic heritage. By acting in a pageant, they "formed a conception of what their past was by getting inside of it and seeing how it felt."

We have the pageants with us once more. They returned not with young maidens as muses. They returned with musket fire and cannons. They returned as war play: something far less European than those memory plays. They became less artistic expressions and more corporate and democratic. The pageants became theme parks and Civil War encampments. Disney imagineers and the weekend Civil War soldier cleaning his musket are in the pageant biz.

As our society has become more ordered and corporate, there is a greater desire for pageantry, for myth, a hunger to touch something of a grand scale, if only for a weekend. Pageants restage the grand movement of time. They put us, the nine-to-five workers, on the stage of great moments. One has extended one's life, taken a timeline and shot it like an arrow into the air.

Antietam on its 135th anniversary is not war recreated, it's not folklore or *fake*lore. This is pageantry. It's the pomp and circumstance of play. In the theatre, the actor plays a character. And though the militia, the Civil War soldiers, the Pilgrims play specific characters, their role really is history.

All pageants could say, as Dylan Thomas does in the opening of *Under Milkwood*, "Time Passes. Listen. Time Passes." One reviewer, describing the dramatic plot of the Peterborough pageant, wrote, "Time passes and the dreams waft him on."

At Antietam, the drama built as we marched to battle, lines of troops converging. Halted in a large field, we cheered as the generals rode by on horseback: *Huzzah! Huzzah!* The battle was booming nearby. The drummers kept up a beat. Standing at rest, we twisted around, taking in the scene. Wow! How many are here? Five thousand in this one field—five thousand, and to think we had even questioned coming here.

Antietam had the sweep of a pageant, it was something larger than one person could imagine. Or rather, as is said of Disney World: There seems to be just too much to do. This is part of the excitement: You're caught up in a grand spectacle.

This is dreamtime. Each of us was saying with our every action, "Come, Oh Dreams."

The past shows itself only fleetingly. Playing your way back into the past is a way of preparing yourself to be tricked. You ready yourself to accept the sleight of hand, the magic trick. "Come visit the past" is what the travel brochures sometimes say, but reenactors are readying themselves for a visit *from* the past. Call it a moment of insight or intuition, or if you believe, a visit from the spirits. One of those surprise moments when, before we even realize, we feel as if we have slipped away.

"You've got to pinch yourself sometimes," Sebor says of some of the battles he has reenacted. "There were times when you were out there you felt like you were really in it. . . . You'd swear to God that you went back in time and there you were. You're out there right now in that battle."

Aliana Wereska is a senior at Pinkerton Academy in Derry, New Hampshire. A group from her school was serving at Antietam as volunteers in the U.S. Sanitary Commission. They ladled out water to the troops along the road. It was much appreciated.

"I was on my way to the medic center and the Union soldiers were coming over the hill and you got the eeriest feeling. And the first thought that came to me was: A lot of these soldiers will not survive the day. Present tense. They're not going to come home."

But, she says, the modern world is always there to break the reverie: a plane overhead, power lines, an automobile.

Several days before the anniversary restaging of Antietam, the organizers issued a public plea. They asked pilots to avoid the area, to spare them the intrusion of the twentieth century buzzing overhead "like a mosquito all day. . . . People want to see it the way it was a hundred and thirty-five years ago."

"We do not have the legal authority, but we have morality on our side," said one organizer, sounding much like a Civil War orator.

The FAA had denied their request for a no-fly zone. Flights are restricted over civilian areas only in special cases, such as a Presidential visit or a natural disaster (which they might qualify for if it rained as it did at Shiloh). There is no provision for calling a "time out" for the late twentieth century.

Terry Barlow reenacts frontiersmen, hunters and trappers, men who lived and prospered by their wits and skill. He started a group where he lives in Maine. They practice forgotten arts like starting a fire without a match, hunting with tomahawks, making your own ropes, knives, and even muskets. He makes his living by reproducing old tools and selling them at different encampments. He has seen a lot of reenactors in his fifty-six years. He opened an antique shop when he was fifteen years old, about the same time he started following black-powder muzzle-loading events, back when there was just the stirring of a revival. More than a dozen years ago, he and his wife had set up their wares at a Revolutionary War encampment in Upstate New York, near Schroon Lake. There was a good turnout, about 2,500 people.

Along toward twilight, he was in front of his tent on the dealers' row. He looked up and there was a Revolutionary War soldier "in uniform just like everybody dresses up at reenactments.

"But he was very thin and tall, gaunt, wearing glasses. He had a blue military jacket on, so he was infantry. And he just looked like he'd been around for a long time. And I happened to comment to my wife, I said, 'look at that fellow, he looks like he's part of it,' you know, really good." They had been there five days, but had not seen him before.

The soldier walked past a dozen tents to Barlow's. He was looking for a mainspring for a Brown Bess musket. Barlow sent him to a gun trader in the next tent, who had a box heap of the small three-inch-long springs.

"There's just potentially hundreds and hundreds of different sizes because a lot of this stuff was handmade. It wouldn't be easy to pick out. He thumbed through it just very quickly, and reached into his pocket and paid him."

"'Boy,' I says, 'your get-up looks really good. It looks authentic.' And he says, 'Well, it's from many long years of wear.' That was all he said to me."

The row of traders' tents faced an open field, ten acres. The soldier headed toward the center of the field.

Barlow turned and joked with the other trader: "Did he pay you in Continental currency?"

"'No, but I expected it,' he said. And I turned to look where he was going and he was gone. This was kind of spooky.

"I was there for another three to four days and never did see him again. I went down into what was the Revolutionary War camp. There was nobody that looked like him or anything like that. And I asked the other traders that evening if they saw the soldier come in," but only three people saw him that night: Barlow, his wife, and the gun trader. "No one else did. Whatever it was."

What it may have been, Barlow suggests, was a visit from an "Ancient One." The Indians have a legend of the Ancient Ones, he says, "They believe that if you're following the teachings of the tribe, their grandfathers, who had gone into what would be heaven to us, will come down and guide the people who are trying to reenact or do things that they have done in the past.

"They will come down to meet people who are trying to portray it as best they can in the original way. Kind of give them guidance and know they've been recognized." That's how they came to call their group of reenactors the Ancient Ones.

Another member of the group, Ray Hamilton, says, "We do believe the Ancient Ones are looking out for us. We do believe they appreciate it."

"I'd like to go back in time. I wouldn't want to stay there, but I'd like to go back. I really would," Hamilton says.

The Ancient Ones are buckskinners, so called for their buckskin clothes. They recreate frontiersmen from the years 1740 to 1840, roughly from the French and Indian War to the last fur traders' rendezvous out West. The Ancient Ones have more than a hundred members, making it the largest such club in New England.

When the club was forced to leave the land where it camped, Ray and his wife Claire bought 89 acres, three miles from any "black road." The land had gone back to forest, but it had a long history of settlement. The Abenakis "had a couple of hundred acres planted to corn and pumpkins," and after they were gone, in the 1850s there was a small village. They restored an old well which was dug by a settler, Ebenezer Conant. "It's just beautiful, beautiful, crystal clear water." The Ancient Ones had guided them to a good place.

"I never planned this to happen," Hamilton says, never planned to own a large teepee, and have his wife and three children dress up on weekends. The two teenage boys have taken first place in shooting competitions.

"As a kid, Boone and Crockett were my heroes. I've got it in my mind now: I had a book on Davey Crockett when he was a boy and it shows him in the prone position on the ground, behind a log with his long rifle. And he's got one leg drawn up and he's firing at a turkey. That's something that's always stuck with me."

A friend encouraged him to go to a "rendezvous." "We walked though the woods and shot at random targets. We had to throw a spear. And we had to shoot a bow and arrow. And there was a knife and tomahawk throwing.

"The beauty of it is, you can do as much as you want or as little as you want. You don't have to shoot. Some of the women, well they used to just cook, most of them. They bought all kinds of Dutch ovens and they'd bake pies. We liked that a lot because the men got to go over and eat them. But now the women are getting more interested in shooting with us.

"Everybody enjoys it and it's a family oriented thing." They encourage the young to join. Without them this restored tradition "will die. We don't want it to die."

They teach visitors frontier skills, like starting a fire with flint and steel and throwing a tomahawk. "It's very simple to stick a tomahawk—stick it in the block. Once somebody does it, it's kind of magical.

"A lot of people can't even believe that we sleep outdoors overnight. They're amazed. We're amazed that they're amazed. Because it's so natural. They'd never sleep outdoors which I find quite surprising, living in Maine. But there's a lot of people that's moved up from the cities, I guess.

"There's so much to learn yet. We're always looking for new things that take us back."

There are many people who want to make this journey, this crossing. They want to go back to visit or to stay. They want to be there in the past.

Donlyn Meyers is the founding editor and publisher of the *Smoke and Fire News*. She has seen reenacting grow in the last dozen years. A spring issue listed upward of eight hundred events for the coming summer: battles, Highland games, pow-wows, rendezvous, Renaissance festivals, agricultural revivals. It's "experimental archeology," she says. "You take a reproduction object and you use it and see what happens."

The medieval organizations have 100,000 members, Meyers estimates. The buckskinners and Colonial-era adherents, including the Continental and British organizations, claim under 30,000. But the Civil War dwarfs them all with 300,000 reenactors.

Some of those playing in our history are Europeans. There's a "mad passion for native American stuff in Germany, and a lot of this mad passion for American Civil War there," she says. In England the "Victoria and Albert" time period is popular, as are "timelines," all of history laid out in one field, tent by tent, for your review: Vikings, Knights, English Civil War, American Civil War. At one event the timeline ended with the Gulf War.

I ask her for a fashion forecast. "The new and upcoming one? There's a lot more Korean War things than there ever used to be" and also more World War I and, with the fiftieth anniversary of World War II, more of that. Anniversaries are big, currently giving the War of 1812 a boost out in the Midwest.

"We're looking for Pirates next year to be the in thing. The last few years have been Scottish because of the movies that influenced it. *Braveheart, Rob Roy*. Everybody wants to be Scottish. Or wants to take a chance and wear a kilt."

These are all homemade festivals. But if fifteen thousand reenactors show up to replay Antietam and there is already a fantasy camp for every sport, and even rock bands, Disney will catch on. The imagineers will build a historical version of the biosphere experiment, a Cliosphere. They'll sign up a hundred or a thousand people and seal them in a big bubble to relive the year 1776 or 1865, or to restage old campaigns and reform movements. Maybe the summer of the Watergate hearings, in 1973, was your moment. Maybe you want to play Richard Nixon or John Dean . . . sign up now.

Disney will notice that this plays in Peoria. The *Smoke and Fire News* calendar listed the first Roman battle planned for North America. On a bluff overlooking Peoria, Illinois, Charles Young planned a skirmish between the Romans and the Picts, a northern Celtic tribe. This is the late Roman Empire, circa the year 400, as it crumbles in Britain. He expected a small event: Eight Picts might make the trip from Arkansas to face Young's eight Romans. ("The Roman Army Needs You," Young advertised.)

The Romans would be outfitted in "natural white tunics. Similar color britches. Oval shields. Minimum requirement is helmets," Young says. "No spears. And only swords and clubs are acceptable. And it's live steel. Not toys. Live steel. No offensive lawn furniture," by which he means the rattan swords another group uses. His steel swords are safe though. They have rounded edges. The Picts, trying for authenticity, would wear only britches on the first weekend in November.

Young had his Roman helmet made by his armorer in England. "Faxed him the dimension of my head. Two weeks later on my doorstep. Absolutely gorgeous. I mean it's a piece of work; a late Roman junior officer's helmet with high steel fan crest with pagan symbols embossed on it." Seven hundred dollars. He is saving up for a bronze, Greek Corinthian helmet.

Young started with this hobby twenty-five years ago when he was twelve, carrying the flag for a Confederate company. He is a design tailor.

He was a "salesman, a writer and everything else. I just decided to go with my true love and that's tailoring and history." He designs and sews all his own clothes and takes orders. He is doing a royal wedding. His wife does the embroidery, and he taught her how to make chain mail.

He was forced to learn to sew when he was seventeen. "My mother sat me in front of the sewing machine, said, 'Here, do it yourself.' When I pestered her to death to make French and Indian War uniforms, or seventeenth-century clothing or whatever. 'Here, do it yourself.'"

Young loves pioneering new reenactments. He does two periods of Romans, both pre-Julius Caesar and late Empire, English Civil War, 1680s French Marines. "Thirty Years War is another favorite." He's "easing back into" the French and Indian War with a Montcalm and Wolfe group. He's part of a Hessian Regiment for the American Revolution. For the War of 1812 "we do the rocketry battery. I designed a rocket that actually works without hurting anybody . . . the candy glitter goes everywhere. Looks like metal shrapnel." He wants to do World War I, German Uhlans, but you need horses and it gets expensive. "I'd still like to do it someday. When my ship comes in, get my horse and go out there and do Uhlan."

World War II is where he draws the line. The veterans have told him it's disrespectful. "They misunderstand it," he says. "What we try to do is commemorate those who've fallen. It's history books in motion. You can't really understand history until you see it standing in front of you.

"For a lot of us, it's a career almost."

"My wife and I, we go back to even the Ice Age," says Terry Barlow of the Ancient Ones. "I just came in here to show her a dart that I was making for an atlatl."

"An atlatl?" I ask.

"Spearchucker. Like the aborigines in Australia use."

He had just the changed the fletching, the tail feathers on the dart, copying one from a thirteenth-century cross-bow which he saw in a book. "And I figured, if they used leather back then, you can do it today."

"It's a step away from reality," he says. A step away from the walled-in and drained lives of our technological society. Barlow lives in the Maine woods, about two hundred miles north of where he grew up. His farm is for sale, it's getting too crowded. He will retreat further north.

Of those who find their way to his antique shop, some are just killing time, some are on treasure hunt, and others are trying to fill a hunger for the past. Almost as if matching his tale of the visit from the Ancient One, he tells of another visit from a contemporary. This man looks like a street person, but he comes up and buys nearly four hundred dollars of Barlow's reproduction eighteenth-century medical instruments. They get to talking and it turns out this fellow is the head of internal medicine at a major hospital, responsible for hundreds of doctors.

"You can walk out of that office and step back two hundred years and you can live as they did on the frontier. Or as we presume we did on the frontier," Barlow says.

"So if it all went to hell you could go out in the backyard and say, Gee, I know how to do this stuff. I can build a fire; I don't need matches. I can kill an animal with a spear. And I can shoot one with a black powder gun. I can dress it out. I can learn how to process the meat. I store it. I don't need refrigeration.

"You're doing stuff that you never even . . . surmised that you might be able to do. Like go out and build a tomahawk out of a stone. Go repair a muzzle-loader—or build a muzzle loader right from scratch. Forge a knife out.

"Basically what you are is a primitive survivalist, is what it amounts to." Barlow is part of "a very loose-knit organization: the Society for Primitive Lifestyles.

"We can teach you," he says. And he means, I believe, not just the skills, but he can teach you how walk away from the late twentieth century.

Some of the reenactors I have met remind me of the first film by George Lucas. In *THX 1138*, a subterranean society is run by computers. Drugs are force-fed; emotions are outlawed. A couple falls in love and races to escape. Nothing exceptional for this kind of dystopia, except for the last scene, memorable for its lack of special effects. The couple flees to the outer precincts of their underground world, which is chilling because it looks like a place we've all been: a big, grey, parking garage. They emerge and for the first time face the sun. They have escaped to the outside. Reenactors are looking for a way outside of our life and times.

People are happy in their war-leisure. The war games I visit are peaceful. The tent grounds have the languid, limpid quality of cow pastures. You don't see people running off with a list of errands, trying to get to the dry-cleaning tent before it closes, late to pick up their child at the day-care tent. There are no wristwatches. At Antietam I lived in a small city of fifteen thousand Americans without machine noise.

Our lives are so noisy that we use another era's turmoil as an escape to peace.

"Nobody brings radios and televisions or Coleman lanterns," says Donlyn Meyers. "It's all by candlelight. Very beautiful after hours, usually. I love going to events because it's so relaxing and you talk to people instead of being *bizzed*. So it's truly a getaway from modern intrusions."

"We're just a bunch of big kids, most of us," Ray Hamilton says. "It's kind of like when you went camping for the first time. We laugh and have a good time."

Among the reenactors at the French and Indian War battle were a husband and wife, an attorney and a banker from a prosperous Boston suburb, who have gotten caught up in the reenactment circuit, traveling all over each summer with their two sons, ages eight and six.

The father is outfitted as a frontier militiaman for the French and Indian War, and for the Revolution, as a French soldier in the Patriots' cause. The mom and children also have costumes.

The mother says that she and the others with young children find security in the encampment.

"You can just let them go off," she says. "You always know where they are and you know that they can turn to anyone else in eighteenth-century dress if they get in trouble. It's great for kids. They don't often get that kind of freedom."

War is safe for children. War is peace.

This is child's play, foolish and brave. This is Clio, played by Miss Bartholomew, calling out for the dreams to begin. And this is us, too, I think. All these white tent encampments, these thousands at play in the fields of Antietam. We invoke the muse of history, but we can never know what comes next. So we play at some dream and dance at the edge of the dark woods.

The Belated Tourist

❧ ❦

I. "Floors suffer."

This earth is no place for a house museum. To the keeper of a historic house, the earth is a science-fiction horror film. Life-giving water rots roofs and dissolves stone; benign sunshine reduces silk curtains to rags, bleaches wood, and cracks leather. Mice and rats and woodworms and moths are hungry for history. Mold floats in the air awaiting its chance. The curators are condemned to live on a planet where the fingertips of earthlings leave behind acid that tarnishes silver, where bronze and pewter are prone to "diseases," and dust can defeat a suit of medieval armor.

Life is a fire. Sunlight, air, and water sustain us and destroy us. Life consumes all we wish to save.

Consider just a few of the admonitions in *The National Trust Manual of Housekeeping*, the revised edition used by that British institution:

"Floors suffer."

"Every time an object is dusted it is at risk. . . ."

"It is unwise to ever trust a handle. . . ."

"It is a mistake to think that metals are hard. . . ."

"Rats and mice will attack books if they are given the chance."

A sink "is often the most dangerous place" for ceramics.

"*Never* touch original upholstery. . . ."

"Do not over-insist" when dipping silver.

"Bronze is specialized and difficult."

The National Trust's manual is an exhortation against the ruins of time and the ravages of light, water, handling, and breakage. The housekeepers of those vast country estates are like lecturing adults: Don't run with scissors! "It really is necessary to concentrate when handling objects; do not turn round to talk to someone, particularly when putting something down."

The manual's tone is firm: Never drag furniture. Don't overexhibit an object. Avoid placing nectar-dripping flowers in vases. "*Never* pick up a plate or bowl by the rim alone, but support it under the base, using both hands." Never rub when dusting metal; a dry duster can erase traces of fine engraving on armor. Never jam books tightly together on the shelf. Never pull books from the shelf by the spine. "Beware of the bacon beetle" which eats the fat under the skin of mounted fish. As for the larvae of beetles and moths: "The best weapon and defence is constant vigilance, good housekeeping and knowing your enemy."

Who can blame them for lecturing? The enemies are many. "Constant vigilance" can be wearying. Visitors point at oil paintings—sometimes with umbrellas!—as if they were maps of the Underground. Housekeepers slap the wet strands of their mops against medieval chests, stripping the finish off the feet. Repairmen, photographers, and "even house staff" on ladders don't see huge chandeliers and crash into them "all too frequently." "All need to be reminded that there is a chandelier in the room."

Nothing is safe; stone is "vulnerable." A marble table-top is a sponge awaiting a spill from a wine glass, or a stain from the "paints and dyes of unsuitable packing materials." "Smoke from a fire can turn it permanently brown or black." Marble is only "a mass of crystals and a blow will bruise the surface."

(If wine is spilled, "immediate action is essential," advises Robert McGiffin in *Furniture Care and Conservation*. "Alcohol, of course, is a solvent for shellac, which is often a component in many furniture finishes. It may liven up a dull party if the only available blotter for an alcohol spill on your furniture is your shirt or blouse. Never hesitate—use it!" But with the correct technique: "blot up alcohol quickly—and be very careful just to *blot; don't rub*.")

Entrusted with the national inheritance, the challenges are great, such as with the "boxing squirrels" at the Castle Ward, part of a tableau in which squirrels are posed in "human activities." (Whoever said the rich were idle?)

The trust's manual takes up the care of the once animate, under the heading "Cleaning mammals." Hair loss is a big problem. Insects, light, and "poor initial curing of the skin . . . can lead to catastrophic loss of hair for which there is no treatment at present." Other aspects are given special attention:

Ears and tails
Be very careful of ears and tails as they are fragile and can tear easily.

Eyes and teeth
Glass eyes and teeth may be dusted with a ponyhair brush. . . .
Noses
Dust with a hogshair brush. . . . If the nose is very dry, consult a taxidermist.
Lions
Lions can have their manes brushed with a soft brush,
but be very careful of the ears which can tear easily.
Elephants and rhinoceroses
Brush with a 50 mm wide paint brush, while at the same time collecting
the dust in a Hoover Dustette fitted with the crevice tool.

The curators' task is impossible: preserve all this stuff *forever*. They are in a pitched battle with the elements. Chemistry is their root knowledge. They realize that everything they handle is fragile, decaying with each moment. They know the cruel poetry of "dust to dust." "A library or an archive is a killing machine," says a paper restorer. "The historic house, when used as actively as it should be, can be a death chamber for old fabrics," says an authority on historic interiors.

In short, the things of this world slowly drive them crazy. They take to talking like this: "Glass crizzles as it crazes," "color is fugitive," "metals have inherent vices." The language has a military-medical bristle; they must prepare for "biological attack," ward off "photo decomposition," and recognize the warnings of "frass."

Or more exactly, they're not crazy, but crizzled.

On a table in the lab for objects conservation at the Museum of Fine Arts in Boston, Ken's shoes weep. Ken is Barbie's boyfriend. Ken's shoes are made of PVC, polyvinyl chloride. The shoes are tacky and wet; the plasticizers are coming out. "There is no known cure for this disease of contemporary materials," says Pam Hatchfield, an objects conservator at the museum. At best, you can extend the life with low humidity. "You have to assume that objects you're using are disposable," she says. "No matter how much you love them."

The little shoes share a fate with a grand inheritance of art. Hatchfield has prepared a slide show for our small tour group, and it's not the usual fine arts review of masterworks. Each slide is a visit to the rot of art. There's a faded drawing by Miro, showing "how fugitive some pigments can be," she says. The green paper has bleached white on top. Next slide: A ceramic face eroding from salt. Next: An ancient statue with pustules growing in its arms, symptoms of "bronze disease." This statue was once buried, and the salt and water in the soil have infiltrated. Now, they are deeply in the object. There's no cure, but as with cancer, one can keep it in remission, she says, in this case with low humidity.

Next up, a cross section of a fourth-century bronze mirror. There is no metal left, it is just an "assembly of corrosion products."

"All metals have inherent vice. They create their own problems. They want to revert back to their natural state as an ore," Hatchfield says, coming close to an allegory for human woe. Don't we all contain the seeds of our own downfall?

The things of this world are besieged from within and without: insects, dust, and earthquake. In California, some museums have netting across the front of storage shelves to catch objects. There are museum-inflicted losses: water damage (art stored in big name museums under sweating pipes), objects defaced by tagging and labeling, taping, shipping, and packing.

Storage can be more hazardous than handling. Materials war with each other. Coin collections, carefully stored in oak drawers, have vanished into dust, destroyed by the oak's tannic acid. Drawers of silvery dust.

"Off-gassing," as it is known, is a big issue, says Hatchfield. The carpeting, adhesives, plastics, and wood in an exhibit area have to be studied. Many modern materials are predators. Formaldehyde is "off-gassing" from storage materials, varnishes, and plywood. An entire conference has been dedicated to the problems caused by formaldehyde. Where there is art there is vice.

At the King's Chapel graveyard, I talk with a graveyard restorer about the problems faced by late-seventeenth-century slate headstones in the heart of Boston. Leave aside the destruction by earlier restorers: In the 1930s, the WPA set all the stones in a row, grouping them by name, so now three Rebeccas move through eternity in bureaucratic order.

Slate is durable, but centuries of freezing and thawing will have their way. It's difficult and often impossible to mend slate. Polyester resin fails; pinning it together rarely works. Nearly half the slate stones are beyond the help of the best experts. As the pieces flake off, the conservators can only sweep up the crumbs, saving the biggest pieces, and burying the smallest.

I look at the slate crumbling like cookies, and I think of a lecture I attended by a photo restorer. "How can I save early color photos from the 1960s?" a man asked. "They're starting to fade." If you keep them in the freezer they will last more than thirty years, the restorer answered, but then you can never look at them. The photos could be copied by scanning them into a computer, but nothing can be done for the original. "It's gone. Sorry."

* * *

Our friend had a glorious cat—an enormous, proud, gleaming black cat. She loved that cat as she had loved no other cat. In a house languid with the presence of cats, on a farm of handsome Connemara ponies, this cat was king.

The big cat got sick early one summer and died while still young. Our friend couldn't part with him. She decided that she would have her cat preserved. She intended it to be a tribute.

She took her cat to a taxidermist. He was a poor man with a family who lived way back in the hills. That is, even by the standards of our friend, who lived off a dirt road, up on her own hill, this was remote.

The taxidermist's children ran over to her when she pulled up. "Is that the kitty! Can we pet him?" "He's a dead kitty," our friend said. "That's okay," the children said, and they petted him: "Nice kitty."

The man brought out his taxidermy catalogs, pages of body shapes for otters, foxes, civets. . . . Styrofoam to fill in where the viscera, the lights, once were. Glass eyes to replace vision. She studied the catalogs and selected the pose for her cat and went home to wait.

Months went by. She dreamed of her cat. She dreamed that when she went to get her cat from the taxidermist, the cat was just a little bit alive. She could hear a faint purring. This is the dream of all restorations. She knew it wasn't going to last.

It was winter before she had her reunion. She went by herself to see her cat again, which would really not be her cat, but her cat entombed; the skin of her cat.

She was disappointed and upset. It was a terrible taxidermy job. It did not look anything like her young cat. It was as flat as a road kill. The ears were crinkly, the eyes were wrong, the head was misshapen. Not only had the cat's spirit and soul departed, but so had the body. She felt awful; she had betrayed her cat. If the ground weren't frozen, she would have buried it right then, she said. The poor cat looked like it was in pain.

Here in this story about a dearly loved cat is the story of house museums. We want the purring, the life everlasting. What we often get is rooms and rooms of furniture. House museums are taxidermy.

The philosophers call it evanescence, the passing from one state to the next. Under the right conditions, ice evanesces to vapor. (Ken's shoes weep.) Evanescence is a wonderful phrase, but when I pry back a board on our old house and reach in, and the beam comes out in moist handfuls like devil's food cake, it's not evanescence, it's rot.

Everything ever created will rot eventually: the Mona Lisa, the Brooklyn Bridge. . . . The world works to recycle itself. We are called on to be curators, guardians, shepherds. And still we can't save our flock.

Without rot, life itself is impossible. Rot probably deserves a better name, something less rotten: progressive deconstruction, returning. Or maybe there should be uplifting books like *Living Your Rotting*, and, *Wherever You Go, There You Rot.*

Things decay, oxidize. Your collapse is the building of something else. Most of life is not showing up, as Woody Allen said, but maintenance.

You can't escape rot, though we try. Fear of decay, denial of death; our monuments and our medicine are of one piece. Time will rot a house; trying to deny time will also bring it to ruin.

Many modern repairs are too strong. Adobe is ancient, mud and straw. It is flexible, expanding and contracting, or in curator-speak, "inherently dynamic." New, improved, "stabilized" adobe brick, mud mixed with cement or asphalt to resist water, is stiff. When used to repair old adobe walls, the bricks cause cracks or bulges and bring the old walls to ruin. It doesn't breathe like the old wall. The old mud may need continual renewal, but that is its essence.

You see this mismatch frequently. In the 1930s, the WPA repaired some old brick crypts in Boston cemeteries. They used hard mortar, instead of the original, softer lime mortar. The cement smashed apart the old bricks. The old mortar had dissolved slowly over time, evanesced. The modern material came apart more quickly, and is harder to repair. The big fix causes big problems. Contradictory materials, warring, forcing things apart. A failure in philosophy.

Restorers can see themselves as bailing the boat, or they can make its sinking part of the scheme. The best restorations, the ones that contain the spark of life, hint at their own fragility. They are part solid and part vapor.

When an earthquake in 1997 destroyed important frescoes in the thirteenth-century Basilica of St. Francis of Assisi, the ceiling came down in thousands of pieces. Firemen carried the fragments outside so the painstaking sorting could begin. Most of the fresco was lost, said the restorers.

One Franciscan nun, Sister Angela Morgenston, said: "Sometimes things need to be destroyed so they can be renewed."

All materials are fugitive. Things fade, dry out, crizzle and craze. Glass is a liquid. Mountains are borne to the sea. Life is fugitive.

The ideal atmosphere for house museums (on this planet) is a chilly coma, the temperature never rising above 59 degrees Fahrenheit, the relative humidity toeing the line between 50 and 65 percent (too dry desiccates fabric, too damp and there's mildew). No ultraviolet light enters. Visitors are few, well mannered, scrubbed and baked in an autoclave before entering. They are suited up in cotton oversuits, arms Velcroed to their sides so they don't touch a thing. To save floors from suffering, they enter only after walking on a scientifically determined length of "absorbent matting." (A minimum of three meters according to the International Wool Secretariat.)

"The most difficult task is to maintain the right environment," says the foreword to The National Trust's manual. "It is a matter of compromising, of finding levels of temperature and humidity, for example which will suit the woodwork, although it would prefer to be more damp, and at the same time keeping paper happy, even though it would like to be drier."

We have all visited house museums like this: The paper is happy, the woodwork is satisfied, but the house is dead; it tells no story. The house is a shrine to its objects, the highboy as a tribal fetish, a trophy engraved with the conservator's names.

When I read about the National Trust tending those large English estates with their furniture covered up, the chandeliers in muslin bags, the blinds drawn, and the thermostat never passing 59 degrees, I think that these old places have become the Miss Havisham of houses, sitting there in the gloom in her yellowing wedding dress by the decaying wedding cake. They are houses jilted by life. But this is unfair. The curators would keep Miss Havisham in better repair. The cake would be an epoxy model and Miss Havisham's dress would be white.

There is a strong element of dollhouse play, a credentialed adult play, in setting up a house museum. Let's pretend it's 1770. Make up a "collections list"—a list of furniture that was, or may have been, in the house. Imagine your family and dress the house accordingly, advise the restorers. "Imagine, for example, the father and mother and eight children gathered in the hall on a night during the Revolution, and what the room must have been like. . . . Was the war being fought nearby, and was the family anxious, or were the battles so far distant that any news was such old news. . . . Were the people clustered before the fire? Where would the furniture have been placed to accommodate such a scene?" asks *Recreating the Historic House Interior*.

Perhaps this is why quite a few houses come out as dollhouses. They start that way. Maybe it would be best to admit it up front and pursue a more imaginative play.

A house museum is in conflict with itself. It is a house divided, part house, part museum. A house, or a home, is in large measure its daily mess: the children's drawings on the fridge, the day's mail on the table, the garbage under the sink, the tomatoes on the window sill. A museum is about control: balanced humidity and temperatures, collections numbered and cataloged. If a museum is a mess, it's in trouble.

Curators are doomed to fulfill contradictory wishes: Stop time, and let a house live; seal it against the elements, and invite the public—the greasy-handed, dirt-clodding public—to tramp through, sometimes by the thousands. And how many houses can take that many visitors?

A museum is a display of artifacts; a house is a place of living, flux. Hence the uneasy fit one finds in house museums. We try to pretend this is still a place of life, even as our presence on a tour denies that. It may not be possible for something to be both a house and a museum, live in time and be stop-time.

II. "The Dumbfoundering Abyss"

Once, when I was in Wales, I found myself quite by accident in the village of Laugharne. The name sounded familiar. Laugharne, Laugharne? it kept echoing in my mind until I came to the village center and the obligatory heritage marker. Of course. Dylan Thomas used to live here. A beautiful, backward place he had called it, and so it was. A little shabby, one fish-and-chips joint village.

There was a sign pointing down a path to his writing studio. The tours were over for the day. I looked in the window of the small shed. A chair—two of its slats missing—was pushed away from a desk. There was an open book on the desk, a pen in a stand, a loose sheaf of paper, written on, and an empty bottle. Crumpled papers were on the floor. The good poet must have just stepped out.

I felt a little ridiculous, like the dupe who has paid 50 cents to see the world's largest lobster. It's A-Mazing! It's Stu-Pendous! The Poet's Stu-*di*-o! See the crumpled paper! See the muse herself!

The poet and critic Randall Jarrell, reviewing the year in poetry in 1955, observed: "Dylan Thomas' *Under Milk Wood* and Wallace Steven's *Collected Poems* were published last year; both poets are dead, now. We put up statues of poets, once they're dead, or buy their houses, but the only way we can really do anything for them is to read them."

In 1895 there were twenty houses preserved as museums in the United States. By 1933, with the boom in finding a "usable past," there were nearly four hundred. Today there are about six thousand house museums in America, six thousand houses in which life has been halted, houses ghosted by objects and their labels. If you were to visit two a day, with Sundays off for good behavior, it would take you nearly ten years to see them all. We once saw ourselves at the lead of the parade we called progress. Now we form committees and hold conferences to discuss the best ways to save the confetti and bunting.

"All of us now have been pre-empted, as I think we are all quite uneasily aware," says the literary critic Harold Bloom. Ours is a "consciously late" age. We suffer from the "recurrent malaise of Western consciousness," says Bloom, "the affliction of belatedness."

Bloom's concern is great writers and their influence. His theories don't send me back to Keats or Milton with renewed vigor, but when his theories are applied to house museums they are nearly perfect.

"Belatedness" may be the central experience of visiting house museums. We arrive and the great poet is not home. To paraphrase a famous sentiment of the Lost Generation, we arrive to find all the great adventures over, all the best Tiffany purchased, and the grand mansions built. We have arrived at the dinner party to find all the seats taken by the dead. We are too late, sometimes hundreds of years too late. We buy our ticket, get on tour, and stand behind the velvet ropes gawking, and listening to the guide's desiccated anecdotes.

Our very existence is a form of belatedness. We do not choose the age into which we are born. We rebel by willfully misunderstanding the legacy of the dead, says Bloom. We rewrite the past by misreading it until it tells us our story.

A poet, Bloom writes in *A Map of Misreading*, is "a man rebelling against being spoken to by a dead man (the precursor) outrageously more alive than himself." He rebels by misreading. "To live, the poet must *misinterpret* the father," says Bloom. He rewrites his father's life.

The dead wrestle with the living. "A poet is strong if other poets must work to avoid him," Bloom says in *Kabbalah and Criticism*. "Strong poets *must* be mis-read." The accepted views of a poet's works are usually the opposite of the poet's intentions, he claims. The museum visitor misreads the exhibit. The misapprehension of the past is our souvenir.

We can be extinguished by the past. "The precursors flood us, and our imaginations can die by drowning in them," Bloom says. He quotes the poet Edward Young (1683–1765), who had a short season of fame before his work was eclipsed by Alexander Pope. The poets of previous generations, said Young, "*engross* our attention, and so prevent a due inspection of ourselves; they *prejudice* our judgment in favor of their abilities, and so lessen the sense of our own; and they *intimidate* us with the splendor of their renown."

I have had this feeling visiting Teddy Roosevelt's house at Sagamore Hill. The scale of Roosevelt's life and ambitions seems out of proportion; the house itself is ample. (The room with the tusks and animal-skin rugs seemed much larger on grade-school field trips.)

On the porch the park service ranger gives a breathless account of Teddy's strenuous life: He would lead some visitors on a straight-line march across the landscape—guests had to climb, swim, jump, hurdle whatever might be in the way. The estate was the home planet revolving around the patriarch: a sprawling family gathered near, servants, important dinner guests, busy trips the world over. TR never tired. Even though he had been shot in the chest during a 1912 campaign stop, Roosevelt rushed to defend his would-be assassin from the crowd, and then, with a bullet in his chest, he delivered an hour-and-a-half speech, before he was persuaded to see a doctor. "He was so alive at all points, and so gifted with the rare faculty of living intensely and entirely in every moment," said Edith Wharton, a childhood friend.

How upsetting it is to find that the dead Teddy Roosevelt is more alive than his living visitors.

So we rebel. People look around and say: So what— *I'm* alive. I may not have won the Nobel Peace Prize or been president or been wealthy, but I have what old TR can never reclaim: breath, blood, presence. I am here, he is not. The sun shines today alright, and I'm going for lunch. Misreading sets us free.

Misreading, or "misprision" as Bloom also calls it, is the opposite of building the same ax generation after generation. The tradition is invention. Not the same ax, but a new ax to replace the old one.

This is bad news if you are in the ax-preserving business. In addition to rot, you have to contend with willful blindness. Many of the objects you struggle to save will remain unseen. Curators have an impossible mandate: First, find the truth about the past, and then communicate that truth to visitors. They are supposed to make objects, documents, and artifacts speak. They are supposed to "sing the unsung" and, in the words of Thomas Hoving, impresario of the blockbuster museum show, make "the mummies dance."

The curators are in a heroic struggle with misreading. Museum visitors *see* the past as nostalgia: a quaint time of simple pleasures, peaceful and carefree. Things were clearer then. The past is a sunlit country morning. The anxiety of today is not present. Just by being the past it implies a happy ending: See they got through, they succeeded, because, after all, we're here.

Contributing to the misreading of house museums and other exhibits is, to borrow a term from aerodynamics, the drag coefficient. How many people on a house tour have been dragged there by a spouse, parent, or friend?

It is just as well that the curators, docents, and volunteers don't know the value of their museum as it is traded in the open market: "OK, OK: I'll give you one hour at the Lord Peevish House if we go shop at Basketville afterward."

I leave it to a gifted student to work out the drag coefficient: $M=$ the museum's mission statement; $q=$ the "impact pressure" of $b\times l$: boredom $\times$ the time approaching lunch; and $S=$ the sweater the visitor saw at the outlet mall—should he go back and buy it?

$$\frac{M}{q(b\times l)+S}=H \text{ (For Huh? Or: How'd they heat that big place?)}$$

I should say that there is misreading and just plain ignorance. At the Grand Canyon, I overheard a visitor puzzling over the local "mule deer": "Mule and deer are mating?" she asked. And a park ranger told us he was asked; "Why do the Indians always live in ruins?" After a half-hour tour of Hoover Dam, we were walking across the top of the dam itself where it stops the Colorado River, when one woman from our tour said; "I don't see why they had to build this big wall here."

We have arrived at what Wallace Stevens calls the "dumbfoundering abyss between ourselves and the object." "For several hundred years now, at least, poems have located themselves smack in the midst" of this abyss, says Bloom. It's where many people write the story of what they are seeing. The object sits there, decaying, vaporizing. We stand behind the velvet rope, across an abyss, uncomprehending. Everything is in motion; sometimes there is a chance collision, a moment of understanding.

After touring dozens of house museums over the years, and reading Bloom, I reluctantly conclude that the house museum that succeeds the most is the one that inhabits the "dumbfoundering abyss." These are the houses that touch people and mean the most to them. The most successful house museums may be the most in error.

III. The Houses of Error: Belated Visits with the River Gods, Elvis, the Eldresses, the General, and the Poet

"A Fruitful Misunderstanding"

"The history of interpretation, the skills by which we keep alive in our minds the light and the dark of past literature and past humanity, is to an incalculable extent, a history of error," Frank Kermode, University of Cambridge professor, says in his sermon on Job's wife, "The Uses of Error." Job's wife has but one line. "Curse God," she says, and this is recorded euphemistically as "Bless God," making the way for thousands of years of misreading. The interpretations have inspired some good art and poetry, says Kermode. "The history of biblical interpretation will provide many instances of fruitful misunderstandings."

"Words bear apparently impossible double senses, especially words having to do with love," says Kermode. "It was of interest to Freud that in Latin the word for 'holy' also means 'accursed,'" he notes. "It would doubtless be convenient if words could only be used to mean one thing at a time; there would be fewer misunderstandings. But there would be much less poetry."

The more recent past is also fruitful with misunderstandings. The founders of this country framed the Constitution, and we are still interpreting it. The American Revolution lasted but seven years and we are still debating its meaning. There have been successive revivals of Colonial American architecture, each cut to a different fashion. "It is part of our experience of the past that we change it as it passes through our hands; and in changing it we may make it more puzzling in making it more our own," says Kermode.

Colonial America has by now passed through many hands. For about one-third of the history of Deerfield, Massachusetts, the village has lived partly as an artifact. Restoration is a business in Deerfield, like running the academy. They are intertwined.

Kermode's sermon could serve as the welcoming invocation for the visitor to this museum village. Historic Deerfield lives because it is in error. It is a brilliant misreading of Colonial history, one that in the end says more than it intended about how America at empire's tide saw its Colonial past: a merry tavern crowded with pewter tankards, a huge hearth, a brick floor, and the finest furniture. All citizens were good fellows, hale and well met. Revolutionary America was a jolly corner in the haunted 1950s (as I. F. Stone called the decade).

"As we turn back to the glowing hearth, light a pipe and perhaps have a friendly warming bit of cheer from generous flip glasses, we wonder whether there is another such unspoiled community? It all seems unique. Is it we ourselves who are here or are we just a shadow of the past?" said Historic Deerfield's founder, Henry Flynt, in 1955.

Henry and his wife Helen set out to make Deerfield a charming picture of the virtuous past. They succeeded. Deerfield is in error, and thank God. It's wonderful. They created a Deerfield that never existed, their own fruitful misreading, Flyntland.

Brave Deerfield was a flag to be saluted. "Is it not possible to sum up the strength of this Republic, its vigor and idealism and enterprise, in a single American community?" asked Flynt. Deerfield stands for "the spirit of free enterprise, the spirit of New England, the spirit which needs to go out into the Nation now," he said. Deerfield was, in the title of a 1952 book on the village, the *Frontier of Freedom*.

The Flynts were introduced to the village when they sent their son to the Deerfield Academy in 1936. Frank Boyden, the academy's legendary headmaster, drew them into the activities of the school and the village. Henry Flynt was soon serving on the school's board of trustees, and active in the village historical society.

"The whole atmosphere is rich in the traditions of courage and of character which made America," said a booklet the academy used for fund raising in 1929. "Somehow the granite of those hills has bred itself into the being of men of New England birth or training." Bruce Barton, one of most successful admen of his era, wrote the booklet. Barton had a bestseller in 1924 and 1925 with *The Man Nobody Knows*, which portrayed Christ as "the founder of modern business" and the greatest salesman and advertising genius of his age. (If there is ever a Hall of Fame for Misreading then Barton's book deserves its own wing.)

The place spoke to Flynt. "There are certain places one goes from time to time which are an inspiration," he wrote to Boyden in June 1940. "Deerfield is such a place with us, due largely to the quiet stately elms no doubt, in no small part to the real bit of England . . . set down in New England—the sun shining through the trees, etc."

The Flynts bought their first Deerfield house in 1942. Flyntland had commenced. Henry had known early that he was a collector. It ran in the family. His father had a hundred clocks, and once had bought an entire room of furniture just to get another clock. "I told my wife never to let me start collecting anything or I might well become a 'gatherer' of heroic proportions," he said. In time the Flynts would buy, restore, and furnish twelve houses, including a few that they moved to the village to replace houses with the wrong pedigree. There are "houses which are unfortunately not in the best Deerfield tradition—these, it is hoped, will be torn down and replaced by more appropriate replicas," Henry said in 1946. Anything later than 1820 or 1830 was a modern horror not in keeping with "the simple, harmonious beauty of Colonial days."

"The Flynts are like fairy godparents," Helen Boyden, the headmaster's wife, said in an after-dinner talk. "You'd say, 'Oh, wouldn't it be nice if that house were gone.' And you'd turn around and it was gone. And 'Wouldn't it be nice if that ugly color was off that house?' And lo and behold, it would be done. And 'Wouldn't it be nice if that porch was missing and you could see the original house?' And it would happen."

Deerfield's life as an artifact had begun long before the Flynts arrived. The village has a dramatic history. A settlement on what was then the western frontier, Deerfield was repeatedly attacked. The worst attack was in 1704 when a French and Indian raiding party killed 48, burned half of the houses, and marched nearly half of the village's population to Canada. The settlers persisted, prospering with the good soil. The Connecticut River Valley became the richest interior settlement in a golden age from 1750 to 1820, home to the "River Gods," as the ruling families were called. In Deerfield, the River Gods built fine homes on "The Street," the mile-long main street of the village; their craftsmen built lively and distinctive furniture.

By the end of the nineteenth century, Deerfield had been bypassed. Rural New England was a pretty ruin. The abandoned farm was the pictu-resque folly of the era. The village was "an historic oasis" for the Colonial revivalists. They arranged rooms to make a pleasing scene; they rebuilt guided by taste and not research. They played with history.

Deerfield is a romance. A theme park is a calculated commodity, each ride and snack stand prefigured. But this is a romance, with the courting and passion that produces poetry and foolishness. I suppose you could call many romances "fruitful misunderstandings." In some ways Deerfield has the heart of an old Broadway show, each house another musical number.

The early restorations have the razzle-dazzle of an outsized stage set. The Flynts were not interested in studying paint chips and nail holes, and excavating kitchen middens. Documentation was "sketchy at best." This is not the cautious, scientific restoration work of today. Guesswork and out-right invention are given full play. This was the past—let's put on a show!

The Colonial era is imagined with tables laden with pewter, shelves thick with delftware and old bottles, high-style, big-city furniture in a farming town, imported fancy goods, rich textiles, oriental rugs, nineteenth-century slate roofs instead of humbler eighteenth-century wooden shin-gles, and the signature jolly hearth. In a period of plenty it is difficult to en-vision a culture of scarcity. This is the underlying misreading of the different Colonial revivals.

The Flynts liked to entertain in one of their big Colonial kitchens, serv-ing elaborate dinners on antique dishes by the light of hand-dipped can-dles. They also favored costume balls, dressing up as they had dressed their houses. They gathered around the past as you would for a fireside chat with friends, for warmth and good cheer.

Like any good production, Deerfield achieved its own look. Bill Gass, who had worked in all the building trades, created the "Deerfield Look" of the 1950s and 1960s. Gass had a feel for the valley's old houses. He moved roofs, walls, stairs, and windows at whim. He used old wood to make his walls and trim look old. Frank Boyden praised Gass as you might praise a Broadway set designer: "I think there can be no doubt but that he more than any one person really understands the Deerfield atmosphere and is a very ingenious and interesting designer."

When the Dwight house, thirty miles down river from Deerfield in Springfield, was facing destruction in 1950, the Flynts "felt so sorry for the house" and rescued it. It was the oldest surviving house in Springfield, built between 1722 and 1733, and had a rough life in its last years as a tenement. The Flynts had an 1868 Italianate house on "The Street" torn down to make way.

Gass moved only the front of the Dwight house to Deerfield, eschewing the rest. He gave the house a nineteenth-century chimney and slate roof—it just looked better than wooden shingles and lasted longer, he said. He made the roof dormers different sizes "just for interest, no other reason," he said. Gass created a big kitchen with a brick floor, large jolly hearth, and exposed ceiling beams. The Dwight house never had such a kitchen. No mid-eighteenth-century house in the Connecticut River Valley—in New England—had that kitchen.

Gass had no formal training. He knew what he knew from growing up near Deerfield and from the previous romantic displays of Colonial revival domesticity. "I figured God gave me hands that could draw and a brain that just knew old things and studied," he said. The Flynts hadn't studied Colonial American architecture either, but knew the displays and houses of the local revivalists. They wanted atmosphere and feeling; Gass delivered.

He did study the old houses for evidence to find the placement of old walls, stairs, and windows. "When he could find no evidence of original work—and sometimes even when he could—Gass designed moldings, paneling, doorways, and other features that were based more on his experience with old houses and his own taste than on actual eighteenth century precedents," says Elizabeth Stillinger in her careful and thorough book, *Historic Deerfield*. "A number of the decorative pedimented doorways that ornament Deerfield houses are Gass's own freely adapted versions of traditonal Connecticut Valley doorways, called by some residents 'Bill Gass originals.'" Gass influenced restoration throughout New England, says Stillinger.

The Flynts loaded these houses with the riches of their collection, creating a "decorative arts fantasy," says one later Deerfield curator—a fantasy that occurred "in nearly all period rooms devised in the first two-thirds of this century," Stillinger says.

The Flynts' interiors mimic the rise of 1950s "Populuxe" culture, in Thomas Hine's brilliant phrase. They go from modest furniture and hooked rugs, to more elaborate schemes late in the decade. There's a 1950s tailfin effect. Just as cars grew more ornate, at Deerfield simple furnishings gave way to the S-curved legs and scrolled pediments of Queen Anne and Chippendale, and china cabinets full of plates and curios. The Dwight house opened with fancy Boston furniture and elaborate drapes by a New York interior designer.

The Flynts' tastes shifted as they got to know the leading collectors of American antiques, a group who in the late 1940s and early 1950s were active in establishing Old Sturbridge Village, Cooperstown, Shelburne in Vermont, and other museums. They influenced one another. The Flynts began collecting more formal furniture, walnut, mahogany and cherry, says Stillinger. Taste inflation set in, creating a kind of Cold War Colonial revival.

Even the meals of this group were opulent and high caloric, seeming to us now like a period piece, such as a dinner for a dozen or so at Katharine Murphy's New York apartment described by Stillinger: "Helped by her devoted retainers, Julia and Samuel, Mrs. Murphy set a sumptuous table with early 18th Century silver, Dr. Wall Worcester, and old ruby glasses. Delicious crab and lobster hors d'oeuvres were followed by a great thick steak or roast—carved by the hostess herself—served in a romantic candlelit atmosphere. Samuel circulated, pouring his famous whiskey sours from pewter pitchers."

The Flynts were building a bigger, better past. "New & improved" was the creed of Populuxe America. "Never before," said *Life* magazine in 1954, "so much for so few." When they opened a "new" house there were crowds, excitement, and requests for plans. People came to see the Dwight house when it opened in 1954 and fell in love with its large hearth and brick kitchen floor. They toured the Ashley house when it opened in 1948 and went home and built Ashley houses. For the World War II veterans, the Ashley house was a welcome picture of home. "There are Ashley houses all over the country," says Bill Flynt, the founder's grandson, who is an architectural conservator at Deerfield.

New is not a misnomer for these eighteenth-century houses. Flyntland was unveiling the latest fashion in the Colonial revival. The Street, the much preened and praised dwelling place of the "River Gods," was like many model house developments of the 1950s. A suburban tract house builder would set out four or five model houses, sometimes around a cul-de-sac. On weekends the dream houses would be mobbed by apartment-weary veterans and their wives.

There are no carports, TV rooms, or split-levels in Flyntland, but the whole display is a primer of home decor, a 3-D shelter magazine. Besides, you might trade up. Move on up to a Dwight kitchen, or maybe a modified Ashley with a two-car garage, and a barbecue pit out back. And in the meantime, you could put in some of that brick-pattern linoleum tile in the kitchen, hang curtains showing spinning wheels and flintlocks, and maybe build some fake exposed beams, or add a butter-churn lamp.

These are houses playing dress up. Deerfield was a jolly place for dress-up games. There were costume balls, drinking in the tavern, candlelight tours. We may have the paint chips and studies to show us a more accurate picture of the past, but their evenings sound like more fun. "It was wonderful and people loved the Flynts and loved Deerfield," said Peter Spang, the museum's first curator.

Flynt and Gass were carrying on a Colonial revival tradition, building new houses under old roofs. Perhaps the essence of this aggrandizing is caught in one early proposal to preserve Mt. Vernon: Tear it down and rebuild it inside a larger, marble Mt. Vernon. This is close to how the Mayans built their pyramids, by encasing an earlier, modest shrine within the new work. The Flynts and other revivalists have surrounded our history with ever more grandiose versions of the past.

Lincoln has suffered a similar fate. His boyhood cabin, eighteen feet by sixteen feet, is enshrined in a classical marble and granite temple with a entrance of fifty-six steps, one for each year of Lincoln's life. The Traditional Birthplace Cabin had to be shortened to fit the temple. No matter, it's almost certainly not the real cabin anyway. The provenance is suspect, as they say in curator talk. Some of the logs are said to be from the cabin. They once toured the country as a sideshow attraction.

At the Lincoln Memorial in Washington, D.C., the nineteen-foot-tall Lincoln looks down the Mall. One time I visited with a friend and her four-year-old daughter, who said, looking up the steps, "He was a big man!"

"She's having a problem with statues and representations," her mother explained.

"We all do," I said, as we trooped up to the statue.

The antiquarians of Flynt's generation unexpectedly share some traits with the Italian Futurists. The Futurists, before Word War I, wanted to level the past, and "invent and rebuild our Modern city like an immense and tumultuous shipyard, active, mobile and everywhere dynamic."

"Get a hold of picks, axes, hammers and demolish, demolish without pity the venerated city," they wrote. The Futurists are the revenge of the belated. Begin by "blowing sky-high . . . all those monuments and monumental pavements, arcades and flights of steps." This goes beyond misreading—just blow it all away, all that crud by Bernini and Michelangelo and da Vinci and Alberti.

Futurists and antiquarians should be opposed. But both misread the past to make way for a future as they see it. Both are Utopianists, one of pewter tankards and glowing hearths, the other of speed and glass. Both want to overturn the present and move on. Revivalists and revolutionaries are latecomers.

The curators of Deerfield today correct and amend and labor to tell a truer story. They are working to reinterpret all the houses. These days they may take ten years to research and restore one house, versus the six to eight months the Flynts took. Their efforts will be added to the history of trying to reach the past.

At the Wells-Thorn house, the curators have reclaimed the kitchen for the realities of 1715–25, when Deerfield, after the attacks, was depopulated and poor. The kitchen has no furniture, only a few cooking utensils, and little food. Sacks of grain hang from the rafters. There is firewood by the stove, and an ax, a hoe, a gun, and a rolled up mattress. No one is likely to go home and remodel their kitchen in this fashion.

But they are keeping that big brick kitchen at the Dwight house. It is a record of aspirations, a double-exposure photo of 1954 looking at circa 1730. Deerfield is a double-exposure photo. More visitors will photograph the Colonial revival dorms of the academy, rather than the actual colonial houses, unaware that the dorms were built in the 1950s. And why not; they've been conditioned by more than one hundred years of the Colonial revival to look for the big, gleaming past.

To restore is to choose. To restore is to create, to compose a new picture out of the pieces we find. Every large restored cultural monument is surrounded by a passionate debate about its authenticity. Each age creates willfully, or by accident, the ruins it likes.

"The Mayans are always building new ruins," says George Ashley, a professor, who with his wife, Pearl, has been living part of the year in the Yucatan for a dozen years. We were visiting for a few days. He handed me a guidebook to the temple ruins of Dzibilchaltun: "It's an old guidebook. There's more now," he said.

Up the road was a small Mayan ruin, a mound covered with trees and topped with a Christian cross. The Yucatan is flat, so anywhere there is a mound, there is a ruin. At the mound there was an altar by a spring where candles would be lit, and chicken feet left as an offering. It was a glimpse of the local, supercharged Catholicism, the old beliefs and the European import in an overheated mix.

The Mayans rebuilt often, the older original temple covered over, Russian-doll-like, a nut inside a shell.

When they began to "restore" the local mound, hundreds of men with wheelbarrows were moving all over, seemingly without direction, said Ashley. It looked like a 1920s anthropology picture, including the head archeologist, a woman from Mexico City, wearing a pith helmet, he said.

"What are you doing?" Ashley asked, when he saw they were starting to cover up a fine intact small temple.

"We're restoring it," she said.

"But how do you know what it looked like?"

"Oh, they're all the same," she said. And besides, she told him, the tourists like big pyramids.

The Colonial revival all over again. The big fireplace or the big pyramid, all part of the big show.

Graceland

We claim popular songs, movies, and books for our own by misreading. This is how a pop chart hit can sell millions, "go" gold or platinum, and still be *our* song, *my* song. There is a space in the popular song that invites our dreaming: We're walking by the river, it's our heart that is broken, somebody done us wrong. Elvis sang *my* pain. Great entertainers draw crowds, fill stadiums, and yet sing to each person individually. Nervous fans, upon meeting the star, sometimes misspeak: You're one of my biggest fans. A misstatement, and a truth: You're mine. Performers are imprisoned by their fans, and the larger their fame, the more secure the prison. They are locked down, sentenced to live with their image. It's the worst King Midas story: All that they touch becomes themselves.

We also claim more serious art the same way, such as documentary photography, which is often presented as a report of the truth. We bring our own story and editing to the photos. In *Documenting America 1935–43*, a collection of essays about the celebrated Depression era photos that have become the "look" of that era, Lawrence W. Levine examines Dorothea Lange's photo of the "migrant mother." We know this photo: a forlorn woman, sitting alone among some luggage under a tent. But what we do really know about this woman? Lange drove up, clicked six shots, and drove off. She didn't even stop to ask for her name, or her story. Is she a victim, destroyed by the Depression? Or is she a heroine, resolute, and dignified? The photo has been read both ways. Lange discarded the other photos she took—they show the woman's children playing nearby, and her teenage daughter with a dreamy look. But they do not live as a type. Poverty has many dimensions, but a good polemical photo (like a popular song) reduces its subject to a symbol, says Levine.

In William Goldman's book about Broadway, *The Season*, he says: "Whatever you call it, the thing that characterizes Popular Theater is this: it wants to tell us either a truth that we already know or a falsehood we want to believe in."

Graceland is a dream space, a misprision, a setting for misreading. The visitor is not outside the story, looking in, as he might be at, say, Calvin Coolidge's home. Each year 700,000 fans come to Graceland and say we love you Elvis; Show us a sign. Graceland is surpassed by only two other house museums, the Hearst Castle and George Vanderbilt's 255-room Biltmore House, each with 850,000 visitors annually. Elvis Presley Enterprises takes in $250 million a year. The company used the last $500,000 of Elvis' estate and $60,000 in advance ticket sales to open. They made their investment back in thirty-eight days.

Graceland is somber. Visitors, each linked to their private tour tape in English, German, Japanese, or Spanish, are as isolated as cars on the freeway. We all pour through Graceland together. You don't tour Graceland, so much as you are loaded in, and played through like the tour tape you are assigned. At no time do the visitors speak a word to each other or meet each other's eyes during the one-and-a-half-hour tour. On this day, at 10 a.m. alone there are twenty-three tours of sixteen each, the size of the buses that shuttle across Elvis Presley Blvd. There are long lines to embark at the sprawling Graceland Plaza, which is part bus station and tourist mart. ("Apply Here. Elvis Mastercard.")

There is no drag coefficient here. These are not visitors whiling away a morning, but pilgrims who have come to see the King. Elvis reached out and grabbed hold of something in people and he never let go. Elvis is deeply felt. There is no clowning, none of those house-tour questions: He lived when? How did they heat the place?

The pilgrims arrive knowing the story and having lived it. In Vernon's office, where his dad answered the fan mail and paid the bills, they see a tape of the press conference Elvis held after he got out of the Army. He is asked, "Did you leave any hearts, shall we say, in Germany?"

"He sure did," answers a woman next to me in English with an accent that may be German. There are many Germans on the tour. Out in the "meditation garden" are wreaths from Belgium and Germany.

The visit is perfectly choreographed to the tape, from Elvis singing "Welcome to my world" as we enter the gates of Graceland, to Priscilla telling us again and again how happy they all were, laughing at the dining room table, laughing as they rode horses, laughing as Daddy played the piano, laughing as they played racquetball. Happy all the time. A Southern, gold-plated Camelot. The tape neatly elides over his downfall and death at age forty-two: "Health problems and dependence on medication were wearing him down."

You are through the house itself before you hardly know it. Graceland, the fourteen-acre estate, is like a miniature golf course when compared to many other house museums on the circuit. The house itself is like a large suburban ranch with those white Southern Colonial Revival columns that pay homage to Tara. Inside, on the main floor, all is white and mirrored and very 1970s gauche. In the living room, there's an expansive fifteen-foot-long white couch, a white carpet, a white TV, mirrors, and two floor-to-ceiling stained-glass peacocks; in the dining room, a mirrored table and one of his fourteen TVs so Elvis could watch as he dined with his friends, the "Memphis Mafia." Priscilla would try to have candles to make it romantic, not easy with that group, she titters.

You pass from the dining room to the kitchen—more happy times— Elvis loved meatloaf so much, Priscilla had to ask the cook to please make something else. You thread downstairs, mirrors on both sides of the stairs. The TV room has more mirrors on one wall and the ceiling, and a painted lightning bolt on another wall, blue and yellow. This is his 1970s logo with the initials TCB—Takin' Care of Business. It's a teen's idea of a cool room: three built-in TVs in a row—President Johnson had three to watch the news, Elvis learned, so he got three to watch football; a built-in jukebox; a bar; and a huge pit of a couch, the ultimate make-out couch.

Across the narrow passage is the pool room, under its 350 square yards of folded cloth. It's like being inside a pin cushion. Elvis didn't like to play pool so much, but he liked being with the guys. You can still see where one of his buddies flubbed a shot and tore the green felt.

You pass back upstairs—green shag carpeting on the walls—to the famous jungle room. Green carpeting on the floor and ceilings. Large, bizarre chairs, sort of 1950s Bali Hi-Polynesian Restaurant crossed with the *African Queen*. Elvis was driving around Memphis, saw the furniture in a window and bought it all.

And then, kerplop! you're outside. The tour continues to the office— IBM Selectric typewriter, old-time adding machine, Cremora, filing cabinets—and on to the trophy room, redesigned as a full-fledged museum with halls of gold records and other awards. For a while Elvis had his slot cars set up here. Slot cars were a cool toy in the 1960s. (Elvis' mom had talked him out of installing amusement-park bumper cars on the back lawn.)

The tour slows to a crawl in the trophy museum. Film clips and old TV appearances stop the faithful in their tracks. There are trophies and plaques ("World's Greatest Car Buyer"), Jaycees' awards, a signed picture of the Thunderbirds, badges and awards from many different police departments and groups like the National Sheriff's Association. There is a selection of gifts that have been sent to Elvis: scrapbooks with elaborate covers, and paintings that show that a lack of technique is no obstacle if you have heart. Elvis called these gifts his "happies."

You do not look at this stuff individually and see its tacky bowling-trophy cheapness. But rather you just look at this hoard in its glittering aggregate. Quantity, not quality, is what counts with populist tributes. Behind the glass are rows of metal and plastic saying: yes! yes! yes!, affirming the pilgrim's belief. When not examined too closely, the awards lined up in the glass cases seem like the plunder of Troy.

The final glass cases show the 1970s white and glittery jump suits and capes from the Bloated Elvis Era. This is placed, without intended irony, opposite Elvis' law and order awards, including his Narcotics Bureau badge presented by President Nixon in 1970. There are no pictures of the Bloated Elvis, not even performing. Instead, with a nice sleight of hand, we are shown his karate and tae kwon do belts.

The tour tape insists that Elvis was a fitness nut, an eighth-degree black belt in karate and tae kwon do (he'd show guests his moves in the foyer of the house), a horseback rider, racquetball player, touch football player and just one of the guys who would shoot Roman candles at each other. (What would it have done to his legend if he had gone in a fireworks accident?) Apparently, even when bloated, Elvis was one happy and physically fit guy.

The tour directs you to Elvis' 1975 racquetball court building where a towering wall of gold records is displayed. They were presented, posthumously, to mark the all-time best-selling recording artist. Elvis sold one billion records worldwide. His "Aloha from Hawaii" TV show in 1973 was watched by more American households than the moon landing, and by 1.5 billion people worldwide, says the tour tape. In 1960 he was given a console TV from RCA Records for selling 50 million records. The TV is in the trophy museum, all nicked up.

The "meditation garden" is at the tour's end, the resting place of Elvis, his mom and dad, and grandma. The setting is like some overpriced catering hall that does proms and weddings: a semicircle of white Ionic columns, backed with a white-brick wall with stained glass windows, which look out into the backyards of a suburban subdivision. At center is a plashing swimming-pool blue fountain.

And here, with the tape off, but earphones still on, people stand in a respectful silence. I've been to European cathedrals where the clatter and the chatter had to be shushed by recorded announcements reminding daytrippers that this is a house of worship, not a medieval amusement park ride. But here there is silence such as you find nowhere else in American public life.

Flowers decorate the bronze tombs. Standing up behind the tombs are some of the floral wreaths that flow into Graceland all year, particularly around the August anniversary of his death. Elvis fan clubs in Belgium and Berlin, Germany, and Clifton, New Jersey, have made and bought and sent blazing red hearts with Elvis at center, and blue flower frames around the King, and fading ribbons that say: We miss you. And: "19 years and still missing you. With love Kelly, Pauline, Bob, Laura." And: "We miss you so. Klaus Kroller & Mike, Berlin, Germany." There's a needlepoint pony, three feet tall, with a red banner on the pony's back:

Love
4
Elvis
Fan Club
Clifton, NJ

Most of the flowers are silk and plastic. They "remain until they begin to show the effects of the weather," we are told. Real floral displays are placed in the air-conditioned racquetball court.

A man from California has left his wallet-worn business card. Under his name it says:

Actor
Comedian Writer Emcee Oldies DJ

A two-line resumé that hints at a lot of striving and scrambling and dreaming and frustration. On his card he has written: "Thank you for helping me my life through. . . . Rest Now, friend."

I had come to see some campy interiors and to understand the South a little. But I came away impressed by the devotion and the heartfelt homage. One steps back in the presence of this emotion.

If the pilgrims were allowed to make more primitive offerings, they would. Bend backward to kiss a stone, or rend their clothing, or draw blood from themselves, they would.

The smooth-voiced narrator on the tape could say, "Now, after leaving the meditation garden, please feel free to make an offering at the votive shrine. Please refrain from the ritual slaughter of small children and family pets. State health and sanitation codes do *not* permit such offerings."

In some ways, Graceland sits there like the Parthenon on the Acropolis Rock, when it was surrounded by the assorted shrines and altars for the local place gods of agriculture and good fortune.

Acropolis Rock was a fifth-century multimedia experience, a processional pageant of dozens of small shrines, fires, brightly colored temples, and statues ornamented with gold and bronze. The pilgrim was impressed with holy majesty, mystery, and awe. Today, as art historian David Watkins notes, we have the Greeks without the blood and sacrifice and superstition. We have the noble Hellenes who gave us democracy, equality, and the agora. The spare ruins of the Acropolis are fitting for the modernist, secular sensibility. Geometry and light.

Graceland with its main shrine, and lesser shrines, ornamented with gold records and bright colors, is like the worship of a local deity—the King, the greatest recording star of all time, the boy who came home from the Army vowing never to leave Memphis.

Graceland also reminded me of a visit we once paid to the home of Josip Broz Tito, who had held Yugoslavia together after World War II until his death in 1980. We were in Belgrade visiting friends who were covering the civil war there. There were protests in the streets, and soldiers just back from the front in Croatia. The café talk said Bosnia was next (which proved true).

Tito's house was deserted. The place was set up for crowds. Our tour guide told us that a hundred a day used to come. "But now we have small visitors, ten to twenty a day." Even that seemed exaggerated. There were four in our tour group, including my wife and myself, and no one else was in sight.

Tito had a suite of houses on a 100-acre estate. There were many outbuildings for amusements: machine shop, billiard house, animal house (a gift from Slovenia for his hunting trophies—"closed but very interesting," we were assured). There were museums filled with paintings, scrapbooks, trophies, gifts from the faithful, and there was Tito's tomb in the Winter Garden. Titoland was also somber, a faded Communist seriousness, mixed with an edginess about what comes next.

In a rigid Communist manner we were instructed: "Now you look at the medals collection, clockwise." We looked. "Now you come here." We came. We were in the "Museum of 25 May," Tito's birthday. There were 101 medals, some that Tito was the "only president in the world to have," honorary diplomas and decrees, each larger than the next, Tito's pipes and cigars, eyeglasses, passport, and his empty uniforms, still puffed out in Tito's profile. A man ran ahead of us turning on lights and turning them off as we left. He said he had an aunt in San Diego "five minutes from Disneyland."

Tito had a better horde than Elvis: a desk set from Haile Selassie, an ivory and wood box from Mahatma Gandhi, a gold coffee service from Saddam Hussein. Mao had sent an intricately carved ivory tusk, which an artist had spent twenty years carving. Richard Nixon had sent a clunky mahogany commode, a copy of a 1792 original that looked like an Ethan Allen factory second. The collection was endless: a silver pan and cover from Liz Taylor and Richard Burton, engraved, "To Marshall Tito . . . Happy Xmas. With great admiration and affection." Anwar Sadat had sent a rather ominous gift, a statue of Osiris, the god of the lower world and judge of the dead. What would Miss Manners say about that?

We were marched to another museum, gifts from the "small people," common folks. The guide turned on the lights and said, "Small people give to Tito their present and write good wishes to Tito and happy birthday and so on. People loved Tito, and something small and something big to give to him."

We looked down a long, long hallway, lined with homemade gifts (men's on one side, women's on the other). We could not see the end of the hallway. Mercifully, time was running short and we were directed to move on. Much of the estate was closed: No zoo, billiard house, animal house, machine shop, photo darkroom house, for us.

Tito was a hobbyist. He hunted wild boar, he collected machine shop tools. He played billiards. ("Tito liked to play billiards in the evening," our guide said, and quickly added, "When he had time. Tito was a worker all his life.") He developed photos. He saved anything ever given to him. And he had houses for it all. Tito's whole compound had the air of some *Popular Science* magazine home handyman's project taken to its limits: Build Yourself A Country Retreat! Entertain Dignitaries!

We followed the crowd-control arrows on the pavement to his tomb at the Winter Garden, a small marble atrium with a red carpet, flowers, and the sound of running water. Four soldiers stood at attention, with bayonets in the air, trying to look soldierly but stealing a glance at the visitors.

At Tito's house and at Graceland, one can accidentally see around the big show, see the hoists and ropes that move the backdrops, and ask: Is that all there is?

You can have anything and you fill your house with slot cars at Graceland, or little hobby houses at Titoland. You sense the exile imposed by fame, and the limits of the imagination and the soul itself. Tito and Elvis lived on desert islands.

The City of Peace

Misreading is misprision, says Bloom. Misreading imprisons a story or an object.

The Shakers built their City of Peace, their utopia of heavenly perfection, on the main road. They wanted the "world's people" to see how they prospered in their faith. The great stone barn and brick dormitories at Hancock, Massachusetts, and all the trim buildings were advertisements, recruitment posters. The Shakers were like so many religious utopians, but they possessed an American pragmatism and a free-spirited innovation.

They lasted but a short time, leaving us their beautiful empty rooms; the elegant and spare furniture, the rows and rows of pegs no longer holding the coats of elders and elderesses. They leave us their work, some still standing true, like the marble steps carved out of one piece, at Hancock and at Canterbury, New Hampshire. Work was a form of worship; they were living in heaven. In their work, and in their faith, these most pragmatic of pilgrims are distant from us. They lived communally, worked twelve hours in the fields, ate silently at 6, 12, and 6, were celibate, and honored an exacting list of rules. At times they prayed wildly and without ceasing. Hard work, fervor, the ecstasies of faith, a life that is a unity—all that is hard to comprehend for the tagged day visitor, shuffling along.

We sit in the empty meetinghouse room, painted white and blue, the colors of heaven, and the guide says: We have no witness to the dance, the "laboring," the "shaking off" of worldly sin that was central to their belief. In the late nineteenth-century, the Shakers stopped dancing; they were too elderly to keep up the "laboring." We do know some hand motions and we have the ten thousand short songs, the guide says.

In the kitchen of the great brick dormitory at Hancock, we talk with a woman who is baking bread and pies and cookies. They are set out on a table. Beautiful-looking food; so perfect, I thought at first that it was fake.

I ask her what they do with this food. "We feed it to the pigs and chickens. Some goes to compost." This woman bakes for pigs. I thought the food would go to a community kitchen, or to the town's overseer of the poor.

I will write a poem, entitled: "In the City of Peace, a Woman Bakes for Pigs." She bakes carefully, following Shaker recipes. And the pigs rejoice, are glad at the trough and sleep the good sleep of a full stomach and a snout covered with bits of muffins.

This is emblematic of the problems of restoration and the making of museums. Things get changed in the handling, original purposes sometimes become their opposite. When you consider all the effort it takes to restore and keep a museum like the Hancock Shaker village going, it is all the more heartbreaking. In a museum dedicated to a religion that made thrift a grace, pigs eat fresh-baked goods.

The Shakers would seem to be an ideal candidate for museum treatment. The nuances of their furniture are made for scholarship. We have their buildings and oral history, and the words to their songs, even if we lack the dance, the spiritual heart. Yet, we forget they were utopians whose presence was meant to challenge society. Their communities were like a work of art, demanding, as Rilke said, that you must change your life.

But museums live on paid admissions, not confrontations. Many museums elicit from their visitors a reaction of "Oh, isn't that interesting" or "That was nice." People take leave of the Shakers thinking of them as that odd group that made nice furniture. Maybe a Shaker rocker would look good out on the sun porch? So much the better than to carry away challenging questions about ways of knowing God.

What are we to do with this collectivist, celibate, euphoric cult? In California they're crazy for kitchen cabinets with Shaker knobs, little signifiers of authenticity. The promise of a serene orderliness: "No dirt in heaven," said Mother Ann Lee. The Shakers are prisoners of their furniture.

The Imprisonment of U. S. Grant

Ulysses S. Grant's cottage is in a prison, the Mt. McGregor Correctional Facility. The razor-wire topped fence of the prison yard is just a hundred feet from the back of the cottage. The cottage itself sits under old trees facing east toward a famous battleground and Vermont.

We do this well in America, the landscape of split intentions; two partners dancing, but each to a different beat. The pastoral and the expedient; the National Park rimmed by a gravel pit; the house that backs up to a highway; drive-thru worship. The cottage, painted a butternut-squash yellow with red trim and green shutters, wrapped by a generous piazza, could be a signboard for the idea of Victorian Domestic Comfort. Crowding in behind rise up the bright, gleaming teeth of razor wire and the gray stories of the prison. An odd couple, these two.

Grant's pleasant cottage was many prisons before it ended up in prison. Here Grant was the prisoner of his last days, dying from throat cancer while he heroically finished his memoirs. He had arrived at this cottage as the showpiece of a speculative venture. He was another Tom Thumb or Jumbo the elephant, a circus act: Come venerate the great general and former president.

His doctor had wanted to move him out of the heat of a New York City summer to some place he could breathe easier. The doctor could do nothing else, except ease his pain with cocaine, morphine, and brandy.

Grant, at age sixty-three, was dying penniless. He had been swindled out of his money, investing in his son's failed banking house. He had lost his money at the same time that he was diagnosed with inoperable cancer. He didn't even have his Army pension, having resigned to run for the presidency. Facing a painful death, and the thought of his widow's poverty, Grant once more in his life did the remarkable. He wrote his memoirs, 400,000 words in eleven months, "perfect in concision and clearness, in its propriety and purity of language," as the critic Edmund Wilson said.

Joseph W. Drexel, a wealthy partner of J. P. Morgan, and a friend of Grant's doctor, offered the general the cottage. Drexel was an investor in a three-hundred-room hotel resort and a railroad on Mt. McGregor, ten miles north of Saratoga Springs, New York, one of the country's most fashionable resorts. The hotel had opened a year earlier and was empty. Saratoga, which was a three-hour train trip from New York City, had casinos, hotels, horse races. People saw no reason to take another train to Mt. McGregor. The cottage was on the hotel's grounds.

"That is just the place I have been looking for," said Grant's doctor. "There is little heat there; it is on the heights, it is free from vapors, and above all, it is among the pines, and the pure air is especially grateful to patients suffering as General Grant is suffering."

Grant arrived on June 16, 1885, and with his wife, children and grandchildren, eleven in all, posed on the front steps for a family portrait. The trip had been trying. The ailing Grant, his neck swollen, could only find some relief propped up in two leather arm chairs. He slept in these chairs, sitting up, or else he might choke to death. The chairs were moved with him, and set up on the train. It was a hot day; when the train stopped in Albany for twenty minutes to switch engines, the temperature rose to 105 degrees in the car. They changed trains at Saratoga. Grant walked as firmly as he could manage. Veterans of the army he had led to victory gathered to cheer. By the time they reached the cottage, he could walk but a few steps, and had to allow himself to be carried in a chair—a journey of 150 feet from the train depot to his cottage.

The hotel was mobbed that summer; business was fabulous. The newspapers kept a front-page death watch. Telegrams and flowers arrived daily. Each day the railroad brought hundreds of sightseers who hoped to glimpse the great man seated on the piazza. "A slight wave of the hand or a nod of recognition was all the return his condition would allow him," cottage custodian O. P. Clarke recalled twenty years later. "Many now living remember the stooping figure as it moved slowly . . . to the pillowed and bolstered chair at the northeast corner of the cottage."

It was a promotional age (then as now). When the New York Pharmaceutical Society passed by the cottage, they did so with hats off in silence, except for one member who implored Grant to try his cancer-curing chewing gum.

The principal owner of the hotel and the railroad was W. J. Arkell, an Upstate real estate speculator, politician, and newspaper publisher. (Drexel only owned a small share of the hotel and railroad, a minor holding for him.) Years later, Arkell recalled his good fortune: "I thought if we could get Grant to come to Mount McGregor, and if he should die there, it might make the place a national shrine and incidentally a success."

Arkell had booked the old president's last days as his nightclub act to pack the house, his marquee amusement. The general and two-term president wound up as the attraction at the end of a speculative railroad. This was a classic strategy: Run a railroad or a trolley line out into the countryside, then build an amusement park or a hotel at the line's end, and with the profits, push on. In this case the Saratoga, Mount McGregor, and Lake George Railroad Company, W. J. Arkell, vice-president, would arrive at Lake George and, ideally, spark a real estate frenzy.

In the center ring, Grant died with dignity. Nearby, a lone sentinel, veteran Samuel Willet, had pitched his tent, to stand guard for his old general. As the summer advanced, he was joined by two regiments of the Grand Army of the Republic.

Grant was wasting away; he had lost 70 pounds, and weighed only 110 pounds a month before he died. He could only eat a raw egg in milk. His voice reduced to a whisper, he communicated by writing notes. In one of his last notes, he wrote, "The fact is I think I am a verb instead of a personal pronoun. A verb is anything that signifies to be; to do; or to suffer. I signify all three." This is as close as he came to saying that he was in constant pain. In his notes, the old commander usually tried to lift the spirits of his family and his doctor. "Do as I do. Take things quietly. Give yourselves not the least concern."

Sometimes Grant would sleep the night; sometimes he would awaken once or more to have his throat cleared. To say he was "resting" was misleading, it implied comfort, said O. P. Clarke. "How little any of us know what it is to be deprived of all this! To sit during the day, and when night comes still to sit, and then again on the morrow; there is suffering in this, though no pain to rack the frame."

He worked on his memoirs, first rewriting the chapters he had written in the spring, and then revising the proofs. His son would read the proofs to him, and Grant would write his changes on slips of paper. He finished four days before his death.

Days before he died, Grant had himself wheeled down to the view from the Eastern Outlook in the "invalid wagon," which looked like a man-sized baby stroller. He was too feeble to walk more than a few steps. Although he spent only twenty minutes or so at the outlook's gazebo, he was exhausted by the trip.

On his return, his son asked that a bed be sent down from the hotel. Grant had been sitting up for months, and now, under an engraving of Abraham Lincoln, he lay down to die. "The bed stands now as it stood then," O. P. Clarke recalled in 1906, "and it requires no very great effort of the imagination to picture that evening scene—the dying man, the anxious, sorrowful group about the bed."

Three days later he died, July 23, 1885. In the pocket of his robe, he left his wedding ring with a formal farewell note to his wife. The memoirs, published by Mark Twain, sold more than 300,000 sets, bringing his widow nearly $450,000 in royalties.

Thrice imprisoned—by illness, by debt, and by being an attraction—Grant was thrice laid to rest. He had three funerals: one at Mt. McGregor, followed by a ceremony in Albany, and finally the funeral in New York City; a nine-hour-long parade led by three presidents: Cleveland, Hayes, and Arthur. Many cities competed to have his tomb, or to build a Grant memorial that would supersede all others. On Mt. McGregor there was even talk of cutting a colossal granite profile of Grant writing his memoirs.

Twelve years later the hotel, under new owners, burned down. It was ruled arson. The railroad folded a few years after that. The Mt. McGregor Railroad never got to Lake George. Arkell was bitter; he had lost a "fortune." Grant's death had "killed" his resort "absolutely," he said. "After his death, as people came to the mountain, the moment they stepped off the train they took off their hats and walked around on tiptoes, looking for something I never could find."

Mt. McGregor is a beautiful mountain, a glorious prospect. The mountain has been used and reused in schemes variously speculative, benevolent, and punitive. Once it proved itself unprofitable, it became a dumping ground: tuberculosis, old vets, retarded children, prisoners.

Beginning in 1913, the mountain was home to the Metropolitan Life Insurance sanatorium for tuberculosis, located on the belief in the restorative powers of good mountain air. From 1945 until the early 1960s, it was a rest home for veterans. Then, until the early 1970s, a state school for retarded children. And from 1976 to today, a minimum security prison.

The cottage has been a museum since 1889. The federal government refused to accept the cottage as a gift from Drexel, so it was managed at first by the G.A.R., and later by a private association. Suye Narita Gambino, a name recalling her American journey, was the caretaker of the cottage from 1941 until her death in 1984. She first came to live on the mountain at age thirteen. "Because of her Japanese ancestry she remained on the mountain under quarantine during World War II," says a cottage information sheet, "but she said she harbored no ill-feelings about her treatment since she loved the mountain and the cottage so much." Another prisoner. She's off the mountain now—you can see her grave from the outlook.

The cottage in the prison does not get many visitors, only 2,700 in a recent year. "We're one of the least visited museums in the state," says the site interpreter. The corrections officers would like to see the cottage moved off the mountain so the prison could be upgraded to a "full medium" facility.

People phone the site interpreter at the cottage: "Are there good signs so we don't get on prison grounds?" She tells them, "'I'm sorry, I can see the barbed wire from here,' and then they don't come."

And it is the strangest approach to any museum that I have ever seen. You stop at the guard house to sign in, and then follow the hand-painted prison-shop signs, which lead you up the old switchback carriage road, through a small parking lot in front of the prison, and to the cottage. There are prisoners walking along the road. It's foolish to nod a small-town hello, foolish to stare, or avert your eyes. These prisoners are serving the last of their sentence. They have maybe a year or two to go. They *could* walk off the mountain, we're told at the Grant cottage. It happens, but not that often. They don't want to serve five years for attempted escape. They can leave; Grant couldn't.

Mt. McGregor: the beautiful mountaintop prison. "This is paradise," says a corrections officer who works at a high-security prison. "It's as different as night and day." Prison as paradise.

The cottage is locked. The site interpreter lets us in, locking the door behind us. The cottage has the original carpets and furniture, all of which Drexel bought in Troy for Grant, except the two leather arm chairs, brought up on the train. The chairs face each other in the center of the room, just as Grant had slept in them. Drexel also had the cottage painted, new wallpaper hung, and a fireplace built. He hooked the house up to the hotel's generator, supplying electricity. (Lights out at 10 p.m., kerosene lamps after that.)

In a display case are Grant's toothbrush, mustache brush, robe, and top hat. On the top of the case is a tall green jar, the cocaine in water, which was applied to his throat. Framed on the wall are a notepad and pen, which he used to communicate in his last weeks, and one of his last notes.

His death bed is in the reception room, along with his favorite wicker chair from the porch. In the dining room, one comes upon the end of the funeral. The floral wreaths are still there. The Victorian way of death was a triumph of display over decay. The coffin was then called a "casket," a container for precious goods. Grant was first placed in an ice casket, then embalmed—his face, brightened with bleach, visible through a window. Thousands came to Mt. McGregor for the first of the last rites. The flowers, too, are a triumph over decay. The original funeral flowers are a small graveyard of Victorian mourning symbolism. Made of dried everlastings, straw flowers, which were dipped in colored wax, they have faded to a dirty white, but they are intact: a cross with a sword from a family member; a big pillow with a sword from the two G.A.R. regiments that stood on guard; a huge gate with urns from the railroad baron Leland Stanford and family. (There is also a cross with a heart, but that's out for restoration work.) These were such accepted tokens of mourning that you could order the arrangements from the Sears catalog, we are told.

Tour over, the site interpreter unlocks the door and we go out on the piazza. She bids us farewell, quickly returns, and locks the door.

We visit the Eastern Outlook, where Grant was wheeled three days before he died. Down the paved walk, past prison-shop-made benches, each anchored with a bright chain, we emerge at a phenomenal view of the valley, and another prison: a six-foot-tall cast-iron fence, padlocked, surrounding a concrete circle, eleven feet across and three feet high. Behind the bars, on the concrete circle, is a marble block, like the blocks that were once used to dismount from horse carriages:

> This stone marks
> The spot where
> General U. S. Grant
> Had his last view
> Of the valley
> July 20, 1885

This a general's prospect, a commanding view of both battles of Saratoga fought in 1777, a turning point in the Revolution, battles fought against a great empire less than a hundred years earlier by a loosely joined federation of 13 colonies. There was a great distance between that republic-in-the-making, and the Gilded Age republic on the make.

These were not likely Grant's thoughts; it's too cinematic. The camera pulling away, looking at the Civil War general looking back at the Revolution, the peaceful green valley below. He may have reviewed the tactical advantages of the battleground; but he was weary of battle. He was looking out from a prospect the healthy do not know, from pain and near-death. The locked palisade of bars is appropriate. Ulysses S. Grant looked out as far as the day allowed.

At the prison gate once more, the guard scrutinizes our car. He looks into the back seat and the floor, and then crouches slightly, turning his head sideways with a quizzical dog-like expression to look underneath. This is a border crossing; you half expect to be asked for your passport, to be asked if you have anything to declare. Free Grant, I think. And we drive away, relieved in our escape. From here, north or south, you can choose meandering Old Route 9, the more direct Route 9, or the Northway, an interstate highway. We choose the highway, choose speed, and roll down the windows.

I Miss the Horses

"Our farm has interesting places to travel to, just like the world, though you do not have to journey so far as in the world," Lesley Frost wrote in her journal at age nine. The farm—thirty acres of pasture, mowing field, and woodland—was the world, and lives in her childhood notebooks. Lesley was sixteen months old when her parents, Robert and Elinor Frost, moved to the farm in Derry, New Hampshire. She was ten years old, with two sisters and a brother, when the family left.

The notebooks record the tranquility and terrors of childhood, much as they are found in fairy tales, fear coming up from behind, just over your shoulder. She writes beautifully of their horses, bluebirds and owls, picking flowers, chestnuting, berrying, swinging with birches, stargazing, watching the wallpaper pattern fade at twilight, and night fears.

"When it shines we go everywhere on our farm though we have been there a hundred times.

"The alders is one of my favorit places to go, because it reminds me of the brook that said 'I sparkle out among the fern to bicker down the vally.' . . . The next best journy I like is going over in the grove. That doesn't remind me of anything, but it is best to play in. You can make little houses and everything with the sticks and pine needles that are over there. . . .

"The big pasture is my next favorite place because there is a little round grove out there of about six trees and they all touch together at the top and make a lovely shade to sit under as soon as it is warm enough, and it is very comefortable. After the big pasture the field over across the road is next best. . . . We go there almost every day to get checker*berrys* or checkberry *leaves* whatever we find there both just as good to us."

As an adult, Lesley wrote, "it was to Mama we all returned at evening, bringing 'bokas' of flowers often crushed in hot and dirty hands but still worthy of being put in a glass of water on the kitchen table. It was to Mama we returned with full accounts of our adventures, adventures encountered on our own or out walking with Papa . . . she *was* home. Going home from anywhere, at any time of day or night, meant returning to her."

The farm was her schooling. The Frost family kept to themselves and taught their children at home. "Mama" ran "Play School," almost every day at 10 o'clock in the front room. The children learned their ABC's and numbers, learned poems by heart just as they learned the constellations by heart, and read aloud from Shakespeare, Byron, Shelley, and Tennyson.

Books were the "jewelry of the house," Lesley said years later. The Frosts read aloud each evening. The library was actually small, just a few shelves, "but it was large in relation to our other possessions." Of the "two nightmares which haunted" Lesley's childhood, "the most terrifying was the loss of our books by fire. With the flames crackling around me, I would take an over-large armful from the bookcase, only to have them buckle and crash at my feet—as I woke up crying."

Lesley was reading by age four, writing at five, and submitting her work to her parents, who were loving critics in disguise. "If we brought Papa something born of half a look, a glance, he sent us back for a whole look. And to look meant to compare, to bring on metaphor," she recalled. "Though we didn't know he was a 'poet,' or even one in the making, we thought he was pretty good at this metaphor game, at this 'imagination thing.'"

Their father "gave" each child a star to "own." Lesley was given Arcturus, brightest star of the constellation Bootes. Her father would bring a brass telescope upstairs to give each child a look at their star. Lesley was awoken to see the return of Halley's Comet, and to see the northern lights—"They streamed right straight up into the air." "Papa and I make believe we can see people on Mars, and houses and everything else on the earth," she wrote in her childhood notebook. "We say these things when we go after the cow at night; we say we will know more than the astronomers do with telescopes."

As in fairy tales, and as in her father's poetry, there is also a darkness in her memories, the near and deep country darkness just down the Derry Road, or just underneath her home. "There is a little cellar that goes in under the kitchen on one side of the main cellar," she wrote at age nine. "Always, when I go down there in the evening, after apples, it makes me feel trembly. . . . I don't want to go back and say that I am afraid to go down. . . . On the way up, it is the same again, and worse. . . . When I get to the top of the stairs . . . my hands are so full that I have to wait till someone opens the door, and then I rush in as if I were being chased by a tiger or lion. When it is over, I am glad, and sit down by the fire to eat my apple and calm my nerves."

The Derry farm is Eden, and Eden stalked by fear. Frost is beloved, or dismissed, for his folksy country ways, an image he made into a brand name, but this is a misreading. He is, as the critic Lionel Trilling said in a toast on Frost's eighty-fifth birthday, "a terrifying poet." "Nature for this poet is neither friend nor foe," explains poet Joseph Brodsky, "nor is it the backdrop for human drama; it is this poet's terrifying self-portrait."

But that is the father at work in his notebooks. In his little girl's careful script she, too, records the fear scratching at the windowpane. "I didn't want to go to bed, because you could hear the wind, outside, whistling around the corner of the house and coming in every crack in the windows and the fine sharp flakes banging against the window panes and then I was such a bad dreamer that I was afraid I might dream."

* * *

"For me, life on the Derry farm was to be a long and passionate borning," Lesley wrote many years later. "Heel and toe would always remember the ruts of the Berry Road, feel the polish of the hermit-brown needles on the floor of the pine grove, where the smoothness seemed to be more a matter of color than texture; feel the cool mud halfway to the knees in the cranberry bog; smell the hot granite outcroppings mixed with the tang of juniper, on Klein's hill; a place where, in other words, earth and poetry were fused in a momentary stay against confusion."

The world knows that farm in the poems, "Mending Wall," "After Apple-Picking," "The Death of the Hired Man," "Home Burial," "Birches," "The Pasture," and many others. Robert Frost, by his own account, wrote more than half of his first book, *A Boy's Will*, and half of the famous second, *North of Boston*, and a little of his third, *Mountain Interval*, drawing from the Derry farm. Forty years after he had left the Derry farm, Frost said, "I might say the core of all my writing was probably the five free years I had there on the farm down the road from Derry village toward Lawrence. The only thing we had plenty of was time and seclusion. I couldn't have figured in advance, I hadn't that kind of foresight. But it turned out as right as a doctor's prescription."

Robert Frost returned in 1938 to spread Elinor's ashes on the farm, at her request. Knocking at the door for the owner's permission, he received a traveling salesman's welcome. The woman who came to the door eyed him suspiciously. She had never heard of him or his poetry. He thought better of it and decided to return to Vermont with his wife's ashes. The farm was sold in 1953 and became a junkyard called "Frosty Acres."

After New Hampshire had purchased the house and farm, Lesley guided the restoration, living in a trailer on the grounds. The state had to truck in new soil to clean up the junkyard. The family who sold the old Frost place to the junkyard are defensive: They loved the place, a son says. His mother was assured the wrecks would be out back, out of sight.

Lesley remembered red floors and red wallpaper in the kitchen. The restorers were skeptical. They pulled up the floor coverings, peeled back the wallpaper and found traces of the red room. Only one company sold red wallpaper like that: Sears, and they still had some left. They had more good fortune. Robert Frost's Morris chair was found in pieces in the attic. He wrote in that chair with a homemade lap desk.

"Most of the object-secrets of the vacant house are never found out," says William Seale, author of *Recreating the Historic House Interior*. "Household things are transient, moved from room to room and house to house. They scatter easily, and we must count ourselves blessed to recover as much as 15 percent of what was in a room at a given time."

Lesley reclaimed the farm in remembrance of her poet father. It fulfills its role admirably. The modesty of the house and its furnishings conveys the spirit. A touring group of more than a dozen crowds any room. If you come away thinking that it was a small place, you would have begun to understand the quiet, poor life of the Frosts just after the turn of the century.

This was a family farm like so many others then. Robert Frost kept three hundred Wyandotte hens, a chicken that had proved itself profitable. The family also had a succession of cows called Bossy, and horses: Billy, Eunice, and Roy. "We loved them all," Lesley recalled.

The barn, now absent of animals, as are many in New Hampshire, is the visitors' center. In a corner where the horses were is the park ranger's desk, and some souvenirs, books, t-shirts, and pins. The rest of the barn has a display about the farm, some old rakes, and a video monitor set up in front of rows of benches.

In "The End of the Ice World" Lesley, age eight, wrote in January 1908: "There once was a big ice world, and I was one of the people on it. But one day I was out on the ice, and I saw great long cracks spreading out from under my feet . . . the ice *all* over the world began sinking down" and "everything began to whiz through open air" until they came to rest in a smaller, more slippery ice world—too slippery to build a house on. But this world also let go, and they fell again, to a red-hot place "shaped like the core of an onion." "There were lots of pieces of ice floating about in open air with people on them." They lowered themselves down from the ice and fire by ropes, and when the ropes caught fire, they jumped down to another level of ice. "One day when we had got all settled down and weren't thinking of any thing," the fire above "fell down and melted all the ice we were living on and burnt all of us and our houses in a second till there was nothing left."

A tour of the Frost farm begins with a video of Lesley being interviewed by Mr. Rogers, the cardigan-clad Perry Como of children's television. Once you get past the initial oddity of this—Did Captain Kangaroo ever host Aleksandr Solzhenitsyn?—you see that Mr. Rogers is a pretty good interviewer. Mr. Rogers had produced a show in 1955 with Frost reading "The Road Not Taken," and the old tape, in its black-and-white serious-ness, is included.

Mr. Rogers and Lesley tour the house on her seventy-seventh birthday. She's near tears as she tells of how her father put 25 cents up the road to coax the children to walk out into the dark world.

The barn is empty and dark. The camera is looking down from above when they first enter. Lesley says, "I wish the horses were here. We were devoted to our horses." She looks into the darkness.

This earth is no place for a house museum. Materials are fugitive. Life is fugitive. The barn is empty when we return and the horses of our youth have fled.

The Birds Keep Their Secrets

I. The Machine When Young

Dayton, Ohio, is a city that has transformed the Wright Brothers' first airplane into a logo and a talisman. There are little Wright Flyers on the street signs for the Wright Brothers Parkway, Wright Flyers on ballcaps, mugs, belt buckles, t-shirts, scarves, and ties.

Everywhere there are holy relics, pieces of the original muslin that covered the wings, a tightly woven cotton known in its day as the "Pride of the West." And there are pieces of shingles and wood from the first hangar on Huffman Prairie. There is a big flag-sized fold of muslin at the Air Force Museum, and at other museums, little two-inch squares under glass, certified authentic by small notes, typed and hand-corrected by Orville.

The Wright Brothers themselves are painted on the side of two hangars, big murals, Orville and Wilbur looking like a sad-eyed Lenin and Marx. The mural at the Air Force Museum, visible across the runways, in particular looks like some banner from Red Square in Moscow.

The Air Force Museum has a strange talking Wilbur Wright mannequin. He looks like a scarecrow. He stares straight ahead as if in a neck brace, his eyes and lips moving like a poorly projected home movie. Wilbur greets you and tells you where the handicapped-accessible toilets are. Dayton makes the mummy dance in a strait jacket.

There are airplanes displayed around town: a 1905 Flyer, rebuilt under Orville Wright's direction, at a park; a much-altered 1911 Wright Model B at the Air Force Museum; and a modern, steel interpretation of that altered 1911 airplane out in a hangar just south of Dayton.

The 1905 Flyer is displayed at Carillon Park in what looks like the bottom of a drained indoor pool. Orville required that it be displayed this way as a condition of his gift. He thought that people would understand the plane better if they saw it from above.

The curator took me down into the well where the Flyer sat. We studied the wing warping device. The Wright wing is unlike any other airplane's wing. The wing flexes like a bird's wing. When the airplane is banking to the right, for example, the trailing edge of the right wing twists upward, while the trailing edge of the left wing twists down. Airplanes today use ailerons, a flap hinged off a stationary wing.

Like others who aspired to fly, Wilbur Wright had watched birds in flight, but he saw something different. The early "bird-men" gliders tried to mimic the balance of birds by shifting their weight. Wilbur saw the birds wheel their wings and flex their wing tips. He devised wing warping on a moment's insight one July day in 1899 while working alone in the bicycle shop. He picked up an empty inner-tube box and began twisting it in his hands. He had his model wing. "Here was the silent birth of all that underlies human flight," Wilbur said.

We know our machines as complete systems—the airline, the airport, the hotel, are an almost continuous enclosure. But the early machines, cars and planes, have something of the animal and something of the craftsman in them. Sometimes the mix is as awkward as a foal finding its legs. We see the spirits mixing, man and beast. We see the machine working to match the animal's motion, hunting for the animal's poise.

I asked the curator how the wing works. Cables ran from the hip cradle of the pilot to flex the wings, but the pilot here was a mannequin. She took hold of the wing tip. "A curator shouldn't be doing this," she said, smiling. She flexed the wing tip. Both wings, top and bottom, moved like a chest heaving, like a body taking a breath. The airplane was animate for that one moment. Fly, oh fly, you wanted to say. We'll open the doors, fly away.

With the cloth covering animal-like ribs, the original Wright Flyers are so much like a rudimentary creature with skin and bones, and for the connective tissue, piano wire. From this start, airplanes evolved away from these almost tender forms in the image of animals. They became machines.

II. "Adjustment Engineering"

I was in Dayton to see the most recent Wright airplane, which started as a replica of a Wright Model B from 1911 and ended up as a hybrid. Though it had similar measurements, the new Model B was made of aviation steel, was more than twice as heavy, had a powerful helicopter motor, ailerons where the original had wing warping, and many other changes.

This was Theseus' ship rebuilt as a destroyer with thirty hi-carbon steel oars.

The group that built the new Model B had reinvented the Wright Brothers. They wanted to fly their replica, but did not want to trust their lives to the technology of 1911, when powered flight was just eight years old. They opted for safety over accuracy. Their changes reveal the perils and contradictions of trying to revisit the recent technological past. More than a few aviation historians say the plane they built is not a Wright machine.

This Wright B was born as a Bicentennial dream. In 1974, Tom Sheetz had envisioned a Wright Flyer leading the big parade down Dayton's Main Street. Sheetz was chief of protocol for the Aeronautical Systems Division at Wright-Patterson Air Force Base. He talked the idea up, and caught the attention of Charles Dempsey, chief of technical plans and programs at the Air Force's Aerospace Research Lab and a B-24 pilot in World War II. Dempsey had always been "infatuated by the Wright Brothers" and couldn't understand why there wasn't a flying replica. "I'm at the birth-place of aviation, and there ain't no airplane flying," he says.

They chose to a build a Model B, the most practical of the early Wright planes. Dempsey began work at his dining-room table. They thought it would take two years and $15,000. They had no money. It took eight years, the work of some six hundred volunteers, and materials, donations, and computer time worth about a million dollars.

Dayton enthusiastically embraced the project. Dempsey was receiving forty-five calls a day from people wanting to volunteer. Everyone from Lt. Gen. James A. Abrahamson (later in charge of the SDI, "Star Wars," program) to Cub Scouts came down to pop rivets into the plane's wings. Corporations showered the group with support. At the start in 1974 when Dempsey and Sheetz met with local business leaders, they were asked just one question: How much money do you want? These leaders were ready to underwrite the entire project, but Dempsey and Sheetz turned them down. They wanted it to be a "people's plane." They gathered $1, $2, and $5 donations, enough so the receipts filled three large plastic trash bags. Bigger donations came their way from more than 200 corporations, including the hangar and the engine.

A close group worked for seven years on the Wright B, developing a strong camaraderie. The hangar is like a genial veterans' club, with constant kidding between the old Navy and Air Force fliers. The group's leaders had thousands of hours of flight time in military craft. They wanted this new Wright B to meet military standards for flight safety, so they adopted all the practices of modern airplane development.

Dempsey wanted to conform to FAA safety regulations and Air Force standards. They wanted to fly the plane at Wright-Patterson Air Force Base, the site of Huffman Prairie, where the Wrights tested their planes and ran a flight school.

The entire Wright B was redesigned to make it better than the Wright Bothers, says Dempsey. The group consulted technical staffs comprising six hundred engineers, had the design reviewed by the Air Force technical evaluation team, and received hundreds of hours of advice and computer time in designing the propellers, controls, and choosing an airfoil.

"We had to take a wooden plane and bring it to FAA Part 23 standard, which is 6 G ultimate," says Dempsey, a big man with a Georgia drawl. "You're not going to have wood, friends. You're going to have chrome molybdenum steel tubes. That's what it says. And to keep the weight down you're going to have aluminum wing ribs. It also says that you're going to have aircraft steel cables. No piano wire.

"The real issue was not making a Wright B Flyer; the real issue was re-designing the original Wright B Flyer to FAA Part 23 standards without it looking different.

"And them old Georgia Tech boys," Dempsey says referring to himself, "are good at adjustment engineering. And that's what it was, baby, adjust-ment engineering."

The new Wright B matches the original in the position of every strut and wire, every dimension, he says, answering critics who say the plane has been "adjusted" beyond recognition. "It is a Wright machine. It takes off at the same air speed, cruises same air speed, stalls same air speed, but it's got all those little adjustment engineering goodies."

The original Wright B is a linen handkerchief with ribs. The wing works just like the 1905 Flyer the curator had showed me. Seeing this new steel Wright B is like seeing a thin track star or a diving champion in foot-ball gear, ready to play nose-tackle. Dempsey proudly recalls a compli-ment he received from a technical inspector: "You Georgia Tech guys make airplanes fly through brick walls." He's not exaggerating. The land-ing gear has been tested by the Air Force to withstand 5 Gs. The wheels were built by a company that supplies wheels for Indy racers. Dempsey designed the pilot seats to withstand 15 Gs. He used to design ejection seats for jets.

But stability was his chief concern. The Wrights' thin airfoil is so ineffi-cient that the plane is unstable, Dempsey says. "The Pentagon said if you're going to fly this at Wright-Patterson you've got to come to neutral stability." The consulting engineers at the Dayton section of the American Institute of Aeronautics and Astronautics selected NACA airfoil 44–12, the same thick airfoil as on a PT-19, the army trainer. "I was happy as hell. I learned to fly on that airfoil," says Dempsey.

To further aid stability, the large engine is centered, the two pilots sit two-and-a-half feet forward of the wing, and more than one hundred pounds of lead was added to the landing struts in the nose. In the Wright's design, the engine sits to the left, and the two seats are on the wing.

The original Wright B was so out of balance that one person could not fly the plane without a copilot for ballast, Dempsey claims. "Frankly, it was an inherently bad aircraft," he says. As proof, he points to a photo showing the plane sitting on the ground with the nose skids in the air. "The plane is not in balance. The airplane will not take off," he says. When he is told of many examples of solo flights, such as Harry Atwood's record 1911 flight from St. Louis to New York, he says they must have added several hundred pounds of ballast. However, Wright historians say the plane was easily flown with one person and no ballast. Dempsey has no patience for questions like this, dismissing the questioners as ignorant "naysayers."

Flying this new version of the Wright B is "like driving an old worn-out tractor across a plowed field," says John Warlick, a retired Navy pilot with 3,500 hours of flying time, which includes dive bombers in World War II. Warlick has done most of the flying for the 250 hours the Wright B has flown, usually while dressed in a replica Second Lt. Signal Corps uniform of the era.

Warlick had to land in two emergencies in the early days. In one the chain broke three hundred feet from the ground; the second time, the propeller shaft broke. Each time he was able to glide down on the flat Ohio farmland. A plaque in the hangar proclaims that he and his copilot, William A. Sloan, Jr., are charter members in the Broken Chain Society.

The chain drive has also been redesigned. There is a 205-horsepower helicopter engine, which is attached to a modified coupling adapted from industrial machinery. This joins a gearbox Dempsey designed, which is similar to that found in the front-wheel-drive Cadillac Eldorados of the 1970s.

There are yet more changes: two Piper Cub J-3 gas tanks in the wings, FAA-approved propellers, full instrumentation, navigation lights, brakes, a larger balanced rudder, heat-shrunk Ceconite wing covering, and small front wheels on the skids. But it's the use of ailerons that sets this far apart from other Wright Bs. Dempsey insists that the Wright B used ailerons, not wing warping. This might be heresy to some in Dayton: It was the Wrights' arch rival, Glenn Curtiss, who used ailerons.

Dempsey has been misled by his source: The modified Wright B in the Air Force Museum, known as the "Lemp machine," does have ailerons. This was the sole model for the group, and it may not even be a Model B. They carefully measured that plane and had high school drafting classes convert 40 pages of measurements into drawings. Their plane is painted to look like the Lemp machine: battleship gray struts and dark brown wings.

The Lemp machine has a curious and unresolved pedigree. It was owned for a time by Harold Rhinehart, who flew it as a flight instructor in 1916 and for the last time at an air race in Dayton in 1924. Using old photos, Wesley Smith, an aviation historian, has studied the evolution of this much-altered plane. At one point ailerons were added. More importantly, he says, this plane has the same wing chord, wing span, wooden blinkers, undercarriage, and overall length of a Wright Model C. "As the aircraft sits today," Smith considers it, "based upon photographic and physical evidence, to be a modified Wright Model C." If he is correct, the Dayton group has built a much changed version of the wrong airplane.

The plane has been controversial. After building the Wright B to Air Force standards, they were not allowed to base the plane at Huffman Prairie or at their second choice, right by the Air Force Museum, which receives one million visitors a year. A few of the museum staff publicly denounced the plane, saying that was not in "any way, shape or form" a Wright machine. Dempsey says that they chose not to base the plane by the museum because they could not afford to meet the "humongous set of rules" for government construction. The Wright B finally found a home some 24 miles from Huffman Prairie in a different county at the Dayton General airport in Miamisburg.

Experts on the Wright Brothers admire the spirit of the Dayton group, but express some reservations. Tom Crouch, author of the Wright biography *The Bishop's Boys* and a Dayton native, flew in the plane. "I got to ride with my feet dangling over the wing of a Wright airplane and from that point of view it's a really neat thing to do. There's nothing else flying that comes to mind that allows you to kind of taste that sort of sensation." But, he cautiously says, "the notion of building the 'all-metal Model B' has some limitations. It is not very accurate."

Peter Jakab, author of *Visions of a Flying Machine: The Wright Brothers and the Process of Invention*, says "What the guys did in Dayton is great, but it's barely a Model B."

Rick Young, a Wright enthusiast and restaurateur who has built and flown several Wright kites and gliders, is less circumspect. "I consider what the guys in Ohio are doing to be exploitative of the memory and work of the Wrights. They built a machine like a carnival ride to be able go out and fly people around. It's not even a Wright Brothers airplane," he says.

What the Dayton group missed was the thrill of reaching a deeper understanding of the Wrights, Young says. When you build an accurate reproduction, "you begin to seek answers for questions that wouldn't even occur to a historian. How a particular piece was fabricated or how it was assembled. Or what material they used or why. When you go to build something you have to answer all of these questions. And then there's all those 'ah hahs' that happen: Oh that's why they did that. Now I see."

When asked how an antique plane should be revived, the Wright experts all point to the work of Ken Hyde, a Virginia airline pilot and experienced restorer who is building an exact replica of Signal Corps #3—a Wright Model B—for the U.S. Army Aviation Museum. At the same time, he's building a reproduction of his own to fly, including a replica of the original engine.

"The Wright Brothers didn't build stuff as nice as he does," says Rick Young. "He has set a standard. Ken's work is meticulous."

I visit Ken Hyde at his own private hangar and airstrip, not far from where he grew up. He built the hangar first, and then his house years later, something his wife will still mention. In the hangar's office, Hyde's desk faces a wall covered with yellow Post-it notes, a testimony to his persistence in tracking down the smallest detail. He is assisted by Greg Cone and Andrew King, whom he praises as "excellent museum quality craftsmen, as well as historians." Indeed, the entire hangar has the air of a museum's restoration department. They have assembled an encyclopedic knowledge of the Wright B and the Wrights' thinking and methods. They have had to: The Wrights were secretive. They left no blueprints of the Wright B.

Hanging on the wall is the broken wing of a Model B that last flew in Iowa in 1916. With its bracing wires hanging all about, it looks like an abstract mobile. This wing has been an important source to study the original fittings. "We measure anything we can get our hands on and record it," says Cone.

In the workshop are five thick loose-leaf binders of letters, documentation, and photos of the Wright factory. Close study of those photos, showing piles of wings or chain guards, has revealed how different parts were fabricated. "There are clues in all of it," says Cone. He has underlined a 1910 factory inventory. "See, it says ash skids. You see an airplane at a museum, you can't very well take out your pocket knife and carve into it." They also refer to their extensive flat files with almost every available drawing of the Wright machines from around the world, including a remarkable 1909 notebook from a British manufacturer and measured drawings of the 1905 Flyer made under Orville's guidance.

"There's so many secrets in there," Cone says. He points out a J-hook at the bottom of an interplane strut. This is part of a swivel mechanism. "Without the drawings you wouldn't know how that went there. The whole plane is just hinged together. That's why they fell into a heap when they crashed." A crashed Wright machine is like a dead bird: the taut animal now limp, loose, and heavy.

People mistakenly think the Wright planes are just big kites with a motor, Cone says. But they miss the heart of the Wrights' technology, all the small details that allow the wing to flex in flight, including such fine points as the grain on the cap strips of the wing ribs.

The spruce cap strips are one-quarter inch by one-half inch. In modern practice, you always put the grain on the wider side, which makes the rib stronger. "When we got these old wings we were looking at them and they put the grain on the quarter-inch side. We decided they made a mistake," says Hyde, whose reserved manner is a match for the Wright Brothers. "So we said, OK, we're going to put the grain like you're supposed to.

"In the middle of the night I woke up: You know there's got to be some reason why they did that. I know they didn't have a lot of previous aviation knowledge, but there's a reason they did this." So they tested the ribs with the grain running each way, hanging weight off different strips. The original flexes almost two inches more.

This is essential since the whole wing flexes: The rib is only attached at the leading edge, and is held in place by a pocket in the wing covering. "Now it doesn't hold up well over long periods of time," Hyde says. But the wing's achievement lies in the control it allowed and its lightness. "If you go out and pick up that wing, I would dare say anybody, even in composite material today, would have a very difficult time matching the weight for the square footage of that wing." And remember, he says, this is only a second- or third-generation airplane. He sees the Wrights as geniuses of fabrication.

Hyde and Cone stand looking at the elegant work of a wing under construction: "And it all gets covered up. That's why people look at it and say there's nothing to it," says Cone.

Much of Hyde's exacting search for the correct components will be covered up, some of it due to the very nature of the Wrights' secretiveness. The Wrights used carriage bows for their wing tips. Hyde found an Amish craftsman still making them. The Wrights specified that "Dairy Tin" be used to join the ribs to the spars. "What is it? Nobody knows," says Cone. Dairy Tin doesn't rust—even the edges don't rust. On the Iowa wing, the nails have rusted, but not the tin. Hyde has a metallurgist studying a sample. Hyde and his assistants have studied old Wright engines, sprockets, and drive shafts, and an original strut with the finish still on it. They have searched out many inconsistencies: There are two Wright Bs left and they have three kinds of wheels. Once they discover the correct wheels, they will be copied by a specialist in recreating antique tires.

It will be the finish that strikes people. The Wright B was a silver ghost: the struts were painted aluminum, and all the fittings were brightly plated nickel. Going to the expense of painting the plane was the Wrights' version of stealth technology. "The film at that time was all silver-backed. If you paint something aluminum it just kind of blends right into the negatives," says Hyde. "You couldn't tell what was ash and what was spruce. So if you're going to just copy their airplane—and there were a lot of people doing that—from their photographs you wouldn't be able to tell. It just disappears. Very effective." The cotton-muslin wings, and the small tires, were white. The two seats were a surprising rich brown corduroy, and the all-brass radiator gleamed.

Hyde has made some modifications to the reproduction he intends to fly, but they are also hidden: a higher grade aviation steel for the hardware, bolts in place of wood screws, shear pins on the prop shaft, and a reinforced wing based on how the yacht designer Starling Burgess built the plane under license. To the eye it will appear exactly the same.

The group that built the metal version thinks Hyde is foolish to fly this antique with the original controls. Hyde is considering making a flight simulator much like that used by the Wrights to train their students. "It's different—it's going to be like patting your head and rubbing your tummy, all at the same time," says Hyde, who has flown for twenty-eight years with American Airlines.

By the time he flies, he'll be no stranger to this airplane. Detail by detail, Hyde has gained an insight into the Wrights. "It's been a very strong history lesson," he says, a lesson he would have missed had he updated everything. "And then you don't have a Wright airplane. I think it's going to be fascinating to hear a four-cylinder vertical Wright engine run. We've never heard one run.

"Every airplane, every piece of machinery smells or looks different," he says. "When you find an old car that hasn't been touched, you get into it— it smells different, it looks different. And the reason it's that way is because they've used horsehair, they've used certain kinds of leathers and they've used certain kinds of glues. Take that car and you put it all together with plastic and T-88 epoxy adhesive, it's not going to smell and look the same.

"That's kind of the way I think it is with antique restoration. You need to try and get as close to the materials that went into it. And that's what we're trying to do with the Wright airplane. I think that comes from doing the paint the way they did, doing the gluing the way they did it, putting horsehair in [the seats] the way they did it, putting the same fabric on." Each piece taken by itself may "not mean a whole lot," Hyde says. But "when you put it together: Wham. It's 1910."

III. "Ninth Wonder of the World"

How did we get from the bird homage of the early machines to the translation of the Model B into steel?

The new Model B is one monument that Dayton has built to the Wrights. As with many monuments, there are two faces in the mirror—one is the Wrights of course, and the other is modern Dayton.

The Air Force culture of modern Dayton couldn't get out of the way to let the Wrights' airplane speak. (A classic example of Harold Bloom's theory of misreading. The restorers had created a new plane out of their misunderstanding.) The Wrights built their plane out of ash and spruce, linen and piano wire. Modern Dayton built planes of chrome molybdenum steel and other materials. Modern Dayton built an airplane by committee and tested it by committee. There were books of standards and specifications, accepted designs, wind tunnel tests, modifications, meetings without end, and procedures to "sign off" on this or that part. The corporate techniques used to develop a supersonic jet fighter had been applied to a biplane from 1911, which flew at a top speed of 45 mph. No wonder that the Model B, like many jets in development, had grown in weight. The Wright Brothers had been processed through the Air Force mentality.

Our century began with men flying kites on the dunes of the Outer Banks. In the years before the Wrights' first powered flight in 1903, the brothers experimented with kites. They built kites like biplanes, twin wings 5 feet across to study wing shapes; they progressed to gliders. To record their experiments, the Wright brothers learned photography. Working with glass plates and a heavy camera on a tripod, they had only one shot to capture a glide. They developed the plates back home in Dayton. The photos the Wrights took on the dunes are beautiful. In one labeled "Orville Wright skimming the ground, Kitty Hawk, October 10, 1902," a glider and its shadow are draped across a dune. In another photo from October 1902, we are watching Wilbur glide away from us downhill. A large dune rises in the distance; the rest is flat. We could be looking at the surface of the moon. The photos preserve the moment of flight; you can feel the lift of the wings above the sand.

The Wrights did not take their most famous photo: the exalted moment the first airplane left the launch rail, December 17, 1903. Orville laying flat on the wing, with Wilbur running alongside. The biplane, just a few feet off the ground, pointed toward the infinite gray. A flight of only 120 feet lasting 12 seconds. Orville had set up the camera, entrusting it to a member of the Kill Devil Hill life saving station. John T. Daniel clicked the shutter as the airplane left the rail, taking one of the century's most reprinted photographs, and likely his only snapshot.

Early flight lives in these photos of long linen-white wings flying shadows on the dunes. So quietly had the century begun. If you had those photos in mind, you would not rebuild a Wright Brothers airplane in steel. To judge the journey, the distance, from those photos to the steel Model B, I only had to drive a few miles from the hangar in South Dayton to the Air Force Museum at the Wright-Patterson Air Force Base, which had at its kernel the few acres of Huffman Prairie. There in 1904 the Wright Brothers made their second most exceptional flight: They flew in a circle. The practical airplane was born. This great accomplishment was only reported in one place, a small apiary journal, *Gleanings in Bee Culture.* They flew for thirty-nine minutes in 1905, flew figure-eights, all in sight of a Dayton trolley line, and the world paid no attention.

The old men who built the steel Model B have loved airplanes since they were kids. They collect anything having to do with flying. Their shrine is the Air Force Museum. "Ninth Wonder of the World," one of them told me, only half in jest. "Can't see it all in two hours or two days. I'm always seeing new stuff there." "You've got to get there at nine a.m.," I'm told one afternoon when I think of driving over. "Wouldn't be enough time," I'm cautioned. You'd just get there and they'd be emptying out. After my visit, I see his point. The Air Force Museum is an entire aesthetic experience that casts a spell.

The Air Force Museum is deceptive. One wades in with little preparation, starting once more, with the Wrights and other early airplanes, but soon it is deep swimming—thermonuclear "devices," the missiles and bombs of Desert Storm, a stealth fighter nesting under the wing of a B-52. Before one is even aware of it, one is steeped in the Air Force ethos. The lethality is hypnotic.

The exhibits seem like a cheery cabinet of curiosities at first. The world's largest aerial camera. The world's largest tire—up to 1941. The only electronic device known to have survived reentry into the atmosphere. The world's most decorated B-29. The museum becomes a hall of natural history wonders. Failed species—big planes that once ruled the earth. Fossils—parts of propellers, wings, wreckage from planes that crashed, killing the crew. Dolls and stuffed toy monkeys that men carried into battle for good luck.

The airplanes are presented like caged exotics. The inventor's hands—our hands—are far removed from this. These planes are treated as heroes, but mostly out of the grisly context of war and bombs and blood and death. Sanitized, polished, the official portrait. We are on the right side of the bomb-bay door.

Even when caged here like zoo tigers in a noon slumber, these are terrifying machines. The B-52 is enormous—its wings go on forever, longer than Orville first flew. Walking through the open nose and up the ramp of a cargo plane, the C-142, one thinks of Jonah and the whale. Inside this whale is a Willys Jeep and a quote from General Eisenhower. (Three of our most important combat tools in Europe and North Africa, he says, were the bulldozer, the Jeep, and the C-142. Oddly, none were built for combat, he concludes.)

There's weapon after weapon. Smart bombs, guided missiles, leaflet bombs. A Mark 53 thermonuclear bomb. Attack helicopters. "Retarder bombs." A B-58 escape capsule with black stenciled letters on a neon-orange background telling the finder to pry it open: "If door is jammed, cut for rescue." Air Force Spam.

I stepped into one little "video pavilion" celebrating the stealth aircraft. The narrator praised computers that went "beyond the boundary of human interpretation capacity." The pilot pulls back his stick—he is not controlling the plane, he is placing an order. The computer makes interpretations, adjustments, flies the thing. One machine was flying another machine, the computer was in command, and the pilot, busy taking in the technical laundry, was along for the ride. Can we be further from the poetry of flight?

I kept coming across a group of fourth graders on a field trip, ten boys and girls led by a museum volunteer. They were standing under a B-36, under the open bomb bay doors, looking up, when I first saw them. Right next to them was a thermonuclear bomb. The guide, a woman in her 60s maybe, who made every sentence an excursion in enthusiasm, was telling the kids that the B-36 was the largest airplane in the museum, larger than the B-52. And how originally it had two tires, big ones that would crack the runway each time it landed—and you can't build a new runway each time a plane lands, can you? The two big wheels were replaced with four smaller wheels. They went over to the big wheel—one of the largest in the world no doubt. If she said anything about the Mark 53 thermonuclear bomb, I didn't hear.

The group moved on to the "Bockscar," the B-29 that dropped the bomb on Nagasaki. We crossed paths again—OK, this time I followed them—as we walked through a B-29 fuselage. The most famous B-29 in the world—it was painted on the side as if it were a circus sideshow:

> World's most decorated bomber
> World's only bomber "jet ace"
> 121 Korean Combat Missions
> 2,500,000 lbs of bombs on target
> USAF Last Combat B-29

The B-29 was a cramped tube, which would have been even narrower when the wings were attached. At the back of the plane the guide was telling the children what they'd have to do to make sure all their bombs had fallen. She made one of the group a bombardier for her story. "Garrett would have to crawl through that tube and tap that bomb loose—because no planes are allowed to return with live bombs!" She said it with a dripping sweetness that was terrifying.

She kept on like this—putting this child in the bomber crew. Two girls were standing at the group's edge. One said to the other: "This is stupid!"

You exit the bomber by a Strategic Air Command exhibit with this quote from Thomas Jefferson: "Eternal vigilance is the price of liberty." (But at what cost to liberty, that's the question.) I made my way out of the museum, through World War II, The Korean "Conflict" and "Vietnam"— that's all it said, just "Vietnam." I wish the museum's tour ended with an ecumenical chapel—no crosses, stars, or prayer rugs—a meditation space washed in the sky blue light of the peaceful heavens. I would place there but one quote from the man who served as president between Washington and Jefferson—John Adams—and ask for a moment of reflection, a prayer for all the dead, and a prayer for forgiveness. On May 12, 1780, Adams wrote his wife Abigail: "I must study politics and war that my sons may have liberty to study mathematics and philosophy. My sons ought to study mathematics and philosophy, geography, natural history, naval architecture, navigation, commerce, and agriculture, in order to give their children a right to study painting, poetry, music, architecture, statuary, tapestry, and porcelain."

IV. "Killing, Killing, Killing"

In 1911, the U.S. Navy, docked in Boston Harbor, was bombed from an airplane. Two aviators in a version of a Wright Model B dropped sacks of flour on the ships. The Navy dismissed it as bad manners; puny airplanes could never destroy ships. A few newspaper editorials took the prank as a warning.

Modern weapons start out like a schoolboy's prank. Like a lark. Some guys messing around, a moment of insight, a patent or two, a crude explosion that wins the attention of a government inspector. This is the machine dream when young and new, when there is just the joy of pursuit. In the first days of an invention, the world is filled with possibilities.

During World War I, two inventors were developing aerial torpedoes, pilotless bombs, for the U.S. Government: Elmer Sperry, the brilliant inventor of gyroscope guidance for airplanes, and Charles F. Kettering, who had numerous patents and later headed the research laboratory of General Motors.

Kettering worked on his aerial torpedo in Dayton with Orville Wright and two of his assistants from the Dayton-Wright Company. They designed a small biplane with a fifteen-foot wingspan, built of steel tubing with wings covered in muslin and brown paper. The torpedo steered with a Sperry gyroscope. A barometer kept the plane at the correct altitude. A small air screw on the wing counted the miles until it reached the preset limit and cut off the engine, sending the little biplane gliding in to kill.

The design was as simple as Kettering could achieve; the operation was so erratic that the torpedo was called "The Bug." On the first full flight, the robot biplane stalled, looped, and dove, scattering the military observers in a panic, before it recovered, stalled once more, and spiraled into the ground. There's a Kettering Bug displayed at the Air Force Museum.

The Bug was a secret military project. If anyone around Dayton saw the little plane in flight, they were to be told it was going to replace motorcycles to speed deliveries to the front.

The next full flight, in October 1918, was even more erratic. C. H. Wills, a former chief designer at Ford who was in charge of the engine, wrote Elmer Sperry about the flight:

"You probably heard of the flight that they made at Dayton last Friday. I think it was terribly funny. A great many were skeptical and thought the engine would not fly, but they have given up that thought now . . . the ship went up about 500 feet and she nosed right straight up into the air and then dropped back, and went up again to about 1,000 feet and tipped over backwards. The instrument board came loose and broke the hose connecting the controls. When all the controls were disconnected the ship sideslipped and started up in circles about a mile in diameter. The machine had been set to drop at 1,000 feet. Mr. Kettering watched it until it was up about 12,000 feet and out of sight and with disgust said, 'Let the thing stay up there' and went home to bed. There were a couple of hundred people there and they got into automobiles and started to chase it and they began to get messages from various towns. One town in the valley telephoned that there was an aeroplane loose there and it was doing all kinds of didos. They finally located it twenty one miles away and there was about a dozen farmers out with lanterns looking for the aviator. There wasn't a thing hurt on the engine, not even the spark plug broken, but the gasoline tank was dry. It would have been going yet probably had it not been for the lack of gasoline. It had traveled approximately 90 miles for it was in flight just one hour. One farmer asked Mr. Kettering who drove it and he told him he did and the farmer wanted to know where he put his legs. I never saw anything that had so many tales and stories about it as that flight. Everybody had a different story about the capers it cut up. Some of the aces in France could have learned a few new tricks."

The Bug was more like a robot Flying Circus than a weapon of terror, but it could fly: The Army ordered one hundred prototypes from the Dayton-Wright Company. The Armistice soon came; the Kettering and Sperry projects were merged and then set aside. In the 1930s, the Nazis' scientists began developing a flying bomb at Peenemunde on a Baltic island, a wilderness of dunes and marshes, and in time had slave labor building the "Vengeance Weapons," the V-1's and V-2's that fell on London, and became the prototype of modern terror; the ICBM, the Scud and the Patriot, as well as the Saturn rocket that sent astronauts to the moon. And here we are in the dark with those Ohio farmers, searching by lantern light for an honest answer to the question: Who is flying? Who controls these missiles?

"I once thought the aeroplane would end wars," Orville Wright said on his seventy-fourth birthday in August 1945, three weeks after the bombing of Hiroshima and Nagasaki. "Now I wonder if the aeroplane and the atom bomb can do it."

A new tool brings unforeseen changes. "Few inventions have been so simple as the stirrup, but few have had so catalytic an influence on history," argues Lynn White in *Medieval Technology and Social Change.* The stirrup changed the way people rode horses. Knights in the eighth century could wear heavy armor. War changed, society changed. The knights became a new power, a class apart. Western Europe was ruled by "an aristocracy of warriors endowed with land so that they might fight in a new and highly specialized way. Inevitably this mobility developed cultural forms and patterns of thought and emotion in harmony with its style of mounted shock combat," White said.

"Things are in the saddle, and ride mankind," said Ralph Waldo Emerson.

The modern war was supposed to be too terrible to be fought.

A few months after the first, celebrated flight across the English Channel, eleven aviators crossed all within one hour. "These aviators were warmly welcomed when they reached one of the London suburbs, but their numbers must have made more than one nervous Britisher see in the peaceful invasion the possibility of a hostile one," *The New York Times* editorialized on July 4, 1911. "This is the disquieting side of mechanical flight. Fortunately, improved instruments for making war do not increase the frequency of wars, but have an opposite tendency.

"Real wholesale slaughter as a part of the everyday business of life ended when men stopped fighting each other with short swords."

There will be no more war, Thomas Edison predicted on a visit to France in August 1911. "Europe will never again indulge in international conflict. For she has learned her lessons from the economic disasters of wars. Germany will never again face what it cost her to march up to but not through the Arc de Triomphe in Paris.

"The day has passed when millions of lives can be sacrificed to foolish military ideas. . . . As things are today the terribly deadly effects of inventions to be used in war are such that no country can afford to wipe out the humanity of another, if only for reciprocal industrial reasons.

"A ultroglycerine bomb dropped from one of our modern airships will do more damage than whole days of fighting did in Napoleon's time.

"In other words, invention has got beyond the thirst of blood; the power of science, that has been let loose, must overwhelm aggressive diplomacy."

Edison was not alone in his faith. His friend Henry Ford concurred, as did Hudson Maxim, inventor of explosives. "The great game of war is all up," said *The New York American* in 1910. England, Germany, and Japan know it. "The enginery of slaughter" had shifted. Fortresses, dreadnoughts costing $10 million, would be useless before the "swift and terrible destruction" of the airplane.

Glenn Martin was a carnival showman. Martin had staged mock air attacks at carnivals, dropping oranges on forts as a signal to his crew below to set off black powder on the ground—"it went woof and blew up some dirt several feet high," said one of his employees. "We weren't taking too much poetic license dropping oranges because nobody knew what a bomb ought to look like anyway." More pranks. With the cooperation of the Navy and the Army, Martin staged a nighttime "battle from the sky spectacle." From a thousand feet, two airplanes "poured a rain of bombs into the 'forbidden city' that entirely destroyed it and brought the spectators to their feet with wild applause," reported the *Los Angeles Tribune*. He was pleased; his show had "attracted the attention of the War Department." Glenn Martin was getting ready for the world we know.

On August 7, 1914, three days after Germany invaded Belgium, the twenty-eight-year-old Martin, who ran a struggling aviation company, wrote about the war in the *Los Angeles Evening Herald*. "The aeroplane will practically decide the war in Europe," Martin predicted. "Veritable flying death will smash armies, wreck mammoth battleships and bring the whole world to a vivid realization of the awful possibilities of a few men and a few swift winging aerial demons."

The aeroplane will terrorize armies with "explosive shells, scattering shrapnel and hurling fire bombs" and "will introduce a new kind of projectile into modern warfare. . . . the needle shell. It kills by wholesale. It comprises a cigar-shaped piece of steel with a needle point and fin-like tail to insure accuracy.

"These projectiles do not explode, but dropped by the basketful upon an army in any formation whatever, from a height of 400 feet, each weighing about half a pound, drive themselves into men and horses, killing, killing, killing."

Martin was wrong; the aeroplane did not win the Great War, but he was ready for the future. By World War II, Glenn Martin was one of the largest bomber builders.

In the earliest photos of aeroplanes, there are often great crowds running. They are running to where an aeroplane has landed, or they are running across fields and dirt roads for their first glimpse of an aeroplane in flight. When an aeroplane is going to fly over, everyone turns out. Millions wait to see a thin little plane go by at thirty or forty miles an hour. They climb roofs, chimneys, trees, ladders, anything to get closer. Men wave their hats, women their handkerchiefs. "Many persons dance when they see an aeroplane in flight," said the *New York Tribune* when the first aviator flew over Manhattan in 1911. "Yesterday there were thousands of such on the river piers and roof tops; thousands waving handkerchiefs."

They run when the plane lands, cheering, at times carrying the aviator on their shoulders. All hail the conquering hero. They gather around and just stare at the aeroplane—sometimes through the night. The dream of wings, "man-flight," "bird-men"—they just can't believe it. Glenn Curtiss recalls that one boy just stood and stared until he fainted. The newspaper editorialists pack their best shot: An epoch begins—we'll all own airplanes—or it doesn't: it's a circus stunt of no value.

Thirty years later the photos show the crowds running away from airplanes. The adolescence of twentieth-century inventions is brief. In the few short years after the Wrights are airborne, the airplane is used experimentally in battle: The Americans pursue Pancho Villa in Mexico, the Italians bomb the Turks at Tripoli. This is a prelude to the quickly evolving combat of World War I. In 1937, during the Spanish Civil War, the Nazis bombed and strafed the streets of Guernica on a market day, killing 1,654 and wounding 899 civilians. We know the rest: The World War II bombing of London, Dresden, Hiroshima. . . . The century had begun so quietly with men flying kites on the dunes, biplane wings on a tether.

At one end of this century people crowded airfields here and in Europe to see any glimpse of an airplane; hundreds of thousands streamed out of

Paris, jammed airfields in Berlin, Moscow, and Rome. A short thirty years later they were hiding in bomb shelters in their own city.

Such is the alchemy of the human imagination; it turns gold into lead, time after time. From the barnstorming era to the first solo crossing of the Atlantic to Guernica. . . . From splitting the atom to Hiroshima. . . . All inventions grow up and go to war.

Airplanes become weapons. That's the heartbreak.

"One second you couldn't see anybody. You were up there having the time of your life, and then like out of nowhere there's this guy on your tail. And two more at 12 o'clock," recalls World War II pilot Jack Sims. "I remember all too well how I felt the first time I got a German pilot in my sights. We were at very close range. I took a deep breath, put my finger on the trigger: I couldn't pull it. After what seemed an eternity I squeezed it off. Then the guy did a sort of slow roll and the plane plunged toward earth.

"There was a second there when I could see the guy's face: he looked shocked that it was all over for him, and then the plane burst into flames and the face was gone. But for a millisecond before his face was consumed, there was the faintest trace of a smile."

V. Sad Witness of the Twentieth Century

As a child on a coffee plantation in Brazil, Alberto Santos-Dumont played the game of "passarinho — voa," "the little bird flies." Sitting around a table, the players would quickly say, Does a pigeon fly? Does a hen fly? and the children would raise a finger. But if someone said, Does a fox fly? and a player's finger was still raised, he lost. Whenever they said, Does man fly? "I would always lift my finger very high, as a sign of absolute conviction. . . . The more they laughed at me, the happier I was, hoping that some day the laugh would be on my side," Santos-Dumont recalled years later in Paris, after he won the Deutsch prize for a guided airship flight. Following a predetermined course, he had steered around the Eiffel Tower and returned to the starting point. No one had done that before his triumph in October 1901. He was a short, thin, serious-looking man who dressed for his flights in a dark suit, high starched collars, tie, and a bowler hat. "Le Petit Santos" was brave, innovative, and stylish. He was celebrated in the City of Light, and honored with a medal back home in Brazil.

"They play the old game now more than ever at home," a friend wrote to him after his flight. "They call it now 'Man flies!'"

* * *

When the young Santos-Dumont first went to Paris with his family, he was surprised to learn that ballooning had not advanced since the Montgolfier Brothers had made their ascents a hundred years earlier. There were no "steerable balloons." A balloonist lived on "the chances of the winds."

Santos-Dumont was determined to go aloft, but the aeronauts discouraged him, so he bought an automobile instead, a three-and-a-half-horsepower Peugeot roadster, a rarity in 1891. "Such was the curiosity they aroused that I was not allowed to stop in public places like the Place de l'Opera for fear of attracting multitudes and obstructing traffic," he said. When his family returned to Brazil, Alberto packed his Peugeot for the voyage.

At age eighteen his father gave him his liberty and his inheritance. He sent his son back to Paris, warning him that Paris was "the most dangerous place for a youth" and giving him this advice: "Do not forget that the world's future is in mechanics." Alberto agreed. He had loved to tinker with the plantation's machinery. He had seen his first working petroleum engine at a Paris exposition. "I stood still before the motor just as if I had been nailed down by fate," he said. He had been nurturing a secret desire to build flying machines. "In the long, sun-bathed Brazilian afternoons, when the hum of insects, punctuated by the far-off cry of some bird, lulled me, I would lie in the shade of the veranda and gaze into the fair sky of Brazil, where the birds fly so high and soar with such ease on their great outstretched wings . . . and you have only to raise your eyes to fall in love with space and freedom. So, musing on the exploration of the aerial ocean, I, too, devised airships and flying machines in my imagination." He kept these thoughts to himself. "In those days, in Brazil, to talk of inventing a flying-machine, or dirigible balloon, would have been to stamp one's self as unbalanced and visionary."

Back in Paris he went aloft. He loved his first balloon ascent, and it seemed as if he "had really been born for aeronautics," he said. "Infinitely gentle is this unfelt movement forward and upward. The illusion is complete: it seems not to be the balloon that moves, but the earth that sinks down and away." Two miles up, the sun cast the balloon's shadows on the "dazzling white clouds" below. "Our own profiles, magnified to giant size, appeared in the center of a triple rainbow!" Alberto had packed a "substantial lunch" for himself and the two aeronauts, consisting of "hard-boiled eggs, cold roast beef and chicken, cheese, ice-cream, fruits, cakes, champagne, coffee and chartreuse." "No dining-room can be so marvelous," he said. "A joyous peal of bells mounted up to us. It was the noonday Angelus, ringing from some village belfry." He finished his little glass of liqueur as they set down. He was hooked. "I cannot describe the

delight, the wonder and intoxication of this free diagonal movement on-
ward and upward. . . . The birds have this sensation when they spread
their wings and go tobogganing in curves and spirals through the sky."

Santos-Dumont was free. He ballooned around Europe. He flew at
night, rising "through the black solitudes of the clouds into a soul-lifting
burst of splendid starlight. There, alone with the constellations, we await
the dawn! And when the dawn comes, red and gold and purple in its glory,
one is almost loath to seek the earth again, although the novelty of landing
in who knows what part of Europe affords still another unique pleasure."
He had crashed and flown in storms. Lost alone at night in a thunderstorm, "I felt myself in great danger, yet the danger was not tangible. With
it there was a fierce kind of joy. What shall I say? How shall I describe it?
Up there in the black solitude, amid the lightning flashes and the thunder-
claps, I was a part of the storm!"

Earlier attempts to invent a steerable balloon had failed. Electric motors
and steam engines had been tried, but they were no match for the "vindic-
tive winds," as the balloonists said. Alberto adopted "so uncertain an engine as the petroleum motor of the year 1900." His experimental method
was direct: he had himself hoisted in his tricycle-automobile up into a tree
to see if the engine would vibrate uncontrollably. It actually ran more
smoothly. This was my first successful flight, he said. (To practice eating
while aloft, his dining room table and chair were suspended on cables
from the high ceiling so he sat six feet up. He walked to the table on stilts.
His valet handed the food up to him.)

He built his airships as he was built: small and lightweight. Le Petit
Santos was 5 foot, 5 inches tall and weighed 110 pounds. He pioneered the
use of lightweight materials. The balloon makers objected, saying the light
Japanese silk he wanted to use wouldn't be strong enough. They tested the
material; it was stronger than the heavy taffetas then in use. He wanted to
build the smallest man-carrying spherical balloon ever, only 100 cubic meters. Balloons were usually 500 to 2000 cubic meters. They said there
wouldn't enough gas to lift him. He called the balloon "Brazil," and it flew
very well. He packed most of it in a suitcase.

Santos-Dumont next built a series of dirigibles that look like flying machines right out of Jules Verne, his favorite childhood author. They were
big cigar-shaped balloons, under which, in a net of ropes, hung a small
wicker basket, just big enough for the little aeronaut to stand. Just behind
the basket was a small gas engine with a propeller of square blades. For
stability his airships had big rudders and trailed about a hundred yards of
"guide rope." We know the sleek German zeppelins that came later.

Santos-Dumont's airships are like the backstage of a show. Nothing is tucked in. His critics said that a gas engine would ignite the hydrogen in the balloon above. They were wrong, but he had other problems. His first flight was a success, even if it ended when the ship folded in two. "I felt nothing but elation—I had navigated the air," he said, and he quickly set to improving his design. The public named the ships after him: Santos-Dumont No. 1, 2, 3 . . . on up to 22. (Skipping No. 8, which he considered unlucky. He wouldn't even fly on the eighth day of the month.) He built a complete aerodrome with an airship hangar, workshops, and a hookup to the gasworks for refills.

He was gallant about his mishaps. He accepted the smaller accidents, regarding them "as a kind of insurance against more terrible ones," he said. On his first attempt to win the Deutsch prize, when he was hung up in M. Edmond de Rothschild's tallest chestnut tree, the royalty next door, Princess Isabel, Comtesse d'Eu, sent over a basket lunch to be hoisted up to him. On his second attempt to win the prize, he crashed into the Hotel Trocadero. His balloon exploded, leaving him dangling on a ledge. He praised the "brave firemen" of Paris for rescuing him.

In competition, he was chivalrous. To win the Deutsch prize he had to announce his flight twenty-four hours in advance, leaving him to the mercy of changing weather. He was "barred by common courtesy" from calling on the judges in the most favorable flying hours, the calm of dawn. "The duelist may call out his friends at that sacred hour, but not the airship captain!" He distributed the prize, 100,000 francs, among the Paris poor and his mechanics. With other prize money he founded his own prize to advance aeronautics.

In his smallest airship, the No. 9, nicknamed the "Baladeuse," the "stroller," he became a regular Parisian sight, a boulevardier of the sky. He promenaded above the Bois de Boulogne at the fashionable hour in the little airship, cruised the Champs Élysées stopping for drinks at cafes, his ship tied to a chair. He would stop at his apartment by the Arc de Triomphe for coffee, while two servants held his ship. He flew to luncheon with friends, visited "fellow clubmen" at St. Cloud, home of the Aero Club, and was invited to fly over a Grand Military Review. "He was the perfect ornament to the City of Light, in its greatest days," says biographer Peter Wykeham.

He was famous. His suits, hats, ties, and high white collars were copied; the collars were known as "Santos-Dumonts." Edison sent a signed picture: "To Santos-Dumont, pioneer of the air, the homage of Edison." The French press had declared his prize-winning flight a red-letter day in history. When others began building dirigibles they were called Santos-Dumonts. He flew a scarlet pennant off his airships, a line of poetry he had learned in childhood, Camoen's *Lusiad,* "the epic poet of my race": "Por mares nunca d'antes navegados!" "O'er seas heretofore unsailed!" He planned to build a flying house, he said, and stay up for weeks at a time. He fancied a flight to the North Pole.

There were rumors in Europe that the Wright Brothers had flown. But who had witnessed it? If the Americans didn't believe the Wright Brothers, why should the French? Octave Chanute, correspondent of the Wrights, had come to Paris to lecture on some of the Wrights' developments months before their flight. No one believed the Wrights could fly, but the aeronauts began to believe an airplane was possible. Santos-Dumont and others began to design heavier-than-air ships.

Ernest Archdeacon, a prominent Paris lawyer, offered a prize for the first powered flight. If the Wrights had really flown they would compete. In 1906 Santos-Dumont won the prize in an ungainly machine. He flew for 60 meters, the world's first public flight. He flew further, 220 meters, winning another prize. "Vole, Vole, Vole!" said the headline in *La Nation,* "Fly, Fly, Fly!" The Wrights were *bluffeurs*; Santos-Dumont was the father of flight. The Wrights had made a flight of 25 *miles* the year before, but no one believed it. Brazil placed Santos-Dumont's face on their money. Paris set his name into memorials. He built another airplane, nicknamed the "Demoiselle," the dragonfly, for its transparent wings of Japanese silk. It was small enough to fit in the back of a touring automobile. People wanted to buy Demoiselles. He offered his plans for free, just as he had done with his airships.

Other Europeans built airplanes; then Wilbur Wright arrived in 1908. After months of delay rebuilding a damaged machine, Wilbur flew in four sweeping curves and the French were awestruck. He flew figure-eights. We have not begun to fly, they said.

Once Wilbur Wright flew, Alberto Santos-Dumont was prehistory. The gallantry of his endeavor with poetry on banners, royalty sending up lunch, fashionable promenades in his little balloon, and his talk of honoring Brazil, belonged to the rapidly fading Belle Époque.

He gave it all up in an afternoon, his Paris aerodrome, and one he had built in Monaco. He gave up his balloons and his airplanes. The word around Paris was that he had suffered a nervous breakdown. His first English-language biographer says that Santos-Dumont was diagnosed with multiple sclerosis. He never flew again.

Le Petit Santos was soon forgotten in Paris. He would revisit Paris, but in time even aviators didn't recognize his name. Brazil hung on to its hero of the "XX Century," arguing into the 1940s that the Wrights had no claim on the first flight.

Depressed, given at times to weeping melancholy, he restlessly moved between Paris and Brazil. Or as he had said of being lost in fog in his balloon, he entered a twenty-two-year-long "limbo of nothingness." He was, as he once said, a prisoner of space.

At the outset of World War I, living in a French seaside town, he was accused of spying. He was on the roof day and night with a telescope. The local police searched his house. Santos-Dumont was outraged. He burned all his papers, all the scientific data, diaries, and letters, and returned to Brazil.

News reached him that zeppelins were being used to bomb cities. He despaired. There was "real mental conflict between the thing created and its creator," says a Brazilian account of this "genius victim of his own talent." He had written in 1905 that the "first practical use of air-ship will be found in war" and that airships would menace fleets, destroy submarines, and rout armies. Now that it was happening, it caused him unending anguish. He held himself responsible.

He called aviation "the daughter of our watchful care." His descriptions of balloons were loving, perhaps erotic. "We set foot on solid ground, and stood there, watching the balloon die, stretched out in the field, like a great bird that dies beating its wings," he wrote of his first flight.

His sorrow had more depth than we, at this distance, can measure. "He now believes, that he is more infamous than the devil. A feeling of repentance invades him and leaves him in a flood of tears," Martin du Gard said. His friends tried to hide the news of any airplane crash from him.

He bought a house, called the "Encantada," in the mountains of a summer resort forty miles from Rio, and there kept to himself, taking short walks, observing the night sky, tinkering with gadgets. He was, say his countrymen, "the sad man of the Encantada," the enchanted house.

In 1926 he wrote to the League of Nations, asking them to ban airplanes in war. The League was discussing limiting other armaments. "It is known, nevertheless, what flying machines are capable of doing: what they did during the last war, enables us to foresee, horrified, the degree of destructive power to which they may attain in the future, as sowers of death, not only among the opposing forces in the field, but also, unfortunately, among the inoffensive people in the zone behind the battle line."

He offered "a prize of 10,000 francs for the best work on the interdiction of flying machines as an arm of combat and bombing purposes."

When two aviators landed in Paris after their around-the-world flight in 1930, he wrote to them, "At the beginning of this century, we, the founders of Aeronautics, had dreamed of a peaceful, magnificent future for same, the war—what could we do?—seized on our work to serve the purpose of fratricidal hatred."

He returned to Europe, and to a Paris he did not know. His condition worsened and he entered a Swiss sanatorium. Santos-Dumont was invited to preside at the gala banquet honoring Charles Lindbergh's solo flight in 1927, but he was too ill. He wept reading the letter. The handwriting of his reply was so shaky that it was barely legible, says Wykeham.

Santos-Dumont improved and returned home. Once more, Brazil welcomed him with honors. A seaplane, named Santos-Dumont for the occasion, flew out to greet him carrying a number of the country's leading intellectuals. With the crowds cheering, and Santos-Dumont looking on, the plane tipped sideways into the water and exploded. It was a national tragedy; all on board were killed. "How many lives sacrificed for my humble self!" he said.

The tragedy haunted him. "The slightest noise upsets him," friends said. He tried to take his life. He had once found tranquility in his beloved Brazil, but in 1930 there was a coup, followed by civil war. Brazil was the second largest importer of U.S. airplanes. The Brazilian government was buying Glenn Martin's bombers. Santos-Dumont had gone to rest at a beach house. Bombers passed overhead. He could hear the bombs falling in the distance. The government was bombing the rebels, Brazilians were killing Brazilians. Santos-Dumont hung himself. He was fifty-nine years old. Brazil was shamed into two days of peace.

"Those who, like myself, were the humble pioneers of the conquest of air, thought more about creating new means for the pacific expansion of peoples, than of giving them new arms of combat," he had said. Everything remains half-discovered. We invent the airplane, television, wonders without end, but know not what use to put them to.

In his last days, Santos-Dumont had been looking for the secrets of the birds and maybe their grace as well. He had risen from his depression for a time and began to experiment again. In his youth he had said that no one would get into the air by flapping like a bird. He knew that from studying the plantation machinery. But now as "he studied deeply all that has to do with birds" he had a change of heart. He built wings from swan feathers, wings connected by wires to a central motor. With these wings, he said, a man can fly free like an eagle, fly over the highest mountain. It was as if he were trying to find his way back to that childhood game. Who flies? Does man fly?

"Exercise common sense," a friend had advised him in his youth. "Does man fly? No. Does the bird fly? Yes. Then, if man would fly, let him imitate the bird. Nature has made the bird. Nature never goes wrong."

VI. The Birds Keep Their Secrets

Flying is our newest antique. At the start of the century, no one had flown in a powered airplane. Now airplanes have changed our lives, but not in the fantastic ways once promised. We have not become birds — bird-men as they said at first. We have become passengers in search of luggage, pilots circling airports, pilots bombing cities.

The miracle of bird flight is so much greater than this: flying by sound, by memory, by stars, by magnetic pull, from a backyard in North America to a tree in a South American rainforest.

Near the end of his life, Santos-Dumont had returned to the original dream of flying like a bird, the dream that awakens when a Wright Brothers wing moves and flexes. Recalling those Wright Brothers photos of a glider skimming the dunes, I signed up for hang gliding school. Hang gliding is early flight. Before the Wrights, Otto Lilienthal in Germany was world famous for his hang gliding with wings shaped like "the out-spread pinions of a soaring bird." He was killed as a result of a crash in 1896. The Wrights pursued a different design with their gliders.

To run downhill with a large wing on your back is to join a large fraternity of the brave and the reckless, of visionaries and fools. You are in a brotherhood with test pilots and backyard crackpots.

On a humid day a dozen of us are running up and down a steep hill trying desperately to fly. We are strapped into harnesses and helmets. When we first pick up the wing, and point it into the wind, it starts to dance, promising easy flight. But the glider is flirting with us. By day's end we will have more in common with moles than eagles.

The teacher, Dave Baxter, runs along with a bullhorn yelling: Flare! Don't let the kite get ahead of the pilot! Lean forward! Lean! *Speed! Speed*! And then he spins around to those awaiting their turn: Did you see that? What did he do wrong?

Baxter urgently wants us to fly in his "kites." He is tough and almost evangelical: He wants to baptize us in the air. He has flown for twenty years. On his longest soaring flight he was aloft for four and a half hours, reaching an altitude of 10,200 feet.

He has an assistant who sometimes runs alongside trying to steady your wing. There is a strong encounter with your youngest self. Someone is running alongside as you try to maintain balance. The last time this ever happened my father was teaching me to ride a bicycle. I can remember the exact spot where I looked behind to see if he was still holding me level; he was standing far away. I was on my own.

We only have to learn five basic steps, Baxter tells us. "Then for the next two or three hours you can't believe the bliss you're in." First, balance the wing as you pick it up at a twenty-degree angle of attack. Second, pick a target. Look ahead; avoid the tendency to look down or up. Where you look is where you go. Envision a runway. Third, take three steps: walk, jog, run. Avoid pushing the nose up. Now "the magic starts," he says. When you reach seven to eight miles per hour the glider is off your shoulder. Fourth, tow the glider with your harness. Lean in, run and pull with the harness. At eight to fourteen miles per hour you'll be weightless—"the fastest weight loss program we know." And fifth: Keep running. You'll be able to take incredibly long strides. Moon walking. "Fifty percent of people lose their mind they're so yahooed!" he says. He adds a sixth step: Relax!

"When you do it right—it feels right—it feels like you've been there before. You feel very connected to the equipment." Sounds simple.

With the eagerness of the born-yesterday, we proceed to write an encyclopedia of how to do the six basic steps wrong. We look like those early silent film clips of the earnestly crazy flapping their wings trying to fly, or bouncing along in a thirteen-decker plane that collapses. We are pulled along by the kites like rodeo cowboys thrown from their horses. We are dragged downhill on our knees looking prayerful. Our class mows the grass low. Baxter calls it "grass surfing." At day's end he lines us up to judge the "grass surfing" champion. One woman has grass stains on her shoulders. We have driven his gliders into the ground like giant lawn darts. We have broken two gliders, bending the leading edge of one and the down bar of another. They are hauled off to the shop for quick repair, just as in the days of early aviation.

The Bleriot flight school in Pau, France, in 1912 may have shared this spirit. "The series of attempts, expectations, disappointments, extends over seven days, and seven dull days they are, during which uncertainty is added to physical exertion," recalled Jean Conneau, a French naval officer. "From time to time an incident breaks the monotony. . . . Over yonder there is a machine rolling in a fantastic manner. Here a pupil alights, his face is black, his clothes saturated with oil, give him the appearance of a demon; he takes them off, but leaves behind him as he goes an unbearable smell. I assure you, learning aviation lacks poetry. Sometimes I would closely inspect the aeroplanes which are put at our disposal. Each of the parts [has] been more than once replaced. One has a brand-new right wing and a dirty, oil-stained left one. Another machine is all the colors of the rainbow."

I am having trouble just balancing the fifty-pound glider on my shoulders—it keeps slipping off. The glider and I have wrestled several rounds. The glider is trying to get me to fly, but I won't listen. Calling it a kite, a children's toy, only adds to the frustration.

As you run along it seems possible—you can feel the glider talk to you—everything seems to be happening faster and higher than it really is. There is a lot that seems to be happening—or about to happen. It's like a car skidding in all directions, is how the Englishman Charles Stewart Rolls described his first time aloft in a Wright machine. (He was later killed in a crash.)

I'm running and as the glider lifts me up, I feel as if I'm being pulled up by the scruff of my neck and my feet are windmilling like a cartoon character. At that moment I think: Oh-my-God-this-will-take-off! I could fly—I'm flyin'—I come thunking down. The ride is over. The instinct is to stop running, not to leave the earth. After all that effort, one wants to stay, if only to see how things turn out.

I have recreated another aspect of early aviation: the disbelieving crowd. "There wasn't anybody there who believed an airplane would really fly," Beckwith Havens said of his first air shows. "But when you flew, oh my, they would carry you off the field." After a day of this I will need to be carried off the field.

I have to get used to this idea: This will fly—I will fly—that is the surprise of hang gliding. You can run down hill and step off into the sky. The only thing holding you back is yourself—a burden of truth anyone would want to leave on the ground.

Sitting down to catch my breath, I review my mistakes. I wasn't calmly balancing the kite. I didn't run through the harness. When the kite started to lift I had no idea of how to control it to keep the nose at the right angle. I was a passenger, not a pilot.

By mid-afternoon, we have burned off the morning's eagerness. Discouraged and fatigued, most of the class now sits down between attempts. We look as if we have been used for tackling practice by a football team. Even our instructor looks discouraged. He probably thinks that we are a bunch of knucklehead grass surfers who belong on the ground. But he picks up a kite and shows us once again. Effortlessly he steps off the hill and into the air. It's witchcraft.

Back in the hangar, Baxter will close the day with a pep-rally talk on the glory of flight. He is an impassioned salesman for his sport. He wants converts. He tells us how we can make it to the top of the hill—the launch for a full flight—in less than a work week, just thirty hours. We can be aloft after just 75 to 125 "flights." We have each made fourteen "flights" already, a mole's air force.

He reassures us. When you get beyond the third lesson, the flying gets more intense. It starts to happen when the launch is second nature, when we have good speed and balance, when we have poise. Less than one work week and you'll be flying, he repeats.

He tells us of the excitement of his first time soaring for hours. You can see the joy in his face. He has the whole class along for the ride. As he talks we forget the frustrations of mowing the grass, our cowboy-clown act. We believe: You take one-two-three steps and you're airborne.

He wants to close, he says, by reading from Wilbur Wright's account of gliding in 1903. As he pulls out the quote, he says: "We're the oldest form of aviation. Otto Lilienthal made 2000 flights. [He doesn't mention his death.] We are not the new guys. We're the old guys, reborn with modern materials, Dacron, Mylar, . . . aviation steel, computer-generated wing shapes. For two to three hundred years, this predates power flight. We're not just some yahoos jumping off hills."

He reads from Wilbur Wright: "By long practice the management of a flying machine should become as instinctive as the balancing movements a man unconsciously employs with every step in walking, but in the early days it is easy to make blunders. . . . While the high flights were more spectacular, the low ones were fully as valuable for training purposes. Skill comes by the constant repetition of familiar feats rather than by a few overbold attempts at feats for which the performer is yet poorly prepared."

We had come to fly like the birds. We had signed our lives away to fly. The "release from liability" form said, "I understand that hang gliding is a potentially risky activity." Sure. "I am aware that hang gliding accidents may cause (and have caused) serious injury . . . and even death." Sure. In bold-face capital letters there was something about: "I expressly and voluntarily assume all risk" . . . blah blah. Let's get flying.

Toward day's end when there is only time for another run or two, someone points out a red-tail hawk riding a thermal on the ridge. Everyone is desperate to strap back into a glider, but we all freeze. A hillside of people concentrating, as if this is the first bird we have ever seen.

We watch. We envy the wild hawk. No one says a word. We are thirsty for the secret. "I can see air," a great airplane designer had said in his youth. He had grown up on the coast watching seabirds by the hour. We want to see as the hawk sees; we want to see the lift in the air.

The hawk sails out of sight. We turn back to our wings and hoist them once more to our tired shoulders. We have only the company of machines. The birds keep their secrets.

FLOW

A Niagara of Ethyl

Niagara Falls was the tourist attraction of the nineteenth century. Niagara was sublime and limitless. Here was the raw power of the New World. The guidebooks fussed about the volume of water racing over the falls (205,000 cubic feet of water a second); a legion of writers, Charles Dickens and Henry James among them, paid homage. Niagara was bounty, abundance. Niagara was America.

Niagara was there for the taking, by tourists, writers, and industrialists. The Niagara Falls we know — as souvenir or factory site — did not exist until it was translated. Niagara became a unit of measure. The world's tallest buildings were illustrated alongside the falls, as if being matched for a heavyweight boxing title. Many products were compared to the falls.

"A Niagara of Ethyl Gasoline — over one billion gallons a year — now flows through the pumps bearing the Ethyl emblem" boasts an advertisement in a 1930 issue of *Business Week* magazine. There is a drawing of Niagara Falls branded with the Ethyl Gasoline Corporation's logo. "The active ingredient used in Ethyl fluid is lead," the ad explains. In those days before corporations put on a smiley face of environmental concern, apparently no one thought it alarming to show a cascade of gasoline and lead. And since Ethyl was then colored red, this would have been a red Niagara.

Niagara's natural bounty was translated into the bounty of industrial production and wealth. All waterfalls were appraised for their flow, for how they could turn a water wheel or a turbine. The machines of the early Industrial Revolution were massive, harnessed to waterfalls, and by brute force transformed landscapes and cranked out goods. Mill cities were, in effect, one machine. Each arm, each life, was joined to a loom, to a belt, to the central power source.

Machines of our era are lithe and everywhere present. They are decentralized, and they control the tempo of all our lives as effectively as the mill city enslaved the mill worker. The automobile, airplane, electricity, television, digital information are about flow and volume. And they threaten to overwhelm us.

American life is about flow: How many, how much, how soon. More goods, more territory, more "experiences," more information, more money.

King Camp Gillette understood the flow of American life. As a bottlecap salesman he knew the importance of moving the goods. He had an epiphany one day in 1896 while killing time on the road, sitting at a hotel window in Scranton, looking at a traffic jam, a knot of horses, wagons, and streetcars blocked by a broken-down grocery wagon. In his mind he followed the route all the goods had taken to be mired in a muddy street. "I traced the flour from the mills to the farmer, the salt to the earth, the sugar to the plantation, the spices across the seas to China and Japan." Then he saw it clearly: All the goods on that truck were the product of "one vast operative mechanism." All the world's industries and governments were part of a single machine. He tried for years to create a utopia based on the idea that an efficient machine would make for a happier society. Fix the flow and you fixed society.

But we know Gillette for the invention and promotion of the safety razor with the disposable blade. It took Gillette years to convince men to buy and later throw out the blades. He assaulted thrift. Gillette advertised heavily (50 cents for each razor he sold in 1906, for a total of a million dollars). He had to change men's habits. First he had to convince them that they were wasting their time with daily shaves at barbershops, which were like workingmen's social clubs. ("If the time, money, energy, and brain-power wasted in the barbershops of America were applied in direct effort, the Panama Canal would be dug in four hours," said one 1906 ad.) After getting men to try his blades, Gillette had to teach them to throw the used ones away. To the company's consternation, many customers had their blades resharpened at hardware stores or bought gadgets to do it themselves.

Even when they were ready to throw out a blade, they didn't know where to put it. In many areas, blades couldn't go into the trash because trash was fed to hogs. Sinclair Lewis had George F. Babbitt tossing them up on top of the cabinet, hoping one day to clean it up. (A blade here and there added up. In the late 1920s the company was using "about 800 tons of the finest steel a year," said Gillette, to make 700 million blades.) Gillette cowrote a magazine article suggesting ways to dispose of blades, and the *New York Telegram* ran a survey in 1927: What do you do with your old razor blades? H. L. Mencken answered that he "put them in the collection plate." The Pullman Company, not wanting loose, dirty blades in its railroad car washrooms, devised a slot in the wall, which became standard in bathroom medicine cabinets. Thousands of old blades are piled up inside the walls of apartments and houses.

Gillette's victory was complete. He was the Throw Away King. His face, pictured on 96 billion packages of blades, became a new international symbol. "America's sedentary days are long since past," Edith Wharton wrote in 1927. "The whole world has become a vast escalator, and Ford motors and Gillette razors have bound together the uttermost parts of the earth."

Industry now worked for "the organized creation of dissatisfaction," as the general director of the General Motors research labs, Charles F. Kettering, said in 1929. A new profession took shape: "Consumer Engineers." Things must wear out faster, consumption must be increased, agreed designer Ernest Elmo Calkins. "Can artificial obsolescence be created? Consumer engineering does not end until we can consume all we can make."

Here was the new Niagara, a limitless flow of products. The Herbert Hoover Committee on Recent Economic Changes reported in 1929 that its research had "proved conclusively . . . that there are new wants which will make way endlessly for newer wants, as fast as they are satisfied. . . . Our situation is fortunate, our momentum is remarkable."

These are just a few of the landmarks of our marketplace. They are noteworthy because they are frank. In short order, words would be spun beyond recognition. (Consumer Engineers became Industrial Designers.) But the razor blade is still the paradigm. During the Bull Stock Market of the late 1990s, the manager of a successful mutual fund was appraising the prospects of a new high-tech product, in this case, satellite-directed navigation for the car. The technology was great, he said, but it did require a lot of work to keep it updated. "Someday it could be a razor blade—you know like once Gillette sells the razor, people have to keep buying the blades," he said.

But can you increase sales, increase the flow? When Gillette introduced a new razor in 1998, it tried something new to accelerate blade sales: a blue strip that fades as a nudge to replace the blade. (The new "improved" blades promised thirteen shaves a blade. Gillette debuted with blades advertised to be good for anywhere from twenty to forty shaves per blade.) The same strategy has been used for a toothbrush with blue bristles that fade, and other indicators that report low batteries and aging air fresheners. Attempting to accelerate the toss-out rate, "freshness dates" are appearing on more products, such as canned beer, which is sealed to last for years. "If you double the throwaway rate, you double sales," says one market analyst.

It is not the pace of invention that has people reeling, but the way these inventions have ordered our lives, the way we have filled our lives with these products. The average American consumes twice as much as he or she did forty years ago. National polls report that Americans are not happier, writes Paul Wachtel, author of *The Poverty of Affluence*: "In 1958, when economist John Kenneth Galbraith appropriately described the United States as 'The Affluent Society,' 9.5 percent of U.S. households had air conditioning, about 4 percent had dishwashers, and fewer than 15 percent had more than one car. By 1980, when Ronald Reagan's successful bid to replace Jimmy Carter was based on the widespread sense that people were suffering economically, the percentage of homes with air conditioning had quintupled, the percentage with dishwashers had increased more than 700 percent and the percentage with two or more cars had about tripled. Yet, despite the astounding economic growth—despite owning more of the gadgets, machines and appliances thought to constitute 'the good life'—Americans felt significantly less well-off than they had twenty-two years earlier."

We are caught up in this flow—the rush hour, the interstate highway, the road widening that threatens houses like some river overrunning its banks. The flow of modern times moves to its own rhythm, and overtakes anything in its path: small towns, family farms, and even the factories of the Industrial Revolution, which are pokey by the modern measure. There have been vast cities in other eras—Rome at its height is said to have had an astonishing 1 million people—but this speed, this volume, this flow is the modern experience.

In Robert Musil's novel *The Man Without Qualities*, he describes the flow of life in Vienna on an August day in 1913, noting the way new machines were changing the city's cadence, changing the way people walk down a street. "Automobiles shot out of deep, narrow streets into the shallows of bright squares. Dark clusters of pedestrians formed cloudlike strings. Where more powerful lines of speed cut across their casual haste they clotted up, then trickled on faster and, after a few oscillations, resumed their steady rhythm. Hundreds of noises wove themselves into a wiry texture of sound with barbs protruding here and there, smart edges running along it and subsiding again, with clear notes splintering off and dissipating."

Musil imagines this modern pace increased in his "daydream" of a "super-American city where everyone rushes about, or stands still, with a stopwatch in hand. Air and earth form an anthill traversed, level upon level, by roads live with traffic. Air trains, ground trains, underground trains, people mailed through tubes special-delivery, and chains of car race along horizontally, while express elevators pump masses of people vertically from one traffic level to another; at the junctions, people leap from one vehicle to the next, instantly sucked in and snatched away by the rhythm of it, which makes a syncope, a pause, a little gap of twenty seconds during which a word might be hastily exchanged with someone else. Questions and answers synchronize like meshing gears . . . meals are taken on the run."

This image of cities buzzing with traffic reoccurs in other novels, science-fiction stories, and films. Sometimes there are highways, twelve lanes wide, racing through skyscrapers on the twentieth story, and commuters rocketing downtown to work. These images were wrong in the details, but right in the truth they reported.

Thomas Merton, the Trappist monk, and Czeslaw Milosz, the poet from Lithuania later to win the Nobel Prize, started up a correspondence in the late 1950s. In one letter, Merton wrote: "What is happening in the world today is a wholesale collapse of man's capacity to love. He has been submerged under material concerns, and by the fantastic proliferation of men and things all around him, so that there are so many of everything that one lives in a state of constant bewilderment and fear." We have remade the world, a Niagara flowing red. Flow is what we mistake for progress.

A Moment's Bright Flash

❧ ❧

I.

Elmwood Junction was once the busy crossing of two railroad lines. The junction had a considerable constellation of buildings: a station with platforms, a station agent's house, coal sheds, water tank and pump house, ice house, oil shed, tool shed, high-level freight platform, two water standpipes, scale house and scales, and a section house. There were sidings leading to these: a sunken track into the coal shed, a coal loading and unloading track, wharf track, passing track, short and long curving wye tracks, an X-shaped diamond crossing regulated by a ball signal, and tracks leading compass-like from Hancock, New Hampshire, to Nashua, Hillsborough, Peterborough, Keene, Boston, and Worcester.

The railroads had overcome a turbulent beginning: a strike that almost turned into a riot, bankruptcy, and litigation. The Keene line ran through rough country, up steep grades and over deep ravines. It cost about $1.2 million dollars to cover twenty-six miles in the 1870s.

Today Elmwood Junction is but a few concrete blocks in the woods, a railroad tie here, a pit that once held coal, a rusty bit of railroad coupling, a rusty bolt. The rail lines are paths, some thick with brush, others kept open by snowmobilers. One stretch of track survives. On a June day the black flies deter any lingering.

William Robinson began farming here in 1807 along the Contoocook River. He named his farm Elmwood for the beautiful elm trees. He had views to the surrounding mountains. William was born across the river. His father, says the family history, found his way north in 1780 by following marked trees. The railroad arrived in 1876. With a salute from Platoon B, First Light Battery of the State Militia, and a reverend's prayer, construction began near Elmwood on the Manchester and Keene Railroad. William sold them the northwest part of his farm. The railroad ran within a couple hundred feet of the Robinsons' house and barn. Another rail-road, the Peterborough and Hillsborough, joined at this spot, and in 1878 both began service.

The Robinsons, by every surviving account, were delighted. William Robinson sold the old homestead to the railroad to use as the station agent's house. It was moved to sit alongside the track. He enlarged another farm building to board some of the company officials, contractors, and survey engineers. Gangs of Italian workers were housed in nearby railroad boarding cars. The telegraph lines followed a year later in 1880, as well as a post office. William's daughter-in-law, Ella, was the first postmaster, followed by her husband.

There were six trains daily between Keene and Boston in 1884, a full daily schedule between Concord, New Hampshire, and Winchendon, Massachusetts, and passengers hastily changing between trains, at times having as little as two minutes. Farmers shipped milk, chickens, and produce on the regular Milk Train, or in a milk car added to a passenger train. Locomotives were fueled with wood at first, then coal. About 1886, sheds and pits for loading coal were built at Elmwood, and the Elmwood Extra, the Hillsborough Passenger, and the Keene Freight stopped to "coal up." Many slow freight trains loaded with coal were routed through the Concord line. On the large X-shaped crossing, trains reversed direction, doing what was known as the "Elmwood Shuffle."

The Robinsons found it exciting. When Postmaster Ella's daughter, Betty, went to the main village of Hancock, she thought it dull. She hurried home to Elmwood Junction where something was always happening.

In the great blizzard of March 1888, 35 travelers, passengers and crew, were snowbound at the Robinsons' farm for four days. The snow drifted above the windows. Some slept in the barn in piles of hay. They passed the time telling stories, singing, playing cards, bringing in firewood and tending the fires. A popular speaker delivered the lecture he was scheduled to give in Concord that day. Ella must have been a whirlwind, cooking supper for thirty-five. She drew on the farm's provisions: a side of beef, a dressed pig, a cellar of potatoes, other vegetables, apples and cider. The farm's seventeen cows were producing seventy-five pounds of butter a week. Plow trains broke through on the fourth day and the travelers dispersed.

The railroad ruled the countryside. Farmers knew it was time to bring the cows home for the evening milking when they heard the whistle of the Concord train pulling in at 4:27. "We live the steadier for it," Henry David Thoreau said of the railroad that touched one side of Walden Pond. "Have not men improved somewhat in punctuality since the railroad was invented? Do they not talk and think faster in the depot than they did in the stage-office? There is something electrifying in the atmosphere of the former place."

A January thaw toppled the empire. Maurice Tuttle was out walking the track on January 9, 1934, when he discovered that a trestle had collapsed. He alerted the station agent. A freight train was stopped. Freight service on the Keene Branch never resumed. Passenger service was abandoned that April. The Great Depression, the flood of 1936, and the hurricane of 1938 finished off various parts of the railroads. Better roads and more cars and buses had arrived. The Keene line was torn up in 1940. After that the demolition accelerated: The water tower, long disused, was cut down, releasing a cloud of bats when it crashed. The ball signal burned down when they were trying to smoke out a hornet's nest. In September 1952 all the remaining track of the old junction, the depot, and all other buildings were bulldozed.

George Rockwell, whose land was next to the Elmwood farm, was a teenager when the railroad came. He carried water for the train gangs. He was ninety years old when the last of Elmwood Junction was leveled. He died the next year. Railroad stations are transitory places, and not only for people and freight: The place itself is in transit. The railroad had ruled for only fifty-six years.

The Boston & Maine, which had operated the railroads since 1900, moved through the country pulling up tracks and tearing down large trestles, as if they were rolling up a carpet. Joe Quinn, a Hancock farmer and all-around hand about town, had a contract in 1940 to pick up the leavings: plates, bolts and pins, tons of iron scrap. "The railroad was the making of Hancock," said Quinn. "This town was awful poor before the railroad."

The town had tried to convince the Boston & Maine to stay. But they were rejected. There is in most railroad recollections something like the lament for an early love. The day's last train would leave Elmwood Junction at 6:27. From her bedroom window at Elmwood farm, Betty Robinson, a young girl, could see the fireman open the firebox to put on coal for a steep grade ahead. On the dark winter nights, the fire glowed. "The whistle would blow again and again as the train got further away and the sound would come back from the hills," she said. "It's so nostalgic as I look back on it now."

The farming days were over at Elmwood. The Robinson family made another sale. In the 1920s Henry Robinson sold the "flowage rights," permitting a paper mill up river to flood 120 acres of the Robinsons' good pasture. The farmhouse is still there, well kept up by the Robinson family, who use it as a summer house. This is the only land in Hancock still owned by the same family for 200 years.

After the railroad, Elmwood did not settle back into a riverine silence. A major north-south state road was put through nearby in 1959. In the woods, which have swallowed the junction more completely than a lost Mayan city, the noise of the road is present and close at hand.

Elmwood Junction proves the truth of American places. Commerce and movement make up the true American place. A railroad junction is a perfect example, a kinetic sculpture. It's all movement.

Today the junction is not even a ruin. Old places, as in Europe, gather memories and associations. Thousands of lives write them as if they were a big historical novel, thousands of feet and hands wear them smooth, re-make them. But most of America's old places decay and are discarded, or are replaced and restored to a false and sparkly new use, all suffering and ambiguity erased, renovated out of existence.

The American place story is about the bright lights of success; it's a thousand gold rush stories. The day the trolley line came and the suburbs were built and the veterans returned and everyone came downtown on Saturday to shop, eat at Schraft's, see the latest movies for a nickel. There is something electrifying in the atmosphere.

The mark of our great places is an edgy milling about. Times Square, Scollay Square . . . not places of repose, parks or cathedrals, but places of unease, dissatisfaction.

When the National Cash Register company built a huge cash-register-shaped building, six stories tall, at the 1939 New York World's Fair, it was a crass monument. The cash register counted the daily attendance—rung us all in—and it did report a truth: Commerce is what we praise above all else.

Steam and smoke and mess—that's the true American place.

II.

The Driscolls' Vermont cow pasture is crowded with machines. There's the snort and chuff of antique engines, puffs of white smoke going up, fly wheels spinning. Little table-top steam engines and a big oil-field engine, almost eight tons, work at nothing. Off the farm, off the belting, out of the mill, they just exist to run and be admired. Rows of small gas engines sit on the ground shimmying and popping, like someone having a private laugh; an antique cement mixer rumbles away mixing nothing. Men on old farm tractors parade through the field. This is a park for machines on a weekend outing. And over it all as the day goes along, worn like laurels, a crown of exhaust.

The engines move to an antique kind of motion—hit or miss, make or break, coasting down, firing to their own beat. Some engines are governed by a throttle and pop along sweetly as if they were born with a more even temperament. All these antique engines seem to clop along like workhorses.

This, to me, is a most American thing to do: take a field and fill it from morning to evening with machine noise, machine motion, and then find in all these pistons and flywheels and flapping belts, in the smell of gas and oil, a kind of lullaby, a cradle rocking at 200 to 500 revolutions per minute—one-fifth the speed of the average lawn mower.

The words to the lullaby are this, usually: This John Deere, this Fairbanks-Morse, this one-lunger was made in 1897 or 1913 or 1931. It ran everything on the farm. Ran the threshing machines, the food grinders, and washing machine. Today my five-year-old lawn mower is shot. My car is rusting out and I just finished paying for it. This Fuller & Johnson, this Waterloo Boy, this still runs. Hit or miss, make or break. This is the sound of the world running right.

This is Doug and Ruth Driscoll's farm. This is the harvest they had in mind. They bought this place five years ago planning to have a yearly antique engine show. They started CRACK, Connecticut River Antique Collectors Klub, with six members; now there are 126 families. "We spelled Klub with a 'K' because we're all a little crazy," Doug says.

Doug is a scrappy-looking fellow, short and wiry. He is unshaven and wears a dusty black bowler, a green CRACK T-shirt with a cigarette pack rolled up in the sleeve, and a coffee mug hooked to his belt loop.

He shows me around. We move at a good clip. Doug greets everyone; he asks what they think. He is the mayor. Everyone is pleased. At the first show they had thirty-five exhibits; today there are nearly three times that on the field, and not only machines.

We have collectors of nearly everything, Doug says. He wants the show to be a family thing, not just a bunch of gear heads. (Family membership is $10 a year, including all unmarried children under twenty-one living at home.) We have salt and pepper shaker collectors, ax collectors, tractor seat collectors, watch fobs, old chow bags, feed caps, chicken and egg equipment, he says. There's a display of lawn sprinklers. "You've got to see them; they're just something." Indeed they are: over fifty lawn sprinklers, shiny brass, laid out on a green Astroturf rug. There's a barbed wire display hung up on peg board. The names are written on tongue depressors, names like ice cream: Merrill's Twist, Nadelhoffer's Twist. In all there are 1,500 kinds of barbed wire, Doug says. There's a man from Quebec with twenty-two chainsaws from 1945 to 1960, some five feet long. They look like some kind of lethal metal fish caught and hauled up on dock.

Doug is called to help start the largest engine. We walk past a collection of steam mill whistles—they will hook them up and play them later; past a shingle mill on a long flatbed; past Elwyn Brown, eighty-four, a retired sawyer turning dowels; past a rare, air-cooled, seven-horsepower engine, running in a pick-up truck bed. The truck sags from the 800-pound weight and wiggles suggestively.

Front and center in the field, under its own roof, a machine shrine, sits a Bessemer oil-field engine. It takes nearly eight tons of machine, a thirteen-inch-long piston, and a flywheel taller than a man to produce only forty horsepower. So the engine doesn't sink into the pasture, it sits on a ten-foot-deep bed of stone. (Club member Gabe Machado moved this behemoth from Pennsylvania to his farm at first. When he unloaded it from his truck, it took out the side of his barn.)

The Bessemer pumped water down into the earth to force oil up. It had not run since 1954. It took eight months to work it free.

They start this machine with another machine. To get the big flywheel moving, they use an air-compressor, a noisy one-cylinder engine— *Wheeze-chuff, Wheeze-chuff.*

The compressor stalls. Patiently, again and again, a man coaxes the compressor's flywheel with his foot. A small crowd of thirty people has gathered to watch.

A balking machine is not a frustration like when a lawn mower dies on the weekend. Starting up an old machine, without the press of work, is like taking a scenic drive. Each sputter or stall is another scenic overlook, just the pleasure of the drive.

Why go looking for trouble? That's what I think. There's so many machines you have to keep running, why invite more into your life? Why revive something as cumbersome and deadly as some of the larger gas and steam-power tractors and threshers? They seem, even at their leisure in these antique engine shows, like fearsome machines.

At another antique engine show, I was touring the field with a friend, Dan Scully, an architect who also builds and races cars. He paused in front of an old tractor, and looking at the big spiked metal rear wheels, Scully recalled a farmer he knew from his childhood. Carl Clark ran an apple orchard by himself. "He had blue irises, and he made me love them. I am not a guy who pays attention to flowers," says Scully. He used to bring the bulbs home to his mother. One day Clark was working out in his field and got caught by one of those spikes on the wheel. He was pulled under his tractor and killed.

After the big Bessemer pump starts up, Doug comes over, smiling broadly, to where folks are watching it run. They are smiling too. "Good job," they tell him. "That's worth the trip," a woman tells him.

Doug hurries to attach an oiler to it, so they don't burn out the large piston. There's a bit of scrambling and improvising the connection. His wife Ruth takes me to tour the museum they've set up.

She shows me the old washing machines first. They take one, a 1918 Coffield, to shows, "belt it up" to an engine. The entire tank rocks. Wears out synthetic clothes fast, Ruth says.

The washing machines are a testament to toil. A 1921 machine from Everybody's Factory, Bellows Falls, Vt., rocks like a cradle. A Black & Decker Cinderella uses a vacuum on top of a tub. Still quite a lot of work, says Ruth, but an improvement. A wooden Dan Patch, named for the race horse, is made so a person could sit in a rocking chair and rock a wooden tub back and forth. The Golden Monarch, another wooden machine, has an agitator shaped like a milking stool. They thought about every way to move the clothes in the water, she says.

The Driscolls try to get Vermont-made things for their museum. They have set up a kitchen. A Hoosier cabinet with all sorts of peelers, pitters, and bottle cappers clamped on, a cast-iron sink with a hand pump, a soap-saver cage, an ice box cabinet. In the adjoining room, they have a display of coffee grinders, including a store-sized one. Until 1972 this building was a general store. It also served as the post office until 1938. There are old Coke signs, toy tractors and trucks, and more machines: a Babcock tester for milk, a knitting machine, a gas-fired popcorn maker from a movie theater, a rope maker.

Doug enters the museum and starts a 1932 one-cylinder, two-cycle, Maytag engine. The gas engine stinks up the room. The exhaust is not hooked to a hose leading outside, as was the practice. We look at some hit-or-miss engines.

"You can run one of these antique engines for an entire weekend on a gallon of gas, because they coast most of the time," Ruth says. They used one engine all over the house and barn. "Now each thing has to have its own." So you wonder about progress, she says.

Doug sweeps me out to the barn. We walk through a century of farm labor in a wink. In a milk house he moved from the Whitcomb farm (complete with the carbon-copy receipts for milk delivery) he has lined up milkers: Surge, Universal, Empire, he names them quickly, points to the aerator used to chill milk, and the milk cooler for the cans. Some were cooled with spring water.

In the next room there's a butter-working table, a Davis swinging churn, and a cream separator. They shipped the cream, gave the skim to pigs. And next, an ice setup: ice saws, creepers, an ice trolley overhead and 3½ tons of ice below the floor, packed in sawdust. The club cut the ice last winter with the old-fashioned equipment. They use the ice to make ice cream the old way at this show.

He walks me past a kerosene incubator for chicks, an egg candler and grader, a hand-powered grain separator, and a suite of machines all run from an overhead shaft: corn sheller, cider press, and a bone cutter. You take your green bones and grind 'em up to put in the chicken feed, he says. Didn't waste anything. He gestures to a wall of hay forks: harpoon, folding tyne, loose grapple, folding grapple.

This tour is like an orientation to a dozen different jobs. Each room in the barn is the first day on the job. I'm still sorting out the hay forks, when he moves on to the hay saws, bull rakes, and hand scythes.

You rake the whole field into rows with a bull rake, Doug says. Then rake out the corner with a little straight hand rake. *Didn't waste anything.* A man comes in: I did that with my father, he says.

Attached to the barn Doug has set up a blacksmith shop in memory of his grandfather, F. W. Brown, a blacksmith who died at age 49. He has more equipment out behind the barn, plows and saws and who knows. A group of teenagers is rebuilding a Morrisville Drag Saw. Doug Driscoll has gathered all this in only eight years.

"People have forgotten how hard people worked to make this nation," Doug says. "I love the heritage of my country," he says. He has the show so the heritage isn't lost. He demonstrates some of these tools at school. Some kids—in Vermont!—don't know how milk is produced, he says.

"Families today are split," he says. It's why we have a drug problem, and the suicide rate. On the old-time farms, families were close. They worked together. "Today parents don't have the time. They give their kids money." An idle mind is the workshop of the devil. J. Edgar Hoover was right, he says. There's no such thing as juvenile delinquency; it's parental delinquency. He concludes by citing the biblical guidance about raising up a child in the way he should go.

A lacy nostalgia has grown up around these machines like the tendrils of a vine. At shows in the Midwest, they restore larger machines: steam traction engines and threshers weighing tons, farm-going locomotives. This stuff is difficult to transport to shows, requiring flat-bed trucks. The steam boilers operate under high pressure and must be meticulously restored and inspected. But the restorers share the same motivation as Doug.

"When the threshing rings operated they required groups of people traveling from farm to farm to accomplish the threshing for each individual farmer. And there was this sense of cooperation . . . and sense of community," says Linda Weidman, managing editor of *The Iron-Men Album Magazine*, which covers the shows. In the magazine, the "steam heads" show photos of their work, swap advice, and passionately argue about the best ways to rebuild steam boilers—"Lap Seam or Butt-Strap?"

The Iron-Men Album has its office in Amish country. When a barn burns down, the community rallies to rebuild the barn and cooks big meals for the workers. The clubs dedicated to the steam machines are "that kind of community," Weidman explains. "I call it spiritual—I don't know what else to call it—that is associated with threshing and which kind of carries over into these reunions. It's really a sharp contrast to the way many people live today."

The Driscolls' engine show is a big family gathering. Once they shut down the machines in the evening, they sit down to a ham and bean supper, bonfire, and pie and coffee. Dorothy Newhall has made ten pies. When she was in the hospital, having her leg amputated due to her diabetes, the members of this club were so good she says, visiting, sending cards. She smiles as she talks and insists that I stay for pie: raspberry, cherry, peach, apple, blueberry, rhubarb. . . . Surely I must have a favorite among those? Her husband, David, is the President of CRACK. He sharpens old saws. He learned from his father and is teaching the skill to his adopted grandson.

Dorothy collects agateware. They have an 1830 house. Anything they collect, they use. "Wished I lived back then," she says. "Life was slower. Pleasures were simpler. Just more fun. We get too caught up in all the running and the money, the TV." The key word is "caught."

This John Deere, this Fuller & Johnson, these machines ran when more families worked together on the farm, when the country built good things and came by its day's wage honestly. This a field of machines, a weekend's play, but it is also about restoring order, community, and a few families finding peace of a kind.

Steam and smoke and mess. Welcome home America. Happiness is motion.

Machine happiness. (*Joie de machine.*) They are happy to sit and regard their engines. Set out two lawn chairs in front of your camper van, trailer, or Winnebago, hang up the wooden sign you've made with your names, and let your machines rip. Catch up with your friends and their machines. Discuss the finer points of replacing the rims on a 1941 Model H John Deere. Sometimes the wife sits in her lawn chair knitting or reading a Danielle Steele paperback, while her man kneels by his machines, tinkering.

I have seen this look of machine happiness on the faces of weekend pilots at the airport. Even if they are not flying that day, that week, or ever again, they are happy to be among airplanes. They will make a preflight tour out of habit—check the weather, check the charts, study the sky, the landing patterns to see which runways are in use.

They are old hands at machine making, farmers, engineers, builders, machinists, with a pride in machine skill. It is a great feeling to take an old motor that has been seized up, stuck, for forty years and get it running right. They are holdovers from an era when America was a nation of small manufactories. There were thousands of machine shops and a legion of workers with a literacy in gears and drive shafts and pulleys. Robert Fulton, steamboat inventor, advised that all aspiring inventors "should sit down among levers, screws, wedges, wheels, etc. like a poet among the letters of the alphabet, considering them as the exhibition of his thoughts, in which a new arrangement transmits a new Idea to the world." Inventors in the nineteenth century would take apart a machine—a telegraph, a pump, a thresher—and find its weak link, redesign it and receive a patent.

These are our poets of gears and torque, old farmers in green work pants and checkered shirts, thick glasses—a notepad in the top pocket with pens and pencils for figuring. Men with white rags hanging out of the back pocket of their overalls. Guys who make a fashion statement by wearing big green John Deere suspenders, or wide yellow suspenders marked off like a ruler. Guys who will spend three hundred hours building toys from scratch—a crane, a scale-model steamboat, toys for themselves—and then drive hours to play with them in public; guys who take old engines and convert them into working models of even older engines; guys who hook engines up to whimsical tasks. So alright, they're not what we usually think of as poets, and I'm fairly sure that "poet" is not the word their wives use to describe them.

It's slow going talking with these men. There are long gaps during which you both stand and stare at the machine going 'round and 'round. They just seem to run out of words, and then look to the machine as if it spoke for them.

Dexter Bennett makes gadgets, like the "Reo Egg Beater," a "Reo Royale De Luxe" gas engine, circa 1950, chained up to run an egg beater.

"When he can't sleep at night, he dreams these things up," his wife Polly says with what I take to be a resigned annoyance. They are sitting in front of their trailer eating lunch.

He starts up another gadget for me, a metal horse standing on a green turntable, surrounded by a gold chain. A winner's circle. The horse is from a weather vane that had blown off their barn. He's got it hooked to a Tecumseh engine from 1949 or so. To fill it he uses an oil can from the Boston & Maine Railroad. "Bet you've never seen one of these," he says proudly. The only other one he's seen is in the Shelburne Museum in Vermont. The Tecumseh kicks right over and the horse prances in its circle. Not much else is said for many horse-turns.

He has six one-lungers at home "but they're getting heavy to move. This stuff moves easy." Each engine is hooked up to work: One runs a butter churn that was on his grandparent's and parent's farm. In 1909 that churn sold for $2.80, he says. The gas engine—a 1927 model—was sold by Sears & Roebuck for $26. This is typical: They can tell you the price of these old engines when they were new.

The Tecumseh pauses, just the slightest hitch in its rhythm. He looks, I look. "You've got moisture in there," he says. There was a heavy rain last night. "I thought I had that cleared up." He starts tinkering with the engine and turntable.

Franklin Hietala rebuilds 1920s Briggs & Stratton engines into older hit-or-miss engines. He has them running in front of his camper. One starts with a Model T ignition coil, the other with a coil from a 1940s Plymouth. Originally they ran 1920s washing machines.

"Where do you get a Model T coil?" I ask.

"Oh, they're all over," he says offhandedly. "You can buy them new."

"I built seven; I couldn't just build two," he tells me. He sold the other five. He has been a machinist, although he declines to call himself one. He is self-taught. Quit school in the eighth grade, worked on a farm fourteen years, then went into business building "stuff for the steel industry." Years ago he sold a $29,000 machine for handling coiled steel. He also used to build and race cars. One of his boys is still building and running racers; the other builds model planes. He's retired and winters in Florida with his wife. He is a member of the Florida Flywheelers and went to twenty-two shows in one winter. "You gotta do something. I'm too old to work, like I say." This is only his fourth show this summer. He just had his second triple heart bypass.

We look back down at the two engines. One is squealing. Compression going by the rings, he explains.

He's got other machines at home. "I like any kind." He has a 1920 knitting machine and another from 1868, which cost $19 when new. A new reproduction knitting machine costs "pert near $700." When they built the reproduction, they had a hard time building it precisely enough to let the needles move. But machinists used to do that all the time, he says. The old machines represent a better order of things to these men.

Each machine, each faded technology, leaves behind a tribe of believers still rocked by its rhythms. Steam engines, threshers, airplanes, automobiles, railroads, computers, neon signs . . .

It gets into your blood, the believers say, with more truth than they may realize. It gets right into the rhythm of their breath and dreams.

"All the old rhythm is gone and in its place is heard the hum of an engine, the whirr of wheels, the explosion of an exhaust," the great songwriter Irving Berlin said in 1924. "The leisurely songs that men hummed to the clatter of horses' hoofs do not fit into this new rhythm. . . . The new age demands new music for new action."

Dan Scully says that rock 'n' roll was impossible without the V-8 engine—*As I was motivatin' over the hill/ I saw Maybellene in a coup de ville.* The machine and the music are united in that rhythm. "The beat of the Flathead Ford V-8 engine is the same beat that Chuck Berry used in *Maybellene*, which is about a Flathead Ford. And it is really the beat of rock 'n' roll," says Scully. "It's staggering how close he got to the rhythm of that engine." The Flathead's valves and pistons were in the block up to 1953, Scully explains. "It's more of a heart pounding than an engine shrieking." When the railroad arrived in a city, more people started smoking cigarettes, say some social historians. Steam for steam.

But these are simple machines, only a few parts are moving at a time. One explosion translated to motion. This is noise, but it is different from today's noise. Today the machinery is the TV, the ad, the movie, the steady occupation of people's dreams and desires.

And here by these machines people find a stillness. They are calm enough to sit.

The peace of antique engine meets is like the peace of the Civil War reenactors' camp. People have found their way out of their era. They have blocked out the noise of our era with another era's noise.

What they are after, I think, is poetry, a kind of American poetry of places: the tock-tock beat that built the country, the noise and steam and soot which chases away the unnerving silence, the silence that the first settlers noted—a forest gloom lacking the sun and bird song of home. We have never quite gotten past that.

With each controlled explosion, a machine works its way free of the past—a past that was animal effort and muscle. With each turn of the flywheel, a machine works to obsolete itself and unsettle the world.

These are the machines that built other machines or built the wealth to build the machines that built modern times. You could say, in homage to the fairy tale, these are the machines that built the house where Jack lives, our house. These are the machines that brought us today.

Most antiques promise a static scene. This is an antique that drags us forward. This is nostalgia for one part of the arc; for one place on the wheel's turn.

All these machines are at work doing nothing, you'd say. But I see them all as pumps, raising the spirit level of the faithful—the tinkerers and visitors. Here in this crazy world something works right. A hit-or-miss engine runs true.

One man at the engine show had built a small scene around a barrel of water. A hired man works a hand pump to fill the barrel, but it never fills.

A pump continuously takes away the water, leaving this machine-driven man at his task eternally.

In the Tao there is this story. A learned master, famous throughout the kingdom for his scholarship, was out for a walk in the country with his disciples. They came upon an old man toiling to water his garden. With great effort, but little result, he was hauling jars of water from the well. The learned master told him he should use a shadoof, a long pole weighted at one end to automatically dip a water bucket at the other end like a see-saw. With a shadoof he could irrigate a hundred gardens with less effort than he used now.

The old gardener gave the master an angry look, then laughed. His teacher had taught him that "ingenious contrivances" were the work of a "scheming mind" and impaired "pure simplicity." "When this pure simplicity is impaired, the spirit becomes unsettled, and the unsettled spirit is not the proper residence of the Tao." He knew of this water-moving "contrivance" but he would be "ashamed to use it." The learned master was humbled into silence. The gardener's simplicity, he said later, was vast and complete.

Here in this one Vermont field is a legion of men ready to rush forward to lift water dozens of different ways, with pumps, water hammers, and water ramps.

This inventiveness is our glory and defeat. This is the one trick we know, the way we've created one kind of wealth, created plenitude, but lost fullness.

"Discontent is the first necessity of progress," said Thomas Edison. "Show me a thoroughly satisfied man, and I will show you a failure."

At the antique engine show they played a game with the tractors. Each competitor drove around with a bag on his head. A blind race. They had to drive to a specific spot. No peripheral vision. A fun game, or a damning image if you think about it.

III.

Waine Morse is a quiet man, given to a Mr. Rogers tone from his years as an elementary school teacher. "Do you know what this is?" he will ask in that gentle way that assures you it's okay not to know. Leaving one of the rooms of his museum, he will say, "And that's what that is about" and he will smack his lips.

He built Old Greenfield Village himself, just as he built his house by himself. He will tell you that only if you press. "Bought a saw and cut down the trees and built the house. So I kept my hammer, saw and level and kept on going. I'm not a trained carpenter. I'll get it right the next time."

Old Greenfield Village has a wonderful homemade feeling. There is nothing provisional or crude about the place. But in scale and materials this is a home handyman's job. The small grassy parking lot has room for about 20 cars, with a fine oak taking up one space. Waine can't bear to cut it down. He has neatly made signs, white with black raised letters: "Park Parallel Here," "No Smoking," and by the corner of the porch on his house: "Turn Back." The different exhibit buildings are numbered to go with his hand-sketched, one-page map of the village, but people still end up on his porch. In each exhibit he has set up a boom box with a tape recording, and left instructions for running the tape on a hand-lettered oak-tag poster. On a few posters he has written some background information, like a photo caption for the exhibit. Do-it-yourself history.

Coming down the walk, he greets me with a forced smile and asks if I want the tour. Yes, I say. He puts on a dirty Greenfield ballcap, and with it he wears a look of a man about to live a rerun. He seems burdened by my visit. We begin at Number 1, the wagon repair shop where his cat Mr. Rascal is lounging.

The map points the way to more than a dozen exhibits: the builder's and wagon repair shop, general store, print shop, 1894 fire company steam pumper, blacksmith and tinsmith shops, pharmacy, church, school, variety store with candy, toys, and a soda fountain, the offices of a dentist, doctor, and optometrist, barbershop, dry goods shop, patternmaker, wheelwright, butcher, steamfitter, plumber, and machinist.

He bought most of this in the 1960s and 1970s as it was passing from the world in Greenfield, Massachusetts and the Connecticut River valley. He and his wife went out every weekend looking for things. The old way of village life was passing with its local production—the blacksmith forging tools and hardware, the pharmacy mixing herbal remedies, the printer setting type, the patternmaker building the wooden forms to cast gears—all this handwork, an entire, faded local economy.

The collection overtook his house, so out in his backyard he built a general store. Two years later he decided to build a complete turn-of-the-century village.

Until he retired, he only had time to build on weekends and summer vacations. He bought his first piece—a coffee grinder—in 1962. He adds it up: "Thirty-five years since I started the collection. A hunk of my life is here."

He goes along opening the door locks and hanging padlocks. He never hunts for a key on his key ring. He shows me into each new place by gesturing for me to lead, as if we were paying a Sunday visit. Waine is thorough; our tour takes two and a half hours. It is mid May, an overcast day. The rooms are chilly, and the ones built into a basement of a building that backs into a hill are chilly and damp (much like the Scottish bed and breakfasts I've known).

His museum is right on the Mohawk Trail, Route 2. Just down the hill are the franchises, which are near a rotary feeding the interstate. As we go in and out of these rooms with their now stilled equipment, all I can hear is the traffic.

The shops he collected intact make the best exhibits. These rooms seem to live more than some of the exhibits for which he had to buy each item separately.

Three-quarters of Number 6 on the tour, the herbal pharmacy, came from a pharmacy that had opened before 1895 and still had cabinets of patent medicines, and original fixtures, including the air conditioning, Waine says, pointing at the twin ceiling fans. "This was truly a find."

The glass-fronted cabinets are stocked with patent medicines: goose oil, Dr. Naylor's Antiseptic Paste, Ox Gall Compound, Lithium Citrate Effervescing Grains, and a best seller of the day, Lydia E. Pinkham's Vegetable Compound. "World's best cure for all female complaints." Made the stern-looking lady on the label rich. Up over the back door are some of the small paper bundles of herbs the pharmacist used to mix his prescriptions.

We look at an object once so common it existed unseen, a phone booth made of oak. "Beautiful. Not a nail or a screw exposed. Looks like a piece of furniture." He regards it. "But. That was then."

He hasn't cleaned it up. The outside edge of the folding door is rimmed with the mark of thousands of hands. The rays of the oak glow in a warm finish, and as far as I can see, there was not an inked phone number, doodle, carving, or scrape anywhere on the phone booth in all those years.

He set up the pharmacy's Italian marble soda fountain in his variety store, which is a child's wonderland of the past: the unwrapped candy is lined up under the glass to have the allure of jewels. There are so many evocative toys: soulful stuffed dogs worn into life, wind-up clowns and singers poised to begin again, a tricycle built as a leaping horse, and some toys from his own childhood: a Shirley Temple blue glass bowl, and an Ovaltine Little Orphan Annie shaker, each in perfect condition. ("I fudged a little," he admits. His toys are not circa 1900, but to a kid, it's all a long time ago.)

Looking around at the shelves of toys, some very rare, he says that now "you can't find many things and if you do they're outrageously high. Wouldn't be any fun to start again," a sentiment he repeats during our tour. He doesn't go to auctions anymore. He gets too tense and everything is too expensive.

The print shop, Number 3 on the tour, was also purchased complete. Arthur Brocklesby was a printer in town who never threw anything out. He had all this stuff in the basement. "Arthur saved his old ink cans," says Waine who has them displayed in the shop. "They look pretty up there."

Brocklesby owned the shop from 1964 to 1992. He bought the printing shop from someone else and so on going back to 1886 when the Prouty press was built in Boston, says Waine.

This shop is like a chain letter that stopped here. All the old trades, once set aside in this museum village, are like a broken chain letter.

Waine has added a 1930s press from the Greenfield Junior High School. (They don't teach printing anymore.) He has hooked up the electrified press, but the motor keeps burning out. The kids "do like to see it open and close and go clank-clank—all the parts move."

Number 4, the blacksmith shop, may be his liveliest exhibit. He bought part of this shop from the last blacksmith in Greenfield. As a boy, Waine used to see him at work. The smithy is set up as diorama, a scene behind the glass. He has made a flat, cut-out figure of the smith at his anvil. Hanging on the visitor's side of the glass is a handle at the end of a string. He tells me to pull it: the flat smith raises his hammer and strikes the anvil. He set this up for the kids. "Chances are they've never hit one and they never will again." He tells me to pull the rope again, harder.

"*Nothing* sounds like an anvil," he says, and smiles for the first time.

The exhibit is not complete. The blacksmith "never swept the floor. I swept it up—two or three inches of beautiful dirt, old metal pieces, wood shavings, parings from a horse's hoof, cigar butts and milk bottle caps—all that he threw down for I don't know how many years. So someday it will go back down again. It was delightful dirt."

(Waine has a fine eye for history. In the 1970s, the Museum of the City of London was collecting street litter: 90 tons a day.)

On a chair in the blacksmith shop is a small jelly jar with a white lid. What's in the jar? I ask. "That bottle has some of his cigar butts." The blacksmith's hat and boots are also on the chair. "That's the end of the man right there—his boots and his butts," he says mischievously.

And sadly, that's what left of our days here on earth. Not the moist living breath, or the remembrance of the scent of apple blossoms on the breeze, but materially, the equivalent of a lost umbrella.

In the rooms, the workshops and stores: The motors, belts, bellows, compressors, taps and dies, sausage maker, soda fountain, cash registers, school bell, and church organ, all are silent. A mausoleum of tools resting in peace.

We fill these places with our story of the past. We line up the objects and say dance. We are the ear that hears the tree fall in the forest. But on this grey day, touring the museum village with Waine is like an episode from the Twilight Zone: You come to town and the blacksmith is gone, the wheelwright is gone, the dentist, the doctor, the patternmaker, butcher, dry goods clerk, pastor, and teacher.

And they've been gone a good long while—the blacksmith's fire is cold ashes, the cracker tins are empty and yellowing, the labels in the pharmacy are fading. Left behind in the exodus are oaktag posters with a few lines of explanation, some recorded tapes to be played, and a couple of manne-quins—the teacher in a black, mourning-like dress, and the hand-painted flat blacksmith. The work of their days abandoned, left for us to ponder. We are lonelier than Rip Van Winkle could have imagined.

In and out of the buildings we go, this ark of yesterday's work, the ma-terials and scale of work indicate that this may have been a stronger, taller race: hardware and tools at monster size—six-foot-long augers, hefty turn buckles and meaty hook-eyes, tackle and rope, wide boards, long runs of flapping, exposed belts, heavy cast iron machines to form other machines. Durable goods shipped in bulk. Thick crackers in barrels and crates. Everything is substantial—Italian marble soda fountain counters, oak tele-phone booths, display cases of graceful, curved glass, small grammar school desks anchored to the floor with cast iron legs, steam boilers, toys of steel. The substantial objects of a life that has evaporated.

If you were visiting a Hindu country, you might think that this was a shrine, an altar to make an offering to bring back the wheelwright deity, the printer deity, or just the past itself.

Waine Morse is thinking of adding one more exhibit. "I'd like to build a jail—that'd be the last thing if I ever do it." He has the parts under wraps in the corner of the parking lot, the old solitary confinement cells from the county jail. Time will have no escape.

Old Greenfield Village is a story of vanished commerce, an exchange of goods that arrived in barrels and boxes, or by the bolt; the making of tools and gears and screws to make other things.

Waine Morse saved many things that would have been scattered to the wind. Though retired, he still teaches, hosting as many as twenty field trips each spring. He has devised all sorts of activities to hold the attention of the third and fourth graders. But I would not be surprised if the children thought of their town of Greenfield in the 1890s as a whisper, a hushed or-derly place.

When Waine has them pull the rope to hit the anvil, or sets the press clanking, he is onto the music of the past, he touches the animating force of his village. *Nothing* sounds like an anvil. That's the sound of the tree falling in the forest, the old life passing.

Set it all running. Join machine to machine. Make one big kinetic sculpture: bellows huffing, anvil singing, dentist's foot-treadle drill boring into enamel and pulp, huge bandsaw cutting into oak, taps and dies spinning through metal blocks leaving curling metal shards, the fire company steam engine pumping water and the sausage maker extruding a long tail of meat.

Orchestrate it all, hand tool and power, and say this is the noise of 1896, this is the way work was done. This is the steam and fire, the strength and muscle of workers and beast applied to wood, steel, iron, tin, granite, bone, tooth, and flesh.

That's the museum I'd build. Go into a room and there's the sound of a big V-8 engine running or a Harley V Twin or a trolley car. There's the stink of the past, the sweat and toil. Unite the Driscolls' field of antique engines with Waine Morse's museum village and we are on the path to a truer restoration of American places.

IV.

American places are machine made and unmade. To the rhythm of the engine, Greenfield had been destroyed and rebuilt, as if the entire town were "belted up" to the engines and had spun faster and faster until it blurred into something new. With each turn of the flywheel, each controlled explosion, Greenfield had been remade. All the workers in their trades were engaged in making carriage wheels or sausages, and did not see that they were each day making another product, a Greenfield they would not recognize. The place moved at a new velocity and left them behind.

American places are fugitive. Even as we are trying to define them, they slip away, they change. The village grows into a suburb, and we are still trying to understand how the village came to be.

Back before we became more sensible about handling chemicals, there was a school laboratory experiment in which students would roll a piece of silvery mercury around on a table. That's our settlement history. The centers of trade and activity slipping all over.

We want our towns to be static. We speak of old towns as being a scene right out of some nostalgic print. We speak of "stepping back into the past." (But if we did we would lose our footing.)

We are like ancient astronomers looking at the sky: From the unspinning earth we look up to where the sun and a few planets orbit us, one sphere nesting in the next. We are Main Street centered, and use nostalgia as our map. Change, flux, uncertainty, are what we exclude from our picture: We don't render those shades. Our past was never as settled as we like to think. The settlers were, in Wendell Berry's phrase, unsettlers.

The historic postcard of Main Street, the stereopticon view of the village common is a record of migration and movement. We would be more accurate if we regarded our historic buildings as if they were parked—our ancestors did, dragging them with oxen all over the place, rebuilding them for new uses. This is the tradition we hide from ourselves.

Many of the New England villages we praise for their serenity have been on the move most of their lives. Some were settled first on a hill, then moved down by the water to run mills. When the railroad came they followed the rails, and when the automobile came to rule, they slopped across the landscape in malls, condos, and food joints.

Some towns were a small Pleiades, a cluster, of a half-dozen little villages, soon eclipsed by a growing central village, which itself burned brightly until the auto age.

Other villages are the story of the rise and fall of one commodity: clothespins, shoes, rocking chairs, buggy whips. American places are often but a rumor of community wrapped around the commerce of the moment.

Point to almost any spot in New England, and you can read some part of this history: New Ipswich, New Hampshire, "settled" 1762. Within its boundaries, it has moved many times. New Ipswich comprised three villages: Smith, Bank, and Center Village. When the Third New Hampshire Turnpike came through, around 1802, the deck was reshuffled. "New roads and streets in the Central Village were cut through, for everyone, it seemed, wanted to reach the turnpike," wrote local historian John Preston. The entire Center Village moved to a new Main Street. Shops, houses, and inns were built close to the turnpike. The "Old Center," as it was now called, was left behind. New Ipswich's other villages were knit together, and within fifty years there were seven villages. "Old wandering roads, which ran parallel to the turnpike were abandoned," wrote Preston, and roads were built for more direct access to the turnpike.

In the booming 1980s one of the town's developers built a shopping center in a sheep pasture, a mile up hill from Main Street, along the route of the old turnpike. The center of economic activity shifted again. Office condos were built along the route. For years Town Meeting has been held in the high school, which also was on the old turnpike.

The American place is always on the road, moving to the machines, the rise and fall of the motive power of the moment. The pace of our lives is governed by the r.p.m. of the engine, by the transport of the reigning fuel: wood, coal, oil, and whatever comes next. Even our villages are "lighting out for the territory," lured by "all that road going."

America is a process, one generation of historians told us: It's a dream, a journey, it's the American inventions of chewing gum and rocking chairs, porch gliders. It's people and places that won't sit still. "We're a town busy being born," reports *Common Threads,* the newsletter of Harrisville, New Hampshire. The way is still clear for invention in the arrangements of daily life. We tend toward the sketch, not the finished work. A sketch leaves free spaces for us to live our private lives, for us to keep a few folded boxes in the closet should we decide to move: cash in, check out, trade up—reinvent ourselves.

We want contradictory things: the peaceful village and the broad road out of town. We crowd into cities and become wedded to the transitory: the sounds of the railroad and trolley, the lunch at a 5 & 10 counter. We are excited by the flow of commerce.

If we feel unsettled today, this is partly the reason. We have yet to settle this country. If we lament the world we are building, and feel restless, then it is false to turn to the past for escape. Strip malls are a continuation of the original surveying of the towns and drawing of the boundaries—the land grants and swaps and deals and clearing of the Indians and trees.

Sprawl is part of our heritage. American places are about access and absence. Getting in and getting out. Flow.

Many of our cities and towns look like the backsides of appliances, all wiring and bolts and warning labels. They are machines for chewing up the earth for the consumer. The earth is sucked dry of its oils, cleared of its trees and sand—the earth is shaped and extruded for you—one more mouth in a vast crawling organism of 6 billion mouths. Landscape as MRE, in military lingo, Meal Ready to Eat. Land of Many Uses, as the signs in the national forests say.

The ideal American place may be a road that is home. A few utopian dreamers have proposed such places: Roadtown, Motopia. Their plans have a child-like rudeness, an overeagerness to speak too directly. Edgar Chambless dreamed up Roadtown in 1910, and campaigned for his patented invention through the early 1930s. Seeking a solution for the congested cities, he had a vision: Take one of those new skyscrapers and lay it on the side: You'd have a linear city, with country and gardens on each side, subways in the basement, roads and a promenade on the roof, and apartments in between. "I had found a workable way of coupling housing and transportation in one mechanism," wrote Chambless.

When the architect Kevin Roche designed Union Carbide's Danbury, Connecticut, headquarters in 1976, he took his cue from the roadtown utopias. The building is a sandwich, with the parking garages at center, and the offices at each side looking out to the woods. Two roads run straight through the building and hook up with ten roads coming from the north and ten from the south. The workers can park within one hundred feet of their office and walk right in. "The American office worker would like very much to be able to drive into his or her office and operate from the automobile," Roche said.

Union Carbide's headquarters would seem to be far from the dignity of the eighteenth-century town street, but each lives for the turnpike road. This modern office building is traditional. It is a fitting building to mark the nation's bicentennial, a try at housing some of our contradictory impulses in one mechanism. A building pierced by a road is a monument to our long tradition of moving towns and buildings.

We look on meetinghouses as symbols of repose and continuity. Great white ships of faith: clapboarded billboards that say New England. Buildings of simple materials and classical proportions, the central house of a strong civic life standing above the tumult of commerce. From just one meetinghouse on a hill in Blandford, Massachusetts, in the early 1800s, a dozen other meetinghouses were visible.

Order. Clarity. Faith. A nice picture. The meetinghouse is that for us. But the picture conceals a story of bitter sectarian rivalry, neglect, and turmoil. Once again the restless American epic of unsettlement, of use and abandonment (and occasionally renewal).

In the seventeenth century, two hundred meetinghouses were built in New England. Only one survives. As more towns were established in the eighteenth century, two thousand meetinghouses were built. About ninety, or only 4 percent, remain. Pretty rough treatment for an icon. The least likely structure to be standing after fifty years was the meetinghouse, says historian Peter Benes, who provides the count. They were burned and discarded; they were converted to ugly churches or useful barns. (The Third Meetinghouse of Hatfield, Massachusetts, served as a tobacco barn until it collapsed in a failed restoration move.) Sometimes they were pulled apart (literally) by feuding parties.

Altered, remodeled, modernized, moved, decayed, destroyed, restored, moved again—these words reoccur in most meetinghouse histories. In the upheaval after the revolution, meetinghouses were almost abandoned, says historian Edmund W. Sinnott.

Wooden buildings are malleable, a fitting material for an evolving republic. The Puritans started with simple requirements: a room, a pulpit, and a table. Meetinghouses were plain, large houses. They were antichurches: no spire, tower, bell, clock, stained glass, statues, frescoes. The main entrance to a church was usually at the narrow, gable end; eighteenth-century meetinghouse entrances were on the long side. Fashions in faith brought changes: Towers and spires were added, buildings were rotated to a more churchly position, entrances and pulpits were moved, pews and furnishings grew ornate.

The great Shinto shrine at Ise shows the ordering of a central authority directing trained craftsmen. Ise is a sacred form: a ritual carried forth precisely. The New England meetinghouse shows us the restless American spirit, an improvisational theatre for the Puritans, the Great Awakening, town meeting, town offices, schools, day care, the secular and the sacred. Paid for by the public to house church and state, it was seldom a comfortable fit. The staid meetinghouse on the common, with all its changes, has moved to a kind of jive and jump.

As Peter Benes tells the meetinghouse story, it is like hearing about the unruly youth of a venerated town elder. The youthful meetinghouse is ungainly, ruled by spite, fashion, and a fierce practicality. Most weren't painted white: They were also yellow, gray, sky blue, red, bright orange, and pea green. (Ashburnham, Massachuseetts, voted for pea green, demonstrating once again that good taste is not a virtue of a democracy.) They were "named like dogs or outhouses," says Benes: Old Yellow, Old Tin, Old Tunnel, Old Brick, and The Ohio (which was in New Hampshire, but was at such a far remove it might as well have been in Ohio). One unpainted house, having weathered darkly, was called "The Coffin," not an inviting place for six hours of Sunday prayer and sermon.

They were a lightning rod for various disputes. "The meetinghouse devil" was said to be at work. (In Ipswich, Massachusetts, the devil left behind his footprints in two stones.) "The spirit of compromise and willingness to consider the general welfare seemed strangely absent in most discussions," says Sinnott. The county court or legislature was often called in to settle disputes. The governor of Massachusetts had to decide the location of Old Ship in Hingham, the only surviving seventeenth-century meetinghouse. (At least once Hingham has voted to tear it down.)

Siting the meetinghouse caused more schisms and break-away congregations than theological arguments, says Sinnott. Attendance was obligatory and roads were crude. The young towns had to find a fair center in a rough territory. Concord was so rare that when Stonington, Connecticut, "amicably" located its meetinghouse, the site was called "Agreement Hill."

The minority would sometimes obstruct the majority. In Mendon, Massachusetts, a group attempted to pull down the frame of a new meetinghouse. In Lebanon, Connecticut, a small group prevented the demolition of the old meetinghouse, just one part of that town's 109-year-long meetinghouse war.

In Richmond, Vermont, sixteen years of indecision led to the building of a unique sixteen-sided meetinghouse, The Old Round Church. (With no corner for the devil to hide in, it was said.) The charter instructed the five denominations to "peaceably enjoy their share." Within eighty years they had all abandoned the sanctuary. Home to town meetings, the building declined, and in the 1970s was condemned. Local citizens rallied to rescue it.

Once the meetinghouse was erected, the matter wasn't settled. Some meetinghouses should have had travel stickers like those used on old steamer trunks.

Lempster, New Hampshire: built in 1794, taken down in 1822 and moved one mile up the road to be near the intersection of two important turnpikes. Old North Vestry, Nantucket: built circa 1711, moved a mile east in 1765. Spire and bell added in 1795, and later removed. West Barnstable, Massachusetts: Congregational church built 1717, sawn in half and pulled apart for a new eighteen-foot section and steeple in 1723. The main entrance moved to the tower in 1834. By 1852 it was run down and demolition was considered. It was saved and remodeled as a typical mid-nineteenth-century church. In 1955 it was restored to its 1723 state. Families in town had saved bits of the original paneling, windows, and pews, and these served as a guide for the restored interior.

Litchfield, Connecticut: built 1829, moved in the 1870s to make way for a Victorian Gothic church. Shorn of its steeple, the meetinghouse survived as the "Colonial Hall" movie house. In 1929 the Victorian was torn down, the meetinghouse rescued, moved back, and restored.

Westmoreland, New Hampshire: Built 1767; twelve years later it was moved several miles, coming to rest part of the way up Park Hill due to a tavern-keeper's bribe (a barrel of rum for the moving crew, says local tradition). Park Hill has been completely remodeled; only the frame is original. "Built in discord, dragged ignominiously over the hills, and deposited upon its present foundation by craft and greed, this church became at last one of the loveliest in New England," says Sinnott.

A few meetinghouses were fortunate in their history. The Jaffrey, New Hampshire, meetinghouse is one of the lucky few, the 4 percent of eighteenth-century meetinghouses that survived.

The day the frame was raised in 1775 they could hear the British ships firing on Bunker Hill near Boston, 40 miles away. The town itself was less than a year old and the only roads were cart paths and marked trails. That's the poetic part, the story you mention to visitors so they go away thinking that this proud white house has stood watch over the rise of the republic. Not close, says Theodore P. Greene, Emeritus Professor of American History, Amherst College, and a direct descendant of Jaffrey's first minister, Reverend Laban Ainsworth, who served for seventy-six years.

Seventeen years after it was built, the Jaffrey meetinghouse was a mess. The roof leaked, the windows had broken glass, it sat on temporary sills awaiting a permanent foundation, and it had never once been painted. The contractors were still owed money. And what's worse: It was in the way of commerce. In 1794 the town gave a Benjamin Cutter permission to move the meetinghouse to expand his tavern. Taverns, or necessaries, were the

center of village life, site of public meetings, lectures, concerts, and weddings. He never did get around to moving it.

The town finally voted to paint the meetinghouse in 1798. The town
doctor mixed the paint. Three years later, as the nineteenth century began,
twenty-six years after it was built, the meetinghouse had its first coat of
paint. The addition of a bell tower in 1822 completed an idyllic picture: the
large white house with a tower at one side, and beyond, Mt. Monadnock.

The surviving photos imply solidity. The photos are few and we are
tricked into seeing them as a deep view. But it is only in our time that
meetinghouses have settled into respectability. For now these great arks
have come to rest. They have become venerated objects, some living as assembly halls, town offices, churches, and others, like the Hancock and
Rindge, New Hampshire, meetinghouses, still a hybrid of church and
state. We are no longer willing to move these arks around the landscape,
chop them up, discard them. A preservation ethic has spread. We express
restlessness elsewhere. This is good for our civic well-being. But what does
it say about our willingness to innovate?

There is something hopeful and American about never finishing your
house, like Jefferson at Monticello. There was an optimism, a buoyancy, in
all the fashionable remodeling and destruction. There was a belief in new
beginnings.

V.

In 2000 B.C. the Minyans arrived in the land that would become Greece.
The scholar Anne G. Ward, writing of Bronze Age Greece, says something
familiar:

"It took the Minyans more than 200 years to feel fully established in their
new country, and in the intervening time they were content with a somewhat temporary way of life, with very little advance. Their towns show no
organization or planning, and their houses were undistinguished."

We are all camping out here, in houses of wood and brick, in office buildings of cement and steel. Tents in the wilderness. It is all temporary. If
we clear a field, the woods will have it back soon enough. If we dam a
river, it bides time and will resume its true course. The land forgets us
even as we are here. We light our fires, brighten our homes and delight in
our conquest. But we are not even a thought in the mind of New England.

The land dreams granite and maple and pine, deer and wolf and beaver. We white settlers are but a momentary incursion. And all our lives are like water over granite.

We take care to say: I've lived here five years, fifteen years, my whole life. In small towns, tenure is conferred at the village store, the dump, the fire station, the church. We take measure against a history that exaggerates continuity.

Local histories are the winners' books. They are the tale of how the first families won the territory, cleared the woods, built the sawmill and meetinghouse. They tell us the story of old, older, and oldest. The winner names the age, the historians say. In local history, the winner names the land: the roads and farms and ponds and houses.

We ignore the cellar holes along the back roads, and off in the woods. They are the equivalent of an adage from before the world wars: "American mechanical progress could be measured by the size of its scrap-heaps." Cellar holes are a scrap heap of lives.

In *The History of Westminister, Mass., 1728–1893*, there is a listing of one hundred "abandoned homesteads."

"A striking feature of the territory of the town at the present day . . . is the appearance, here and there in all directions, of old cellars, wells, orchards, or other tokens of dwellings once existing, but now gone forever."

Westminister had seen much migration within its borders. The first landholders were dispersed throughout the town; "nearly every one of the sixty-acre tracts laid out in the first division of land had a resident owner upon it."

When the Revolutionary War ended, "a spirit of enterprise and of improvement sprang up in all directions," says the town history. "The work of centralization began." Small manufacturers were established, running off newly harnessed water power; roads were built, including the important Fifth Massachusetts Turnpike, which brought travelers and trade, a need for a hotel, and several new stores along a "Main street." Westminister came to have a thriving center.

In the "outlying districts . . . many once well-tilled fields and farms" were abandoned, as the farmers moved closer to the center, or took that turnpike out of town to the promises of the West.

"So great have been the changes thus indicated many names once familiar here and representing large families, such as Brooks, Graves, Heywood, Hoar, Taylor, are no longer to be found." At most, perhaps fifteen families still lived on land an ancestor had settled.

In the small agate type we reserve for stock market reports or baseball box scores, there follows a detailed accounting of one hundred "abandoned homesteads." Such as:

No. 19 . . . On the cross road to Ashburnham Center there was a dwelling a hundred years ago, supposed to have been erected by Oliver Whitcomb, a resident in town before 1780. It was owned or occupied successively by him, Caleb Wilder, Thomas Keyes, and perhaps others, before being left to final decay. Tokens of its exact site have been sought but not found.

No. 63. At the same date [1748] upon which Paul Gibbs sold the N.E. corner of lot No. 20 to Mr. Brown, he conveyed the corresponding N.W. corner to Jeremiah Gager, who built a house, etc., thereon, and no doubt resided there for a few years. Subsequent owners, in their order, were Elias Farnsworth, John Rand, Dr. Israel Green, Edmund Bemis, and Michael Gill. In 1796 the latter sold to the town for the purpose of enlarging the "burying ground." The house and barn were then standing, but were at once sold and taken down.

Lot by lot, the listing piles up the language we seldom acknowledge in our portrait of the New England landscape: ". . . about 1848, the family moved away. . . . Only transients lived there afterwards and the buildings gradually went to decay. . . . No corresponding cellar-hole or other token of a habitation has been found. But there exist certain indefinite remembrances of such. . . .The house was burned more than 50 years ago, and the barn, in 1876. . . . Remnants of an old orchard, seen soon after beginning to ascend the hill, mark the general location of the buildings. . . . The original house was probably of cheap construction, and so abandoned at an early day for a better one near the opposite end of the lot. . . . After the death of Mrs. Walker, in 1826, the buildings were removed and all signs of their existence were obliterated. . . . If he had any successors, they were but temporary ones. . . . Nothing further known."

"No one living knows anything about it."

"Overturn, Overturn, Overturn! is the maxim of New York," wrote former mayor Philip Hone in 1845. "The very bones of our ancestors are not permitted to lie quiet a quarter of a century, and one generation of men seem studious to remove all the relics of those who precede them."

Hone was not only speaking metaphorically. The young Walt Whitman wrote indignantly about a woman forced to defend the graves of her husband and family. Workmen had arrived to dig up the burial ground. She held them off with a pistol. A mob joined her and rioted.

But the land speculators, the Hudson Fire Insurance Company, won. They "actually set people to work with spades and pick axes to dig down and pitch out the decayed relics of bodies buried there . . . as loafers pitch pennies upon the dock," Whitman wrote in 1842. Houses were built, houses themselves long since overturned and removed.

Overturn! Overturn! This is our anthem, this is what we should rise and sing before ballgames.

"The lesson is this: when migration turns to a new region, do not clutch the dying past. Let go and move on," advises real estate investor Jack Lessinger.

"Steadfast in its consensus, the economy becomes a veritable bulldozer programmed to scrape out, heap up and reshape the world to its own special images," says Lessinger. You can either feed the scrapheap or be on it.

I went for a walking tour on a December Sunday when the sky was low and roiled overhead and frozen rain fell. I would have rather found a fireside, a room suffused with the yellow light of domesticity, and piled with familiar objects. Instead a dozen of us stood on a former railroad yard, now a big lot in the center of Keene, New Hampshire. We looked at a historic photo of the trains and factories, and then at the weedy lot, the few remaining factories, the graffiti on the back of one building. The small photo was crowded with activity, the tracks laid out like harp strings. The lot we stood in seemed much smaller than the photograph in our hands. We heard of a half-dozen conflicting plans for the site. And we listened to a historian talk and talk of the romance of steam engines—how, as a boy, he thrilled to the sound of the steam whistle, and the smoke far off; and where all the trains came from and went to, the labor to lay the track and build bridges, the passengers and the freight. Keene was once the "rocking chair city." Millions of chairs were once made and shipped out, set in motion. The frozen rain made a tinkling sound. Our small circle began to shift from foot to foot. The damp cold seeped up into our boots. We were looking for old commerce, old flow, long gone.

American places are about the exchange of goods. They're about everyone thinking they're going to own the joint. Eye on the main chance.

Flow—that's our creed. More and more. A messy vitality. Broadway boogie-woogie. That's what people talk about vanishing—all the people, trains, trolleys, canals. Flow. To give a true picture of our civilization, how do we preserve that?

Industrial sites—furnaces, railyards, smelters—settle toward a deceiving repose. The sky is blue, birds nest on silent smokestacks, and can be heard singing. Grass grows up on the railroad siding. Trees wedge apart concrete.

The railroad had a long run in Keene, one hundred years of passenger service, 1848 to 1958. The last freight limped out in 1982. The trains crossed Main Street on grade, and, for a time, ran right through the station.

When the railroad was abandoned, and the station closed, they shoveled all the railroad records out of the windows and into wagons and took them right to the dump. Commerce was ended; the real life was over.

The tock-tock beat that had built the country was silenced.

In another small city I once spent time gathering stories of the vanished life. And again it was like standing in a weedy lot and talking of what used to be. This city once made things—cars, typewriters, furniture—useful and beautiful things, some of which are now avidly collected. Today, the downtown is cut up by interstate highways and ringed by shopping malls. But hold up the old photo, look at the empty lots and listen to the city in the memory of the speaker:

"Downtown was the most exciting place, but remember I'm a little kid. It was the most exciting place in the world. Downtown was bustling with people, and you know in those days there were stores that don't exist now. And the thing that I remember the most was that you had the streetcar. And of course trolleys always *bang-bang*, but to me it was a kind of music. The newspaper boys at least one on every corner were yelling at the top of their lungs: read about the latest murder or whatever. When something really happened they put out extras. The presses seemed to be running all the time in those days. All you had to do was yell about something exciting and a guy could sell his papers in nothing flat. And the streets at that time, even at night, were usually crowded with people. There was a lot of theaters and they were in full swing: the Keiths, Loews, the Strand, the Empire, the Paramount and the Eckel. I loved vaudeville; my father loved it. Soft shoe, tap dance, comedy acts, the usual run of dog acts, acrobats and so forth.

"The newspapers, like in the World Series they would put this huge scoreboard up in the street. And they would get the score by tickertape. And it wasn't unusual to see this mob of people out there and this guy walking along the platform. The Yankees made four runs in the second, so he'd put a big 4 there. A big crowd—they'd stay right there till the series was over.

"I was train crazy. The trains ran through on the street. They had to hold up traffic and street cars and everything at all the street crossings. Of course when I was a kid I was thrilled by those giants moving down the street. They moved very slow. They kept the smoke down. But I remember all those buildings were pretty smoke stained.

"And I'll tell you a story that's a little off color but my father-in-law was telling me. He was an engineer. Those locomotives were quite high and a lot of the houses on Railroad Street were houses of prostitution. And he said that it was not unusual for him that he could in many instances, riding high enough, look into second story windows, and in these you saw a lot of action there.

"Then at the arena, which the building is still there, they held prize fights. I have a brother who's 15 years older and he was a prize fighter. He fought at the arena. He was just a fair to middlin' fighter. He would fight on the undercard, in the prelims. And I can remember they paid him off in silver dollars. He'd bring home a cigar box of silver dollars. The sporting figures hung out—it's gone now, the building's gone—it was the Kunch & Cross Pool Room. That was a high class place. Some of the great billiard and pool players of the world played there. And that was next to the hotel——that's gone now, that's torn down. They had a tremendously long bar in there. They used to say it was the longest bar in the country. That was a great gathering place for the politicians. But the war changed a lot of things.

"My wife and I were eating at a diner—it's gone now—and we had just gotten into our meal when the guy that owned the diner came over and he said, 'Look it just came over the radio: the war is over.' He said, 'You people take your time, eat your dinner, but I'm going to close the diner.'

"Everybody poured downtown. They danced all night in the street. They lifted trolley cars off the track. I went down and came back. I had a profound sense of sadness that night, because I mean I was glad the war was over, and elated like everybody else, but I'd lost several very close friends, and I simply couldn't get this out of mind. The war's over. Great. But these guys are not coming back.

"I can't pinpoint when downtown changed. First vaudeville was gone, the streetcars were gone, the newsboys were gone. Now of course you huddle around the television set. And it's more convenient, but the color isn't there. The liveliness, the excitement is gone.

"All in all it was paradise valley to me. It did have life day and night at that time. You can go downtown now and you can pick your night. Shoot a cannon down the street; you couldn't hit anybody."

VI.

The Nevada Test Site is the country of the atomic bomb. The site is 1,350 square miles, larger than Luxembourg, and "one of the largest secured areas in the United States." The test site is 65 miles northwest of Las Vegas. The mushroom clouds of some atomic bombs could be seen from the Strip. This land was once sacred to the Shoshone. By freshwater springs, archeologists have saved a few sites. The springs were also a relay post in the 1850s for the Salt Lake City to Los Angeles mail route. No one lives here now, but there are hundreds miles of roads, two airports, ten heliports, and 1,100 buildings.

For forty years in the desert, 925 atomic bombs were exploded. The land is marked with so many craters that the Apollo astronauts trained for the moon here. Like the moon, some of the craters have names. Sedan is the largest, a quarter of a mile across. Twelve million tons of earth were blasted away by a 104-kiloton bomb in 1962. Radiation at the crater's edge is now approaching background levels.

One hundred and twenty-six bombs were exploded in the atmosphere before the above-ground test-ban treaty. Five metric tons of plutonium were thrown into the atmosphere. Communities downwind in Nevada and Utah were exposed to 12 billion curies of radiation, or 148 times the radiation released from the meltdown at Chernobyl in 1986. Like the little hit-or-miss gas engines in Doug Driscoll's pasture, the bombs had names: Priscilla, Smoky, Diablo, Gnome. . . . Officially they were all "tests," not bombs. The engineers called them anything but bombs: devices, gadgets, shots, ploot, shakes, jerks, kilo and mega jerks, barn wall. Infernal machines are what concealed or disguised bombs were called in the nineteenth century.

Atomic explosions became commonplace for the "downwinders." The government encouraged people to come out and watch the bombs. Darlene Phillips saw the blasts when she was a teenager. "You would see the whole sky light up as if the sun were coming up backwards, and even the shadows of the trees would be wrong, casting their shadow in the other direction. And I should have known then that the world was upside down, that it was wrong, but I didn't," Phillips told Carole Gallagher, author of *American Ground Zero, The Secret Nuclear War.*

Diane Nielson was a child. "After the bomb, there it would be, the fallout. We would play like that was our snow. It would be thick enough you could write your name in it. It would burn your fingers and you would have to wash your hands." After another explosion, pink hail rained down so pretty some children ate it.

Russell Jack Dann was a soldier 3.8 miles from Smoky, a 44-kiloton explosion. "Nobody knew how big the bomb was. We wore no protective clothing or anything, no gloves, no gas masks. We were in completely open space, right on top of the hill. . . . When the bomb went off the light was like a thousand suns and the sound was like a million cannons. Then we saw this tidal wave of dirt and dust and sagebrush and rattlesnakes and wires coming after us, it could have been any damn thing out there, but it was coming and [the sergeant] hollered, 'Hit it!' We went down like damn bowling pins. First of all, you could see right through your arm as if it was an X-ray, the sound was just earth shattering and deafening and a tremendous roar. The wind was blowing 150 miles an hour, peppered the hell out of us and everything went flying, everything you could hold on to. There was nothing to hold on to."

Twisted bridge girders, smashed cement bunkers, crushed aluminum, shards of glass blinking in the desert sun mark the Nevada Test Site. At Frenchman Flat, twenty-seven nuclear explosions fused the sand into a bubbly glass. The top six to eight inches of the desert soil in an area as big as thirty square miles was scrapped off by road graders and buried in some of the "subsidence craters." Signs fade in the desert sun, warning: "Radiation Hazard. Touching or removing scrap objects is prohibited. . . ." "Caution: Contaminated area." Sage and mesquite grow in old blast zones. Birds nest amid the curly, melted metal of a railroad trestle.

They blew up airplanes, locomotives, cars, army tanks. They built a traditional Japanese town, houses of paper. They set out live animals in cruel experiments, and in Priscilla, soldiers only 2,500 yards from the blast. Soldiers returned to camp bleeding from their eyes, ears, and nose.

For the Apple II bomb, May 5, 1955, the Federal Civil Defense Administration built a "typical American community": Survival City. An oxymoron; it was built to be destroyed. Some of the houses sat on Doomsday Drive. A true boom town, hometown for the infernal machine. The explosion was nationally televised. ("7–8:55. Morning Show—Today: Atomic test at 8:15 [if held] . . . 8–8:30—Groucho Marx; *You Bet Your Life.*")

Survival City had houses of brick and wood, trailer homes, fallout shelters, a radio tower, power systems. Mannequins from the Darling Company were set up in the houses. Fresh food was placed in the kitchens and dining rooms. One hundred and fifty businesses and trade associations had donated their products "for guidance in styling . . . in the era of threatened atomic warfare." When the bomb hit, some of the mannequins, called the "Darling family," were dressed as if for Sunday dinner, posed in conversation around the dining room table.

The explosion swelled from a pinpoint of light into a "rolling, orange-red fireball of dazzling brilliance more than 1000 feet in diameter. It continued to churn viciously for 20 seconds" as it was "enveloped in an iridescent gaseous purple sheath," reported *The New York Times.* White fire shot up from the sands. The houses caught fire, swayed in the blast like palm trees in a hurricane gale, and were blown away. "A vast cloud of dust welled up from the desert floor, covering the test town like a brown shroud," reported the Associated Press. Civil defense workers moved through the rubble looking for mannequin-survivors. There were none. Doomsday Drive was destroyed. The glass in a house more than mile from the blast was smashed into pebble-sized bits.

Gilbert Fraga, a radiation monitor for the Atomic Energy Commission, toured Survival City a week after the blast. "The mannequins were just cut to shreds by the glass from the windows blowing in. Shards of glass were stuck along the opposite end of the dining room." Apple II was a small bomb for its day ("a firecracker" said the *Times*), 29,000 tons of TNT, only a third larger than the Hiroshima bomb.

Close to the blast, two houses survived, one of brick and one of wood. The wooden house was about a mile from ground zero. It still stands with the paint scorched off, windows blown in, and a twisted brick chimney. Ground zero is still highly radioactive.

The scientists performed nearly one thousand "tests" to answer the most basic question: Would the bomb work; were the calculations true. The Nevada Test Site was a vast machine, and each controlled explosion unsettled the world. "We used to say Nevada equals truth," said Mike Sohn, a computer expert.

If American places are about flow, movement, exchange and reaction, then this is the most American place. It was all over in an instant here, just like so many downtowns, main streets, closed woolen mills and cold-as-bones steel mills.

American places are but a moment's bright flash, followed by long, confused memories.

Old Home Day, Every Day

~❦~

Each August in my town we celebrate Old Home Day. Main Street is thick with visitors. We set out every event that a small town of 1,500 can muster. We start with an ice cream social on Friday evening and on Saturday morning let those who wish run off that ice cream in a five-kilometer road race. This is quickly followed by a parade with a marching band, fire engines, and floats. The minister steps up to the bandstand on the common to deliver a brief invocation. Around the common, and in the horse sheds behind the Meetinghouse, are booths selling food, plants, crafts and art. The historical society and the old train depot have open house. There are shows of children's coloring and adults' photos, hayrides, a clown, field games (greased pole, pie eating, egg toss), a hot-air balloon ascension, and so forth. The volunteer fire department barbecues enough chicken for dinner to put a blueish haze over the town.

The parade in recent years has had a theme, usually something about finding our way home again. A few families and town businesses assemble floats.

One float, about coming home, showed a Christmas tableau in the pickup truck bed with a decorated tree, gifts underneath, and stockings hung on the mantel. Limping behind the Christmas truck, on one crutch, was a returning, wounded veteran, followed by a bride, then a prisoner wearing state pen stripes and a yellow ribbon. Someplace along the way was a little girl dressed in red, white, and blue.

This was a pop cultural meltdown: Frank Capra's movies, Norman Rockwell's illustrations, and a 1970s pop music hit. And it is right in the tradition of Old Home Day, which began not as a time to celebrate the joys of being home, but as a call to return home. The first Old Home Days worried over the impossibility of return, and the fading of the home and the village.

Even if people had never left their village and still lived in the house in

which they were born, they were longing for home. They were like that
veteran in the parade limping toward the Christmas welcome just steps in
front of him, but always out of reach. Home was leaving them.

Those first Old Home celebrations at the end of the nineteenth century
were a kind of courtship. The orators, poets, singers, musicians, and amateur actors were all wooing the idea of homecoming. They lighted bonfires, prayed, sang, paraded, reminisced, and told jokes. They implored and
proposed; they were evocative and prescriptive.

They were Victorians. We should be distanced by the great bulk of their
words, by their ornate sentiment. But each year, it seems to me, brings us
closer to the first Old Home Day. Our parades travel further than the
length of Main Street; they bring us full circle. Old Home Day is a modern holiday.

I. "The Hospitality of Sincere Hearts"

"I wish that in the ear of every son and daughter of New Hampshire, in
the summer days, might be heard whispered the persuasive words: Come
back, come back!" Frank Rollins wrote in 1897. "Do you not hear the call?
What has become of the old home where you were born? . . . Do you not
remember it—the old farm back among the hills, with its rambling buildings, its well-sweep casting its long shadows, the row of stiff poplar trees,
the lilacs and the willows?"

Frank Rollins invented Old Home Day. He rallied others to his idea,
founded an Old Home Week Association, and as governor of New Hampshire presided over the state's first homecoming. Towns had held annual
picnics and "Old People's Gatherings" before, but this was new. The state
issued its invitation across the nation to its sons and daughters toiling in
the cities, in the fields of the Midwest and the mining camps of Montana.

"All claiming descent from her loins are heartily and cordially invited to
return and spend at least one day in the place made hallowed by associations of birth or ancestry," Rollins wrote in his invitation for the fourth
Old Home Day in 1902. "Hospitality will abound, good fellowship will
predominate, old friends will extend greetings, old hopes and ideals will
come back, the weariness and cares of age will fall away as a garment, and
all taste again the sweets of youth's glad springtime. Is it not worth the
time and trouble?"

He held out the sweetest reunion in the language of an embrace—"*the
weariness and cares of age will fall away as a garment. . . .*" If they returned,
he promised that they would find communion with their younger selves.
"When you think of the old home, you bring back the tenderest memories

possessed by man; true love, perfect faith, holy reverence, high ambitions," he said in 1899.

"These Granite Hills remain unchanged / Like words of Gospel Truth," said a 1908 Old Home Day song set to the music of *Auld Lang Syne*.

Each New Hampshire village issued invitations. "To former residents of Deerfield," read an invitation from August 1, 1902, "We offer no special attractions, but what is better the hospitality of sincere hearts."

The first Old Home Days were haunted. They were haunted by all those who had left New Hampshire, by a feeling that the old home was running down like an unwound watch. All the more reason to sing of the unchanging granite hills. Rural New Hampshire was fading away, shrinking. There were abandoned farms, homesteads that had caved into cellar holes, and towns that were but a shadow of their former selves. (*The Vanished Form* is the title of a 1902 Old Home Day poem.) By century's end, America was traveling at a new velocity, an emerging imperial power having just defeated Spain the year before. New England was left behind.

"There is no experience in life that is worth more than the greeting that we receive as we return to the old home," said Professor Franklin W. Hooper at Walpole's first Old Home Day in 1899. "And when we reflect concerning those who have gone, I do not wonder that there have been great civilizations in the past who have come to believe in ancestral worship.

"Returning to the old home shortly after some loved one has passed away, the place seems filled with a beautiful presence. The familiar rooms, the ticking of the old clock, the flowers in the yard, the clover blossoms, the singing of the birds, the play of the sunshine and the shadows on the hills, the fleecy clouds, the stars by night, all speak of the one who is gone, whose life was indissolubly connected with these things, and with yourself. So when we return to the old home we come truly into the presence of those who have gone before, and as truly as God did appear unto Abraham, Isaac, and Jacob, so truly do those we have loved return to us in our beloved homes."

This is a festival of homesickness. There are great rolling orations, long poems, songs, pageants, tableaux vivants, parades, all about home: *The Hills Are Home, Home Dearest Home, This Dear Spot, The Old Farmstead, The Old Oaken Bucket.* These titles and many more were sung and recited at picnics in groves by lakes, and under the hot August sun on the common by people bolted into their Sunday best ready to listen to two hours of speeches. Some had returned a long way to be home, but many had traveled little in their entire life. They were homesick at home.

"No local industry has flourished in the same degree as the manufacturing of Old Home Week verse," said one observer in 1906. "In every New England town observing the festival the local poet has been burning the midnight oil so assiduously that it is no wonder the price of kerosene has been advanced a cent or so a gallon."

The celebration had "roused feelings long dormant," said Rollins, who read "hundreds of poems, sonnets, songs, and marches dedicated to our state." Some of them were later published in an Old Home Week song-book. The best we can say is that they were written without a grant. They came from the heart.

The poems worked a set of images, much in the manner of the Old Home Day Christmas float filled with the images we recognize. Peterborough in 1900 heard hometown boy Elias H. Cheney, U.S. Consul at Curaçao, Virgin Islands, read *The Old Home's a Good Home.* Marlow in 1902 sang both *My Old New Hampshire Home* and *There's a Home in Old New Hampshire.*

Come Home to Your Mother! from 1902 is typical. It begins: "Come home, boys, come home." Third verse: "There's the pond where you skated, The lake where you fish'd: And the great elm shadows, where you swung all you wished." Return to your happy childhood, dear farmhouses, mountain glory. "Home and mother are the two sweetest, tenderest words in the English language," Rollins said, "so when we ask you to come home, it is your mother's voice" calling.

There were even tributes in fireworks. The first Old Home Day in Concord on August 31, 1899, concluded with a fifty-three-part fireworks spectacular. Each was identified by number and a description in the official program, such as "No. 22 Design Portrait of Admiral Dewey, the hero of Manilla"; "No. 45 Starry Flags"; No. 52 "Aladdin Jeweled Trees"; and No. 15 "Grand Special Piece, 40 × 20, plan furnished by the committee,—old cottage, barn, well-sweep. 'We never forget the old home.'"

At the following year's celebration in Concord, a speaker asked: What one thing would you have loved to have written? It is not recorded if he paused to let the audience think: A Shakespeare sonnet or play? Something from Dickens or Twain? Lincoln's Gettysburg address? "The verdict reached by the judges appointed for the purpose, after consideration of the votes handed in, was that it lay between the childhood prayer, 'Now I lay me down to sleep,' and *Home, Sweet Home.*"

The American heart is a homesick heart. Homesickness sets in early. It is there in the first letters *home* to Europe in which the settlers decry the rude wilderness, and are hostile or, at best, blind to the savages who had been home here for thousands of years. As the savages were killed and forced west, they stole away with their secrets. We are a nation of the up-rooted who have uprooted others. Old Home Day is the holiday for the uprooted.

Homesickness took the form we know today as early as the 1820s. The last heroes of the Revolution were dying, and the young republic was still a crude frontier, and as European visitors loved to taunt: It was still not Europe, or even Europe's young cousin.

The Knickerbockers in New York gave us the some of the first monu-ments of longing, a particular literature of lament. There's Samuel Woodworth's *The Old Oaken Bucket* (1818), Washington Irving's *Rip Van Winkle* (1819), John Howard Payne's *Home, Sweet Home* (1823), and a poem by George Pope Morris, *The Oak*, which we know as *Woodman, Spare That Tree!* (1837). The great popularity of these ballads in the nineteenth century suggests that Americans felt themselves to be so far from home.

Rip Van Winkle is an essential story about American places. They change beyond our recognition. We become strangers in our native village. Rip Van Winkle falls asleep in the hills for twenty years. On his return he finds his old home "empty and forlorn," and new houses everywhere. The old village is a place bustling with strangers. We know in our bones that Rip Van Winkle is a story with some truth. New lives press in behind us and will not be denied. All that we hold and love falls from our grasp. Home leaves us.

The other stories we tell ourselves about home are travelers' tales. Home is the unchanging oasis. Home is where our youthful idealism like some spirit life still walks the earth. Governor Rollins' invitations had promised as much. Home waits for us.

Home is the memory of *The Old Oaken Bucket*. Samuel Woodworth wrote *The Old Oaken Bucket* in New York City. The poem is a "tear of re-gret" for the cool waters of his boyhood well back in Scituate, Massachu-setts.

> How dear to this heart are the scenes of my childhood,
> When fond recollection presents them to view;
> The orchard, the meadow, the deep-tangled wild-wood,
> And every loved spot which my infancy knew. . . .
> The old oaken bucket, the iron-bound bucket,
> The moss-covered bucket which hung in the well.
>
> That moss-covered vessel I hail as a treasure;
> For often, at noon, when returned from the field,
> I found it the source of an exquisite pleasure,
> The purest and sweetest that nature can yield.
> How ardent I seized it with hands that were glowing,
> And quick to the white pebbled bottom it fell;
> Then soon, with the emblem of truth overflowing,
> And dripping with coolness, it rose from the well. . . .

He wrote his song after a hot day's walk back to his apartment and a drink of municipal water. "The Bucket" was beloved, memorized in schools, sung at gatherings, and was held in peoples' hearts for many generations. Pilgrims wore a path to Woodworth's grave and continued to visit as late as the 1920s. They would carry away snippets of ivy and climbing rose that grew on his tomb. The poem irritated some writers who came forward with realistic portrayals of farm and village life, such as Hamlin Garland's *Main-Traveled Roads* (1891).

Woodworth had hidden his own harsh tale. "Born into a section of the country the most rugged and unlovely of any that I have ever witnessed— and I have traveled some—it required unceasing toil, combined with the strictest economy, on the part of my parents, to feed and clothe us, while we were yet too young to lend a helping hand," he wrote under a pseudonym. The only other words he has for his native place are "vulgar," "sterile," "obscure," and "ugly." He hated Scituate. (A visitor today finds a lovely place of beaches, bays, and wooded hills.)

His recollection of farming is that of many country mice in the city. It is not the pure spring, but rather "earthly drudgery," and the boredom of "bean-porridge," a "soup meagre" of white beans and dried, salted pork fat. "I have often vainly entreated to be permitted to *fast*, to avoid swallowing the nauseous compound."

The "dear" scenes of childhood, were, in truth, painful ones. "Rickety from my birth . . . with a debilitated system . . . I never could learn to catch a ball, or strike one with a bat; never could spin a top, leap a rail-fence, run, wrestle, box, skate, or ride horseback," he wrote. "Every failure in competition with my fellows, almost broke my heart; especially when followed by such unfeeling taunts and jeers. . . . In those moments I have often ardently and sincerely prayed for *death*. . . . 'Why am *I alone*, of all the human race, thus singled out for tortures like these!'"

Once, at about age 15, escorting his "first flame," he was tormented by the "obscene jests" of four toughs. He was helpless. His girlfriend tried to make peace by giving the tormentors peaches, which were intended as a gift for her mother. "They accepted and devoured the fruit; and then, one after another, threw the skins in my face!" he wrote. Woodworth retreated to cry.

Even without prompting, his friends often found him alone in a corner "giving vent to a passion of tears, without being able to assign any cause or reason. I can recollect numerous instances when I was not interrupted until the paroxysm had subsided, the cloud dispersed, and the sunshine of peace settled on my countenance," he wrote in a series of seventeen autobiographical essays published under a pseudonym toward the end of his life. Without his knowledge, a friend chose the heading "Memoirs of a Sensitive Man About Town."

The Old Oaken Bucket implies a happy, sunlit world. The poem is all fore-ground and no background. Although Woodworth alludes to many dear childhood memories, there is only the well in the poem: no friends, no fam-ily (except his father's cot), no scenes of village, home, or even farming. He is happy because has returned from the "drudgery" of the fields. The poem entices us to create a pastoral scene, to fill in the blanks beyond the well.

Woodworth, who never had the education he desired, left home to ap-prentice himself to a printer in Boston, and went on to a string of failures. He had a few successes in the theatre, but he was always poor with a large family to support, and in his last years he was paralyzed by a series of strokes. Friends rallied several times to raise money for him with theatrical benefits. Woodworth had vowed that he would not return home until he had won his fame and fortune. I have not found any account of Woodworth's homecoming.

George Pope Morris was one of Woodworth's friends who had aided him. The two had founded the *New-York Mirror*. Morris published his fa-mous poem in the *Mirror* under the department of "Original Songs," ti-tled *The Oak* with "musick by Henry Russell."

> My mother kiss'd me here;
>   My father press'd my hand—
> Forgive this foolish tear,
>   But let that old oak stand!

Another of Woodworth's friends, John Howard Payne, wrote *Home, Sweet Home*. The two had met as young men when Woodworth was an ap-prentice. *Home, Sweet Home* was written by an American for an English play that was based on a French "ballet-pantomime." The song itself is set to a "Sicilian air." *Home, Sweet Home* is a cosmopolitan creation. Payne spent years writing in London. The song appeared in *Clari, or the Maid of Milan*, which opened in London. The play is "a piece of slight texture" says one theatre history, but "the one sincere note that is struck in the play is the longing for home on the part of Clari."

By the fiftieth anniversary of the Declaration of Independence, Ameri-cans had created a significant body of nostalgia. This longing intensified throughout the nineteenth century. Americans have sung about losing their hometowns almost as long as they have had hometowns.

An arsenal of the literature of longing awaited the first celebrations of Old Home Day. The songs and poems written for Old Home Day are al-most all variations of *The Old Oaken Bucket* and *Home, Sweet Home*.

At the second Old Home Day in 1900, one guest speaker in Concord told a story that "no doubt" would be known to his audience. It was about the Civil War "in which some of you here participated, and of which we all have memories." The speaker, Thomas Nelson Page, was from Virginia, but took care to tell his audience that he had a summer home "within ten miles of your state border," as well as a father-in-law who was born in New Hampshire.

"The two hostile opposing armies of Americans lay entrenched opposite each other on the slopes above the Rapidan, ready to spring for that death grapple. . . . It is said that one evening as the hush of evening fell, the bands of both sides were heard playing an air,—an air which each held as its own,—*Home, Sweet Home*," said Page. All fell silent before that music, "and the two armies began to cheer each other." They had "a common heritage, the heritage of home and . . . around that sacred shekinah they united as one family." In Judaism, the Shekinah is the divine made visible, the presence of the Lord. "As long as we retain that principle—our love of home—our people are safe and our country is secure."

II. "Hustleville"

Old Home Day was Governor Frank Rollins' prayer for restoration. Rollins was a Harvard-educated lawyer and banker who knew the smart talk of his day: New England's talent and money were being drained away to build up the rest of the country. Why, one of Chicago's newest tall buildings was called the "Monadnock Building," after the mountain in New Hampshire. Boston money was building Chicago. Chicago was to be envied; it had the go-getter spirit of the age. Boston, by contrast, was settling into a premature hoary antiquity. And New Hampshire, it was said, "was a good state to emigrate from."

A standard part of many Old Home Day speeches was a roster of the "native genius" who had gone on to fame in New York, Ohio, Illinois, California, and many other states. "To examine the list of men and women New Hampshire has contributed to people the West and South is to wonder that we have any state left," said Rollins on the first Old Home Day. "Never was a commonwealth asked to make such sacrifices for her country. We have contributed of our best blood to every state in the Union." They "owe us a debt which can never be cancelled."

"In good old colonial times the voice of New Hampshire was often heard, and seldom without effect," said Rollins. "Nowadays we seem to occupy less space in the public eye."

In the New England tradition, Old Home Day is part scolding and lament, part moral reform and booster's scheme. The holiday succeeded because Rollins mixed sentiment and utility well. But all inventions require tinkering; there are ungainly predecessors.

Rollins began 1899, the year of the first Old Home Day, by scolding his state. Each year in February the state observed Fast Day, a day of prayer and reflection. Fast Day was older than the state or the nation. It had begun in 1681 when the first Colonial governor, John Cutt, was ill and a day of fasting was called. Governor Cutt died, but Fast Day persisted for more than three hundred years. The governor's proclamation for Fast Day routinely called for the citizens to count their blessings. Rollins stunned everyone by proclaiming that Christianity in the state was in serious trouble. "There are towns where no church-bell sends forth its solemn call from January to January," he said. 'No matter what our belief may be in religious matters, every good citizen knows that when the restraining influences of religion are withdrawn from a community, its decay, moral, mental and financial, is swift and sure."

His proclamation was a surprise. It first appears on page 5 of the *Concord Evening Monitor* under an advertisement for "Dogs. Dogs. Dogs." ("Five trained Japanese Spaniels who are never sick but full of play. They live entirely on Austin's Dog Biscuit. . . . They will remain in our windows Wednesday and Thursday. . . .") But the decree quickly became a subject of national discussion. The *Monitor* could headline its stories simply "That Proclamation"—so many stories that you could well think Rollins had declared a Fast Month. Every pastor and editorial writer in the state weighed in. The Massachusetts papers had a field day roasting their wicked northern neighbor.

Rollins had hit a nerve. "Degeneracy" and "spiritual decadence" were watchwords. ("Are the Massachusetts Country Towns Degenerating?" asked one article in *New England Magazine*.) He also realized that he hadn't got it quite right. Politically speaking, his Fast Day message was just too negative.

He had grown up in a political family. His father was a U.S. Senator and a "zealous" Republican party leader. The Rollins home, a few blocks from the state house, was a political salon. One of the oldest houses in Concord—"beneath spreading branches of grand old guardian elms"—it was torn down just a few years before he thought of his homecoming holiday. Rollins was a diligent banker, a translator of French stories, and a short-story writer, but in fellowship he found the "fullest enjoyment." He was an active member of clubs in three cities, and here he took his clue for his holiday: fellowship with a purpose.

The state government was in debt, as were three-quarters of the towns. The governor preached the old-time religion of self-reliance, and something new. He had a vision for New Hampshire, for the day "our manufacturing may pass away, our spindles may be silent, the whirr of our looms may cease." Once it was enough to accept the summer visitors who came your way. But this was a new age and his state would have to advertise, and remake itself for the comfort of tourists.

"The business man who succeeds today must push and hustle. He must advertise and spend money, or he is 'left at the post.' It is also true of states and towns. It's a world of activity," the governor warned, "and if we would keep abreast of the times, we must be up and doing." The new is supplanting the old. Today businesses must replace machinery after only ten years. "We must seize our opportunity as it it gallops by. . . . And I might add that opportunity is galloping by our New Hampshire towns with their matchless scenery and superb summer climate all the time.

"I would spend a million dollars in good roads, distributed over a term of years." The state spent nothing on roads; they were the responsibility of the towns. The roads were usually repaired by men working off their taxes. "I would make a park of the White Mountains and of Lake Winnepesaukee and protect them from ruin. In other words, a liberal expenditure now is the greatest economy for the future.

"The great White Mountains are being denuded and burned over, and the summer visitor turns away in sadness and disgust," Rollins said. "The path cut by the lumberman is like that of a glacier. Nothing living is left.

"Some one will say 'We can't afford to spend money for these things.' I am tired of hearing that. You can't afford not to." If you had only one well, and it was being polluted, "would you let your family be contaminated to save a few dollars?"

As a reformer, nothing passed his notice, from mountains to crockery. The governor saw himself as the housekeeper-in-chief.

"A word should be said to the keeper of the summer hotel and the summer boardinghouse. The average summer visitor . . . wants wholesome food, properly cooked and well served—well served, not thrown at him by a slattern in a dirty dress, and on cracked, heavy crockery. Give him plain country fare, plenty of chicken *broiled*, plenty of fresh eggs, good butter, good bread, fresh vegetables out of your own garden . . . have it served by as pretty a girl, a farmer's daughter, as you can find, neatly and prettily dressed; and have your table immaculately white and clean—and don't forget to throw in a few flowers for the morning. Throw away your frying pan; go bury it in the pasture twenty feet deep. . . . Make your place attractive; pull down old, rattletrap buildings; paint the barn, straighten the fence; put a swing for the children . . . be polite."

He proposed a statewide system of scenic roads with a bicycle path at one side. "At suitable intervals I would have picturesque and well-kept taverns, a treat to the eye as a comfort to the inner man." Each tavern would have a bicycle repair shop and blacksmith. Guideposts would point the way to scenic spots. He would eliminate all roadside advertisements. They were "an outrage and reproach."

"Can you not see yourself skimming like a swallow along the perfectly

kept bicycle path? Can you not feel the spring of your muscles and the bub-
bling over of exuberant life? . . . Can you not smell the wild roses by the
moss-covered walls, see the white pond-lilies titling on the wayside ponds,
see the quick summer shower come scurrying over the hilltops while you
huddle close to the big pine, see the sun come bursting out, turning the
drops on every leaf into flashing diamonds. . . .

"In fact, good roads represent civilization," he said, epitomizing the belief of the "good road movement." Even the bonfires that kicked off the
first Old Home Day were called "good roads of gorgeous glimmer." Old
Home Day was the good road home.

The housekeeper-in-chief was delighted to see that Old Home Day
brought renewed activity to places where "pride was dormant, sleeping."
"Drowsy" towns one critic called them. "For a month or more before the
date of the reunion they begin to 'spruce up' their homes and the town itself," said a 1906 report. "Houses are painted, shutters repaired, unsightly
fences removed, the huge brass knocker on the front door polished up, the
broken flag pole replaced . . . and in a few days the place has such a clean
face that the residents hardly know it." "Hustleville" is born.

The homecomers found "their townsmen waiting to receive them with
open arms and brass bands, decorations, street parades, public meetings
and banquets." They returned from the big states and from the big cities.
One woman returned after forty years—from Vermont. She was drawn by
the invitation, a promise that you could return and not be as lost as Rip
Van Winkle. The visitors purchased abandoned farms, made donations to
the schools, libraries, and churches, helped pay for historic markers, road
repair, and trees. A banker in a western city sent his hometown one hundred cherry trees.

"All doors were open, all hearts were glad. Hospitality was infectious,"
said a jubilant Rollins. He visited a different town or city every day during
the week-long celebration. "It was one of the happiest weeks of my life—
for everyone was happy about me." For one shining week it seemed as if
fifty towns in New Hampshire had outrun the old maxim: You *could* go
home again. The holiday was Rollins' triumph. "I consider it the greatest
happiness of my life that the idea of Old Home Week occurred to me."

Old Home Day was adopted by other New England states, and by
towns in Pennsylvania, Ohio, Indiana, and parts of Canada. In distant California, Granite State natives unable to make the trip home held their own
Old Home Day reunions. New Hampshire was back in the public eye.

The country towns had renewed hope and courage, a broader outlook
and higher ideals, said Rollins.

"We learn that we are not forgotten," he said, "that the pulse of all those
who are scattered over the world still beats true to their native state."

* * *

"Last year it was an experiment; this year it is an established fact, an established custom, or institution," said Rollins at the second Old Home Day in 1900. We invent our traditions that quickly. And just as our traditions gain some age, they are faced with new challenges.

By the fiftieth anniversary of the homecoming holiday, there was a new world. Fifty years had brought two world wars, a depression, and the start of a terrifying Cold War. In Gilford, a Harvard professor of sociology who was a summer resident spoke about "the Small Community in the Atomic Age." In Fremont, they heard their congressman, Chester E. Merrow, say, "If Russia decides to use military force (towards her goal of world domination) there is nothing, in my opinion, which will keep them from reaching the English Channel within a month." After that speech, it would have been hard to sing any antique hymns.

Or perhaps they were in sympathy with the song in the Old Home Week Association's 1947 songbook, *Let's All Sing*. The song was *Now That We Are Home*: "Oh that we might all remain where our hearts are happiest."

After the fiftieth anniversary, we know what happens to America: The roads grow wider, the elms die, ranch houses with picture windows become the flag of prosperity, the piano in the parlor gives way to the television in the living room, and much of the hometown, homemade culture fades by the light of nationally televised spectacles.

The good roads were built, without the bicycle paths. The White Mountains were saved. The vast mills did fall silent. Tourists have become New Hampshire's cash crop. In any given year you can attend a conference or a business breakfast and hear state officials advocating Governor Rollins' program: Hustle for the summer people, the leaf peepers, the skiers. They are still housekeeping the state; packaging, branding, theme-parking, we call it today.

In the hands of Wallace Nutting, Norman Rockwell, the nostalgists of the Colonial revival and others, New England has been shaped into the idealized American home: the home for Thanksgiving, for Christmas, and the picturesque scene of summer and fall. The good roads deliver millions to these scenes of home. We have come back.

From Frank Rollins and his generation we have inherited a useful sentimentality. We have the Old Home in Hustleville.

After a hundred years, Old Home Day should be a Victorian curio, but it resonates with a great place hunger, an even wider homesickness. We know the impossibility of return, and the hope for renewal. We are shadowed by Rip Van Winkle.

III. "Where Is the *Here*, Now?"

Conversation on board a plane in flight, Boston to Seattle. Two passengers are standing in the aisle talking:

"Where are you based now?"

"Well I've been here for a year."

"Where is the *here*, now?"

Let us admit that this is the way we live now—by the odometer, by the speedometer, by the jet trail in ozone. We live by the timetable. We protest that we love the homeplace, even as we greedily seek out the turquoise blue-water promises of the travel ads. At a party in our town, I listen to my neighbors talk of their trips: They are back from Greece and Turkey, Cambodia, Brazil, Scotland, Iceland, and France; they are off to Nepal; they are thinking of going to Ecuador.

In a neighboring town, Harrisville, an acquaintance, Jack Calhoun, had organized a "futuring" conference. About 75 people would meet intensively over three days to plan for their town. Harrisville is a beautiful out-of-the-way place, small even when measured against other small towns. Residents were flying in from Russia the night before to get to the conference, Calhoun said. Some of his neighbors are professionals who can run their business anywhere. They have a desire for a small town and have chosen it, he said, but often don't know how to take part.

We are pressed for time. That's what we've been telling each other. Experts say we don't sleep enough—they tell us this in those thirty-second TV news reports and sixty-second all-news radio spots. Parents race from work to daycare, shuttle their kids from one scheduled activity to another. We abhor quiet.

What we may really lack is place. We are not at home in any one place. We are here in these small towns, but not here. We are uplinked, downloaded, commuting, encapsulated by shell after shell of our clever devices. Sometimes Calhoun asks his neighbors who work at home to count the number of people they talk to each day. How many are in town?

Donald Paine, a landscape gardener in Blue Hill, Maine, has seen a surprising change in his region. Corporate executives arrive from the cities, and wall themselves off. They demand something previously unknown in the local landscape: privacy hedges across the old Maine pastures. On thirty acres they reproduce a suburban house plot, placing a fenced-in house with shrubs on one patch. The rest of the land is a pasture/moat.

Life is lived in "segments," they tell Paine. Of course, you'll have four or five jobs or careers in a lifetime. They live in towns as if they've checked into a country inn. Instead of a weekend, they'll stay four or five years. Safe in the privacy of their hedges, abstaining from town life, just where are they?

This is how we live—in segments. A few years here, a few there. And so we find ourselves at 30,000 feet, someplace over the continent, asking "where is the here, now?" This is the question that haunts our Old Home Days.

Rollins and his generation seemed to believe they could make the world right by oratory. They tried to talk New England into a revival. They talked of home. We talk of "sense of place." We, too, are trying to talk our way home.

These are the books Rip Van Winkle might write: *Recovering a Sense of Place, A Place of Sense, A Good Place to Live, A Better Place to Live, The Great Good Place, Staying Put.* These books have been published in the last few years and on the whole they are good thoughtful books. They remind me of the title of a memoir: *Is There No Place on Earth for Me?*

Home has left us. The native is now exotic, the ordinary is extraordinary. This is only a sampling of the books that look intensely at a place as if to caress the face of the landscape. They worship locality, are thirsty for details. They are hungry for sun up and sun down, for grass and dirt. Hungry for a routine that their grandparents may have fled—a routine that sends millions toward cities in poor countries each year.

When the country was rural, when most Americans lived on farms, we had harsher things to say. Village life was an entangling grotesque. In the 1920s Sinclair Lewis, Edgar Lee Masters, and Sherwood Anderson wrote of the narrow, hobbling small town life in what has been called "the revolt from the village." Now the nation is urban and suburban: We love small towns, and are moving there in record numbers.

These "sense of place" books chant "only connect," and at times, only over-connect. They want to know all the names of the mountains and the hollows, the old family names on the earliest houses. They desire a possession that goes far beyond the rights of property. Staying put has become a cause taken up by poets.

"The prose of other people's everyday lives can seem like poetry to those, like myself, who have never experienced such ordinariness so unself-consciously," Kathleen Stocking writes in her charming book *Letters from the Leelanau.*

Stocking limns the beauties of the Leelanau, the peninsula in northern Michigan home to the Sleeping Bear Dunes, and home to many new converts to staying put. They are like earth-deprived space voyagers just returned, ready to sing praise for the dunes, trees, anything—including people—sitting in one place long enough to be shaped by the seasons. A friend tells her, "We're here because we have this relationship to the land. I can't go a day without knowing the phase of the moon and what flowers are in bloom, because they impose themselves on us." She later says, "I feel we're connecting more to the land and more to people who've come before us, and will come after us." These converts seem to be talking themselves into this "rootedness," trying to drive off the urban nomad in themselves. You could easily imagine them in a support group for former suburban mall rats and freeway hounds. Will some of them move on to the next fad in their lives? "Oh, we've done the land thing."

From the 1930s to the 1950s, Lewis Mumford's architecture criticism in *The New Yorker* assailed the failure of various projects to meet the genius of a place. Now we must recreate place out of whole cloth. *The New Yorker* has a new department heading, "Annals of Place." Place is no longer a given. A native, returned to the Leelanau after twenty years in Boston, tells her children, "'Look at that steam rising off the lake in the narrows,' because someday you won't see this."

Look at the earth now, children. This the manifesto for the "sense of place" books. In *Winter, Notes from Montana*, Rick Bass seeks his valley as a balm. We're hiding out here, Bass says. He doesn't want to think about a proposed mining operation some miles south, or of the clear cuts that have silted the river in town, he says. He wants to be snowed in, to feel the sting of 20 below, to earn the valley. He cuts wood and more wood as one would eat to partake of the world. He treasures the details about chainsaws, generators, and trucks. Bass wants nothing less than to become the rhythm of the land. This like the afterlife up here, he says.

Like the Old Home Day speeches, these "sense of place" books are a kind of courtship. We want the land to smile back at us. We desire "tuwanasaapi," says John Hanson Mitchell in his fine book, *Walking Towards Walden, A Pilgrimage in Search of Place*. Tuwanasaapi is the Hopi word he translates as "The place where you belong. The spiritual core of the universe. When you get there, you will know it."

When the New England Society of Brooklyn met in the 1890s, they sang *The Old Granite State*, also known as the *Mountaineer's Farewell*. Newly arrived immigrants rallied around their own newspapers, churches, synagogues, and stores. They could speak the comforting language of the "old country" in these places. The Yankees met for their own rites. Men and women in from the farms kept up their home ties with Vermont, Granite State, and New England societies. In the cities, many Americans were also immigrants. Rollins first proposed his Old Home holiday in Boston at a meeting of the Sons of New Hampshire. The first celebration was funded by the state's immigration bureau, "as the best means of promoting" the bureau's mission.

We meet for similar rites, but we don't sing about the old mountain home. Several professors at Franklin Pierce College, in our corner of New Hampshire in sight of Mt. Monadnock, are questing after the meaning of place, of where the here is now. They have set up the Monadnock Institute of Nature, Place, and Culture, a rather searching name. For one meeting they asked their advisory board, of which I am a member, to come prepared with a definition of place. (Teachers reflexively assign homework.)

For a couple of hours, twenty people, each in turn, talked their way around the circle, creating a composite American Place biography. We talked about how we had come to be here. Some, like the director of a local conservation center, Meade Cadot, had their home place moved from them. Rapid suburban development had covered over country lanes with houses and highways. Others had moved for work, always thinking, well, where to next? And some who had moved have never felt at home. John Hanson Mitchell's parents lived in New Jersey for a half a century, but always spoke of Maryland's Eastern Shore as "Down Home." Chris Salem had been in New England for ten years. She had left behind her family in Nebraska, where they have been settled for five generations. She said she felt like one of those trees that are uprooted, cut back, and balled up in burlap. She can feel those lost roots like phantom limbs, she said. "This isn't home, but that isn't home either."

In the third, and smallest, category were those who lived where they had grown up. Jane Brox, author of *Here And Nowhere Else*, returned to her family farm in Dracut, Massachusetts. She has a lover's quarrel with her home place. Chick Colony's family had built the mills that had once run in his hometown. He said that he knew his roots were in Harrisville when he went next door to show his newborn to Fannie Luoma, a ninety-year-old Finnish woman. "Janni," she said—that's what she called Chick, whose given name is John. (People who stay in their hometowns sometimes accumulate names like the old roads hereabouts.)—"Janni, he looks just like your father looked at that age." Chick asked, "You can remember that far back?" "Oh yes," she said.

Elizabeth Marshall Thomas, author of *The Harmless People* and *The Hidden Life of Dogs*, spoke of clearing the meadow that she looks out upon as she writes. She worked with her father, and drove the tractor. "This place is who I am. It's like the food you eat," Thomas said. There is a pull toward home, an "atavistic sense" that she has observed in birds and cats. The travels of limpets, small mollusks, have been studied. They move with the tide to feed, but return to the exact same spot, their home, on the rock.

Here was the American place biography. We moved; we stayed. Our home moved away from us, changed beyond recognition. Here was the story of Rip Van Winkle, the story of settlers and immigrants coming to a new place and learning that place. Does the itch to move fade? Does your job take you up and down the corridors of employment? Few of us are where we began. Whether we are first generation, or fifteenth-generation Americans, we are immigrants and settlers.

These searching discussions are our version of the Old Home Day songs and poems. What did this place mean to us? We tried to answer.

It's the place where you see fishers and moose, the conservationist Cadot said. It's a place where town, forest, and to some extent pasture are still in the right proportion on the land, I said. It's the summer cultural events; the stock car race track in Winchester, said others. To some it's the sight of a meetinghouse spire; to others it's just where they are and have always been. Some move in and live as you could almost anywhere in North America—commuting to work, watching TV—oblivious to these little towns of a few thousand people.

Our understanding of this place is like *umweld*, said one biologist, the world unique to each animal, the way each animal perceives the world.

And so around the room we went, offering illustrations of migration, settlement, place hunger, soul hunger, solace, repose, and the pilgrim's quest on the road.

Place is where the rivers run, it's where the soul finds nourishment. It's a balm and a burden, it's limiting and liberating. Cleaving to one place can lead to war or to one hundred years of peace.

Place is the *real*. We live in a time of image and data; of rehearsed dialogues and scenes; of a torrent of spectacles. It used to be the circus came to town but once a year; now, if we wish, all the time.

So what is a sense of place? It's who you are and where you have been and where you *think* you are now.

We are soil and light and dreams, as has been said by the poets and psalmists. Live in one place long enough and you are a certain slant of light; a certain flintiness may grow up in you.

Places call forth different attributes within us. The right place is like the right marriage—it's an evolving, loving relationship. Once in a thousand times it's interesting, as Thornton Wilder said in *Our Town*.

Jack Calhoun's children, Peter and Nelly, ages seven and five, said it best. Bit by bit, he drew this answer out of them:

"A sense of place is where . . . the people we love and who love us, too, live. It is where our friends and neighbors are. It is our house and the trees that show us the changing seasons. It is the view of the hills and Mt. Monadnock, the pond in the backyard where we swim, and the village. It

is the sounds of the road out front, and the sound of quiet at night. It is
rain on the slate roof, the bird sounds in the morning, the wind outside
during a blizzard, and all the bright stars in the whole sky. It is where we
feel safe."

Places gather memories.

"The invitation sent out to us invited us to 'come home.' . . . But where is
home?" asked the Rev. George A. Putnam at Dunbarton in 1899, where he
had been born and raised. Is home with mother and father? They are dead.
"Essentially, home is where love is," he said, "the *things* I love, the *people* I
love, and the people who love me. . . . I '*come home*' whenever I come back
to the memory of" this love, he said.

Home is our sacred Jerusalem, the reverend said. "We read of Daniel,
that when he prayed he opened his windows toward Jerusalem. If I were
to open my windows I should open them towards Dunbarton, and set my
face to this spot." Capuchin monks ship loads of Jerusalem's soil to Rome
so they may be buried in the sacred soil, the Rev. Putnam said. "If I ever do
anything of that sort, my ships will come to Dunbarton."

Places gather memories, and that is why they are sacred. But if we today
live "hither and yon," where is home? If we live our lives out in segments—program our days and years in blocks as if we were TV network executives—do we deep down feel that we have scattered our meaning, the
work of our days, our love, to the winds?

"The stamp of this place is upon me," the reverend told his friends in
Dunbarton. He believed in "the influence and impress of material things,"
the power of our home to shape us. On the coast of Maine he had talked
with painters. Isn't painting more than capturing the rocks and crags, the
"essential, namable things," he asks. Isn't it the atmosphere too? A painter
replied, "Almost everything depends on that atmosphere."

The same is true of people, he said: Character depends not only upon
virtue, "but also on the subtle atmosphere, on that mysterious coloring
and inspiration that trees and flowers and mountains and valleys bring to
the life of those who grow up among them." He didn't follow his metaphor through, but he had reversed our usual manner of thinking. We usually say that we shape places; we take nature or our land or house as the
blank canvas and create our scene. But all the while, we are the canvas, we
are the scene painted. Do we in these days feel uncreated? unpainted?

Places gather memories. If we live our days in no place, nowhere, are we
then ungathered? Are we like a painting without atmosphere, just a cold
report? If a place has not touched our soul, do we even know where our
soul is?

* * *

Thirty people have gathered for "The Awakening of a Sense of Place." This is "a roundtable discussion on the Experience of the Sense of Place as an antidote to the current personal and collective alienation from the healing rhythms of life and nature." This discussion will be followed by an all-day workshop, and an evening concert, "Heart of Earth." ("Celebrating the awakening of a place of awakening.")

One era rhapsodizes the old oaken bucket at the well, another era enshrines the songlines of Australia's aborigines. The language of many Old Home Day speeches is to us florid, earnest, and suffused with longing. One hundred years later, this how some people try to go home and this is their language of longing.

Ross Jennings leads the proceedings. Ross is an "earthwright"—"It was important that someone break the ice and coin the phrase," which he did ten years ago, he says. He sees a change coming. "We took a detour," he says. To reconnect with ancient teachings—"the mything link"—Ross founded the "Dancing Dragon Center for the Art of Placemaking." He's a short man with grey hair and a goatee. He wears a purple velour tunic with batwing sleeves.

"It's important that each person cultivates their sense of place," Ross says. The weekend will be worthwhile if just one person steps forward and shares their relationship with the earth, something they've never expressed before, he says.

He starts by talking about a trip he took to the Yucatan last year. Though this is about place, the panelists for this discussion travel a lot, including my wife, Sy Montgomery, an author of books set in India, Africa, and Indonesia. No one confronts the irony of the place-eroding effects of all this twentieth-century travel. One panelist jumps the globe to praise people who are rooted to one place: Findhorn, Scotland; Arcosanti in Arizona; and 11 trips to Auroville, India. More than a thousand people from thirty-five nations "gave their lives to reforesting" Auroville. They planted two million trees. She admires their "real commitment to stay in one place"—not that she's advocating it for everyone.

Ross talks about a bird he saw in the Yucatan and how easily it rode the thermals. Each of the panelists tonight is going to take us aloft, he says, on a "psychic thermal."

It's like the vulture and what does the vulture see? Ross asks.

"Carrion," my wife answers sensibly. No one laughs. The earthwright carries on with his uplifting metaphor.

Displayed on the floor are the usual suspects of cool native people's instruments from here and Australia—two didgeridoos, two drums, one with lizards chasing each other. In the middle of the instruments, on a small blue towel, sits a rock shaped like a heart (or India). One yellow carnation has been placed in front of the rock.

Ross found the stone in a forest he helped to save from logging. "The stone had laid in a certain state of enchantment for 30 thousand years—I was called to change it," he says. He didn't go looking to move it, he says. He just picked it up and it balanced. "If something that ungainly can be that balanced," he says, so can we. "Of course it represents how I feel," he says of the stone. "We've just scratched the potentiality . . . I know this is the place of awakening."

We have to do a little "low-grade exorcism," Ross says. Children do "eurythmy," dance, in this Waldorf school classroom. We need "different energies." He intones: "Those energies, take five, step back. We'll ask those kind of beings and energies to depart." We'll focus ourselves on this now, not whether we left the stove on, he says, unintentionally introducing a new worry to the room. "The sound will convey the intention." He kneels on the floor. A woman with long gray hair and a heavy-set man come forward to play their instruments.

Ross swings a twangy wire and rubber band thing over his head. Then he blows through the didgeridoo. It is part fog horn, part rumbly African beast of the Savannah, deeply resonant. People sit with their eyes closed. The man gently touches the drum, finger tips only. The woman plays a small stone whistle.

This is a ridiculous scene—like a clichéd Hollywood rendering of a New Age gathering—but the room feels relaxed, quiet.

Ross resumes by talking about the Songlines of the Aborigines. This is de rigueur for a sense-of-place gathering. If the Aborigines don't attend to a place, it sickens and dies, Ross says. He likens it to the performer on the Ed Sullivan show who kept all the plates spinning.

Ross introduces his friend, Steven McFadden, who has recently finished a walk across the country in stages with Native Americans. He talks in a practiced manner, eye contact all over the room, dramatic pauses, and he finishes by saying, "I have spoken."

McFadden reads us a birth poem that he says is from the Souhegan band of the Algonquin people, who once lived here. We should know the myths of this place, he says. We've arrived only in the last three to four hundred years, but they had been here thousands of years and had things mostly worked out.

At a bend in the Ashuelot River, south of Keene, New Hampshire, where the river makes an abrupt turn, there is evidence of campfires and caribou bones dated to 10,500 years ago, McFadden says. But the "timekeepers," have told him, no, the site dates to 40,000 years ago.

There are sites all over, we just have to know how to look for them, he says. There are stone fences the natives built with prayer seats in them, like a seat you'd ride for a journey.

Ross thanks him, saying that there are legends of place and we are adding to the legends tonight. He introduces the next speaker, Pam Mayer, an elderly woman whose long gray hair gives her a wise, medicine-woman look.

When Pam and her husband returned to Vermont fifteen years ago, she was devoted to her garden, or, as she says, she was "interactive with her garden." She was ill and so was her garden. A little tree by her garden was dying. She sat down and looked at the tree and we "had a sense we were communicating."

"The next morning I had an image of the tree—it was a person—a man turned upside down—and the place in it that was damaged was the same place I was damaged." She went to the doctor and was diagnosed with cancer. "I realized that tree was trying to tell me something." The tree died.

For health care, Pam and her husband moved to a retirement community. She was heartbroken to leave her garden. "I knew there had to be rituals," Pam said. Her friends performed a protracted series of "rituals." Finally the movers were there. A friend came to help say good-bye to the house and garden. In her garden a pileated woodpecker was gasping for breath, dying.

There was nothing we could do to help the bird, so we just sat down and watched it die, she says. They left the dead bird on a stone that was central to a now-dismantled labyrinth.

On her drive to the retirement home she was joyful for the first time in months. A week later she returned to her former garden. The bird was gone. There was nothing. "This bird had been an angelic being and came to take off my pain to wherever angels go and freed me to start my new life."

She doesn't consider that someone—fox, rat, red squirrel, weasel, dog, cat, vulture, crow—carried off the poor bird and ate it.

Her ignorance is her freedom. She has seen a miracle. But while saints and seers talk in this manner, this is reductive, a non-vision. The bird died for her. The tree died for her. The land leans toward her. Mystics and prophets astonish us by the sudden connections they make, the unity of their visions, the exalted view. This is about "me," like all self-help, self-reflective visions.

Pam kept a cabin in the woods on their land in Vermont. No more gardening. The land "was going to make me—all I had to do was be present to do what it was asking."

She is a dowser. She loves following "energy lines." You find wonderful places, she says, magical places. "Was it magical, and the lines came to it or the other way around, I don't know." She knew there was a master line from the high point on the land, which she called "The Dragon's Head."

But it is hard to stay on one line. She was searching for the one story, the unified field theory of her land. It's what we crave: a strong central story line.

One day she was scrambling up a trail she had not followed before and there was a porcupine looking at her. She had "never had a prolonged eye contact with an animal before. This porcupine was walking toward me. Part of me got nervous. I thought there must be some *meaning* to this."

She got up on a rock and the porcupine walked past, looking at her with "disgust."

"I got home and looked up porcupine in my book. Porcupine means *trust*—all the things I wasn't exhibiting."

She went back—she had to go back—to where she had seen the porcupine. "I saw two quartz rocks" lined up. This was her major line. "That was what I was looking for all summer. Most sacred sites on my property line up," she says.

She built a sweat lodge. "The land has *profoundly* changed because of the intentionality of what has been happening there, the ceremonies and rituals."

"Our purpose," she says, is to "allow healing to happen: healing of land and people." A dance goes on; the people change; the land changes. A relative visited the land after a five-year absence. The land is so different, he said. "Like a curtain going up on a new play," she says. "So it's *profoundly* nourishing for those involved in it."

"There is a reciprocal process—the land becomes more vital," Ross says. "If you respond, you will change, you will have capacity that will be awakened." If we didn't have that capacity, we wouldn't be here now on earth, Ross says. We can all do this.

"It's possible to rediscover the same relation that ancient peoples have had with the earth," the earthwright says confidently.

Here the self-help conceit meets the old Romantic notion, born of the Industrial Revolution. We can return to the primitive, the natural, the native. We can sail for Tahiti, make honest, premachine art and furniture. We can tread lightly. We can go home again.

Paradise, utopia, spiritual self-help, the earthwright taps into it all. If he lines his circuits up right—his lines of magic—he could have a season of PBS fame: a stroll in the woods with Bill Moyers, a thin bestselling book, earthwright conferences. He could be a New Age Norman Vincent Peale. He is probably closer than he realizes to a kind of pop culture, snap, crackle, and boom.

Ross expresses what many want to believe: Rocks and trees love us. The earth speaks to you *personally*. A place will reciprocate your love.

Our overrefined Western culture seems to work its way into this corner several times a century. Nature is rediscovered, and Nature's face is, so often, that culture's face. Sometimes this rediscovery produces great art, better lives, and sometimes a pile of New Age mumbo jumbo and fractured social science that is puny in the face of the smallest bulldozer.

The woods are full of portents and signs, porcupines as prophets, and God speaks everywhere to everyone. We have only to listen, Ross assures us. Be your own shaman, your own Native American treading noiselessly. But even they had only a few select among them as shamans.

We turn to the land, and as the joke has it, we say "but enough about me — what do *you* think about me?"

When Moses sees the burning bush in the desert, he is not receiving some self-help pointers, getting lessons to overcome his speech impediment. When God speaks to the prophets, they are a vessel for the message. They are the eye and the ear. Sometimes they are remade, and sometimes destroyed. The self is a prison, the old religions teach, and escape is difficult.

Americans are hungry for community, hungry to be a part of something larger than themselves. Another serving of self-help will only leave them starving at the table.

"We can imbue the energy field with any intention we want to give it," Ross says. We can "enhance the destiny of this place." "You move in interplay of the process and you begin an interplay. . . ." Words tumble out of the earthwright in search of order and logic.

Now, he says, "You must release the beings of place."

The woman with the stone whistle stands up again, "This is a musical rendition of what you just said."

We ask too much of places. The Old Oaken Bucket — "emblem of truth overflowing." A heart-shaped rock. The Old Home. The Songlines. The unchanging granite hills. Shaman porcupines. The hospitality of sincere hearts. Your mother's voice calling you home. True love. Perfect faith. Jerusalem and Utopia. *Home, Sweet Home.* This is our Old Home Day parade.

The residents of Dunbarton on Old Home Day in 1899 heard their town praised by the Reverend Putnam as a Jerusalem, and by the Honorable Henry M. Putney as a "veritable rural Utopia." "A town whose people were so peaceable and sensible no lawyer could live among them . . . and whose annual town meetings were perfect illustrations of the spirit of a pure democracy." A town without poverty, whose men and women "typified all that was great, grand, strong, ennobling and productive in the Old Puritan." Dunbarton and the small hilltowns, he said, were "fountains from which virtue and virility flow into the cities."

Dunbarton—utopia, fountain of virtue, Jerusalem. It is a wonder that the hard-working farmers of this village didn't collapse under the weight of their assignment: Grow food and soul enough for a nation on land that was "not forthcoming."

Country life was real. The city was evil. "Men are realizing that the life in the cities is forced, artificial, unreal, unhealthful, and they are harking back to first principles, getting back to nature," said Governor Rollins in Woodstock, New Hampshire in 1900. "Every man that you take away from the city and plant in the country is a distinct gain for civilization," he said in Hanover that same year. "The true life of man is lived out of doors, upon the soil, where he can study the ways of plants and animals, the movements of the heavenly bodies. . . . A man can have no particular attachment to a house designated by a number in a city street in a row of brick structures—it has no identity, no significance."

Rollins is blind to the cities, blind to the majority of his own state. He has little to say for the great mill cities of Manchester and Nashua, except to note that they are prosperous. ("They speak for themselves.") He ignores the French-Canadians, nearly one-third of Manchester's population, the state's largest city. He refers obliquely to "an alien race" who are adopting the hard-working Yankee ethic as New Hampshire loses its "best-bred stock." He believes that the hilltowns have emptied out directly into the mills. "Where have the people to build up these and other cities come from? From the hill farms, from the farming towns," Rollins says. Mathematically this is improbable.

The problems of the cities, and all the big issues of the 1890s, are absent from the Old Home Day orations: strikes, trusts, temperance, wealth and poverty, child labor, immigration, race. This is nothing less than the reform agenda that shaped twentieth-century America. I have found only one speaker in 1900 who mentions these issues. A rare woman speaker in 1911 spoke the Progressive line.

Though the subject is home, few women ever get to speak. The "home" in Old Home Day is not about the domestic life of the hearth and the raising of children. The Old Home Day orators are talking about being at home in the *world*: finding one small, unchanging place to sit awhile and regain their balance.

They left out the political issues of the day in favor of *The Old Oaken Bucket, Home, Sweet Home*, and recollections we are quick to dismiss as nostalgia. They were describing the essence of feeling at home: a stillness, a quietness. When we say life was simpler and we were happier when young, we mean, I believe, that we were in touch with this quiet. We were like Rip Van Winkle asleep.

The orators did not refer to Rip Van Winkle. But Rip Van Winkle comes to all Old Home Day parades. At our old Home Day, on a pleasing August morning, there was that homecoming veteran on one crutch, the bride, the prisoner in state-pen stripes, all trailing the Christmas scene on the truck. They were Rip Van Winkle returning:

"The very village was altered; it was larger and more populous. There were rows of houses which he had never seen before, and those which had been his familiar haunts had disappeared. Strange names were over the doors—strange faces at the windows—everything was strange. His mind now misgave him; he began to doubt whether both he and the world around him were not bewitched. Surely this was his native village, which he had left but the day before."

He had returned to his old home in Hustleville.

On that first Old Home Day, as the hard-won farms grew back into brush, it may be the word "settlement" that eluded them; settlement eludes us. We have made an ugly landscape. We live with houses, products, and franchise businesses tricked out to make us think that we are home.

Today we are looking for the rituals of Old Home Day, looking for a homecoming, a peace that is within ourselves and a peace with our surroundings.

"Life was a struggle" on those old hill farms where the "soil was cold and unready to give up its secrets," said Rollins in 1900. But "life was lived amidst the most beautiful scenery and surroundings" and it marked one "indelibly." If New Hampshire's sons and daughters, abroad in the world, are ever "discouraged or ill . . . their feet turn toward the old hill farm. There, they know, is peace, there is balm, there is healing."

Rollins set aside one week a year to talk of home. We talk endlessly about place and community. In this desperation for solace we mark Old Home Day, every day.

The Lost Language of Villages

~❧ ❧~

Architect David Howard is sliding a transparent yogurt cup lid over a map of Nantucket. The lid covers six and a half acres by the map's scale. He counts the houses, marveling at the compactness of this graceful town. He slides it over India, Hussey, and Quince Streets and counts houses: forty-five. A tax map, he says, is "an essay about the ways people live together." The lid glides over the map like a pointer on a Ouija board: Howard is trying to conjure the magic of this old place. He wants to build beautiful small towns again.

"The whole nineteenth century and early twentieth century was a process of building villages," Howard says. "We're just not building villages anymore."

We are in Nantucket, rambling around, looking at the town. Howard brings questions to the street: Why is that house only fifteen feet from the next one when they had the entire island to build on? What were they thinking about? On other excursions, he has taken a lawn chair and planted it in front of a house and stared for a half hour or more.

He is looking beyond the pretty picture to begin to understand how our towns were designed. "I look at calendar pictures and I see something very sophisticated that took thousands and thousands of years. I don't just see a pretty picture."

For thousands of years there were no words for the design of villages because this was simply the way people lived. To talk about how to design a village would have been like issuing instructions on how to breathe. Nantucket evolved as a tight fishing village not because it would later make a nice postcard, but because it was shaped by a way of life. But in the modern age we live differently: We left Main Street for the highway and the suburb.

Howard believes we can find our way back. We can learn again how to build villages. "It is an evolving tradition. You can work in it like a musician," he says. He sees New England's villages not as a group of antiques to be protected, as in a historic district, but as a text to be read, a guide and an inspiration for the future. These villages are like town elders and they have much advice, if we would only listen.

David Howard is a one-man round table, a chorus, a crowd of discussions. He can carry on enough stories, spin out enough ideas to fill an entire restaurant with talk. We meet one day for lunch at an inn near his house in Walpole, New Hampshire. Most of the time the other tables are quiet, yet I feel like I'm trying to tune in on two simultaneous conversations—but only Howard is talking.

He is explaining his theories of how good villages evolve, but along the way he tells me about his ancestors, about skipping out of MIT for two years to run off to Europe where he helped support himself by doing sidewalk chalk drawings (patron saints a big money maker), about a house he designed for a Southerner whose life is a novel (it is, but as he tells the story, it would dwarf War and Peace), about why education and insulation are usually done incorrectly, about Alaskans (losers!), and about the adolescence of modern architecture. He does great voices and laughs freely. David Howard is an athletic talker.

Like many architects, he talks with a mechanical pencil in his hand, sketching as he goes. When he's describing a new house to a prospective client, he'll reach across the table and draw upside down. He refers to the custom-made notebooks he carries with him, two hundred pages of leather-bound graph paper, filled with sketches, house plans, lectures, lists of ideas, all in an urgent hand, and all indexed in front.

Howard, who is fifty-five years old, has designed more than 300 houses in thirty-six states, including thirty-two on Nantucket. He started out designing timber frames. Then for a time he imported old barns from England.

He is known also for the first impression he makes: sloppiness. One client said to him: "David, your shirttail is always hanging out." He replied, "Well, how are you supposed to clean your glasses?"

But his sloppiness and his absorption in his ideas serve him well: This is the classic portrait of the genius at work. It also levels the field for prospective clients. They may well think: We can barely keep up with this guy, but he is charming and hell, at least *I* can tuck in my shirt.

His office has the same shirttails-out quality. Four rooms with stuff everywhere: blueprints, model airplanes hanging up, toy cars, cameras, books, CDs, timber frame models. The office is like a Howard conversation—it seems at first to be crowded with unrelated parts, but one quickly sees a great unity, a playfulness and an experimentation.

One day when I mention that my lawn mower is in for repair once again, he tells me that he has a system for mowing his four acres. "I finally figured out how to mow the lawn," he says. "I bought five old mowers at yard sales. Fixed them up. I blow the whistle. Get the whole family out there mowing. We're done in twenty minutes and then I load everyone up and we go to the Chinese restaurant." Costs about $45 to have the lawn mowed, he says. So he spends it on a family dinner. He takes his own path to traditional Yankee thrift.

One of the things Howard tells me right off is that he is from an "old New England family of great purpose." One uncle, Herbert Howard, was a medical pioneer commemorated with a big portrait at Massachusetts General Hospital. Howard remembers the big Thanksgiving dinners at his uncle's house. After dinner, he says, "the men retired to the drawing room. . . . The eldest member would come look at you: 'What are you doing? Is it worth anything?'"

He surprised his family when he went to MIT and shocked them when he took off for Europe. But it was in Europe that his real education began. During the reign of the International Style when the crisp glass box was exalted, Howard was drawn to the ancient villages. "I became absolutely fascinated by them." He filled 4,000 pages with notes and sketches in his search for a "village vocabulary."

When he says vocabulary, he means that parts of the landscape function like parts of speech: Main Street, the town common, the meeting house, all combine to tell the story of a place.

If we can rediscover the lost language of villages, Howard believes, we can return to building places like the ones we love. "The founding fathers thought out the village plans we admire. They thought about this deeply: how rich and poor can live together."

One hundred years from now, he says, "the world will most likely re-vere" the New England of 1750 to 1850, just as we revere ancient Greece. "No one had ever achieved this equality before. It's a hundred year thing. A nineteenth-century spectacular. We built these villages without zoning or historic districts. That's the mystery."

We are walking down Liberty Street in Nantucket. Look at this street, he says. The houses are right on the narrow street. A typical house has forty to fifty feet of frontage—he paces it off—one hundred feet deep, say: four thousand-square-foot lots, about the size of a basketball court. On this street were a dozen or more violations of our modern zoning codes: houses too close to each other, no setback from the street, no parking. . . . You can't build this street today. You wouldn't be allowed. Some parts of town have as many as ten houses to an acre. "And it's wonderful. People are drawn from the big power suburbs to this—its antithesis—why?" he asks.

"These houses have humility," he says. "You're constantly getting a feeling that this is a group of people." These houses are similar in shape and size, yet there are differences in the size of the lots and the setbacks, and in the treatment of doors. And there are the exceptions to the order of the street. "Every town has a pink house," he says.

"This is what a group of people looks like—all the same size, yet all different." The New England town is ensemble acting, a troupe of actors, each building with its own role, each coming forward to speak its part.

Today in our suburban landscape we have only soliloquies, isolated houses and stores, endless strip malls. "It's adolescent," he says. All of it is look-at-me architecture. "Suburbia is adolescent. What is adolescence? I don't have to care about anything but myself. That's an important part of our life, but that should last only five years," he says. "We are a nation born of people who always left before they faced their community responsibilities."

In a village the house exists in the right relation to its neighbors. "The house is just a private part of town. You're at home in the whole town. You say: I live in town."

We turn the corner onto a new street, Woodbury Lane, at the edge of the old settlement, and the place just dies. The feeling is different. It's like a taut rope had gone slack.

Here are new versions of the older houses. They are good-looking houses—trim, well-detailed, but they are speaking different lines.

The street is much wider, the sidewalks wider and the houses are set back behind a green moat of a lawn. The rhythm is gone. If the old town is like a Bach concerto, then this is a novice's practice session, missing notes and off tempo. This is suburbia, plain and simple-minded. "I feel like an intruder here," Howard says.

We walk back to the old streets, which is walking back to Nantucket itself. "This street has dignity," Howard says. "There's some real harmony here."

"The biggest house is ten times bigger than the smallest house, one block away. Yet you never felt they were drastically different houses." Today in the newer developments the rich hide in gated communities and the poor are miles away, but five hundred feet is all that separates them in the village.

"There's a sense that being an honorable person is more important than being the richest person," Howard says, sounding very much like the nephew who has absorbed the lessons of those after-dinner drawing room talks.

"What do these people in gated communities say to their children?"

* * *

What do we tell ourselves about the world we have built?

In *Secrets of the Nest*, Joan Dunning recalls her time in Vermont. For a couple of years she slept on the second floor of a cabin with a small door open to trees filled with the sounds of the wood thrush and the hermit thrush, the state bird of Vermont.

"The song of the wood thrush typified all that I hoped Vermont represented. It sounded like the easy, relaxed movement of a porch swing. I imagined an old woman, one foot down to the floor of the porch, gently pushing, keeping the swing in motion. There had been no such sound in Southern California."

This is a good summary of peoples' aspirations for Vermont, and for all of small-town New England. This is why visitors traverse New England looking for the ideal inn, the finest common, the best view on the peak day of autumn. They seek that gentle rocking motion and all it signifies, from infancy on to an adult state of acquired calm, of knowing where you are.

"America is starved for a better community," says Howard. Sometimes "Americans think of New England as hard. But people from Beverly Hills were in tears when they saw Walpole [New Hampshire]. Los Angeles is high-tech. They come to New England looking for high-touch."

We love these towns: We pay homage in the long lines to board the Nantucket ferry, in all the cute Vermont products, in continuing to think of ourselves in some ways as a nation of small agrarian towns. In the 1980s people moved into rural areas in record numbers. More than five hundred rural counties across the country grew by 14 percent. People left the suburbs for the empty places on the map. Rural traffic within fifty miles of a city has grown five times faster than city traffic in the last twenty years.

Migrations bring change. Some small towns have been stretched like Silly Putty until residents find themselves living in a distorted place that is both familiar and strange, increasingly resembling the cities that they left. People have been asking tough questions: What makes this place a community? Are we losing that?

Throughout New England, towns, neighborhoods, advocacy groups, and governments are scrambling to sustain community life. New Hampshire's Community Cornerstones program is typical: Residents gather to list their towns treasures—old buildings, ponds, views—and then see if they can be saved. Barrington, for example, bought the development rights for a heron rookery. The inventory energized a volunteer group that grew to more than eighty. They assisted at the food pantry, planned a spring peeper festival, looked after some of Barrington's many small cemeteries, ran an Arbor Day program at the middle school and so on. Not all the community treasures are physical properties: Unity identified its annual town meeting and old ballot box; Haverhill its Fourth of July parade; and Sunapee's pride is the opening day of fishing season.

"Can we hang on?" asks Philip B. Herr, a planner from Newton Corner, Massachusetts, who has advised Nantucket, Westwood and Norwood, Massachusetts, and Block Island. More people are realizing the "functional rationale" for compact centers, but the trick is accommodating the car. "The trade-offs keep pushing us apart," Herr says. "It's easier to be dispersed than to be compact. How do we put a twenty-first-century form in a nineteenth-century form? A lot of us are struggling with that."

"We have a romantic sense" of small towns, says Herr. He was helping Peterborough, New Hampshire, plan its future development when he noticed a room hung with paintings of the town. "People come to places like Peterborough and want to take away a piece of it. They'll take a painting of how wonderful it is. There's no cars in any of them."

There is a hunger for community. In Maine, Peter Cox, founder of *The Maine Times*, has held a class of eighth graders spellbound with his description of a tradition in many Italian villages, the *passegiata*. In the evening, at seven, everyone gathers for a stroll around the square. "The kids' faces light up. They all live five miles apart. They were fascinated. They don't know the parents of their friends. They can't just drop in on each other. They can't walk to be near friends."

One of the drawings of a town David Howard has designed shows Main Street in the sweep of a bird's-eye view. At the church a wedding party is departing the front steps. In the back an undertaker is bringing in a coffin for a funeral. That in sum is what Howard is trying to restore to the places we live: life, the ceremonies and the days in between. The village as the stage for all of life, not as a stage set, or tourist attraction or bedroom community of commuters. ("This drawing here," he says, "I could talk to you for 12 solid hours.")

The last forty years of suburban development have wiped out our memory of how to build towns. We are like a stroke victim relearning the rudiments of language again. There is a growing movement of architects like Howard who are looking to revive traditional town design.

We are a long way from the society that built the first villages. In his classic work, *Town Planning in Frontier America*, John W. Reps writes that "public welfare was paramount" in these eighteenth-century villages. "A rough but workable democracy prevailed . . . rarely since that time have important decisions been made about community planning in America with such harmony."

American society is on a much larger scale now, but Howard puts his hope in something that is often overlooked: "New England happened awfully quick," he says. Many villages were built in fifty to seventy years. In Walpole the first houses were built in the 1760s, and the majority of the village followed from about 1780 to 1850. It took just a fraction of New England's long history to build beautiful villages. This is comparable to the average build-out time for a modern residential or office park development, about twenty or thirty years.

The ideal village, as conceived by Howard, takes his town of Walpole for inspiration. Walpole is 185 acres, with 300 dwelling units, five churches, shops, a dairy farm, and a corporate headquarters. His village will cover 200 acres. No one will be more than 1,500 feet from open space. Ten percent of the land in the township will be developed in a compact town, 90 percent in conservation and farming.

There are no opportunities to build new villages this way in New England. The land is too expensive, he says. Howard's firm, the Village Company of New England, is studying the Midwest. They want to take a few farms and build a town that will be a descendant of Nantucket or Walpole: compact, beautiful, and true to its setting. He will not build a Farmtucket pastiche.

Howard has proposed village projects in Canada, the Midwest, and Georgia. Towns are seeing their open space swallowed by the same old sprawling developments. But when they see the village plans with a 1:10 ratio of building lots to open space, they welcome you right in, Howard says. "You go talk about this and everyone thinks you've come from heaven, instead of from the bank. You've got an answer. You're building railroads across the country!" he says, referring to the great railroad building of the 1850s, when the government would do anything to encourage railroads.

After three centuries of settlement on the East Coast, towns are running out of open space. By comparison, there have been twenty centuries of city and town building on the British Isles, and yet there is plenty of open space. We consume land with the passion of a frontier society. "The world population is going to double," says Howard. "We have to build this world all over again."

Howard is not saying that building villages is the solution to all our troubles. "Let's say this village idea applies to only 5 percent of us—that's 12.5 million people—that's a lot."

As he talks he is sketching out a village, showing the flexible design: odd-shaped lots, a bend in the street, big and little houses. "You're building in richness," he says, all the different things people want in their houses and lots, variations on a common theme. He sketches away. "What would you like?" Under his pencil grow the idiosyncrasies of the villages we know and love.

Driving home from Nantucket, we stop to eat at a Chinese restaurant in a shopping plaza right off the interstate. There are only a few other people in the place, lone men, each in a suit and tie, some looking over their paperwork. It's 4 p.m., the salesman's hour of ennui, the lonely hour when the motivational tapes and lectures no longer motivate.

Howard, at least on this trip, never sags. He's still talking about how to stop the way we are consuming the countryside. Just in the few years that I have known him, his town, Walpole, has been walloped by a new shopping plaza out in a cornfield. The stores in town moved out. The familiar catastrophe: the fraying of small-town life. And Nantucket is in the grip of a land rush, large new estates and ordinary houses going for millions. "The place has become a Coca-Cola," Howard says, "something people take for refreshment."

Nantucket missed a chance to follow its own example. Before the recent building boom, land could have been set aside to create two to four other villages, Howard says. No houses would be built on the moors or beach front. "It could have been something that would have lasted for centuries and be an example," he says. The island is 40,000 acres, which is the size of most townships, Howard says, doing one of his customary calculations. You build on 800 acres, one-fortieth of the land. There could be 24,000 people all within walking distance. Then there's 45 square miles left.

Howard is sketching again on napkins as he talks. He may be talking of the next American Revolution, the next change in the way we live, but to get there he will have to be another salesman on the road, selling not restaurant supplies or insurance, but towns.

New England villages are admirable because they are limited. They were built in tight confines, against the surrounding wilderness. They were built of the simplest materials: wood, nails, plaster, brick, stone, mortar, and glass. If this doesn't seem unusual, try to inventory the materials in a modern office, or take stock of the epoxies, solvents, plastics, and fasteners in any aisle of one of those warehouse hardware stores. The graceful place is born of limits: in materials, knowledge, and time.

These old houses are by contemporary taste plain, even severe. One size windows repeated across the front, buttoned up tight with clapboards, but all tied together with a fitness of proportion and a rightness of form. These are houses with no ornament—except the doorway.

The door was ornamental along the best lines, the finest architecture—columns, pediments, dentils, fan lights—allusions to Greek temples, to democratic ideals, to the finest houses in the young republic's city.

A door built this way, Howard says, represents the finest you can have in life. You can't afford this level of detail for the rest of your house, but here in this door is your Mozart. And this doorway is your gift to your neighbors. These doors are what we admire 200 years later. "There's no reason why one out of ten can't be the best. One set of the best silver. That's a rational development of life. You've got to have a little front door in life."

From this start, the towns have seasoned and matured as places. Time has worked them smooth and you cannot imagine, say, that house on the common anywhere else, cannot imagine the earth without that house. The land wears the house.

Old wooden houses in their life of decay and renewal grow toward repose, settle toward the earth. They shape lives toward them, and lives shape them.

Sometimes we know a place has repose at first sight. And other times, a place seeps into us, detail by detail, until we learn, as one carpenter said to me, "the reverence of a nail."

Over "long periods of intimate association between human beings and nature" a landscape may acquire "a quality of blessedness," the biologist Rene Dubos wrote. Taking a phrase from the Indian poet Rabindranath Tagore, he calls this "the wooing of the earth." The phrase, a translation, sounds archaic. We have no contemporary term for gently developing land. We have the bulldozer.

The lost language of villages is symptomatic of a greater loss: a blessedness in the land. Our places lack repose—many of our places are placeless, no where, a manufactured gloom engineered for quick transit.

You can't legislate blessedness. But we can learn to recognize it and make our towns ready to receive it—like grace. Build well, derive a good life from that, and leave it to the next generations to decide how well we have done.

David Howard may get a few new towns built. The first residents, raised on calendar-perfect images, may be a little disappointed. There will not be any hundred-year-old lilacs shouldering close to old houses that sag and waver. There'll be no layering of old family names and half-remembered town legends.

They will find themselves to be the true heirs of the earliest settlers of the first villages. They will face a raw, half-made world surrounded by the wilderness, but not one of the deeps and silences of the forest, but rather of the chaos we have created. They will face the hardest task, and perhaps the most American of all moments: living on the knife-edge of improvisation.

Solace on the Block

❦

Auctioneers love to tell stories. They are like baseball players, door-to-door salesman, and pilots—anyone whose meal ticket is his self-confidence. A humble salesman will never get his foot in the door, and a doubting pilot is better off on the ground.

They spend a lot of time waiting. A busy auctioneer is only actually selling three and a half hours a week—the rest is set-up. Ballplayers are forever waiting on the field, in the dugout, on the bus, in the airport. And pilots are earthbound more than they like. So they talk. Pilots call it hangar flying.

Over lunch, not far from their auction house and school, Col. Ken Martin and his wife Col. Ann Rozelle are talking about the great treasure hunt that is their lives. They are always looking to make a great buy, this time in an ice storm. Perfect weather for bargains.

I have enrolled in their school. This includes lunches, and a chance to also be called colonel, a title some auctioneers have taken since the Civil War.

"We go up to a New Year's auction. It was a snowstorm," Col. Ann says.

"Ice on the roads. Stay off the highways. There'll be nobody there," says Col. Ken.

"We're going to rob and plunder," says Col. Ann.

"Oh yeah! Steal! Plunder! Rob!" Col. Ken says, a happy Viking over his cottage cheese and fruit salad. "We get there and you can't get near the place."

"First of all everybody was there. Second of all," says Col. Ann, "the wind knocked the power out."

"A big Quonset hut with no windows. Pitch black," says Col. Ken.

So what do they do? What sane adults would do when faced with the prospect of freezing to death in an ice storm: They started bidding.

The auctioneer held up pieces of antique glass over kerosene lamps. People in the dark would call out bids. "When you held some of this glass over the kerosene lamps it was like a jewel," says Col. Ann.

A room full of auctioneers, antique dealers, and even a few "civilians" bidding in the dark. This story was my introduction to the Yankee School of Auctioneering in Concord, New Hampshire.

A week in auction school lets you become a witness to one of the most elemental scenes of trade: two people or twenty or forty competing to buy one object. Each auction is a story of greed and desire, loss and gain, and at the center stands the auctioneer.

"That's what gives the auction power," says Emma Bailey, a retired auctioneer. "You go to an auction and you will just simply be aware of all the tension, all the eagerness, all the disappointment that people are suffering. The joy of the person who got a high price but didn't think they were going to get anything because it was a lot of junk. The joy of the person who bought it because they didn't think they'd get it at that easy price."

Pound Em! And What I Assume You Shall Assume

"Last night we knew we had to pound the audience," says Col. Ken. He is sixty-five, a hefty man who has worked as a commercial fisherman. He says the word "pound" with some force and you take notice. "Sometimes you can feel money in the audience and I was right." Col. Ken says that last night he did his best dollar volume ever in the hall. His "hall" is an industrial park between an interstate and the city's sewer works, which makes its presence known on some windy days.

He has applied the lessons of one of New Hampshire's oldest established auctioneers. Nearly 4,000 auctions ago, back in 1951, George Michael learned his most important lesson: "When the chickens are sitting out there, you pluck them."

This is the rough talk of the freest market: The audience is pounded, plucked, intimidated, rushed into a sale. And people love it. Who needs an amusement park?

The auctioneer's creed could be a line from Whitman's *Song of Myself*:

> I celebrate myself, and sing myself
> And what I assume you shall assume.

"I don't let my audience think," Col. Ken boasts. "I am always in control of your mind, whether you know it or not."

The auctioneer establishes his pace—"trains his audience" as Col. Ken says. He gets his audience to bid quickly. After a few bids if Col. Ken repeats the price three times—thirty-five—thirty-five—thirty-five!—the next word will be: sold. And he tells his audience what the object should sell for. "Who'll start this hundred-dollar chair at twenty-five dollars," he'll say.

Traders, salesmen—people who live in the free market—not checkout clerks, not mall sales clerks—understand how with each sale you have to win hearts and minds, sell the sizzle not the steak. There isn't a worldly good that's not wrapped up in human desires.

The auctioneer confronted with a room of full of old furniture and bric-a-brac, worn, exhausted goods, knows that the sizzle of an auction is speed: Act now! Act now! That's what the auctioneer's voice drums out. "I would! I would!" says Col. Ken, as he tries to raise a bid five dollars. And you believe at that moment he would. *And what I assume you shall assume.* But what would he want with three Batman pillowcases?

His hands underlie the urgency, waving people in; come on, come on. He climbs the numbers quickly. "You don't want the sucker to think"—he quickly corrects himself—"the buyer, so called," he tells his class. "You don't want the buyer to get buyer's remorse. What am I doing spending a hundred dollars? Don't let 'em think. Keep talking. If they think, you'll lose them every time."

The worse case of buyer's remorse on record occurred in 193 A.D. when Julius Didas bought the entire Roman Empire at an auction. He bid against the leader of the military coup that had just overthrown the government. The new owner of the empire then "passed a sleepless night; revolving most probably in his mind his own rash folly," reports Edward Gibbon in *The Decline and Fall of the Roman Empire.*

Old Julius Didas had gotten caught up in the moment, caught a little auction fever. He had no time to think and that's what auctioneers want. Pace is everything. Col. Ken fills the room with his voice. Like all auctioneers he has a few "filler" words that he uses like a drum: "And; Now; Dollar."

"Dollar-dollar-dollar, has a nice kick to it," says Col. Ken. "Bid-a-dollar, bid-a-dollar, bid-a-dollar"—he sings—"almost like three-quarter time."

He makes a rocking motion with his hands, his voice picks up the rhythm and becomes a chant:

"Hum, hum, hum," he warms up. "Forty-five—forty-five—forty-five." Good numbers to chant. But "a nasally sixty—fifty—seventy: Horrible. A hun ten, a hun twenty, hun thirty, hun forty." That goes well, but "fifty-five is a horrible number to say." His voice goes up a tone toward the end of each number. Each number has a life. Forty-five conveys a sense of excitement that you had never noticed. And you're not even bidding on anything.

The auctioneer's bid call is like the call of a horse race. In one chute is the object of desire, in the others are the bidders. And they're off! Out comes the cherry breakfront server, and round the track come the bidders: thirty-five—thirty-five now forty-five now forty-five and fifty-five—sixty-five—seventy-five—seventy-five—seventy-five. Sold! And one bidder crosses the finish line with his prize.

People look on and think about joining the race, particularly when the bidding is slow to start, and the auctioneer asks for $5 or $10: "Let's get it going—thirty dollars." No takers. "Ten—I have ten all over the room. Now 15." In silence dozens of people are thinking a variation of this thought: "Thirty dollars—I don't need that—it's nice, sure, but where would it go—ten dollars—hey for ten dollars I could sell that—twenty dollars—Should I jump in? What's it worth?" Sold—$25. "That's all?—I should have bought it. I can't believe I let it go." Next item.

"I'm clicking those numbers off," says Col. Ken, "and I'm thinking: how do I get this guy to bid and why isn't that person bidding and I'm still going forty-five—fifty-five—sixty-five—seventy-five—eighty-five. . . .

"Within a half hour, I can tell you through the bidding, who buys what. I find out you're a furniture buyer. I've got you pegged now. For the rest of the night the minute a piece of furniture comes up, I'm going to pound on you. I'm looking right at you, asking for the first bid. I look at you while I sell to another. I take these blues and I lay them right on you."

On an average night Col. Ken will move four hundred lots. He arrives at work knowing he has to move a heap of tired objects out the door: a bad abstract painting of horses, glass slippers, spatterware, old Coke bottles, crockery and geegaws so awful they should be sold with a BB gun for target practice, half-finished plastic ship models, old photos of grim-faced ancestors now nameless, old colored postcards of London and French cathedrals, panoramic scenes of World War I cemeteries, rickety furniture that makes kindling look noble.

But Col. Ken sees past all that. He has it worked out to a science. "I now relate everything to dollars per minute," he says. He has to make a $5 commission a minute just to break even. Things flow out to the audience, dollars flow in. Col. Ken is the pump. He is handed computer reports every half hour to see if he is ahead or behind. At the end of an auction he'll speed up, moving four, five, or even six small items a minute, a geegaw firecracker finale.

"Anybody can sell quality. But not anybody can sell junk," he says. Once he visited a graduate of his school at an auction. They had Col. Ken stand in, and then stuck him with a bad Scandinavian bedroom set: "Sell it, Ken." He started at $10, almost sold at $25, and finally clawed his way, at $1 a bid to $77. "It was a challenge," he says, smiling.

Selling junk is essential. When it comes time to build the National

Shrine to the Persevering Salesman, those words should inscribed: It takes talent to sell junk. Willy Loman couldn't have said it better.

"The biggest thing you learn in this business is: smile, smile, smile," says Col. Ken. "When you're picking their pockets, you want them to think you're happy when the money is flowing from their pockets to yours.

"Most people pay far too much because of the auctioneer. They work on your greed."

Col. Ken makes it sound easy: pound 'em, pluck 'em. But most salesman's talk has a certain inflationary tendency. Remember they are always building confidence, creating the belief in themselves and their listeners that they are masters of psychology, able to make great sales in a single bound.

There are nights when the chickens keep their feathers. Reggie Geno who runs the Blackwater Auction Company in Enfield, New Hampshire, has had auctions when the "whole crowd sits there with their arms folded: Go ahead and make me bid." At one auction Geno "put up a twenty dollar bill and got twelve-fifty for it. I said, 'You folks are dumb! That's cash! You can go out and buy groceries. Anyone else want one: twenty dollars for twelve-fifty?' No sir—not a hand. So that's how bad it can get."

"Ken enjoys selling furniture," says Col. Ann.

Why?

"I can sell a $250 piece in thirty seconds," Col. Ken says.

Because of the price?

"Greed!—greed!—greed!—greed!—greed!" he leans toward you and stares as if he were calling an auction. "*Greed!*"

"If I sell a $10 item in thirty seconds—$10 I make . . . $2.50 commission. If I sell a $250 item in thirty seconds at 20 percent commission. That's $50. Which one am I going to sell? Come on! Why do you think we sell that stuff first?

"The whole business is a business of greed," he says. He's had other jobs, sold commercial fishing nets and was an engineer before he started in the auction business in 1982, auctioning off fish in Portland, Maine.

"Money. Greed. You can see it every single Thursday in here" on auction night. "It erupts like green slime all over the place. Greed everywhere you look."

Col. Ken's regulars are a restless bunch. On auction night, in a crowd of two hundred to three hundred, there are people in motion all over the hall. A man emerges from the bathroom to bid; another regular is a concealed bidder, shyly signaling from behind a pole. A woman in a black, backless gown moves around so that everyone can see her many times. A couple argues in the fifth row: "Why didn't you bid?" "Why didn't *you*—you said it was such a deal." Up on the block, Col. Ken takes it all in. Out of this swimming confusion, he keeps track of the bidders. Many large men are eating heaps of heart-stopping food. "You gotta have food. You gotta keep people happy," says Col. Ken. The large men load up on food and then load up their "cube vans" with heaps of stuff. Appetite. Greed.

The credo of the auction goer, the bidder, could be: The auctioneer is a sucker. He doesn't know what he has. Gustav Stickley or a pile of sticks, Tiffany glass or a Flintstones jelly jar. He can't know it all. Pluck 'im, pound 'im. They are hunting for a bargain, to strike it rich, hit the mother lode of Annalee dolls, Shaker chairs, Depression glass. And it happens often enough to keep the prospectors out in the hills: the Stickley Morris chair bought at a parking lot flea market for a song, sold for thousands, the Hawthorne letter found behind a painting, the "Tippicanoe & Tyler Too" bottle which was going to be sold for fifty cents, but was rescued by an auction manager and sold on the block for $41,000. These tales make the auction circuit, more campfire gold-rush tales with the same message: Keep looking.

The auctioneers feed the prospecting spirit. Before an auction Ronald Rosenbleeth announces the policy at his Henniker, New Hampshire, hall. "If it's chipped you keep it. But also if I say it's silver plate and it's sterling silver you keep it."

Col. Ken says directly: "I like to fan the fires of greed." When someone requests that an item be put up, or someone has left a bid, Col. Ken makes a point of telling everyone. "The greed kicks in: Ah, somebody wants that, it must be worth something."

Here one enters the circular logic of the marketplace: Something is in demand because people want it. The auctioneer just jumps in and stirs the pot. An item is worth what people think it's worth. If there are two people competing he's got a chase. (If there's just one, well, he has a few tricks.)

"What sets value is not rarity. What creates value is desirability," says George Michael.

When two people are bidding furiously against each other, the emotions of an auction are hung out like laundry.

"What you see is the whole audience is hushing down and they're look-ing at that box lot [a box of small items] and it's 185—195—205—215—225—235—245," says Col. Ken.

They're following the auctioneer's hands like they're watching a tennis match. The place quiets down. "You can hear a pin crash to the floor," he says. It's as if the dance floor had cleared to watch one couple tango.

"They're thinking 'What the hell was in there that I didn't see?'"

"I looked in that box," says Col. Ann. "The auctioneer is saying, 'I looked in that box.' The crew is saying, 'What the hell is in that box?'"

Merchants who are burdened with longer work weeks and far greater overhead look at such scenes with disbelief. Back in 1828, merchants were losing so much business to the auction trade they tried to have them banned. The crowds "obey his call with a degree of obsequiousness that allows him to do as much business in three hours as the majority of shopkeepers do in a week," they charged. The auctioneers defended their buyers: "We contend, that in this free and happy republic, every man has a right to be ruined in his own way."

Not only is greed in play, but also jealousy. Ninety percent of Col. Ken's regulars are antique dealers. Sometimes if they see their colleagues getting a good buy, they'll jump in and "bump" the price, raise the price just to take away a bargain. He's seen competitors pay thousands more than something was worth just to win out in a grudge match. "Malice," he says. "You pray for it."

Sometimes the bidding needs a little jump start. Some auctioneers will take a bid from the wall, or "bounce one off the rafters." It doesn't happen often at auctions and it is difficult to spot. I have never seen Col. Ken do it, but he tells his class: "You get bored on the block. You've got to do some things for fun. Don't get too Puritanical. Just have fun. For Chrissake what's two and half dollars if you took the bid off the wall. It's not illegal. It's just not ethical."

Many years ago, George Michael was at an auction. Someone in the audience challenged the auctioneer. "Who gave you that three-dollar bid?"

"My Aunt Sophie," the auctioneer replied. "She's sitting up there in the rafters. Would Aunt Sophie please stand up? A huge lumberjack stood up. There were no further questions."

Possession

What do people want? Why are they drawn to the auction? Why sit in the dark in an ice storm?

Greed is an easy answer. But why be greedy about all this old stuff? Why Hummel figurines or old Coca-Cola signs? There are many other things to be greedy about—money, for example—it's easier to hoard, or wine.

For the collector, auction going is a quest for completeness. That's the power of a collection—it closes the circle, makes one thing perfect, sets the collector on a quest: You must have Dedham dinner plates—you'll die if you don't find more in the bunny pattern. But of course you won't really die. It's a manageable quest. And this is why so many collectors when they reach the promised land, sell their collections and set off into the desert once more.

"Don't sell five chairs or seven dishes," George Michael says. "Take one out. Five chairs kill it. Round the set off. Now it's a perfect set. If I sold them five they'd be hunting the rest of their life for the sixth and be mad as hell at me."

Once after an auction, Michael called a woman over who had bought a set of china. "I'm going to give you a present," he said. "Here's a few extra pieces."

"'You deceived me!' the woman said angrily. 'I thought I bid on a complete set.' She stomped off indignant."

Chairs and dishes at least have a use. The collector has that excuse. But what about a piece of cheese more than five hundred years old?

At a Sotheby's auction in 1993, Simon Perry of Maidstone, Kent, England bought a one-inch cube of Tibetan cheese. He paid $1,500, but he "would have paid anything for it," he said.

His cheese club had taken up a collection and he went off to London to bid. The cheese had been in England a hundred years. The French were also bidding. "We couldn't let the cheese leave England," he said.

But why this cheese? he was asked.

It's a "named cheese," he said, just like diamonds have names. This one was called "Eye of the Tiger." It's a true relic. Some records indicate that it may go back to the thirteenth century and the fall of Constantinople. He thinks the cheese is made of either goat milk or rancid yak milk.

Would he eat it?

Oh no. It's too dried out. (The little cube is wrapped with a string around it.) Possessing it is the most important thing, he said. There'll be a celebration tonight at the pub, he said. No champagne though, orange squash raised to toast a piece of centuries-old rancid yak milk.

Col. Ken and Col. Ann go to auctions on their day off. They once went to a *worm* auction: worm castings sold to the highest bidder.

He got started as auctioneer because he had piled up so much stuff that his wife made him become an auctioneer so he could sell it. "If we don't do something we're going to collapse the barn," Col. Ann told him.

"He's collected almost everything I can think of," she says. "He collected yardsticks. He collected slide rulers, ice picks. Heavy metal—"

"Wrought iron, tools, equipment, machinery, old industrial things," explains Col. Ken. "If I gave you a twenty-minute tour of my barn, you'd just go out shaking your head and say, 'This man's an idiot.'" He laughs a little.

"Have you ever been to an auction and somebody points to pile of old metal and says 'Anybody give me five dollars for it?' Well," says Col. Ann, "he'd take ten truckloads of crap, heavy metal."

Is it usable?

"In my mind . . . maybe," says Col. Ken. "It's debatable." He thinks some more: "It's still in the barn." He seems pleased as he contemplates his hoard.

A giddiness sets in with some collectors. As one gets closer to the edge, a feeling overcomes one: I can have 1,500 radios, 300 cats, 800 Barbie Dolls, Majolica soup tureens without end. There's no one to tell me not to. And many people do sail over the edge. Given the prevalence of our many national psychoses, this has to be one of the more benign. Some people want power, some want money, some just want to be left alone, and some want that rare Barbie doll, the first one with the holes in the feet for the stand. (This is your squirrel brain talking, that part of the cerebral cortex known to neurologists as the Medulla Rodentia.)

Driving to lunch one day, we stop at a traffic light across from where a gas station is being demolished. Big yellow machines are eating into brick, cinderblock, plumbing, window frames. Hunks fall to the ground, as if out of a hog's mouth. Piles of debris. "Look at that," says Col. Ken. "They're just going to throw that away." When the light changes to green, Col. Ann has to tell him. In his mind he may be weighing the rubble, sorting it, auctioning it off.

Col. Ken even has the first thing he ever bought at an auction: a square trunk for one dollar. It says "human blood" on it.

Why did he buy that?

"I still don't know."

We Never Forget the Old Home

Many collections are restorations, trying for some harmony, some idea of the world made whole again, sometimes from childhood. Toys are "hot" right now, auctioneers will tell you.

You can sense this desire most acutely at auctions held on site at the house. Auctioneers like house auctions because items coming right out of a house are more desirable to dealers and collectors. The auctioneer stands to make 20 percent more than if the auction were held in a hall, says Col. Ken.

An auction at an old house speaks deeply to people. There is a hunger for home, the accretion of generations—someone else's family bible and family picture. Clutter that is wood and porcelain and silver.

I remember one auction at a house in Nelson, New Hampshire. There were maybe five hundred people all looking through the crumbling innards of a household dragged out under a tent: a draft card notice from 1910, a porch load of moldering books—to be sold in one lot—framed photos in sepia of old stern women, photos of houses standing in piebald hills—the same houses now in the woods.

The whole still had coherence, had grown in toward itself. This was one complete natural outcropping. By the evening it had gone to the winds, to Massachusetts, New York, and Connecticut.

The antiquing hordes, *Kovels' Guide* in hand, were ready to jump for Shaker measures, Depression glass, and all manner of sagging wicker, worn maple, soapstone, silver, paper—all saying age and stability and the stolidness of a thousand baked-bean and ham dinners.

These are the kind of cluttered, close rooms that caused people in the 1950s to flee to new tract houses in the suburbs with big picture windows and a few spidery pieces of Danish modern furniture. Houses that were all light and airy as if the preceding centuries had never occurred.

Emma Bailey knows what some auction goers are looking for: solace. Bailey was an auctioneer in Brattleboro, Vermont, in the 1950s. She billed herself as America's first woman auctioneer. She sold from a barn at her house, back in an era when the pounding and plucking of an audience was a little more leisurely. Auctioneers today, she says, "just want to sell, sell, sell."

When she was a little girl, Bailey glimpsed her first auction. She was in a horse-drawn wagon on the way home from school, when the driver stopped at a house with a picket fence. The front yard "was scattered with furniture and farm tools, as if a cyclone had just struck out of the blue."

She wanted to know what had happened. "There's no family left to care," she was told.

For years after, Bailey hated auctions; they meant the dissolution of a family, the end of a story. But once she was older with a family, she caught the auction bug and came to see it differently: These objects went on to a new life with another family, "passing on to do more good." "Sold for twenty dollars to where they will be used, loved, and passed on," she would sometimes say at her auctions.

People are seeking the solace of old things, Bailey says. They want a connection to the past, to own something from their grandmother's generation. (Is all this pursuit of old objects about touch? Looking for a reassuring touch, warmth, love, continuity.) Driven by such sentiment, they'll often pay too much, she says.

The most fervent collectors are driven by love and denial, she says. "There's always a sense of having been denied that makes them want to have it. It's a sense of denial from childhood or a sense of love . . . the mother did have it and she may have sold it." Once they buy the object, they will quiet that feeling, she says.

She remembers a man from the Midwest who brought her an unusual assignment. His grandmother had left Vermont for the West, and always mourned the move. He had found his grandmother's diary, which listed in detail every piece of furniture that had been auctioned seventy-five years earlier. She had carefully noted who bought each piece. He had Bailey buy back every piece she could find. He retired to Vermont and built a house on his grandmother's land. "He wanted forgiveness from something or other," says Bailey.

That's the way it is at auctions. People bid and you have to guess about hidden meanings. A rocker may be just a rocker, but to one person it may represent the home they lost, the unrecoverable past, and to another, the home they hope to create. Each auction is a story of greed and desire, loss and gain.

When they hold up old mirrors at Col. Ken's auctions you can see those emotions: The whole crowd is reflected, pensive and wondering. The mirrors are eerie. In their wavering surfaces, a ripple in the stream of time, the old life and the new mingle. Do they reflect old lives — in the way we see light every night from stars long dead?

Looking into those old mirrors, sometimes I think about that man who bought back his grandmother's antiques and undid her Western exile. I have just one question. There, in the house, with the old things back in place, did he live happily ever after?

REPOSE

I. The World at Six

Some required scenes from the evening TV news:

Police. Always on the scene too late. The men in blue are in the background. The detectives speak to the camera, and at times seem like Catholic school boys just off the playground, their jackets and ties askew from basketball. They talk cop: "The perpetrator entered the premises, fired two shots. . . ."

Police, ten-second version. Just police cars surrounding the crime scene, which is marked off with yellow tape.

Neighbors. They exist to say: 1. But he was such a quiet boy. 2. How could this happen here? 3. Everything is different now.

The Dead. Not shown, increasing their presence. Sometimes we see the spot where they were slain—usually just another ordinary slab of sidewalk, or acre of woods; the banality of horror.

The Community. A big hall, a meeting. Outside, a teacher or student or a parent says, "This is awful. He was so nice." The other flavor: the angry zoning/school board meeting. Film clip: righteous citizen; irritated, snapping board member. Pan of crowd, hooting, or clapping.

The State Legislature. Old men in ornate rooms. Inquisitors on a podium behind a long desk. Gavel pounding. Mystifying rituals. Sometimes citizens stand outside with signs to protest, or speak to "demand" something.

Sometimes a legislator is indicted. He's seen running through a gauntlet of cameras. No legislation is ever followed or explained. Only emotions register.

The Experts. "Boil all water." "The x, y, or z planned to cut up your neighborhood will not harm you." "Take all sensible precautions." Who hired the experts? Why are they experts? What's their expertise, their track record? No one asks.

Religion. Good for certain set pieces: Confrontations with fundamentalists. Fifteen seconds of a St. Patrick's Day parade. Film-blip of the Christmas toy drive. Funerals. Prayer vigils at crime scenes—a third-day story. Jews make an appearance when a vandal desecrates a temple or graveyard.

The Weather. The only fully "rounded" character on the news. The Weather has moods, dimensions, Old Testament vengeance and beneficence. Every crevice of the Weather's personality is explored. The ancient Greeks similarly discussed their Gods. Much data is presented: record temperatures, how the rest of the country fares at His hands and did in 1910 or 1888. Only the Weather has a history. Communities, religions, governments do not. Victims have obits: a two- or three-step walk to a cruel fate.

Sports. In season: quick-cut footage of scoring. Locker room: a sweaty athlete says, yeah we won, we lost. In court: dressed up, restrained with his handlers/lawyers at his side. Seen going and coming from court. Maybe a short lawyer statement: Not guilty of assault, rape, drunk driving. . . .

Highlight films: Much merriment with films of men falling down, crashing into walls, each other. Send in the clowns.

Culture. A new movie opens. A stale Broadway play arrives in town. A rock star old enough to receive *Modern Maturity* from the AARP fills the arena with a show conceived to hide his ripped-up voice: giant-screen TVs, fireworks, etc. The star promotes the movie/play/rock show by offering a snippet of victimology: She/He is back! having overcome drugs, drink, riches, rickets, a lack of talent.

The World. No foreign news. Or at most fifteen seconds: 100,000 people in the street marching for freedom, risking their lives. Ho-hum. Just where the hell is that country anyway?

"Special Report." After the news. The anchor urgently divulges his information: Shots fired. Witnesses say as many as nine shots fired. People injured. One may be a cop. To repeat. Shots fired. . . . He is delivering the telegraph of a disaster, the disordered way facts and rumors come in before they are a report—or even a sentence.

We are all well trained in this drill from political assassinations and natural disasters.

The camera is a live feed—ambulances racing away, cops standing around, movement. The picture is sharp. "Here's the ambulance bringing one person to the hospital," says the anchor, who has nothing to report.

Then an eyewitness is saying what he saw or rather heard. Nine shots maybe. He was up in the office building. Now he's spelling his last name, as the anchor starts talking again: Shots fired. . . .

What is served by these on-the-scene reports? We get a sense of the disorder of the moment, we partake in the uncertainty. If there is enough blood, we are voyeurs. A short sentence and a bulletin with some known facts would be better, even if the news team must wait twenty minutes before going on the air.

Sum total of the World at Six: People die in the streets, at bars, in bed at home. Actors and sports stars strut the stage. Lawyers tell us no one is guilty. Religious leaders are on call for mourning. Citizens are thrust forward to personify emotions: sorrow, fear, anger, hate. The Weather looms. We look on, knowing that the police will arrive too late. That it will rain on our one day off, and that there is no belief, or government, no higher calling or achievement. Our main concern is to stay on the right side of the yellow crime scene tape.

II. The World Beyond the World at Six

Peter Acker has risen at 2 a.m. in Vermont. He drives for hours through the darkness toward Walden Pond in Massachusetts. "I'm desperate to find those windows of quiet which will allow you to kind of shoot yourself back and imagine yourself at a point in time where Walden and the woods around it were just beautiful harmonious places to be, where the woods rang with the wood thrush, and on a windy day the wind is all that you hear.

"But we'll see what kind of wind we have this morning," he tells me. "Hopefully everyone stayed out late last night and are too tired to get up early."

He is seeking something that may be impossible: the sounds of Walden as Henry David Thoreau may have heard them. The sound of the world before the automobile and airplane, lawnmower and chainsaw, radio and cell phone.

"If I am lucky, I'll get a minute of usable sound," he says.

He will be in the woods by 5 a.m. These are hunter's hours and Peter Acker is hunting silence. "What I'm hunting for is a vanishing species. There's less and less every year. There are spots close to my home, that I go to purely for recreation, when I just want to go out and listen, that in years past have been quiet. Granted, not quiet for ten, fifteen minutes at a stretch without hearing a truck or a plane, but pretty darn quiet. And a lot of those places are gone."

He is recording Walden as part of a project to capture the natural sounds of the places Thoreau portrayed in his travels around Concord, at Cape Cod, and in the Maine Woods. For other projects, he has also re-corded the sounds of winter and spring at Acadia National Park, and the rainforest canopy in Peru.

As we drive through the dark, Acker talks quietly with the assured tone of a professional radio voice. He makes his living by doing radio voice-overs and commercials, and narrating corporate videos. Or as he says, he's half Madison Avenue and half in the woods. "I create the noise, but then I try to get away from it." His business is called Radio-land Productions.

For his nature recordings, he does not mix in sound. He will not fabri-cate a scene, layering in bird calls from different places, editing out ma-chine noise. This is his great challenge. "For me, success is uninterrupted quiet for three or four minutes," he says. He drives nearly 40,000 miles a year, he says regretfully, often to come away with nothing.

Walden Pond, pressed in by Route 2, not far from Interstate 95, is his most difficult subject. "I'm walking through the woods and I turn every-thing on and it seems like 95 is just screaming at me through the head-phones."

At Walden, he was pushed back into the trenches, literally: into a natural gully of only 500 square feet on the other side of the railroad tracks. In the middle of the day, when the air is denser and sound doesn't travel as far, "it's this little pocket of quiet. I've gotten a couple of minutes of decent sound there."

"You can find little patches of quiet in the most amazing spots," Acker says. The province of quiet is shrinking. Silence survives like now-rare prairie plants living along railroad tracks.

He started first with *The Maine Woods*, delighted by Thoreau's extensive descriptions of sound. "He awoke in the middle of the night to hear the sound of wings flapping as it passed over his head. In northern Maine, at that period of time, it's almost the absence of sound that is there most of the time. And when sound does occur it's like a bold stroke of a red paint brush on a white wall. It stands out."

In our time, the Maine woods are not as quiet. On the west branch of the Penobscot, near Chesuncook Lake, he was staying up all night to record loons. "Because they're so elusive, all you can do is get yourself to what you think is a good spot and just hope." Along about midnight, one jet after another broke the silence, seventeen in just one hour. He was under an international jet path. "And there were some beautiful loon choruses during that hour."

His most successful recording was on Cape Cod: eighteen unbroken minutes of the world sounding like the world. It was 4:30 a.m. The waves were only one to two feet, breaking every five seconds; very gentle, rhythmic waves, he says, very much the hunter.

He set his microphone in dunes under a camouflage netting in a thicket of low shrubs. Chickadees landed on the shrubs and on the microphone. On the recording, you can hear their wing beats.

"When you're out on the shoreline when it's early in the morning and you're the only one on the beach and the waves are crashing and the birds are waking up in the dunes behind you, you can imagine yourself there in the mid-to-late 1800s when Thoreau was there, you can almost envision yourself in that time. But you retreat from the beach a few hundred yards and it's very clear you're in the twentieth century."

We have stopped in the Estabrook Woods. After his frustration at Walden Pond, Acker has widened his search to include the woods where Thoreau walked. Acker unloads his gear from the pick-up truck: a mannequin's head on a pole, and a shoulder bag. The head is a $6,000 microphone he has named Max. This binaural stereo set-up allows him to make a "three-dimensional sound portrait. This is the closest you can get to human hearing." He places a black curly wig on top of the head, which aids the sound. It looks like some kind of techno-voodoo act, as if he was prospecting for spirits. Acker puts on headphones, checks a few settings on the recording equipment in his bag, and he sets out down the dirt road into the woods holding the head aloft. He is, he acknowledges, a strange sight.

He stops and kneels down beside the microphone pole, listening to his headphones. It is a chilly May morning. He can see his breath.

It's only 5 a.m. but there's a distant thrumming. It's Route 2, miles away. It's the low-frequency noise that carries, Acker had said earlier, "it's the rumble, almost this constant vibration of civilization, just this chugging, churning of humanity." This low roar is what our world now sounds like: always something on the move.

We walk to the shore of a pond. Acker had scouted out this location on another visit. Mist is moving over the water. There are geese and ducks. Across the pond, the sun is rising, a blade of pale yellow light cutting across clouds of mauve, and a deeper purple. Acker crouches at the pond's edge. The mannequin head looks out at the sunrise.

The geese are calling. One flies in low right over his head, calling to two geese out on the pond and landing with a loud splash. This is perfect. Listening to the recording with headphones, you would hear the goose as it passed from back to front. But a jet is taking off at an air base some miles away, and that noise washes right in. For a moment we had joined up with a time before this time, but we are wrenched back.

Flights are starting at Hanscom, Acker says. He may come away with nothing this morning.

Among the small group of nature recordists, they talk of saving places for quietude, Acker said on our drive down. "We all want to see areas preserved, but how do you do that? It's a difficult thing because the average person is not aware of how far sound travels. Road noise can travel eight to twelve miles. You can hear the hum of a powerline up to a quarter, a half, a mile away. Chainsaws, two or three miles. Jet airplanes, ten to fifteen miles. If you're standing on a spot that's quiet, how do you go about protecting that, short of buying all the land for miles around?

"How do we as a civilization, or a community of people, place a value on that, when there are people who want to live out on the edge of that woods?

"I wish I had the answer. I think we'd all be better for it. If we afford that same protection for what we see, shouldn't we also be sensitive to the scenes that we hear? Sound is a forgotten resource. I don't think people are aware of it."

We start to leave. The jets overhead, the thrumming of distant autos, have won again. Walking down the road, he stops, and without a word, returns to the pond. "When I go out, I'm really led around by my ears," he had told me earlier.

The sky brightens. There are blues and reds, yellows and oranges, and the sun itself above the horizon. The robins are waking up. Red-wing blackbirds sing, geese call. And for a moment the world belongs to the birds alone. We are looking in at a scene of a thousand, thousand mornings. He walks back from the pond smiling. He can't tell until he returns to the studio, but he may have a small moment of repose. Peter Acker has his trophy for the morning: ordinary time.

This century has been a race to fill the world with noise. When the airplane was new, thousands would wait all day just for a glimpse of flight. During nine days in August 1911, three million people jammed Chicago to see an unprecedented gathering of aviators in America, more than thirty in all. There were even eight airplanes in the sky at once. The "heavens fill with commerce," Alfred Lord Tennyson had prophesied, "the heavens fill with shouting." Today, the sky, the wilderness, our national parks, the ocean, are all filled with noise.

On winter weekends, Yellowstone National Park has the highest carbon monoxide levels in the nation, higher than any city. Each year 140,000 snowmobiles crowd the park—gatekeepers at the park entrances get headaches, dizziness, and nausea from the exhaust. The town of West Yellowstone, Montana, rents 1,400 snowmobiles on a good weekend. Winter brings the town $30 million. Noise is good business.

Sight-seeing flights are overwhelming the Grand Canyon. There are nearly 100,000 flights over the canyon each year, a $250 million industry which is growing faster than predicted. The Park Service and the FAA devised a map of allowed air corridors, but that failed to restore the "natural quiet."

The Grand Canyon is so noisy that the National Park Service, after years of study, proposals, legislation, and complicated interagency agreements, could at most stake out this "policy decision": "a substantial restoration of natural quiet in the Grand Canyon will require that there be natural quiet in half or more of the park for most of the day."

Almost as many visitors say they come to the park for "natural quiet" (90 percent) as those who come to "view natural beauty." But quiet means different things to people. Twenty percent of visitors say they are annoyed by the sounds of low-flying helicopters and airplanes. They want to complain to somebody. But another 20 percent hear the noise and want to sign up for a flight.

If the Park Service plan were carried out, with limits on flights, changed air corridors, and incentives for quiet planes being phased in for fifteen years, the best that could be hoped for is that eventually "forty-four percent of the park would experience natural quiet 100 percent of the time." If no action is taken "less than one percent of the park would experience 100 percent natural quiet."

"It is a serious problem in search of a measured solution," says a report to Congress. "The National Park Service considers it akin to the proverbial canary in the mine; finding solutions should not be delayed while the duration of the canary's song is measured." The Park Service plan was denied in favor of some modest changes. The Grand Canyon is just one of ninety-eight national parks compromised by airplane noise.

Trying to achieve a percentage of quiet seems like a reasonable approach, until one realizes that "natural quiet," as the park service calls it, is an absolute. You either have it or you don't. Consider the sanity of Taos Pueblo.

Taos Pueblo, one of the oldest settlements in North America, was suffering from airplane noise. The FAA had proposed a commercial flight route over the Blue Lake Wilderness. Private sight-seeing flights were also increasing. "During our annual Blue Lake pilgrimage, our People were buzzed by low-flying Cessna aircraft, sixty to eighty feet high attempting to film the sacred 'Journey to Life,'" they wrote to Senator Daniel Inouye in 1992. And two military bases were sending forty to seventy flights a day. B-1 bombers were refueling high overhead, echoing off the mountain passes, and making low level runs through the canyons.

"Under the traditional ways of Taos Pueblo, air is part of the 'sacred realm,'" they wrote to the National Congress of American Indians in 1992. "Our ceremonial ways protect all things of the Earth and all things overlying the earth. It is impossible for us to conceive of adequately carrying forth our traditional responsibilities when we can no longer control what happens within the sacred realm of the 'upper domain.' Among our people, it is understood that there is no separation between Earth and the realm overlying Earth. It is an inseparable extension of life and the responsibilities toward life."

We have destroyed the repose of even bigger places than the Grand Canyon. We have filled the oceans—70 percent of the planet—with noise. Until fairly recently the ocean was too big, too deep for us to pollute with noise. The mysteries of the ocean live beyond our hearing.

"Whales are acoustic animals," says Katy Payne, who discovered the songs of the humpback whales. "Their lives are informed not by what they see but by what they hear." The courtship songs of humpback whales change from year to year, rhyming and refraining like our own poetry. Dolphins and orcas chart their realm with echoes, finding food, communicating, avoiding predators. Blue and finback whales don't have annual gathering spots for mating and feeding; they find each other using very-low-frequency sound, which travels across oceans. Seals, walruses, fish, sea turtles, and shrimp use sound in ways that are not yet understood.

Into the ocean we have thrown the noise of deep-sea oil rigs, supertankers, and many smaller ships. "Each sound by itself is probably not a matter for concern," said Sylvia Earle, formerly chief scientist at the National Oceanic and Atmospheric Administration. But taken together, "the high level of noise is bound to have a hard, sweeping impact on life in the sea."

Two recent underwater projects may add so much noise that some scientists say they could fundamentally alter the life of the seas. Attempting to measure global warming, in 1995 scientists began one of the biggest experiments ever: broadcasting loud, low-frequency sound waves from California to New Zealand. The Acoustic Thermometry of Ocean Climate (ATOC) measures the ocean's temperature.

But even this experiment is dwarfed by a new sonar system the Navy is testing: low-frequency active sonar. It is ten thousand times more powerful than the scientific experiment. The Navy plans to use it in 80 percent of the world's oceans.

And yet: "At this time, essentially nothing is known about the auditory after-effects of exposure to intense sound in marine mammals, fish, or invertebrates," reported a panel of specialists convened by the National Research Council in 1994.

There have been a few studies that show that the smallest sounds can cause significant disruption: Whales change course to avoid the noise of an average outboard motor, and abandon breeding grounds when boat traffic increases. On a larger scale, when low-frequency sounds were broadcast through five ocean basins in a 1994 acoustical experiment, sperm whales fell silent for thirty-six hours. These whales locate food by sound. This silence may have represented an enforced fast.

Sailors used to hear the mermaids singing, the sirens calling. We have grown deaf. If we had to depend on our hearing to survive, we would be dead.

What has been lost? Quiet. The sound of running water and bird song. But the loss is even greater than this. It is the loss of emptiness, of what the Japanese call *ma*.

"Ma is in the gaps between the stepping stones, in the silence between the notes in music, in what is made when a door slides open," Michael Benedikt writes in *For an Architecture of Reality*. "When a child's swing

reaches the point of neither rising nor falling and is momentarily weightless . . . there is ma. . . . When we speak of the 'draw' of a good fireplace,
when we feel the pull of an empty room for us to enter and dwell there,
when we see in something incomplete the chance for continuation or find
in things closed a gate . . . there is emptiness." There is *ma*.

Emptiness. Space for nothing. That sounds extravagant; it is essential.
The particular cadence of a place lives in such silences. When we are
touched by the spirit of holy places, it's this emptiness that often allows us
to enter that space. In casual conversation, we sometimes call such places
"breathing spaces," which is exactly correct.

We see this on vacations; people crowd the seashore or mountains,
milling about as if they were looking for something they had lost. Even
heretics want to be believers on their vacation. They want to "get away"
but also get to someplace else—find a way into that vanished emptiness,
stillness, silence. They may end up buying little trinkets for their living
room, but I see that as a small talisman of their hunger for that missing
solace.

When we have overrun ourselves with ourselves, killed the thing we
love, we have lost silence, lost *ma*. We have excommunicated ourselves
from the once-beloved place, and we can find no way home again.

We have invented our way here. All this noise is recent. It began with the
steam engine, with the gas engine, with the ringing of a telephone bell.
From the book of unintended consequences:

"It was Dr. Bell's custom to work at night when there were no distract-
ing noises, though there were few of these at Hammondsport even during
the day," aviator Glenn Curtiss recalled in 1912. Alexander Graham Bell
had founded the Aerial Experiment Association. Bell would sleep to noon.
"No one was allowed to wake him for any reason."

"The rest of us were up early in order to take advantage of the favorable
flying conditions during the early morning hours. Dr. Bell had a strong
aversion to the ringing of the telephone bell. . . . I occasionally went into his
room and found the bell stuffed with paper, or wound around with towels.

"'Little did I think when I invented this thing,' said Dr. Bell, one day
when he had been awakened by the jingling of the bell, "that it would rise
up to mock and annoy me.'"

Dr. Bell is a fussing old Luddite by today's standard. What would he do
in a world of beeping pagers and watches, cell-phone chatter, elevator
Muzak, car alarms, and television that is spreading into once-public
places? Advertisers are eager to add to the four hours of television a day
that Americans watch on average. That adds up to sixty days a year, two

months lost to television. Advertisers are like oil field geologists: Once the big fields have been pumped dry, they find new ways to squeeze oil out of the ground. In places where people were once unplugged—doctors' offices, airport lounges, the food courts of shopping malls—special TV networks have been set up. Mercifully, an effort to create the Checkout Channel in supermarkets folded. (But there are, reportedly, free blood pressure checkers, that once inflated, play a commercial at their prey.)

"Nobody tries silence," says Henry LaBalme, director of TV Free America which organizes the National TV Turnoff Week. "Silence doesn't make any money."

"Nothing has changed the nature of man so much as the loss of silence," Max Picard wrote in *The World of Silence*. "The earth was once no less occupied than it is today, but it was occupied by silence. . . . Man did not need to know everything; the silence knew it all for him. And as man was connected with the silence, he knew many things through the silence."

The world revealed itself in omens. In the silent age, omens had power. "The silent flight of birds and the quiet motions of nature, could easily move into the human world" and be at home there.

"In silence" we are "confronted once again by the original beginning of all things: everything can begin again, everything can be re-created."

The World of Silence was first published in 1948, in German, after the noise of war. The book is a series of pensées. There are chapters on children, peasants, the human face, ego, love, illness, and hope, but there is no chapter on war and silence. Picard's book is a prayer for peace, a peace deeper than political treaties.

"The heaven of silence no longer covers the world of ideas and things today, restraining them with its weight and pressure.

"Two menacing structures face each other today: the non-world of verbal machinery, which is out to dissolve everything into the noise of words, and the non-world of mechanized things, which, detached from language, is waiting only for a loud explosion to create a language of its own."

War must have been most painful to Picard, who is as finely attuned to the qualities of silence as a plein-air painter is to the richness of light. This how Picard describes the art of the old world:

"In the pictures of the old masters, people seem as though they had just come out of the opening in a wall; as if they had wriggled their way out with difficulty. They seem unsafe and hesitant because they have come out too far and still belong more to silence than to themselves. . . . If you look at a group of these people together in a picture by one of the old masters—people who have each as it were just stepped out of the wall of silence—it is as though they were all gathered together in a waiting room, waiting for the great opening of silence to appear before them through which they can all disappear again." Today, he says, we believe in "movement for its own sake."

For Picard, silence is lying in wait like a "forgotten animal from the beginning of time. . . . Sometimes all the noise of the world today seems like the mere buzzing of insects on the broad back of silence."

Good poems, worthy conversations, friendship itself, Picard says, have repose, places of emptiness, *ma*.

"Speech came out of silence, out of the fullness of silence. There is something silent in every word, as an abiding token of the origin of speech. . . . When two people are conversing with one another, however, a third is always present: Silence is listening. That is what gives breadth to a conversation. . . .

"Words that merely come from other words are hard and aggressive. Such words are also lonely, and a great part of the melancholy in the world today is due to the fact that man has made words lonely by separating them from silence."

Picard's gospel of silence is in retreat. All that is left is muteness, he says. The particular copy of his book that I read has itself been mute. Called from storage at a state university library, it has been taken out only three times in the last forty years.

"Is it not likely that when the country was new and men were often alone in the fields and forest they got a sense of bigness outside themselves that has now in some way been lost," Sherwood Anderson wrote in a letter in the 1920s. "I can remember old fellows in my home town speaking feelingly of an evening spent on the big empty plains. It had taken the shrillness out of them. They had learned the trick of quiet."

In the biographies of men and women of this era, one often comes across a large silence. There are years on the farm, or in a small town, or a crowded tenement, years hidden from view, hinted at only in a letter or two, or a neighbor's recollection. In later life, when tested by tragedy, the person—a president, a reformer, an artist—retreats again from the biographer's view. Though the biographer may quote friends, diaries, and psychologists, he is held at a distance. There is a resolve that hides from explanation. This is the core of silence; it's where we each know our own true self as well it can be known. It is where also, if defeated, people retreat, leaving only the outer self, the public hero, to carry forth making speeches, collecting honors and the daily mail.

"There is also more silence in one person than can be used in a single life," writes Picard. "That is why every human utterance is surrounded by a mystery."

I was talking with someone who had visited Grover Cleveland's fishing camp in New Hampshire. We are used to Presidential pomp: helicopters and jets, sprawling family compounds. President Cleveland's fishing camp from the 1890s was a little cabin with a few cots. He would get up early and go fish—not to entertain some visiting politician, not for a photo op, and not as part of some plan to be a well-rounded person. The man wanted to be left alone to fish. We would do well if the next man or woman we call on to lead us has also a passion for solitude.

"The age into which we are born is fundamentally opposed to tranquillity," wrote Karlfried Graf Von Durckheim in *The Japanese Cult of Tranquility*. "Yet perhaps at no time more than today are men so filled with longing for stillness, and so ready to yield themselves to it."

"Behind it all lurks an awareness of total destruction. Millions of men and women seem paralyzed at the annihilation of everything that once gave purpose to their lives. They are hypnotized by the destructive forces obliterating the past and undermining the future, and they are powerless to break the spell," Von Durckheim wrote in 1960. "Our innermost human self is imperiled."

Threatened from without and poisoned from within, we have lost our ability to perceive tranquility, he says. We fear it, says Von Durckheim, "as though stillness were a terrifying void." But we never lose our desire for "what is indestructible": tranquility.

"Deep in the heart of man there exists a hidden knowledge that true tranquility such as the soul desires is something more than a mere beneficial lack of noise . . . that it is even more than the pre-supposition of spiritual life . . . it is the actual experiencing of fulfillment of life." "True happiness" lies in "genuine stillness."

A note at the Vernal Equinox:

More light. World still frozen. Days of icy rain. The snow is like glazed, heavy crockery. We walk on top of the snow; kick a piece of ice and it skitters downhill and off into the woods. We are ice bound. Houses, cars, snowmobiles scuttled, frozen in, locked in place. I think of a belt clamp I have, pulled tight.

Birds empty the feeder with gusto: cardinals, finches, blue jays, juncos, and a rakish evening grosbeak. Saw the comet last night. Eclipse also.

There's a group of us for dinner before we go out to watch the stars.

One friend balances an egg on the table. Some people believe that you can only balance an egg on its end during an equinox. Scientists say this is not true, but no one in the room wants to hear. There's no poetry in that. An egg balanced on the equality of night and day appeals to the poetic sensibilities of our era, which wants to touch a stillness at nature's center and believe all is beautiful equipoise.

Special Report. Shots fired. More at Eleven.

Buzzland
Or, A Prop's Short Memoir

❧ ❧ ❧

The producer, a thin woman with wide-set eyes and the thin, angular face of a fawn or a mouse, greets me. "Mr. Mansfield?" She extends her hand. "It's a very interesting book and you'll be interviewed by our hosts Robert and Alice—*both* of them?" She checks her clipboard. "Yes, both. And you'll be sitting on a couch and it's a very interesting book." I nod so her tape-loop recording won't repeat.

Depositing me in the "green room" to wait, she says she's heard that there's "a lot of good buzz around the book." Meaning: somewhere a person or two had read it and had written a review or two. She is mercilessly accurate; a writer in the television kingdom is a fly buzzing in the room.

You need a hook, you need a big hit, you need youth, you need buzz: Good buzz is the hive humming your name. You have to be a supernova visible by day or else you're nothing. The word "star" doesn't cut it—there are millions of stars in the sky. And your book, your precious little book, is a 25-watt light bulb powered by a stationary bicycle that you and your publisher furiously peddle. That is why I had driven four hundred miles to talk for several minutes on one stuffed couch to two stuffed hosts. I am an advertisement for an ecologically poisonous way to proceed.

The green room is littered with dead flies and dim bulbs. There are two shelves of recently published self-help books, along with a sprinkling of conspiracy theory books. Some are self-published, like the "Great Washington Cover-up" and a spiral-bound report on the real story behind the Lincoln assassination. Floating on this sea of anorexia, child abuse, inner-child love, and job success are the only two volumes of substance, a Frederick Douglass biography, and a Library of America volume of Richard Wright, remnants no doubt of Black History Month.

The walls are hung with some of the show's trophy heads, black-and-white 8 × 10 photos signed by a motley assortment of media stars: Wolfman Jack, Ed Asner ("God what a grilling," he wrote), Cab Calloway, Regis Philbin, Howard Cosell, Larry King, and Jerry Mathers (signed "the Beaver").

I am on the talk show with a woman who arranges flowers, "Petals Plus," a woman who runs a test kitchen—"Food Plus" or something—a high school chamber orchestra, a well-known sportswriter, and a satellite feed of some guy showing off expensive gadgets.

The set is a living room with pink walls, an overly large wardrobe, and bookshelves. ("See, they've got books," another guest says to me.) The host and hostess make a seamless flow of happy talk. They enthuse niceness. "Tomorrow you'll find out why waffles aren't just for breakfast anymore!" Somewhere out there in the nonstudio world where the colors aren't as vivid, the American Waffle Council had done its job.

In the green room I watch the start of the show. They are interviewing the sportswriter. He has written a novel about Japan on the eve of World War II, told from the viewpoint of a Japanese woman. (Yet he was incredulous that a nonnative New Englander could write about New England.)

He is a tall man who dresses like someone who got his cues about being dashing in the 1940s. His hair is swept back and kind of shiny. He has a pencil-thin moustache and a silk tie. He looks like a "swell." In person he is impressive. On the TV monitor he looks a little rumpled. There's a spot on his shoulder, and the camera comes upon him at first as he's making a face like he's just belched.

I have looked much worse. One time I drove for hours over ice-caked roads on a freezing day. The great hermetic trip—out of the car into the studio, one box to another. Later, when I see the show, some public TV book chat, I look like a guy who has driven for hours over ice.

Actually, with my curly hair, each strand marching to a different drummer, I look like a Cotswold sheep that's been tangled up in the gorse through a spell of rainy weather. There I am on TV, a talking sheep, in a tie and a tweedy jacket.

But he's a pro at this. The hostess is impressed. She asks: Will there be a movie? He says, "We're talking mini-series."

Anna from Petals Plus is next. She has brought in enough greenery to fill Central Park. The set looks like the winner's circle at the Kentucky Derby. She is wearing a Santa-red dress. She actually looks good in it.

I'm up soon to talk about New England history. They pin a mike on me. I sit down on the couch and I watch the host as he reads from the Teleprompter, "They say that those who do not remember history are condemned to repeat it." Watching someone being prompted to recall

George Santayana's famous statement about memory is an irony overload.

And then I'm talking on. I've said these things about museums and historical markers so often that I can watch myself talking. I talk about how we create our history, and illustrate my points with stories of Johnny Appleseed and the contents of little museums. I am careful to marry each idea to a concrete image. Horse and cart.

I've lost the hostess. The lights are on, but she's not home and my answers are piling up on her doorstep like a week of newspapers.

She asks a question about personal history, and I fumble a gooey-stew of an answer—*what am I saying?* I think.

In the last of my minutes under the hot lights I feel that my nose may be running: There's nothing that I can do. Is the hostess horrified? Bravely I talk on.

You really don't have to answer the questions. Whatever you say, the next question will be right along.

You could advocate the violent overthrow of the government, or announce the cure for cancer, or sell a new lint remover—it doesn't matter. It's all pitched at the same level, one mellifluous net of happy talk. White noise. A box of mixed biscuits, a persecuted people, a scandal, a new movie, a disease; it's all equally weightless.

Breaking this even modulation, this code of geniality, is deemed bad manners.

The answers don't matter. The questions don't matter. The subject is only a pretext. The flow is all that matters. The hosts and guests must maintain a nice burble of chatter.

The real message is: The world is friendly. The world is a happy place, a safe place for waffles any time. It's going to be all right. Time passes—but there'll be no consequences, no reckoning. Tick tock, tick tock. Happy, happy, happy.

So when the host asks you what your book is about, you are a fool to labor for answers.

He can say: "Where do you get your ideas?"

You can answer: "I had cottage cheese this morning."

The host will continue, with a glance at the Teleprompter: "How long did your research take?"

You can say: "I had small curd cottage cheese."

Host: "Is that unusual?"

You: "Small or large curd—That is the question."

Host: "And you've had a good reception to your work?"

You: "Large curd, though—it's too pushy, entirely too assertive for cottage cheese. I mean—really!"

Host: "Wonderful! Best of luck with it!"

You: "Thank you. I enjoyed being here."

Host: "The book is *Dachshund Angst* by Mortimer Peebles. Next Up: Eight new ways to make toast!"

I do answer the questions, of course. That was the lesson of my Cold War public schooling: Fill in all blanks, guess if you have to, use a Number Two pencil only, you have sixty minutes, begin.

The host ends by asking me about multiculturalism—nothing in particular—just: what about it? I act my part, the laboring fool. I vainly try to join up that debate with earlier debates about the themes of American history. We're always rewriting our history, choosing our ancestors, I say.

"Watch out for the revisionists!" the host warbles, and we're off the air. He's so seamless. "That went well," he says.

I sign a book for him. I see that he has read only the first fifteen pages. The hosts go off to do a food segment.

Why do we put so much effort into creating and packaging these walls of attractive talk? Our landscape and cities are in disorder. But our airwaves are bright, shiny rooms filled with endless chatter. Television is a void to fill a void.

You think words have weight, density, texture, rhythm. You drive away from the studio weighing your words, rewriting in your mind, wishing your answers had more shape, more topography. You are a stone mason, a sculptor in an age that has moved beyond all materials, an age that manipulates electronic particles of images. You are like some monk come down from the abbey, the keeper of the books, and you watch as the word is transcribed into its atomic particles, the buzzing of atoms.

The TV talk show hosts use words as an aerosol room spray. They spray out words, each one as weightless as the next. Words evaporate, just another liquid on the move. They talk as if the words will never run out. Words are the lesser partner of the entertainment team: Pictures-and-words, Music-and-words. Words are manufactured goods, uniform commodities. All poetry, sacredness, surprise, rigor, and athleticism is drained from talk.

In the zero-gravity chamber of media chat, words billow away, a gas cloud. Whoosh! Wee! One talks and talks. The task is never done. Talk begets talk.

In three minutes—no, in thirty seconds—no one will remember what you said or that you were ever there. You are reduced to your electronic imprint, some magnetically charged atoms, easily erased.

"All that is solid melts into air," Karl Marx wrote in *The Communist Manifesto*. Marx was writing about "modern bourgeois society." "All that is holy is profaned."

Talking over the airwaves is the signature feeling of modernity: All that is solid melts into air.

After a TV interview you feel insubstantial, diffuse. You feel that you are not even composed of your atoms, not the buzzing cloud-like orbits of your electrons, but rather it's as if you're aware of the spaces in between them. Is it true that there is more space between our atoms than atoms themselves? It would figure.

In the same era that Marx sat writing in the British Museum, Ralph Waldo Emerson, wrote in his journal, March 20–23, 1842: "In N.Y. lately, as in cities generally, one seems to lose all substance, & become surface in a world of surfaces. Every thing is external, and I remember my hat & coat, and all my other surfaces, & nothing else. If suddenly a reasonable question is addressed to me, what refreshment & relief! I visited twice & parted with a most polite lady without giving her reason to believe that she had met any other in me than a worshipper of surfaces, like all Broadway. It stings me yet."

I am the most minor of props, but my experience is representative. It is similar to, though far less frenetic, than a friend who had a book that was a best-seller. I have weathered radio call-in shows, phoned-in interviews during AM drive-time ("phoners"), earnest public television shows, cable TV, live radio on location, and days at the hands of a production crew from a regional magazine show. I have served up sound bites, and been one of those know-it-all talking heads.

It's not surprising that the TV world is false, "a freshet of shams," as Thoreau said before there were reruns. Nor is it surprising that many TV people talk to you with that smarmy glad-handing nice-to-meet-you-Bob, sit-here-Bob, manner of life insurance salesman. No, what wears you down if you're trying to say something, is that TV is about itself, its *TV-ness*. Like any creature or monster, it lives to perpetuate the species. And it will eat anything it must to survive—no item of trivia is too small, no sorrow too vast, not to be swallowed entire. One happy meal after another, the trivial broadcast as the tragic, and the tragic diced into trivia.

Scheherazade had only one thousand and one nights of air time to fill to save her neck. If the Sultan had lost interest, she would have been killed. She didn't dare flirt with reruns. But if she were looking at years and years of programming, she might have run out of stories and given herself over to a talk-show format: On the next *Scheherazade!* Does your man want to behead you? And: quick make-overs for the recently beheaded.

* * *

The first thing you notice about Cable Access TV is that it is is dirtier than regular TV—not the programs, but the building. The lobby of this Boston-area C.A.T. is like a grimy stop on the T. No one has cleaned the glass in ages. There's litter and the sticky stains from spilled soda.

Cable Access looks like public transit. Other television stations deport themselves like a slick bank or an airline. This is the bus.

The woman at the reception desk is, true to the TV reception form, watching TV. Great job! Mostly people come in to ask about their remote controls. This channel or that doesn't come up. Cable Access is true to its name here. People walk in at will. No sign-ins, no security guards.

Cable Access people have ordinary, civilian hair. On "real" TV, the "personalities" have big hair. I once visited a network affiliate, which, with its broadcast license, is like an occupying army. Any idea is shot on sight.

As I waited in the lobby, the young receptionist, Amber, sat with a slack-mouthed look of wonder watching a large TV—showing, of course, the TV station's broadcast. She watched it all as if newly arrived from some Pacific island grass-hut culture.

The phone rang. Not taking her eyes off the TV, Amber pushed a button, picked up the receiver, and murmured the stations call letters, but the receiver slid off her shoulder, out of her hand, hitting the table. In another office, you would say, surely Amber was hired because she is someone's daughter or niece. Here in Buzzland she has the potential to do the nightly news. She does have good hair. And hair is key. You can't teach good hair; it's a talent.

I was led to the studios by a woman who had hair of a black-gold color that looked as if had been shellacked into place. This is apparently the look. The woman anchor on the news had hair that looked like it was extruded. It was shaped on her head with two curving jug handles above her shoulders. They may hang her up by her hair at night.

On Cable Access there is no hair spray, and no preliminaries. The show that I am on is a standard format for cable—two guys talking. The other format is two women talking.

The studio is small and hot. One of my hosts acts as a cameraman. There's a crew of recent college grads at the control board. The hallway bulletin board has a sign-up sheet to work on "shoots." There must be sixty names there.

The whole setup reminds me of the first TV show I was ever on. In college, I was on a student TV show at the communications school. They had an enormous TV studio, the size of a regulation basketball court.

They had asked me to come to discuss a Freedom of Information Act request that we, at the student newspaper, had filed with the CIA. Other documents had come to light showing a CIA presence on campus.

This was back when I thought content still mattered. I thought we were studying to be journalists, not packagers of celebrity babble, diet tips, and vague gruntings in the night about "them" and "big government" ruining everything for *us*.

The host asked stupid questions: Why should we ask what the government is doing? I couldn't believe this was a fellow student at a school of public communications. He had no sense of what the First Amendment was, or any concept of what he should be communicating to the public.

When a press baron had announced his donation to establish this school, A. J. Liebling skeptically noted that "journalism" had been replaced by "communications"—a "neutral" term with "no intrinsic relation to truth." He imagined this exchange:

Q—What do you do for a living?

A—I am a communicator.

Q—What do you communicate? Scarlet fever? Apprehension?

As students we thought it was a wisecrack, but as usual, Liebling was right.

I was talking about the Bill of Rights, and the freedom of Americans to talk to whom they wish or to think what they will, without being shadowed by their own government here at home, when I was distracted by a man with a headset who was swimming around below the table waving at me.

I stopped mid-sentence. Resumed. But he was still waving at me, miming: *Your feet are on the table*! I stopped again.

I didn't remove them. I looked at the host. "Excuse me, but there's a man frantically waving at me," I said.

"Your feet are on the table," he said.

Sunday morning is radio's public service ghetto. The FCC no longer requires stations to address serious issues as part of the rent for using the public's airwaves, but a few stations have a vestigial conscience. I go to record a show at a Boston oldies station.

Middle-aged radio guys on soft rock/oldies stations are like high school seniors grown a little wider, a little softer, playing the music of their youth over and over. They have a lifetime hold on "senioritis": "Isn't this job a goof?" they seem to say. I meet Jack, the DJ and interviewer, in his narrow office. The door is a collage, top to bottom, of newspaper and magazine clips: editorial cartoons, "babes" in bathing suits, lots of vampires with teeth. There are photos of him with his former guests, including

G. Gordon Liddy: "Halfway through the show, I'm thinking—I'm alone in the room with this guy. He could kill me with his bare hands. You know he never took off his trench coat the whole time he was here." And the "'Buns of Steel' girl": "I was surfing the channels the night before she was coming on the show, and the first thing I see is her ass in a thong bikini: This is going to be a good interview." Promoting hard buns is a public service. Beautify America.

I'm there to talk about Thoreau, Town Meeting, majestic old elms. Things like that. I can offer no spies or buns of steel. Thoreau walked everywhere, split wood. He could have been buff.

Isaac Babel in Odessa: Tell me of your first love and I will make you dinner. The young writer was exchanging gifts. A story for a meal, an even match, nourishment for nourishment. Today Babel could tune in *Geraldo*, or some call-in radio psychologist, or some Internet chat "lounge," or go to the half-dozen support, twelve-step, Life-Anon, victim-a-thon groups listed under "activities" or "events" in any city.

Today we can't shut up. Vaudeville never died. We are all in Vaudeville now: politicians, teachers, preachers, doctors, generals, and their therapists.

"I can well remember the times we went to bed in the dark because there was no quarter to put in the gas meter; or even more vividly, some evening meals eaten by candlelight for the same reason," Moss Hart wrote in his autobiography *Act One*. Hart was a successful playwright, writing Broadway hits with George S. Kaufman, such as *The Man Who Came to Dinner*, and musicals with Irving Berlin and Cole Porter. The first shows Hart remembers in his autobiography are from the time before radio, movies, and television, before he even saw his first play.

His Aunt Kate had come to live with them, and even though they were all poor, Aunt Kate always made it to the theatre.

"Never once did she offer to forgo the theatre, no matter how dire the financial crisis might be, and, equally astonishing, it seems to me, was the fact that she was not expected to," wrote Hart. "We were grateful for this small patch of lunatic brightness in the unending drabness of those years."

His aunt would bring the show home with her and "recreate the entire evening for us," unwrapping each detail like a separate gift. "Little did escape her and she regaled us with all of it, from the audience arriving to the footlights dimming, and then the story of the play itself. She would smooth out the program on the kitchen table, and there we would sit, sometimes until two o'clock in the morning, reliving the play with her, goggle-eyed at the second act climax, as ready to applaud the curtain calls as the audience itself had been."

The scene in the Hart's kitchen has more in common with the home-spun era—the family gathered by the fire—than it does with our own era. Things happened one-at-a-time then.

"It is hard to realize now in these days of television, movies, radio and organized play groups what all this meant to a child of those days," wrote Hart, who was born in 1904. "It was not only the one available source of pleasure and wonder, it was all of them rolled into one."

Today, everything comes in. Nothing sinks in. We are in the media co-coon. We are media-dipped. Said the critic John Leonard: We're so wet we don't even know that we're immersed.

In winter twilight, I walk to pick up our mail in town. The post office is in an old Grange hall on the rise above a pond. A few grey clouds retreating in the east catch the last light. I scan the pond to see if anyone is skating. No one in the gathering dark. And then I detect one figure moving wraith-like. I can hear his blades on the ice as I stand near Main Street. That's how quiet our town is.

Just as your eye adjusts to the night sky and stars are revealed, I see two other fainter skaters moving slower, no metal-on-ice sound, and then I hear a small child, giggling.

I walk home up the steep hill that sits at the head of our Main Street. I am buoyant, a cork on the tide of good feelings. It's going to be a cold night. The chimney smoke rises straight up into the starry dark, making each house seem like a small ship at sea.

Everyone is snugly in their houses, and I confess that I'd throw a glance into lighted windows where I'd see the side of a wingback chair, and a gray head looking at a newspaper. There was the glow of the fireside in a couple of houses.

In more than a few houses—I didn't count—the room flickered in television's peculiar light. We have emptied out great spaces of our life for this, giving up the only thing we really have: time. In what we call "tradi-tional cultures," villagers gather to tell stories. We have the same desires, but we sit watching rehearsed dialogue; fast food where once there was a feast, an electron-thin wallboard of pretty faces where once there was holy architecture. And a laugh track where once there were drums and feathers.

The little TV satellite discs have begun appearing on houses, sticking off the roof or the side of a wall like small mushrooms. All yearning off to the same degree, lives ruled by the orbit of an artificial star. And with each disc I feel that another has left us. Another blank spot in our public life, an ink blot that spreads.

What are we missing?: The present, the light praising this moment here on earth.

A Trappist monk, Father Thomas, was on the radio, talking about silence. He lectures on contemplative prayer, trying to bring some of the benefits of the monk's life to the rest of us. He wants people to free themselves from the idea that we are in a movie, our psyche always reacting. Actually, he said, we're in a theatre watching a lousy movie and can leave anytime.

We need to be quiet to hear God's voice, he said. The interviewer was flummoxed by the idea of silence. After all, she worked in radio. Silence is a technical difficulty. Dead Air.

"Radio has occupied the whole space of silence. There is no silence any longer," wrote Max Picard in 1948. Radio noise is "limitless," he wrote. "Content hardly matters any longer; the production of noise is the main concern."

"It's as if men were afraid that silence might break out somewhere and destroy the noise of radio. And so all space is filled with noise, it dares not be silent, it is constantly on guard against silence."

Without silence, the sacred word is destroyed, says Picard. "Radio fills up the space within [us] where the word used to be." It educates us to "not listen to words"; it takes us "away from Thou, from Love." "God, the eternally Continuous, has been deposed, and continuous radio noise has been installed in His place." Radio destroys silence, and so destroys us, he says. "This is what makes the man who lives in this world of radio so bad-tempered, so ill at ease: everything is thrown at him by the radio but nothing is really there at all. Everything slips away."

The producer from a television news magazine calls. We go over the script. The segment is six minutes and seems to dance from concept to concept. It alights here, then there.

A few times he says to me: "This is TV, you know" and "You've got to understand this is TV." Reading the script he says: "Then there's a short burst of sound."

"A short burst of sound?" I ask.

"That's you," he says.

＊　＊　＊

On a frozen morning early in January, my wife and I go to be interviewed on a radio station that has one of those wall-of-talk formats: CBS news on the hour, little two-minute features like "The Osgood File," "Animals Around Us," bits and bites that are woven into a net of talk over the city. Sitting in the studio, I imagine the city under this big-top of talk, a broadcast circus: news acts, animals acts, chat acts, in lieu of bears riding bicycles.

These all-talk stations are our century's equivalent of the early fires of the cave dwellers: Keep the fire burning, keep away the darkness. We need to keep these radio beacons going to keep away the darkness of doubt, despair and emptiness. "It's just another ordinary day": That's what we want the radio to tell us. The world is our cozy living room. Silence is feared. In the silence we might sense how estranged we are from our homeplace, from ourselves. In the silence of a January morning, we can feel the intensity of a New Hampshire winter and we know it can eat us alive. Eat us alive, freeze us out, crush us, without remorse or celebration, without notice. To be of less consequence than a granite boulder is too much to bear, so we turn up the top-40 music stations with their carnival-barker commercials, turn up the Mozart, and the unending talk that melts into air.

I have come to believe in the silences.

Tomorrow's Another Working Day

❧

Keene, New Hampshire, is an invisible city. It is invisible to most of its citizens. They take it for granted. Why think about Keene? It's like thinking about the granite hills that ring the city.

The citizens accept Keene as you accept the geology of your region. Once long ago these rocks were formed and here they are. Once long ago Keene was formed. To ask how it could have been different, or how we can change the city today, is to them a foolish question. How could granite be different?

Keene is not a city of destiny. People don't come to Keene to make a fortune, win fame, or fall in love. Keene is like a good pair of overalls worn over the years. No one praises the overalls for style, or even discusses them.

You don't think of people falling in love in Keene, but of course they do. There are other cities known for their romance or beauty, cafes to tarry in, grand *allées* of trees to stroll beneath, men playing chess in the park, little art galleries on side streets.

Some cities are riddles: the city seen from hills and rivers, unfolding with each new perspective; or the city as a walker's mystery, an intricate puzzle of intimate and grand spaces, alleys and squares. But Keene is wide open. You can see all of Keene in a loop or two, and yet because it is a quiet city, you will miss it.

Keene's citizens are guarded. Not for them sitting out in public places playing bocce or chess, or feeding the pigeons. That's loitering. If you want to talk—I mean if you really must—then go to a support group. There you can emote. In American life, even emotions are zoned. There are zones for religion—churches and synagogues—one day a week—and zones for neighborly concerns, for dealing with "problems." (Emotions are "problems.") Just as we drive all over the landscape for errands, so we have spread out our emotional life and spiritual life. In other cultures such sorting out would be incomprehensible.

Keene does not have one knock-out, signature feature—a beautiful waterfront, a handsome skyline—the kind of natural or man-made features you make sure you drive visitors by, the scenes sketched by artists and codified on postcards.

Keene's beauty is muted, as befits a city of quiet people. Keene has a handsome vista up its Main Street, presided over by a white church spire that commands the street and makes the city feel like a large village.

But drive visitors up the street and they're likely to miss the view. They will remember the traffic lights. Confronted with a vast natural cataract and a traffic light, most will see the light. Put a traffic light in front of, say, Monet's "Water Lilies" and it is no contest.

One Sunday, a group of us took a walking tour of Keene—a radical idea. We walked out of history and into traffic, which is appropriate since auto traffic is the death of cities and civilizations built for walking. A dozen of us started out at the historical society in the Keene of the early 1700s and we made our way up Main Street and then out West Street. We were lead by Alan Rumrill, director of the Historical Society of Cheshire County, and Peter Ryner, the city's planner.

We were recreating the history of Keene, moving up the street as the city had moved, driven always by changing transportation: wagons, the railroad, and now the automobile. In each era, all the region's goods came to Keene, first by animal power, then by kerosene, wood and now oil. Each change in technology transformed the entire layout of the city. When the train arrived in 1848, the old Colonial settlement was left behind as the city grew around the Central Square that now sits at the head of Main Street.

People drove by and stared at us. You don't see walking tours in Keene. The idea that Keene is worthy of close attention would be strikingly odd to many people. They might go to San Francisco or New York and walk about gawking. Those cities are like dancers. They are always performing before an audience or, failing that, a mirror. They live for attention. But who would go on a tour taking in the quieter charms of Keene, with its handsome brick Greek Revival houses, each window neatly trimmed with granite?

One way to transform a city like Keene is to look at it. A group staring at a building lifts that building up from invisibility. Others might look again where they haven't looked in decades, and an ordinary house or storefront is unveiled for them.

Restoration is, in part, about looking anew, refreshing our sight, seeing the neglected close at hand. Sometimes we have to physically unearth old buildings, remove the tar on skylights, the dropped ceilings hiding the mosaics, the metal siding and plastic office partitions. The building comes back to life. Who knew? people say of the new-old building. Tear it down—did we say that? We can't live without it. It's the community's emblem, the pride of place, used for weddings, parties, the place we show visitors first. When a building is restored to a community it's like the restoration of vision.

The Greek Revival was once the proper uniform for the house of a doctor or lawyer. The two- and three-story brick houses with their pedimental temple ends facing the street are crisp, self-assured, and proper. They are houses dressed for Sunday dinner, the shirt buttoned all the way up to the top button. The taut geometry of the houses reminds one of the starched collars and dresses with high necks of the era. The upright effect is further emphasized by the tall chimneys.

These houses have today an elegance, a certitude that we lack. Each one should be sought out, photographed, measured, celebrated, and never allowed to fall. Mostly, of course, these buildings are ignored, and a few have been demolished. In an era when new buildings in the American city have become a carnival sideshow of freaks and novelty acts, such reticent architecture is easily lost.

As we walked down West Street, with each block the old city fell away—the street widened, the sidewalk narrowed, curb cuts and parking lots became prevalent. The wires emerged from the ground and hung overhead. The fast-food signs marked the route and the air tasted of exhaust. Our historian said less and less and the city planner spoke more. The talk was of traffic volume, traffic studies, road conditions, turn lanes, curb cuts, and pedestrian bridges.

We had walked out of history, out beyond the city formed by wagons and trains into the auto world that is Keene's most familiar face.

The city had always been shaped by the dominant transportation of the day, and now it mirrored the frenetic motion of the auto age. For a city occupying a small flood-plain, Keene has spread out with the extravagance of a prairie town. It has done well saving the surrounding hills, but the flat buildable land has gone in a spree. In the last twenty years the city has added only two thousand people, but the area it counts as its central business district has tripled in size. From a traffic light on the state's major east-west road, you can see the usual shopping centers and fast-food places, and off in the distance, if you look for it, just over the Dunkin Donuts sign, is the old church spire of Central Square.

This is the view that most people see of Keene, and it is what the city's planner Peter Ryner first saw when he arrived. He was ready to leave. "I'll be damned if I'll work in a place that looks like this," he said. The next morning he found the old Main Street, walked around, and stayed a decade.

When he was preparing the city's master plan, Ryner looked at all that vanished farmland, home to some of the city's twenty-five dairy farms as recently as the 1950s, and he asked: Who will feed us? What species of urbanism is this that assumes our food will come from elsewhere? He wanted to make a provision for food as an essential concern in the master plan, along with such things as jobs, clean air, parks, and transportation.

"Keene doesn't do food," he was told.

Keene does not have a great tragic history. There were no bloody labor strikes, just the usual fall of the New England mills, the pride of the leading families, and no doubt somewhere in there, some missed opportunities, missed futures.

In short, there are not the high and lows that would distinguish a typical portrait. None of the scenarios for telling about a city seem to fit: No vanished splendor (except the elms). No center of wealth bypassed. No noble American experiment in democracy gone flat and no tale of hurly-burly nineteenth-century raw industrial might.

No, the story of Keene, as far as I can tell, is this: Keene gets up in the morning and goes to work, the same job for twenty, thirty, forty years. Maybe later Keene goes to the movies, has a pizza and a beer or watches TV, but mostly Keene goes to work. ("What's the best night spot?" the local daily polled its readers. "Home" was tied with a brew pub. "Why do you live here?" "It's quiet," said many.)

Tomorrow's another working day: That's what it should say on a sign welcoming you to Keene.

As an example, take this story from page 1 of *The Keene Sentinel* back a few years ago. A venerable local company, Kingsbury, had to reduce some workmen's hours, having them come in only every other week. Kingsbury makes auto parts for Detroit, as well as "sophisticated machine and robot systems for the . . . small engine, appliance and aerospace industries."

Faced with a halving of their salaries, here is the combative voice of Keene labor:

"I would much rather see them save jobs than do more layoffs," said a nineteen-year veteran. He did say it would be tough, he would have to raid his savings. A thirty-year veteran responded: "You have to do what you have to do."

Maybe that's what it should say on the sign to the city:

Set your alarm clocks to rise early.

You're in Keene.

You have to do what you have to do.

Tomorrow's another working day.

Other cities claim to be the hub of the universe, the big apple, A-number-one, top-of-the heap. Keene gets up in the morning and goes to work.

Once even alarm clocks would have been considered frivolous.

One man remembers when he came to Keene to work in the 1930s. He wanted to buy an alarm clock. What do you want with an alarm clock? said one merchant, dismissing the fancy ways of this new generation. You don't need an alarm clock. You get up with the roosters, he said. People don't rely on roosters anymore, but that practicality remains. Long after the granite hills wash away down the Connecticut River, that steadfastness will remain.

The people of Keene will do what they have to do. I can see that in the faces of the shoppers in a supermarket in the afternoon. The shoppers are mostly elderly. They are as twisted as *krummholz*, those trees that cling to sides of mountains, each cell and fiber permanently bent by the storms. But they know no exalted view. They seem mostly disappointed, some lonely, even those who are couples. They seem weary. There is no "attitude," no buzz as in hip locales, no quick talk, swagger, bizarre haircuts, or flashy jewelry and cars.

Here the people are like natural formations. Some are like old trees that have grown galls, or grown around barbed wire stapled to the trunk long ago. Others are like granite—once in a far-off youth, molten, fiery, changing, forming. Now, rock solid, only worn away by ice and the steady dripping of the years.

I was waiting in the hospital for a neighbor one day when I struck up a conversation with the man sitting next to me who, judging by his skin color and his story, was, I'm afraid, done for.

He was wearing the green pants and thick-soled black shoes of a factory worker. He was sitting quietly, drawn in a little so that even though he was a big guy and had been here before, you could see he didn't like it. All his movements had a restricted quality.

He had prostate cancer. He had been in for thirty-seven treatments—and had not missed a day of work.

In fact he had worked at a factory for thirty-three years. The first twenty-nine years he only missed three days. He was out with the flu. "Took me right down," he said.

But now the cancer had spread. Just flared up again. He had to come in for treatments lasting a half hour. Both sides of his rib cage and one leg had to be irradiated. He was on disability now. If he lifted anything he'd be exhausted, he said apologetically.

His two daughters were Marines. One served for fourteen years and was now with the same company as her father. The other works in data processing. If there's a war, she could be called up. She is a crack shot. She learned from her grandfather, his father. She used to go hunting with him.

He had also learned some shooting lessons from his father. When he was married in 1952, his father took him to a town dump and taught him how to shoot. He set up six bottles standing in a row and gave him a .22 pistol. He shot four of the six bottles.

Then his father set up six more bottles. These were lying on their sides, with the open necks facing them. His father took the pistol and shot out the bottoms of all six bottles. Didn't even touch the necks.

His father had all sorts of sharpshooting ribbons from different fairs, and now his granddaughter was rated an expert at the range.

Twenty-nine years of work and only three days sick. With his quiet dignity, he seemed to me to be the spirit of Keene—steady as she goes. Tomorrow's another working day. You have to do what you have to do.

And in the long procession of those working days, there are some moments of true grace. The graceful is often invisible to us, lost from notice like those old Greek Revival houses. Even at a town dump, on a day you are just shooting out old beer bottles, you can aim for grace.

Freegrace Farm: My Prayer Sincere

~❧ ❦~

Freegrace Marble Farm. I am drawn by the name. I drive nearly a hundred miles through decaying mill cities and sprawling commercial strips, through the America we have built for ourselves, heading toward Freegrace. The farm is named for the first landholder, Freegrace Marble, who received the land from King George II.

Freegrace. The name has a sweetness to it, the name may have been a blessing on this land, a guidance for the future. Names are sometimes destiny.

Leona Dona has loved this farm for sixty-one years. She is eighty-one years old, four feet eleven inches and seventy-nine pounds, and resolute. She has a beautiful smile, clear blue eyes, and a radiance that her wrinkles only accentuate. One friend says of her: This woman is a blessing to everyone who knows her. Another friend says of visiting the farm, "Then you know you are in heaven. The beauty you see and feel is that Leona has seen and felt for a long time."

Through her great efforts, Freegrace Marble Farm in Sutton, Massachusetts, has been preserved, the sixty-three acres left in care of the Society for the Preservation of New England Antiquities.

On an overcast chilly day in the middle of May, Leona shows me her farm. We walk up to the high pastures and the small family cemetery. We are accompanied by a procession of black flies.

As we pass one stone wall, she points to a hollow place and remembers the foxes that lived there one year: a vixen and three kits. She'd give them bread and they'd come running, just like her geese come running.

The geese are grass eaters, but she loves feeding them. She calls out with excitement: *Come on guys! Come on guys!* She says that they'd usually be here quicker. Up the path they come running, honking.

We walk along the traces of an old road in the woods—the original colonial road in the area, she says. She points out where the Nipmuc Indians camped, a shelter of rocks with a fresh spring by the brook.

She loves the history of the place. The cemetery is the first thing she tells you about. Leona has spent much time recording their epitaphs, researching their lives. Visitors always love the cemetery. "I have a granddaughter. When she comes here, she will go to the cemetery and bring a book and read. She loves the tranquility. And the beauty—the beauty."

We come out on the pasture and walk up to her apple trees: Northern Spy, Baldwin, Rhode Island Greening, Honey Russet, old trees now, dropping limbs. "In the fall I don't pick all the apples," she says. "And I like this field cut and the hay left here for the deer." From the old orchard, the hill rolls down to the pond with her guys, the geese, and then up a gentle slope to the house and barns, which repose under tall trees. She used to ski with her two children through the openings in the stone walls.

I admire a tree and she says, "This tree was only as thick as my arm when I arrived at the farm." Her lilacs are crowded with blooms—she does nothing with them, just lets them go their own way. Her other plants are robust: yellow violets, Japanese quince, a cranberry bush she planted for the birds, may apples, dogwood in bloom, large hickory trees. She gathers the nuts each fall as she has done since the lean times. When she came to the farm as a bride of twenty, she found and restored the herb gardens from Freegrace Marble's day. She still cultivates that garden.

She was married in 1932. "The little money we had, we lost," she says, when the banks closed. "We lost it all."

"So I said to my husband: we're lucky. We have the farm. We have each other." She began researching the old herbs and food that sustained the Indians on that same land. Sassafras and wild chamomile for tea; wild asparagus, cowslips, ferns, and dandelions for fresh greens; slippery elm bark for chewing gum; and wild Concord grapes, from which she still makes a celebrated grape pie. They also raised chickens, hogs, and cows. She never used pesticides or chemicals. She gardened using companion plants to ward off insects. She harvested rush, dried it (you have to season it for two years) and wove chair seats.

"We used everything we possibly could," she says.

She also worked off the farm: Twenty-five years driving a school bus in the morning, working in the cafeteria and then driving the kids home. After that, twenty-one years teaching the practical arts: "when to pick it, how to pick it, how to preserve it."

We enter the cemetery, which lies behind a tall stone wall, and there are the old stones of Freegrace Marble and his descendants, Major Alpheus Marble, Civil War Captain Samuel Marble, as well as a few Nipmuc Indians, including a chief. But they have been vandalized. Three years ago some children viciously smashed the stones, dragged a few off and dug up a grave. One stone is riven with a long fissure between the word

"Memory" and the watching cherub looking heavenward. That is one of the least damaged stones.

Freegrace Marble's stone lies on the ground like a crumbled cookie, the slate pieces look like they are floating on the ground, like a wreath on water.

We stand and look at the broken memorial. From up here you can hear the roar of traffic on Route 146, a strip of stores and gas stations about three miles away. The farm is only twenty minutes south of downtown Worcester.

When Leona spoke of the cemetery, she said how tranquil it was. She never mentioned the vandalism, this recent wound.

She is saddened to see the destruction, the broken teeth of the stones. One child was caught and confessed to his father. His father made him apologize. "But that's beside the point. What's an apology when they've done this damage?"

They have smashed the repose of the place, ruined it as surely as if they had run through a gallery of paintings with knives slashing everything beautiful.

We walk out of the cemetery, across the high pasture and orchard. The cemetery visit has changed the views, the composition of the green pastures, the geese and the old white farm house. The vandalism is a strong poison. The breeze carries its odor, spreading a meanness like ash that clings to everything, the violets, the trees in apple blossom.

Leona bends down, "Aren't these buttercups beautiful? This field in August is covered with dark-eyed Susans."

There is a strong current of destruction pulling at this land, even if it is protected. We walk back along the paved town road that curves through the farm. By the Sibley Reservoir, near another Indian encampment where artifacts have been found, people have thrown in some trash and tires. She shows me where the town cut two big healthy trees. One tree, an ash, lies in logs three feet in diameter. A perfectly good tree, she says.

In another spot a town truck has smashed in a stone wall, an old loading area by the barn, promising over a year and a half ago that they'd return to set it right. Her stone walls are beautifully maintained, even with developers who "have helped themselves" to the stone.

"Now this here was a horse pond," she says, pointing at the paved edge of the road which runs into some scrub. There used to be gravel that led gradually down to the water. "When you were going to market with your horse and wagon, you'd stop on your way and let them drink and go on. But they destroyed it—the town did." When Leona was a little girl, growing up on a farm in this valley, she and her sister used to deliver spring water and milk in a one-horse wagon.

That horse pond can be put back, she says.

We walk on. "I walk every morning and I pick up all the cans and papers, but I didn't walk this morning," she says apologetically.

These are only small signs of the larger battle she has waged to save this farm. Her ex-husband wanted to sell the farm to developers. She fought him. It was a long, painful, legal battle, but she won't say anything about it. The farm she loved was a hostage of their divorce. To settle their dispute, the court ordered the farm sold at auction. At the front door of the house, a divided family fought each other for the farm. It was a dark scene. Neighbors rallied to her side, spoke out before the auction, offering money to Leona. She doesn't express any anger toward her ex-husband, but rather she steps around any mention of him. He is a void in her stories.

"It's the educated people, the lawyers that I really am disappointed in," she says. "All they thought of was the money! They had no compassion!" she says with a disbelief that is refreshing. She expected those lawyers to have a moral compass.

In the end, she was able to preserve the farm. She donated her half of the farm. Her husband sold his half to the antiquities society. She will continue to live in the 1731 house as long as she wishes. Eventually the house will be sold, with strict preservation guidelines.

When did she first know that she wanted to save the Freegrace Marble Farm?

"Always," she says. "When I came here I had a vision. I knew what I wanted to do," and she whispers, "*I fell in love with the farm.*" Saving this heritage, she wrote in a poem, "has been my prayer sincere."

She started clearing away brush, repairing the stone wall, restoring the house. The house was just a shell, no running water, plumbing. "Every winter I would prepare all my supplies and materials I needed and I'd do one room in January and February." She stripped off eight layers of buttermilk paint, uncovering the old wainscotting and gunstock beams.

She was away from the farm only three times for any extended period, when she visited her cousin, a bishop in Ghana. Of course she missed her home. "I couldn't get back fast enough."

After she saw what the people in Ghana were suffering, she came home and raised money for them. She held several open-house craft fairs at her farm. She has always delighted in showing people the farm, in leading them to see what she sees. And people have responded. She has been celebrated locally and honored by the Boy Scouts she invites to camp on her land. She's an honorary grandmother for Cub Scout Pack 274. "I love them all," she says. She proudly shows a quilt they made for her to commemorate their visit to the farm, each square a small homage to a different place on the farm: the pond, the cemetery, the Indian campground.

While she makes some black tea, I look out her kitchen window at the lilacs, the barn, the green hills.

What makes a place beautiful? I ask.

The way people live there, she says. "When all help each other. The giving and doing without expecting any compensation. Live your life in peace and harmony and enjoy what the Lord has given us. I'm a great believer," she says, and we sit quietly.

Names are sometimes destiny. Freegrace is the song of the place.

MENDING

Tikkun

In the beginning was exile. Before the Lord could create the earth and its creatures, He had to withdraw. He sent forth his creation as light to fill the "vessels." The divine light was overwhelming, breaking the vessels, spilling downward. The perfect order was destroyed; evil entered the world. In the beginning was evil. To gather the spilled light, to erase evil from all creation, the Lord created Adam. And Adam could have made creation whole again; Adam could have reunited the Creator with his creation by the first Sabbath, but Adam sinned and more light was spilled, more "sparks" fell down, and evil grew stronger. Adam and Eve were banished; human history began in exile. The Lord tried once more to restore the harmony of creation. He chose the Israelis in the desert and gave them the Ten Commandments, and had they believed, creation would have been made whole, but the Israelis sinned, worshipping the Golden Calf. More light was spilled; evil grew even stronger. Each act was an attempt to repair the catastrophe of creation. In the beginning was exile, evil, and catastrophe. It is our work on earth to repair this flawed creation, to reclaim the world through the restoration known as *Tikkun*.

This, very briefly, is the teaching of Rabbi Isaac Luria, a sixteenth-century mystic whose words are shaping lives down to this hour. Rabbi Luria was a Kabbalist, a Jewish mystic, and in his teachings he altered the Kabbalah's tale of creation, adding the initial exile of the Lord, and the idea of *Tikkun* (pronounced tee-KOUN).

Rabbi Luria came to Safed, Palestine, which was then a center for the Kabbalists, in 1570. He was thirty-six years old. Of his life before Safed, little is known. It was said that Luria could read people's secret sins in their faces and prescribe a *Tikkun* for each. He conversed with the ancient prophets, and knew the language of the birds. Souls are present everywhere, he said. Luria gathered a dozen disciples and became known as ha-Ari, the Lion. He lived only two more years, and wrote almost nothing down, and yet Luria's ideas "became in subsequent generations almost the only basis of Jewish ethics," says scholar Joseph Dan. "*Tikkun* is the most powerful idea ever presented in Jewish thought."

Tikkun is the mending of the world, the repair of the broken vessels. Each moral act, each prayer and ritual, works toward *Tikkun*, or restoration. Gershom Scholem, the pioneering scholar, defines *Tikkun* as "the restoration of the right order, the true unity of things" and also as "a perfecting, a betterment, and a correction." An ideal representation of *Tikkun* is the story of Enoch, told by the thirteenth-century German Hasidim. Enoch was a cobbler who, with "every stitch of his awl," joined the upper leather with the sole, but also "all upper things with all lower things." With each stitch he meditated until he was called heavenward to become an angel.

"Every human deed or misdeed may change the whole universal balance between good and evil and be decisive concerning the fate of the earth and the heavens together," writes Joseph Dan. An individual's deeds shape "the fate of divinity itself." The world may be at "any one moment just one step away from the complete redemption, and a minute sin performed at that very moment by some individual would prevent and delay the redemption," says Dan. "There is no neutral ground, there are no deeds or thoughts which do not contribute to one side or the other." Each person's actions carry the weight of the entire community's redemption. The mending of the world is a communal act. Each day we rise to finish creation.

"History, according to Luria, is the story of the repeated attempts of the good divine powers to rescue the sparks and to bring unity to the earthly and divine worlds," says Dan. "Luria and his disciples were absolutely certain that they were living in the last moments of the last attempt, which this time could not fail." In their lifetime, all the spilled light would be lifted by prayer and good deed. Evil would be conquered and the Messiah would arrive.

This is a radical reconception; instead of waiting for the Messiah, each act of each Jew would bring the Messiah. Redemption is no a longer a catastrophe, the end-time of history. "To Luria the coming of the Messiah means no more than a signature under a document that we ourselves write," says Scholem.

The Kabbalists—who found 613 commandments in the Ten Commandments, and 600,000 "faces," or meanings, to each word in the Torah— had a rigorous scheme of prayers and rituals to "lift the sparks." Each person also had a particular *Tikkun* to perform, a responsibility to erase a specific evil.

In the post-Holocaust world, *Tikkun*, mending the world, has taken on a new secular meaning. In the face of overwhelming evil, how does one person begin? *Tikkun* provides a way to see each individual small act, each little congregation of worshippers, as united in a vast restoration. The more impossible the task, the more Luria's idea of *Tikkun* lives. "The kabbalistic *Tikkun* shows its profoundest energy" in meeting the challenge of despair, says the Holocaust scholar Emil C. Fackenheim. If the world is broken unto itself, and if we ourselves are also flawed, then "all powers must be summoned for a mending." The worse things are, the clearer is the need for *Tikkun* to begin. The healing and repair of the world is the only work to be done.

Tikkun has been modified since Rabbi Luria's time, but like that farmer's twice-repaired ax, there's a rightness to it. With apologies to Rabbi Luria, I take *Tikkun* as the measure of all restoration in this imperfect, material world: Does it restore harmony? Is it on the side of life? All good restoration is *Tikkun*.

How do we mend the world? When everything needs doing, when the sky is falling, where do you start? There is a formula in urban forestry: When a mature shade tree falls, you do not replace it with another tree—with one spindly, wrist-thin sapling. To restore the shade of that older tree you have to plant dozens of young trees.

Perhaps this is a model. When we lose a good soul, we have to go forth and mend and restore this world in all the ways we know. We have to plant anew—we know this. But with the crisis all around us, we have to plant groves.

An Arkload of Noahs

⁓➤ ᴇ⁓

Here's a survey question Noah himself could have received at his post office box in Mesopotamia:

What needs to be saved in your community? (Check ✓ for yes, ✗ for no)

historic properties	river valleys
farmland	shorelines
forests	water supply
ridgelines	greenspaces separating villages
views and vistas	wildlife habitat
scenic approaches	old roads for recreational trails
mill yards	other
ponds and lakes	

This survey was sent out by a preservation organization in my state, and it seems to ask: When everything needs saving, where do you start? All of the above?

Within sixty miles of where I live, there are people saving land, children, turtles, homeless ferrets, sawmills, butterflies nearing extinction, steam engines, furniture, town commons, old types of apples. I can draw the circle wider, draw it any size, and round up more Noahs. And I suspect that my part of the world is not unlike yours. People are saving neon signs, historic roads, Yiddish books, lighthouses, cars, souls, the earth's atmosphere, countries, languages, rhinos, gorillas, viruses, bogs, bear cubs, toys, wallpaper, dances, shipwrecks, dogs, cats. . . . Has there ever been a time when there were so many Noah's in the land?

From rhinos to neon signs to Yiddish books to the very sound of the wild world, we are writing the same story over and over: Noah building his ark. There are nearly one million buildings on the National Register of

Historic Places, singly or in districts. The National Wildlife Federation has "certified" more than 20,000 backyard habitats since 1973 to help restore places for small wildlife to live. The names of several efforts in my state reveal the aspirations of our era: Community Stewardship, Community Cornerstones, Inherit New Hampshire. Once it was enough to save a historic building, then it was historic districts; now we are talking of valleys, states, bio-regions. As the forces destroying the old life have grown, so has the response, but always lagging, always groping to find a way to answer the language of quantity.

At my post office box I find an envelope declaring: "There are 175 covered bridges, 150 lighthouses, 6,800 miles of shoreline, 34 million acres of forest, and 15,000 bull moose in New England at the moment. And every one of them is going to be protected if I have anything to say about it." This pledge to out-Noah the old ark-builder is from the vice-president of a credit card company. If I sign on, and pay an annual fee for the privilege of borrowing money at 15.9 percent, he'll save a moose. (Did Noah offer preferred seating to those with a gold card?)

There are so many Noahs among us building arks; we believe that we are approaching flood time. "After us, the deluge!" Governor Frank Rollins said in 1897. He was talking about the rapacious logging of the White Mountains. The sight of the piebald mountains, and rivers clogged with the eroding soil, led after long effort to the establishment of the first national forests. But this can also be read as a statement of how we feel: "After us, the deluge."

The great flood, with its promise of a blessing for a new start, is one of our central stories, one of the first Sunday school lessons. Flood stories are common in antiquity—there are 302 by one count—telling of many local floods or one great flood.

Searching for flood waters, the archeologists have measured the alluvial silt of other eras, and the scholars of ancient texts have calibrated each reference, but they may miss an essential point: Many societies have feared a coming deluge, sensing that it all was about to fall in, as it has so many times in history.

We don't always recognize the Noahs among us. These people are sometimes portrayed as eccentric button savers. From time to time you read a newspaper story about a local "character," the "mayor" of his or her block. This old-world soul sits out on the street as if in Italy, or at an English pub. The street is the usual expedient American street, given over more to quick passage and parked cars than to life.

The newspaper stories talk about the "mayors" greeting and knowing everyone on their street. They are not the eccentrics; we are. They sense an order, an evident rightness invisible to us. It is the same with the Noahs.

The greater Noahs who save lives, mend landscapes—and the lesser Noahs, who save pottery or buttons—they are aware of the coming deluge. Their eccentricity is that they are sane. They are in advance of us. They have a deep sense of self-preservation.

Throughout this book we have met Noahs—people like Frank Rollins intent on saving his state's villages and mountains, Peter Acker capturing the sounds of the woods near Walden, Leona Dona giving us the gift of Freegrace Farm, and quite a few others. These Noahs I have visited are performing the greatest act of restoration: optimism. "Everybody should build one steeple in their lifetime. They should know what goes into making that," Waine Morse told me at his Old Greenfield Village. We were standing in front of the chapel he had built on a hill looking out over the Connecticut River Valley.

We may be at flood time. But some of the most optimistic people also have a deep measure of our disaster. They realize we can't afford pessimism. Worldwide, two out of three bird species are in decline, one-third of all fish, one-eighth of all plants. Nineteen-ninety-eight was the warmest year on record. The sky *is* falling, but it is a beautiful sky.

"These dangerous times for Earth call not just for passion, imagination, intelligence and hard work, but—more profoundly—a sense of optimism that is willing to act without a full understanding, but with faith in the effect of small individual actions on the global picture," says Victor Papanek, an industrial designer who has worked tirelessly to create environmentally ethical designs at home and abroad. These ark builders have earned their optimism.

I offer no tidy solutions, just a few honest people taking sometimes ordinary, sometimes heroic, measures to mend the world. The Noahs I have met say, in the words of photographer Ralph Steiner, "In spite of everything, yes."

More Than a Train

Sitting in the sandy lot of a gravel pit, the train is astonishing. Only three cars long, a complete design, the stainless steel still gleams, even though it is dented and the painted logos have faded. After sixty years the Flying Yankee still looks like the future was supposed to look: an efficiency that approached grace, the elegance of a 1930s cocktail shaker. This is a machine-age ruin, a train that has not run in forty years, but all the "go" is not gone.

The inside is a little stuffy, a little humid. It's a ruin as you would expect, but one sitting at attention, the musty brown seats upright. All the paint is faded and alligatored, and the once-bright metal is dulled. The cork and "battleship" linoleum flooring has crumbled. The windows are foggy with cataracts; the pioneering glass-and-plastic laminations are coming apart. Here and there a few have cracked or have been shot at.

In its prime, the Flying Yankee was dressed to the nines inside: blue-green walls, coach seats in "mulberry taupe mohair" with brown leather arm rests, lemon-gold drapes with three pairs of horizontal stripes, green and sand-colored carpeting. Fluorescent lighting was tucked into the ivory ceilings. Stainless steel moldings ran the length of the car, above and below the windows.

The observation lounge, which was a more expensive ticket, was finished with two-tone blue walls, individual movable arm chairs in green upholstery, and a henna-rust carpet with a lighter shade stripe just in front of the chairs. Between each pair of chairs was an ashtray, and a stand to put your drink. This was the sophistication we glimpse in the old black-and-white movies: men with wide-brimmed hats, ladies with white gloves. Cigarettes and cocktails, Nick and Nora, Clark Gable, Art Deco, Art Moderne . . . sleek and quick, racing down the tracks past hard times.

My host, Robert Morrell, Sr., has walked through this train hundreds of times before and he is excited to return. He looks around and sees the train as it was when it was new and the leap of faith it represents.

Morrell is a youthful 77 years old. He seems more like someone who is years away from retiring. He has the pleasant can-do, we-can-make-it-work demeanor of a businessman who, with his wife, started a thriving amusement park out of nothing more than some bad pasture land, a set of German dolls, and very long hours. He is, by his own description, a "gung-ho optimist," and the way his northern New Hampshire accent clips some words streamlines his speech. He wants to restore this train, get it back on the tracks, running. When he talks about the train, I see that look again, the wonder, that older men get around machines.

"It's a cream puff. It only holds 135 people. But they traveled in great comfort. It was more than just a *railroad*," he emphasizes. After being on dirty coal-fired steam engines, riding in this train was like taking your first airplane flight, he says. "My God, we're off the ground—look at what we're doing! It's that wavelength. That was the kind of experience.

"That's why we're not interested in rebuilding a steam engine. They are fascinating, but they don't represent a step forward."

The Flying Yankee is a monument to a hard-won optimism. "At the very depth of the Depression . . . people had to scramble, I mean really scramble," he says. One out of four workers was unemployed, output fell by one-third, 10,000 banks folded. "There were no jobs, no opportunity. Today young people need to understand this. And the railroads were one of the things that took a very bad hit." Passenger travel in 1932 fell to an all-time low, less than half of what it had been in 1929. "And so some of the best brains at General Motors, GE, Westinghouse, the Budd Company in Philadelphia, mines, construction, dams, all of this stuff—some of the best minds sat down and said we've got to change the direction we're going. And the Flying Yankee is a result of that level of thinking.

"General Motors calls up the guy from the Budd Company in Philadelphia and said, 'Hey, can I use that engine that you used to generate electricity? We want to put that in a train.' 'Well, I guess you could, we'll have to adapt it.' And so out of all of that they changed *everything.*" One hundred years of steam-engine power was coming to an end with the Flying Yankee and its predecessor the Zephyr, as well as the Union Pacific's M-10,000.

He is looking around the train as he tells me most of this, but he stops and turns toward me. "It's a little bit like climbing a cliff. I was in the mountain troops in World War II, as was my brother and a lot of other friends. We had to learn climbing techniques. The thing is: You look at something like that and say never in God's name can you get up it. Get up close and you find that you get a toehold, then you get a fingerhold and then another toehold—that's what we should be teaching. That's what this is: This provided people, an industry, a chance to get a toehold and go from there. That's the biggest purpose of this right now: is to see what was done then and to go ahead and do other things." As he walks on ahead, he says, "There's no such thing as everything having been invented. That's a crock of shit." A few steps later he says, "We learn, we get a perspective by this kind of thing.

"In other words it was a psychological change. Now take today. We're having psychological changes in our society, mostly because of the computer and communications. I mean whoever would have thought of satellites in 1930. Now we don't think anything about it. . . . But this opens up so many other doors, that people say: oh we can't do this and we can't do that," his voice singsongs. "And it's very confusing for a younger generation. There are so many options, so many directions to go, that you don't know how to get a toehold."

This is more than a train; this was the future. The "Silver Slipper," this bright wonder speeding through the countryside, is now sitting, decaying in a dirt lot by the woods. The Flying Yankee was built on a future faith, a way of going at our problems, inventing new things, finding our way forward.

When this train first came to town, schools let out, crowds gathered, brass bands played. In the summer of 1934, some 15 million saw its twin, the

Zephyr. The train's debut at the Century of Progress fair in Chicago brought on a public appetite for streamlined automobiles, toasters, tricycles, and refrigerators with "speed lines." The hot toy of 1936 was the Zephyr and Flying Yankee.

"Everyday at five o'clock it hums by at eighty miles an hour," the Budd Manufacturing Company advertised in *Fortune* magazine. "Sleek and gleaming, this train of stainless steel brings a fresh thrill to the countryside. Millions, seeing it, sense a new impulse that has come to the rails. For this swift, smooth thing of beauty is not just another train. It is the embodiment of a new principle bringing about revolution in all forms of transportation."

The train was a breakthrough, setting the pattern that is still followed today. The Zephyr and Flying Yankee were dramatically lighter than older rolling stock. The entire three-car, 199-foot-long Flying Yankee weighed 113 tons, about the same as a single 85-foot-long sleeper car. The train was streamlined to cut down on wind resistance: 3 feet lower than the old cars, with a rounded prow, bobtail back, and a stainless-steel belly. Half of the train's weight is in stainless steel, the rest in an extensive chromium-manganese steel frame. The Budd Company, excited by stainless steel, had patented a "shotwelding system," overcoming the difficulties of handling the material at high temperatures.

The Flying Yankee was faster, more efficient, and wonderfully profitable. The Boston and Maine, which had to take out a government loan to buy the train, paid off its debt in just two years.

"The amazing thing about this is that it is complete," says Morrell. The Flying Yankee has escaped extensive renovations, and pilfering by railroad fans. The train still has the luggage racks, the curtain hangers, and even the removable seat trays, an elaborately articulated steel construction.

Morrell points out each detail with care. "See how it was made?" he says, directing my attention to the floor. "The decking was all stainless steel. Then they covered it with this stuff—about one-half-inch of cork . . . and then what I call battleship linoleum . . . it was used in schools, I presume on battleships. The stuff just lasts and lasts."

In two places on the train, four people could sit facing each other across a removable table. "Let me take out one of the tables. This is incredible— this is incredible," he says. The table easily slides into the two slots on the wall. We examine the construction: plywood covered with masonite (a new material back then), finished with an aluminum inlay along the edge. "Look at the aluminum inlays put around here and the pedestal. . . . *It was fancy,*" he says admiringly.

Because the train was air conditioned, it required the first insulated windows, a sandwich of glass and plastic. "*Oooh* was that new. And just think—to bend those back windows!" Morrell says of the curving windows at the rounded end of the observation lounge. "That's the magic, that's the catch to this whole thing—how did they do this? All the work that you see here was done with human hands—there were no robots."

We walk forward. I welcome a breeze as we pass the one open door, and linger. "Just think," he says, showing me how the door was engineered, "this platform here and the step folded up so it was just like an airplane and . . . you had stainless steel all throughout this place here." Outside later as we look at the traction motors, the train's wheels, he says, "the way they cast this, as far as I am concerned, is a miracle."

We squeeze into the claustrophobic compartment up front. Under a low, five-foot ceiling are seats on each side of a big bulkhead for the engineer and the fireman. It feels as if you were being pushed to the very edge of the train, squeezed forward like toothpaste. On the old steam engines, the engineer sat way back behind a boiler. "If you hit a cow with this thing, you're the first one to see the cow," he says. The noise also drove some guys crazy, he says. The tiny compartment sits right in front of the enormous diesel engine. The exhaust pipes went straight up off the piston, creating "a dull roar." School kids could hear the train coming up the valley. The Flying Yankee ran through the Mount Washington Valley from 1941 to 1944. His father worked a little on this train in his long railroad career.

Standing in this humid sealed chamber, we hear a train whistle going by. I look through the clouded window and see people sitting at open windows in old-style cars, pulled by a diesel engine on the Conway Scenic Railroad. "That's an old train, it's diesel electric. It's *just* a train. And what we need is something that's more than *just a train*. . . . This is what I call sexy. This has got some verve to it." It's a strange moment of the future passed—the once-shining future derailed as the old-timey past, the nostalgic past, reprises itself.

We are standing outside at the streamlined prow that still retains an expressive face, like that in a children's book illustration. "It really is in good shape and it's too bad to junk it," Morrell says like a true Yankee. "We just could not let this go by." The logo has weathered off like a ghost sign on a barn or a brick wall. I reach forward to feel the stainless steel ribs, but I realize that my motion, and then his as he pats it, is more like greeting a horse at a fence. We know the myth of the artist who wants to bring his statue alive, but what of the dream of returning a machine to its machine-hood?

I ask him if he thinks that we have lost our faith in our ability to find fresh solutions, if we have lost what he calls our American ingenuity. "I think we need it to be renewed all the time," he answers. "The challenges ahead for us in the environment are just monumental. What're we going to be able to do about this finite thing called gasoline?" he says, referring to studies that show pollution soaring if China and India take up the automobile as we have.

"These are challenges out there for the kids that are in school today. You need—I hate to use the expression—but we've got to get people with balls to step out of conventional ways of thinking and dare to do something different.

"I wish I were younger because I would like to tackle the future for fuels in the whole world. We need to do something about that. Those are the unknowns. Pure water in the world—we keep patching that up because we don't tackle the basic problem," which is the growth of the world's population and the suffering in many African countries.

"The whole complex subject is related to something like the Flying Yankee. You may find that a thin thread to put together; for me it is just another reference point that we need. And there are lot of others. But it's one.

"See, I spent an awful lot of time as a youngster and up through my younger years when we had the threat of war constantly. And you think a lot different under those circumstances than when you feel safe, quiet. You know there was always a challenge out there: in the Depression to survive, and after that to survive with your life during World War II, the Korean War, and all the rest.

"It's easy to slide back where you don't want to take any risk. And you want to take the safe route. What we need is people who will plunge in ahead like the Bill Gates who go right off the end of the chart. That's what this thing does. If this is streaking down a line, some kid's gonna say: *Wow*. And that may apply to what he thinks about."

Robert Morrell died a year after we talked, but his train project continues.

Desert Island Talk

Stephen Mack was rescuing a fine eighteenth-century house that was now surrounded by strip malls and was just a few feet from an ever-growing road. "The house had entirely lost its context," he says. He was getting ready to disassemble the house, and move it. One day an older woman knocked on the door of the empty house. "She had once lived there," Mack says. "She used to rent it quite a few years ago. And she said that after she had moved all of her stuff out, and went back in for a last check, the house was just as welcoming with no furnishings in it at all."

In his careful restorations Mack seeks the calm and dignity of places that are never really empty, but possess *"ma,"* the necessary silences. The welcoming, empty rooms of that old house are a measure of what we have lost.

"In a sense, life is made up of two sectors," Mack says. "One is filled with car keys, credit cards, bills, telephone calls, lost children on milk cartons, work weeks . . . the bombardment of daily life. And another part of life is filled with wind, earthworms, clouds, cold, rain, bugs, time, a full belly.

"And the first aspect, I think, overwhelms, these days, the second aspect enormously. It's not healthy for the mind or the body for those who are, as I say, locked in the front end of it." You can turn on any newscast, any time, he says, and see "the reasons why being locked into the first aspect too much is too much."

The houses he rebuilds offer his clients a way to reconnect. Some just see an old house and are happy with that, and some have their lives changed, Mack says. In any case, he doesn't lecture. He lets his craft and the house speak.

"What I try to do, what I like to do is to create a haven of sorts using these houses and this architecture as a medium. To be honest with you, I could just as easily work in a different architectural medium. But these houses are very earthbound. . . . They seem to have all of the aspects necessary to have the living space be firmly planted in a natural environment. They tend to not call for Chem Lawn to come and poison everything, to try to have one particular strain of grass. They don't require nonindigenous bushes that screw in like light bulbs.

"Eighteenth century houses are a marvelous place to live. They're wonderful. In their own way, they're very, very elegant. Elegant in their simplicity."

Too many contemporary houses are spiritless places, cut off from from the outside, "denatured," he says. "It's been a disaster since the Second World War," he says, during which time three-quarters of the country's housing was built. "We should have gone from Victorian architecture to a more 'earthbound' architecture, using technology to get closer to the trees, birds, sky, that we like. Didn't happen. We're in this place now where things are built and no one really likes them.

"People come into houses and apartments and instead of feeling the space, they count the toilets. They make a decision on whether this is what they're going to buy based on how many toilet bowls they get for the price."

We have come to a divide with the eighteenth-century house on one side and us on the other. "I think it's pretty much all a result of industrialization. A long time ago when you bought a broom, you knew what a broom wanted to be like in order to last, in order to get your money's worth. And therefore, of the various broom makers there was one or two that made a really good broom. And they cost more or less the same. All at once somebody comes up with a machine that can make brooms that are lousy brooms but they're so cheap who could say no.

"After a certain length of time nobody knows a good broom from a bad broom. Welcome to the twentieth century."

This is why Mack moves and rebuilds old houses: to save a few good brooms. On an acre he has stored the parts of more than twenty-five houses and barns, all wrapped up under black tarps, each one numbered in white paint, a staging area for an invasion from the old life. It looks like a wartime materiel depot, I tell him. "Like a Normandy beachhead," he says good-naturedly.

Each covered pile is the parts of a different house or barn; the entire field is mapped.

"This is a Dutch barn that I took down the summer before last," he says, lifting the tarp to reveal huge timbers shaped like tongue depressors at the ends.

"Aren't they wonderful?" he asks.

"Incredible," I answer, "like sculptures."

"They are, they're absolutely sculptural," he says. (I learn later that he is also a sculptor.)

We walk on and he lifts another tarp, the framework of the Jaquith Buck house, circa 1812. "Wonderful house. Wonderful detail. Perfect condition. Victim of a development outside Boston."

Each building is meticulously documented and photographed. Each timber is numbered and keyed to a drawing. If there is a stone chimney, each stone is numbered. Mack, directing a crew, removes the interior woodwork in pieces as large as possible. The taller objects under wraps are stairways. ("There's a stairway, there's a stairway," he says, pointing around the field.) If something is broken, it is repaired on site. All the houses are recorded, some with as many as twenty pages of drawings and three hundred photographs. Mack even saves the small surprises that are revealed when old walls and floors are opened: seeds, bits of pottery, glass, porcelain, coins, oyster shells, shoe lasts, Indian artifacts and ax heads. He passes these on to the next dwellers when the house is resurrected "to shelter a new family, to sing with the summer breeze."

I visit his farm on an early spring day of apple blossom, lilac, grass three inches tall waving in the strong breeze, and the light green of the trees. Though I had only the thinnest directions, I knew I would recognize his place once I found his road. Each object, each view, on his farm is composed. His touch is present like a narrator's voice in an old-fashioned novel. It's there in the fence gate with the old iron latch, and the fence with its odd-sized old hand-split boards. Even his wood box, no more than a yard tall, matches a plan for it that still hangs on the wall.

The view out the back door of his house is a landscape painting, with a perfectly balanced foreground, middleground, and background. The foreground is framed by a stone wall, his office in a small cabin with a stone chimney that he moved to the site, a barn, and a flat-bottomed boat up on jacks. Sheep and a few lambs are sheltering under the boat. Just beyond there are a half-dozen cows lounging about, then a small water course, a pond, and a second pasture and trees.

"Context" is an important word for Mack, and here at home he is careful to select the context. He walks me to certain places around his pastures. He leads us past the sheep, over two, small broad bridges, past the cows and over stones, and we sit in the second pasture and look back: waving grass, cows, the studio, barn, sheep, and, on a small rise, his red house.

Later we will move to a small pond, and once more to his eighteenth-century center-chimney Cape Cod. It was a wreck when he found it and began his first restoration. He began to learn his craft with his own house. The pasture was all overgrown and it took a lot to bring it back.

"You don't own the land," Mack says. "The land has come from forever and is going to forever. The house that I own was built well over two hundred years ago, and with a little luck it will be here well over two hundred years from now. So I'm living in it, but I don't consider it precisely to be mine. I'm simply living there. There's a certain degree of stewardship in most things."

Inside his house, light spills through clear panes of twelve-over-twelve windows—wavy, bubbly glass that leaves you with no doubt that glass is a liquid. Old plaster, whitewashed walls, and the milk paint on the woodwork catch the light. There is no dust, no disorder. Each floor has a fascinating texture. The kitchen has a granite sink older than the house. Dishes are stacked on open shelves up to the ceiling, and the shelves are finished with a neat strip that curves back to the wall. He uses the same detail in his small library and study, where there is small drafting desk by the window. Around the house are a few of the maritime antiques he collects. Mack has been a collector since his childhood. If he had designed his place only to advertise that old houses feel good to live in, you would sign up immediately.

"Everybody wishes they were Israel Sack in 1920, '25, going around the North Shore with a wagon picking up some of the most spectacular furniture that's ever been built in this country for 50 bucks each, or going out and finding a Pierce Arrow in a barn," he says. "And while they are wishing that they were in that situation, the opportunity actually still exists, in the largest pieces of furniture that have been built in this country, which are some of the houses that have been built. And it's especially true here in New England, but is actually true in many places all around the country."

Stephen Mack is a careful speaker. He revises, applies caveats, exceptions, takes care not to be classed as an elite tastemaker, a fussy complainer. And one time he says: These are like desert island discussions. How would you rebuild the world? What do you do first? Plant a tree? Reform the soil? Teach people to see that a tree will grow there?

"You have to start someplace, and starting is at once an act of optimism, and an admission or acceptance of defeat," he says. "By starting here, you know that no matter the task, it cannot be saved or completed in your lifetime.

"The potential of what one does in their work is not the work, but how the work can influence others," he says. "I've always felt that I've done much more good in my work by example than I have in fact. I mean, how many houses in a lifetime could I possibly save or build or create or anything else?"

Mack wants to show people a way out of the boxes we have built. Consider the closed-in life of many suburban and country houses, he says. After rising, dressing, eating, all indoors of course, "you walk into the garage, you get in the car. You push the button, the door opens. You drive the car, which is also a closed environment just like the house is — you drive the car to the building where you work, you then may actually be in a parking garage underneath it in the extreme, or have a short walk from the parking lot into the building. And then you look back from a closed environment.

"And in that scenario you are living inside a man-made closed environment. You've got forty hours a week working, you've got eight hours a day sleeping — there goes another forty hours a week and then you've got all your meals — basically you're living inside a completely conditioned environment."

The houses and offices we live in are a radical break from the past. "It is only now in the last . . . seventy-five or eighty years when we've lived in houses where the plaster is getting dead flat and perfect with no warp, it's cleaned by machine. . . . Nothing has any depth to it," he says.

"I don't think people realize some of what they lose," he says. "So rather than going out and trying to convince people about what they're missing, it's more logical to create a scenario where they don't lose it as much and let them discover what they're gaining for themselves." If a community has good walking paths through fields and forests, people will use them. The right environment is a far better teacher than a heap of manifestos.

And that's what his old houses do: They open a view to a better way of living. "All the details are the heart and soul of the house," he says, and he works not to lose that. He takes care with "innumerable aspects—floorboard, plaster surfaces." For example, Mack hand-planes the boards and uses a scrub plane to take all the roughness off the board. Look at an early door, he says, the imperceptible concave marks in wood give it a texture. The uninitiated eye doesn't acknowledge these details, but it responds. "The personality, the visual effect of the house . . . consists of idiosyncrasies and patina," the spirits of old places that live in stairs worn by feet, and latches smoothed by hands. "Such houses have unimpeachable character," he says.

"In this room," he says, pointing about his house, "the plaster has an almost imperceptible wave to it. You don't notice it. You don't say to yourself, gosh, that wall's got a bit of wave in it. However, it affects you. The woodwork, the floorboard, the stones in the fireplace, all these aspects have a lot more movement to them."

"It's always a compromise: saving the house, saving the feel and putting the house back in context," as well as working in the modern utilities and comforts. "So in the end, as with all things in my work, and perhaps all things anyway, it's a study in compromise. Something with purpose is *perfection of compromise*. Just like the Constitution and other things that seem to be that perfect," which he notes we are still debating two hundred years later.

"I think that we don't make any compromises when we build new architecture and the result is not good. That is to say, we decide that we want to pepper the roof with skylights or the wall with windows, and we focus on what the interior looks like and not make the compromises, in order that the outside might have some sense or order, symmetry or elegance. Or, we might decide that we want the outside to look a particular way and not relate to the way the inside works."

The "concept of sympathetic architecture" is lacking. "And the damn trouble is while it's not happening, things are getting built. And it's not like a bad dress—you don't just throw it away. You're stuck with it. When they build a school, a hospital, a strip mall, those things last for forty or fifty years. And then you only get a face lift after twenty-five or thirty years. . . .

"Nobody likes any of these shopping centers, strip malls. They don't like

them, but they don't even discuss it. They accept it. It's worse than if everyone were questioning it. The war would be won. The fact is, everyone is
not questioning it at this time. And the ground is lost as more things, important parts of the built environment and the natural environment, are
lost. I'm not singing a song of that's the end."

I tell him how hard it is for people to express why they are dissatisfied.
Watching a public meeting discussing the design of a planned school or a
store is like revisiting the environmental movement before Rachel Carson
wrote *Silent Spring*.

"That's exactly correct. We just haven't gotten there," Mack says. Saving old houses, saving endangered species, these efforts are "running parallel" he says. "And the trouble is an enormous amount of damage happens before people say, 'Oh alright I guess we have to do something.'

"There are a lot of people trying to save a lot of things. . . . We have
now at long last come to a time that we're trying to save, and it's a new experience for society, I think. Not entirely new, but on a large scale it's new.
Just to try to save our environment alone, and I'm talking about an international and global standpoint, is a massive endeavor and a very serious
issue.

"It is interesting but very frustrating to be in the beginning of this
movement—it's slow. In comparison to some other things, it feels like
it's going at a glacial speed. It suffers all the ups and downs of various
political parties coming and going, budgetary constraints. . . . and the
longer it takes . . . the more damage will be done, and the less will be left
to save," which leads to things that have been said many times. "But the
fact is, it's late in the day and dark at night and there's no other way to
put it. And if you have to say the same thing over and over again, that's
what it takes."

Are you optimistic? I ask.

"For somebody who complains bitterly without taking a breath for up
to fifteen minutes, I'm actually pretty optimistic, yes, I think so. Because
there's no other alternative. Because it's live or die—and I'm taking the live
direction.

"This is an amazing time to live in because you can live in 1850 visually
and be in the year 2000 medically and foodwise, and you can be sitting in
front of a giant fireplace and eating vegetables that you froze from last
summer from your own garden, looking out the window at a snowstorm
wearing a hand-woven wool shirt if you want to. It's really amazing you
can take the greatest advantage of all those things at once. I don't have any
desire to live in another period.

"Now we're at a glacial pace discovering how we can segue back into
the prior, positive aspects of what we have given up. I think we can if we

want to. There isn't anything standing in our way except us. We can do this if we want to do it.

"If people start taking the chance, and I don't think it's a big chance, if they start allowing themselves to do things that they believe in, I think they'll get a great deal of acclaim for their work and be very successful at doing it. I would encourage anyone to take a breath and give it a try. I just don't see that there's anything to lose."

Weaving

Patryc Wiggins is a weaver with ambition. She is remaking her hometown of Newport, New Hampshire. On her loom the small milltown is reborn in a more colorful and generous light. She is weaving a tapestry of Newport. She is weaving Newport itself, bringing together millworkers, bankers, leading families, machinists, artists, students, teachers, mixing them together until they are more vibrant than when separate. Her tapestry is an act of community building. Newport, she says, has been ashamed of its mill history. She is finding the ceremony for Newport.

In your hometown a part of you remains, always, the child who went forth. "My family story is really the story of Newport, and Newport's story is really New England's story, and New England's story is the story of America," she says. Patryc went forth from a green house pulled up close to a busy road. No yard, just room enough to park a car. Other houses crowd the road, and the brick mill. You could miss it all in a wink on the way to downtown Newport not knowing that you had driven through Guild (pronounced Guy-ld), and past the Dorr Woolen Mill, one of three working woolen mills left in New Hampshire. You might miss this place, unless you were with Patryc Wiggins.

Here she took her first steps at eight months, showing early a certain family trait for stubbornness. Her mother, determined to use the name Patrick, created a new spelling for her daughter. From her second-floor bedroom with a wallpaper pattern of hot-air balloons, she could see her dad at work in the second shift of the spinning room at the mill. The mill was only two doors down. She could see her grandmother coming home. Grandmother Wiggins worked 32 years in the mill and lived next door. She could see other children playing, laundry hanging out, and the Sugar River, running red or green or purple, depending on the dyes and waste dumped that day. (Kids used to bet on what color the river would be.)

All that is thirty years ago now, but it is a scene Patryc lives everyday, part of the great tapestry she is weaving. This bold project, which began in 1988, is unlike anything else in the country. The tapestry will be large, 6 feet by 13 feet, executed in the French Aubusson method, like the great narrative tapestries of the middle ages. It takes about an hour to weave one square inch. In the central scene of the tapestry, a little girl looks out her window toward the woolen mill, the Sugar River, and the rest of Guild. The window is a "magnifying lens," she says, a way to see into history.

Her parents, Frank and Celestine, still live in the same house. They are one of eight married couples from the class of 1947 at Newport's Towle High School (and none has divorced, as Frank notes). His machine shop is next door, Z & W Machine & Tool. Around the shop, above the various drills, lathes, and calibrating measures, he has framed and hung the drawings his daughter sent home from when she lived in San Francisco, pencil sketches of street scenes. Such art might seem incongruous at first, but in Patryc's drawings of her Mission neighborhood, the houses posses the same jumbled angularity of the village the mill owners built in Guild. In the Mission neighborhood she learned much about seeing Guild.

To create the tapestry, Patryc had to draw a "cartoon," a hand-colored, wall-sized mural of what she will weave. This image was then enlarged, traced, and reversed before it went on the loom—sideways. She is working on an image sideways and reversed. This kind of transformation is not unusual—a writer may spend decades turning over childhood scenes in her mind. For Patryc, age forty-four, the many steps before the weaving itself represent her long journey. She did not go straight from Guild to this loom.

Michelle McDonald's American literature class has come to see Patryc in her studio at the Richards Free Library. Twenty-five students, mostly juniors, many outfitted by the sneaker companies, shuffle in, quiet and compliant. Newport's high school has one of the higher dropout rates in the state. The teacher brings the class to learn local history, but also to see that someone from their town is doing *something*.

Patryc has an open studio each Thursday afternoon. The library is in a mansion donated by the Richards, one of the mill-owning families that shaped Newport and left their names on the schools, and the mercantile blocks that line Newport's wide main street. Her studio is in what used to be the servants' quarters, appropriate since Patryc is on a mission to have Newport acknowledge its working-class, mill history.

She tells the class right out how she got pregnant in her junior year, at age seventeen, and fought the school to stay and finish her education. "I was the first girl allowed to continue school, pregnant. Before that you were out the door, expelled." Her daughter is now twenty-six. Two years ago—after twenty-four years—Patryc finished her B.A. degree.

She introduces the tapestry by showing them slides of Guild and her family. She smiles often when she talks, and seems to be a natural speaker.

"Why are the mills here?" she asks.

Silence. And then weakly, one voice: The Sugar River.

"Why?"

Silence.

To power the mills, she says. "Where does the Sugar River start?"

No one knows.

It starts at Lake Sunapee harbor, before running right under Newport's Main Street on the way to the Connecticut River. The river falls dramatically—eight hundred feet in twenty-four miles—which once powered mills that drew workers from all over the world. Newport once had the largest Finnish population in New Hampshire. She shows them a slide of the Finnish socialist hall, since torn down. "When my mother was in school, the majority of kids couldn't speak English." It was rough at times. The Ku Klux Klan burned crosses on nearby mountains. "That's part of our history we need to know."

The students' silence is what drives her forward. That silence is what she wants Newport to overcome.

"I was phobic about speaking. I can remember coming in here," Patryc says of the library, "and thinking this wasn't my place, and coming up to the counter and being *petrified*." Like the visiting students, she was also silent.

After she overcame a learning disability and learned to read in the third grade, she became a good student. Placed in the "smart" classes, she felt out of place, and was silent. Even as sophomore class president, she never made a speech, never held a meeting. She managed to graduate after having her child, and also won a state skiing championship in 1972.

Still, she had lost any hope of going to college, and went straight to work in the Dorr Mill, the third generation of her family to do so. She later worked in a machine shop, cleaned houses, and delivered the mail. They were tough years; she had a bad marriage. She began reading at the library, "African-American autobiographies—people who overcame, transcended difficult experiences." She read all of Richard Wright, Malcolm X's autobiography, Maya Angelou. They became her models.

And she began weaving. She would get up at 4:30 am, before work, to weave. She knew nothing, worked with cheap acrylic yarn, made up knots and techniques as she went along, and loved every stolen moment.

Her marriage ended, she remarried, "escaped" to San Francisco, and had a son. "I didn't even realize I was working class until I went to San Francisco. It was like going from Tuesday night bingo to a country club.

"I looked up weaving in the San Francisco yellow pages: San Francisco Tapestry Workshop." She thought, "I don't know what tapestry is, but it's under weaving." She had found her way to "the most important weaver in the world," Jean-Pierre Larochette, who is the fourth generation of his family to weave tapestries. He apprenticed with his father, as had his father before him. Weavers came from all over to study with Larochette, but no one just walked in off the street.

"What I remember most of Patryc is seeing really how she blossomed," Larochette says. "She was extremely shy—a person coming to the work-shop just to see what was happening, probably without even really think-ing that she could be part of it." She evolved "rapidly into one of the bet-ter weavers we had. Very soon I was arranging for her to weave other people's work, which is part of the program."

She was hired by other weavers and artists, and by the Hearst Castle to copy a section of fourteenth-century tapestry. She could have lived well "weaving corporate commissions of benign landscapes," but Newport was never far from her thoughts and art. She loved the many Latino mu-rals in her neighborhood, admired their verve, their strong colors and the sweep of their storytelling. She wanted to bring this provocative public art back home. That meant pushing herself harder.

She enrolled in San Francisco's free City College to study feminist and labor issues, and fine arts. But she was so unsure of herself that she was afraid to even get out of the car to pick up a class schedule. Her husband had to go in for her. She said nothing in her classes for two years, and fi-nally sought out counseling to free her up. She worked at that for years.

When the time came to unveil the first sample square of the tapestry in Newport, she knew she would have to make a short public speech. She took a speech class at Lebanon College, and was "petrified" for weeks, be-fore she spoke for five minutes before a roomful of her supporters. "Ok, I've got to completely abandon my fears," she realized. "Being afraid is not a reason for not doing anything. You've got to be fearless."

Since then Patryc has lectured twice at the Smithsonian Institution, served a year-long residency in the Newport schools, and has sat twice on grant review panels for the National Endowment for the Arts. She had to borrow money and clothes to help award two million dollars in grants. She is courted by foundations studying community-based art. Patryc will talk with anyone willing to listen about the Mill Tapestry Project: She ap-proached the library to help her; she convinced a yarn company to give her miles of yarn at a discount; and she helped to create the space for the finished tapestry in the new Sugar River Valley Technical Center.

"Patryc has this amazing courage and insight and drive to accomplish things," says James Garvin, New Hampshire's state architectural historian. "She's remarkable and her project is remarkable. From this one spark the whole community is beginning to see that its daily life is inseparable from the arts, inseparable from a broader story that goes beyond the day-to-day drudgery of things, and actually is a saga."

"What she's doing is wonderful," says Larochette, who has visited her Newport studio. "Tapestry is like a book, it's a traditional way to bring about memory, to record history. Having the community involved is extremely valuable. And I think it's quite unique. I travel quite a bit. I haven't seen anything like this abroad either. For somebody to take on herself a project like this, I think is quite amazing."

As part of the project, she took on a further challenge, co-producing the New England Artists Trust Congress, which brought nearly four hundred artists to Newport. There was an exhibit on the town's machine tool industry, poetry by four generations of residents, murals painted by an artist in residence, and a live opera performance at the recently restored Newport Opera House. Downtown was specially illuminated with lighting designed by high school art students. Patryc involved everyone. (She had her dad helping out on the machine tool exhibit.) The Arts Congress was, she says, "weaving of another sort, literally the social fabric of the community."

"Our history is of value to the state and region if we have the guts to share it in a honest way. The good memories and the bad are all important for us to embrace. Our strength is being authentic."

But there are people who would rather Newport remained silent about its history.

"I deal daily with resentment," she says. When she started weaving she didn't call herself a craftsman for a decade. Then she went to San Francisco, where it was "easy to say I'm an artist. In San Francisco everyone's an artist." When she came home saying she was an artist, some said, "Yeah. Sure you are."

She was stepping out of her place. She has been told outright: We have known you all your life and you can't do a tapestry. Not her, "one of those pregnant teens . . . who went to work at the mill."

Mostly "it's an invisible thing that isn't discussed," she says, carefully weighing her words. "But it's something that I think about daily. And I know that it's so important in the end. That is the triumph of this whole thing: It is my stamina to move forward when the psychological, social, cultural forces have oftentimes—not always—have done their damnedest to not let it happen." Patryc Wiggins has the stamina of a long-distance runner.

In the last few years she has seen her efforts starting to succeed. At the beginning it was difficult to even talk about Newport's history—in her dreams she was pushing boulders and blocks uphill. Good work seemed to evaporate. A successful discussion or program seemed as if it were forgotten a month later. But it adds up, she says.

"You start realizing that those teachers that hated you during the residency, you find out that they've found the curriculum you've wrote and they're actually doing the chapter. In fact the teacher is yelling out the window, saying, hey, the kids loved it!"

Outside Newport, others are impressed with how things are changing. "What we've seen in the state preservation office," says James Garvin, is "the power of an image, the power of an idea, the power of a celebration of work, and of community and tradition—all those things coming from this little part of Newport which nobody ever paid attention to, this little neighborhood of Guild. That's the last place we would have expected that kind of revitalization of community to have come from.

"Even people who are indifferent to the tapestry project, or possibly hostile or jealous of Patryc as an individual seem to be, in their own fields perceiving . . . a bright interesting future in that community."

Patryc thinks back on that silent class that visited her and is sad. "I just know I had something that they can use. I have a sense of other people's ability that they don't have. They don't see it."

Samantha Dumais, Erin Mullen, and Heather Jarvis (fourth grade) are the first to visit Patryc one afternoon during her open studio. They are regular visitors and catch Patryc up on their lives: Heather's rabbit just had baby rabbits. She's not sure how many, because they are hidden by the mom and the hay. Samantha's cat just had kittens. "Spring is here," Patryc says, smiling. And there was a big spelling bee at school.

They are soon joined by Shaina and Lyndsy Stoddard (fifth and fourth grade) and Tracy Carter (second grade) on their first visit. Patryc shows them the cartoon mural.

The six little girls stand before the cartoon asking about different things in the scene. Patryc answers their questions with stories: There's Bonnie Miller's horse, Shiloh. She loved Shiloh. She cut a hole in the barn wall so Shiloh could stick his head in the kitchen and visit. But the flies got to be a bother, so she had to close it up. Next door to the horse, a little girl is doing cartwheels. "That's Patryc showing off," she says. And the girl looking on is her sister "Reesee."

She shows the girls the tapestry on the loom. The verdict: "Aw—cool—awesome." Which is close to what adults say when they lean in close to the tapestry.

"Isn't that gorgeous. Who-who! Boy, oh boy!" says Bob Falkenburg from a nearby town. He is retired and volunteers his time tutoring adults.

The night the chamber of commerce gave him an award for his work, Patryc was speaking. Today Falkenburg and his wife are showing two visiting friends around town. They are familiar with weaving, so talk turns to weft, skeins, colors. A moment ago Patryc was talking with schoolgirls. She easily matches her visitors' interests.

The space behind the loom is narrow, and the ohhs and ahhs of visitors sound as if they're seeing a small fireworks display. "Isn't it so pretty? Mom, you've got to go behind there and look," says Brittany Dunn, her next visitor. "It's beautiful! I love it! I love it! I love it!"

"Well, thank you," says Patryc. "You must have grown an inch since last week." Brittany first saw the tapestry project when she was in the third grade, three years ago, and likely thinks it's natural that the town library has a weaver at work.

By now the small room is crowded, and her older brother Frank (Fuzzy by family lore) shows up. They good-naturedly chide each other about who was considered the good child, and the smart child. They recount more of their family's "can-do" attitude: their mom going off to college at age forty, her resolute stand as a rare Democrat, and the heated political discussions around the kitchen table with neighbors.

The talk touches on scenes in the tapestry, mixing family, work, town and politics, mixing the living and the dead. They talk of Grandma Kennedy, Nanny, who was beloved around town. "I ran into Mrs. Stetson, she mentioned Nanny saying how much she missed her and got tears in her eyes," says Patryc.

A few years ago Patryc visited an exclusive Connecticut suburb. There were many prohibitions: no above-ground pools, no repairing cars in your front yard, no hanging out laundry, no TV antennas, no powerlines. And she thought: Everything that is not allowed, that is Guild.

And yet under her hand, on the loom, the Guild that is taking shape is beautiful, even down to the river choking on dyes.

"I'm honoring the effort of working people often doing really boring, monotonous, sometimes crazy-making work, day after week, after generation. Everyday I think of my grandparents . . . people of just immense integrity and depth, living out lives that didn't match their potential or worth."

For all that has happened to her grandparents, to her, to Newport, Patryc could create a dark art about the hard life of millworkers. But she doesn't see it that way.

"There is so much joy just in the process, not only of art-making, but just in life . . . if you can open yourself up to see those joys as they happen.

"I was driving up the road yesterday and I just got so much joy—it just came over me—to be driving on this road, this same road that I rode my bike and walked on when I was just a kid, and I was thinking of the guy who was my best friend. . . . I allowed myself to feel happy even though I was in the middle of a manic-paced day," she laughs. "You could just forget that, not allow that in. But I am thinking that's what life is." Her talk takes her from childhood to history, and the quiet, daily courage of many lives.

It is like when she weaves—her happiest time. "I do a lot of thinking. A lot of times I have a pad beside me because as I'm weaving it all ties in. I'm thinking about the stuff I'm actually weaving, which brings up Guild, which brings up Newport history, which brings up family, which brings up questions.

"You can choose to look at life with no history to it, or no connections, or you can open it up and see that everything is connected to everything.

"Things don't fall apart. I hated that," she says in reference to William Butler Yeats' famous poem, *The Second Coming*. "There's connections. People are so isolated. People want to connect. That's about mending and weaving and not falling apart. But you gotta fight for it."

This is a good place to end, a tale of good works, the good fight. But one more story, about a poor woman who found her treasure at the town dump. She, too, was a Noah.

The Button Saver

Noah gathered two of all that lived, following some of the most specific instructions in the bible. We aren't always so carefully guided. Voices, visions, burning bushes are given only to a few.

Sadie Huntoon lived the hard life of the backwoods: no running water, no indoor plumbing, a small house with thin walls. In her twenties she fell in love with a "dashing hero of World War I, Corporal Aubrey Huntoon," William M. Sullivan has written of his great aunt. Sadie had grown up in a large working class family that had known hardship; four of her eleven brothers and sisters had died before age five. She was a small woman, not five feet tall, shy, and was poorly schooled. Sadie posed for a studio photo at age twenty in a plain dress and high black shoes. She stands as if she has just put down a heavy load—her shoulders are bent, her arms hang down. She meets the camera stoically.

Her war hero had been decorated for his valor, but he had also been wasted by a mustard gas attack. He could never work. They lived narrowly on his pension, and what money they could get from occasional jobs like picking blueberries. He was unfaithful and an alcoholic, says Sullivan.

After Aubery died early, Sadie lived by herself for the next thirty-two years. Well into her eighties she chopped her own wood. Each week she walked six miles into town to buy her groceries and six miles home.

Sadie began to visit the town dump several times a week. The dump was just over a mile's walk away. In this she was not unusual; "picking" is an accepted practice at most small town dumps. A few people make some money this way; most people just pick for the sport of it, to see what comes along, but it gets a hold of a few people until they've recreated the dump back home.

Dump picking got a hold of Sadie. She stuffed her house, basement, and three sheds with her treasures. Furniture and boxes were stacked so high that there was no way to get very far into her sheds, says Sullivan. She had to stack her wood in a "derelict 1940 Dodge station wagon behind her house."

She collected "gallons and gallons of buttons she clipped off discarded clothes," as well as "eyeglasses, pots and pans, tools, screws and bolts, cigar and other wooden boxes and a variety of chairs, radios and furniture," says Sullivan. She brought home two old china cabinets and filled them with discarded dishes. She also saved books, and one of her saves was priceless: the handwritten *Record of the Winchester Anti-Slavery Society,* April 1838. Winchester, New Hampshire, had one of the many town chapters of the American Anti-Slavery Society. The Winchester society distributed anti-slavery tracts, raised money to build a new school for "colored children" in New York, and petitioned Congress to end slavery. Without Sadie, this important historical document would have vanished.

In her last years, Sadie "became secretive, combative and paranoid," says Sullivan. She burned $3,000 in old bills "because the money, seemingly, like herself, was old and worn." On of one her long walks to get groceries she had been attacked by two men who tried to force her into their car. She was never the same after this attack. "She departed from this life unheralded, unsung and virtually unnoticed," says Sullivan. Her few relatives were left to clean up the "gallons and gallons of buttons," and all the rest of the hoard.

All Noahs are like Sadie Huntoon. They pull from the wreck we have made of the world what they can, and time will judge its value. Sometimes they collect buttons, not even knowing that they are trying to hold the world together.

Some Concluding Restoration Principles, Pleas, and Prayers

~ॐ ॐ~

1. *Restoration is praise.* "Ancient religion and modern science agree: We are here to give praise. Or, to slightly tip the expression, to pay attention," writes John Updike.

2. *The future.* Good restoration schools us in the graces of the old ways, freeing us to build anew. When we bring our loving attention to that which is old, it is not the past we are restoring but the future. Good restoration saves the future.

3. *Mending.* Good restoration is a two-way street; the object being mended in turn mends the worker. As important as a restored building may be, the real value lies in how this work restores and awakens us. When preservationists talk on about technique and tax codes and architectural history, they have often lost sight of why we save old things. They have lost touch with the animating spirit that called them to the old ways. We save these old things to save ourselves.

4. *Evanescence.* On some winter days, snow passes right to vapor. Evanescence. All things worthy of restoration are so because we are seeing them as they pass, each in its own time, from years to eons—houses, waterfalls, trees, and the earth itself.

Good restoration should contain its opposite: going away, softening, decay. Even the most meticulously preserved object, all glittering and pristine, should hint of its fate. Evanescence instead of epoxy-essence.

Can we restore the evanescence of a sunset to our lives?

5. *Epoxy-essence.* The newly restored nineteenth-century hotel gleams. Everything is freshly painted and scrubbed. The marble is polished to brilliance, the wood stripped of one hundred coats of paint. We like our old

buildings to look new. Prosperity in America is represented by the slick surface. As society ages, and has to accept wrinkles and sags and a stiffness in the joints, will we accept the same in our buildings? Historic preservation has too much in common with plastic surgery.

6. *Neglect.* Treasured objects need the proper level of neglect. Much of our cultural heritage has come down to us because it was sheltered in an attic or protected by a layer of later fashion. It was saved from the wrecking crane, and the ruinous good intentions of restorers.

An era of renewed attention usually brings on a flurry of scraping and removal to achieve an often incorrect color or finish or form. The history of restoration is frequently the history of misreading.

Less scraping, less constructing new buildings in old shells. Let the coral reef be our model: Life built on life.

7. *Loss.* We must let go of some things—some beloved things—to allow the birth of the new, which at times will be shocking and awkward.

8. *Paradox.* There are many photos of the early Chicago tall buildings that I admire. The best buildings are at once rude in their new power, and poised. In one photo, taken around 1880, there is a Studebaker showroom. In the window are new wagons, awaiting their horses.

There are places in which history changes—you can see the rift as clearly as the line of an advancing storm front. We could make weather maps of such rifts, a new idea or invention spilling with fury into a settled atmosphere. Let us honor the wagon in the skyscraper window, the horse and wagon pulling the Wright Brothers aeroplane. A true American restoration would catch the flux and uncertainty of our lives. We dwell in contradictions.

9. *More igloos, less frozen time.* More axes repaired and in use; fewer in a glass case.

10. *Original purposes first.* A grain mill without grain is not a mill, a smelter without fire is not a smelter. No more food courts, festival marketplaces, gift boutiques, shopping malls inside old walls, please. You can't shop your way back to the past. History is not a mall. We have enough of those fake San Francisco-style trolley-buses rolling on rubber tires through neighborhoods on safaris after the quaint. Stop the spread of FTD—Fake Trolley Disease.

11. *Machine spirit.* A working mill is alive. When the penstock is opened to the water and the turbine is set turning, the floor hums and the

belts overhead flap and clack with the contentment of machines easy in their motion. Overhead and below, the place vibrates. We are standing inside the machine.

Deceived by tranquil, mirror-smooth millponds, we may forget that mills are machines. If the sunlight falls right, it too is set in motion by the belts, producing a dappled light like that under an elevated train.

The mill is astride the water. There is a waterfall just outside the open door: water visible through the broken windows, water rumbling beneath the rough floor. A Venice of barn boards, wood shavings, old gummy oiled gears and big wide belts.

This moment when a mill comes to life should be a measure for restorations: Is the building alive? Does it breathe?

The spirits of many American places live with the first ignition of a machine.

12. *Nothing is ever saved.* At a seventeenth-century house restored by experts, they have put a little sandpaper grit in the clay of a repaired chimney, a microscopic calling card, evidence of the twentieth century "flashing back" at the next generation of workers. "You need to leave messages," say the restorers. Restoration is a legacy. The job isn't finished; it is handed off to the next caretakers. Rot is our inheritance. Rejoice!

13. *Time.* This is a dream I had shortly before waking. I go to visit an old man we know who lives in a nearby town. As I enter, he is watching a television show. He greets me and I join him. At first the show seems to be about young boys playing summer games at a lake. Then I recognize one of the boys is his recently married son. There are other scenes from the boy's life as he grows up.

In the last scene we are at the lake's edge again. The boy is standing up on a rock out in the waters. He is holding up a fine, old-fashioned watch, with a rectangular face and a silky, deep burnished steel. He holds the watch up—he is wet, the watch is wet. The watch slips from his hand into the waters. Another man pulls the watch from the lake bottom. He is a boy when he finds the watch, but we see him in that instant as a grown man. The watch makes all the difference in his life.

The show ends. I look up. The old man had left the room. I knew then that we had been seeing scenes from his life. He was the young boy who had let time slip through his fingers.

This is the one restoration no one can achieve: Time. You can plane the boards to perfection, repoint the bricks, reset the terra cotta, dust and protect, rebuild, sketch and speculate. But time has gone by.

"Different and ever different waters flow down," Heraclitus may have said. You can only step in the same river twice if that river is epoxy, a frozen river.

14. *Renewal.* Ours is an age of broken connections, lost connections between heart and work, soul and politics, community and the self. Restoration is renewal—an effort to mend the world—or else it is not worth doing. Good restoration is a prayer, an offering. It's praise, attention paid; it revels in the glory and spirit of this life.

Bibiliography

The Same Ax, Twice

Arnold, David. "Wind-Borne Once More." *The Boston Globe*. August 19, 1996.
———. "At the Helm of History." *The Boston Globe*. July 22, 1997.
———. "History to See; Old Ironsides." *The Boston Globe*. July 20, 1997.
Boorstin, Daniel, ed. *Visiting Our Past: America's Historylands*. Washington, D.C.: National Geographic Society, 1977.
Chandler, Hugh. "Plutarch's Clothespin." *Analysis* 44, 1984.
Chapelle, Howard I. *The History of the American Sailing Navy*. New York: W. W. Norton & Co., 1949.
Economakis, Richard, ed. *Acropolis Restoration: The CCAM Interventions*. London: Academy Editions, 1994.
Fraser, J. T., ed. *The Voices of Time*. New York: George Braziller, 1966.
Fitzhugh, William, and Susan A. Kaplan. *Inua: Spirit World of the Bering Sea Eskimo*. Washington, D.C: Smithsonian Institution Press, 1982.
Golen, Jimmy. "New House, Same Old Parquet." *The Keene Sentinel*. April 22, 1997.
Highsmith, Carole M., and Ted Landphair. *America Restored*. Washington, D.C.: Preservation Press, 1994.
Hoyt, Edwin P. *Old Ironsides*. New York: Pinnacle Books, 1976.
Humphreys, Joshua. "Letter Book 1793–7: USS Constitution: Dimensions and Sizes of Materials for Building a Frigate of Forty-Four Guns." Naval Historical Center Detachment Boston, USS Constitution Maintenance & Repair Facility.
Kahn, Charles H. *The Art and Thought of Heraclitus*. London: Cambridge University Press, 1979.
MacQuarrie, Brian. "Today's Big Day for Old Ironsides." *The Boston Globe*. July 21, 1997.
Morford, Mark P. O., and Robert J. Lenardon. *Classical Mythology*. New York: David McKay, 1971.
Mullin, David G. "Rigs: Past and Present of the USS Constitution." Naval Historical Center Detachment Boston, USS Constitution Maintenance & Repair Facility, August 30, 1994.
Oliver, Paul. *Dwellings: The House Across the World*. Oxford: Phaidon, 1987.
Onians, R. B. *The Origins of European Thought About the Body, the Mind, the Soul, the World, Time, and Fate*. Cambridge: Cambridge University Press, 1951.
Robinson, T. M. *Heraclitus Fragments*. Toronto: University of Toronto Press, 1987.
Rose, H. J. *A Handbook of Greek Literature*. 1934. Revised, London: Methuen, 1961.
Rowley, John. *Taxidermy and Museum Exhibition*. New York: Appleton, 1925.
Smart, Brian. "How to Reidentify the Ship of Theseus." *Analysis* 32, 1972.
Stille, Alexander. "Faking It." *The New Yorker*. June 15, 1998.
Walker, Henry J. *Theseus and Athens*. New York: Oxford University Press, 1995.
Ward, Anne G., et al. *The Quest for Theseus*. New York: Praeger, 1970.

Watanabe, Yasutada. *Shinto Art: Ise and Izumo Shrines.* New York: Weatherhill, 1974.
Wiggins, David. *Sameness and Substance.* Cambridge, Mass.: Harvard University Press, 1980.

Unearthing the Mammoth

Agenbroad, Larry D. "Mammoth Site." *Natural History.* October 1997.
Associated Press, "Looking for Levittown." *The Keene Sentinel.* January 21, 1997.
Attinger, Joelle. "When the Sky's the Limit." *Time.* February 29, 1988.
Bearss, Edwin C. *Hardluck Ironclad: The Sinking and Salvage of the Cairo.* Baton Rouge: Louisiana State University Press, 1980.
Bloch, Nina. "Mammoth Hunter." *Earthwatch.* May/June 1998.
Borden, Jack. "Wanted: Skywatchers." *Sky & Telescope.* June 1991.
Browne, Malcolm W. "Astronomers Rage Against the Light." *The New York Times.* May 9, 1993.
——. "Cost of Wide Phone Service May Be Astronomer Static." *The New York Times.* June 29, 1997.
Cahan, Richard. *They All Fall Down: Richard Nickel's Struggle to Save America's Architecture.* Washington, D.C.: Preservation Press, 1994.
Cummings, Abbott Lowell. *The Framed Houses of Massachussetts Bay, 1625– 1725.* Cambridge, Mass.: Belknap Press, 1979.
——. "The Gedney House." Society for the Preservation of New England Antiquities, 141 Cambridge St., Boston, Mass. 02114.
Ferris, Timothy. *Coming of Age in the Milky Way.* New York: William Morrow & Co., 1988.
——. *The Whole Shebang.* New York: Simon & Schuster, 1997.
Grady, Anne A. "The Boardman House." Society for the Preservation of New England Antiquities, 141 Cambridge St., Boston, Mass. 02114.
Howe, Peter J. "Blinded by the Light." *The Boston Globe.* August 26, 1996.
Ingalls, Albert G. "'The Heavens Declare the Glory of God.'" *Scientific American.* November 1925.
International Dark Sky Association. Home Page, www.darksky.org.
Kuznik, Frank. "Sky Raves." *Air & Space Smithsonian.* December 1997/January 1998.
Land-Works. "A Report on Ski Area Lighting in Vermont." Submitted to the Vermont Agency of Natural Resources, Middlebury, Vt., April 1994.
Mammoth Site of Hot Springs, South Dakota. "Development and History of the Mammoth Site." www.mammothsite.com.
Mansfield, Howard. "When the Telescope Nuts Come Back to Stellafane." *Yankee.* August 1996.
New England Light Pollution Advisory Group. Circular Nos. 8–14. Editor, Daniel W. E. Green. Smithsonian Astrophysical Observatory, 60 Garden St., Cambridge, Mass. 02138.
——. "Good Neighbor Outdoor Lighting." Draft 4, August 1994.
Raymo, Chet. *The Soul of the Night: An Astronomical Pilgrimage.* Englewood Cliffs, N.J.: Prentice Hall, 1985.
Ross, W.D., ed. *The Works of Aristotle.* Vol. 9. *Ethica Nicomachea, Magna Moralia, Ethica Eudemia.* Oxford: Clarendon Press, 1915.
Schwartz, Cornelia. "That's My Sky!" *Orion Nature Quarterly.* Winter 1984.

The Stellafane News, Newsletter of the Springfield Telescope Makers. October 6, 1993; December 13, 1993; March 24, 1994.

Tuan, Yi-Fu. *Passing Strange and Wonderful.* New York: Kodansha Globe, 1995.

Upgren, Arthur R. "Night Blindness." *The Amicus Journal.* Winter 1996.

U.S. Department of the Interior/National Park Service. "Astronomy and Astrophysics: A National Historic Landmark Theme Study, 1989." Washington, D.C.

Wald, Matthew L. "Seeing the Sky: Not a Limit but Infinity." *The New York Times.* June 21, 1987.

Ward, C. Whitney, and Jack Borden. *For Spacious Skies Activity Guide.* For Spacious Skies, 1990. 54 Webb St., Lexington, Mass. 02173.

Weil, Simone. *The Need for Roots,* New York: G. P. Putnam's Sons, 1952.

Wilford, John Noble. "In a Golden Age of Discovery, Faraway Worlds Beckon." *The New York Times.* February 9, 1997.

Willard, Berton C. *Russell W. Porter.* Freeport, Me.: Bond Wheelwright, 1976.

Verdet, Jean-Pierre. *The Sky: Mystery, Magic, and Myth.* New York: Abrams, 1992.

Building the Elephant

Baker, George P. *The Pilgrim Spirit: A Pageant in Celebration of the Landing of the Pilgrims in Plymouth, Massachusetts, December 21, 1620.* Boston: Marshall Jones, 1921.

Bodnar, John. *Remaking America.* Princeton, N.J.: Princeton University Press, 1992.

Bourne, Randolph. *The Radical Will: Selected Writings, 1911–18.* New York: Urizen Books, 1977.

Glassberg, David. *American Historical Pageantry.* Chapel Hill: University of North Carolina Press, 1990.

Kammen, Michael. *Mystic Chords of Memory.* New York: Alfred A. Knopf, 1991.

McConnell, Stuart. *Glorious Contentment.* Chapel Hill: University of North Carolina Press, 1992.

McPherson, James M. *Battle Cry of Freedom.* New York: Oxford University Press, 1988.

Sears, Stephen W. *Landscape Turned Red: The Battle of Antietam.* New York: Ticknor & Fields, 1983.

Sebor, Michael. "Rally Round The Flag: A Civil War Living History in Peterborough." Peterborough, N.H.: Sixth N.H. Volunteer Infantry Historical Association, 1997.

Snow, Stephen Eddy. *Performing the Pilgrims.* Jackson: University Press of Mississippi, 1993.

Peterborough Historical Society. The Hovey, Holt, Cummings Collection. MSS 96. Peterborough, N.H.

———. MacDowell Colony Collection. MSS 17. Peterborough, N.H.

Waite, Otis Frederick Reed. *New Hampshire in the Great Rebellion.* Claremont, N.H.: Tracy, Chase, and Co., 1870.

The Belated Tourist

Andrews, Edward Deming, and Faith Andrews. *Religion in Wood: A Book of Shaker Furniture.* Bloomington: Indiana University Press, 1966.

Axelrod, Alan, ed. *The Colonial Revival in America.* New York: W. W. Norton, 1985.

Bloom, Harold. *The Anxiety of Influence.* New York: Oxford University Press, 1973.
———. *Kabbalah and Criticism.* New York: Seabury Press, 1975.
———. *A Map of Misreading.* New York: Oxford University Press, 1975.
Brodsky, Joseph. *On Grief and Reason.* New York: Farrar, Straus, and Giroux, 1995.
Brown, Patricia Leigh. "Reliving Myth of the Presidential Log Cabin." *The New York Times.* May 25, 1997.
Butcher-Younghans, Sherry. *Historic House Museums: A Practical Handbook for Their Care, Preservation and Management.* New York: Oxford University Press, 1993.
Clarke, O. P. *General Grant at Mount MacGregor.* 1906. Reprinted, Saratoga Springs, N.Y: The Saratogian Print, 1994.
Coleman, Laurence Vail. *Historic House Museums.* Washington, D.C.: American Association of Museums, 1933.
Curtis, John O. *Moving Historic Buildings.* Technical Preservation Services, U.S. Department of the Interior, Technical Report. Washington, D.C., 1979.
Demos, John. *The Unredeemed Captive.* New York: Alfred A. Knopf, 1994.
Fleischauer, Carl, ed. *Documenting America, 1935–43.* Berkeley: University of California Press, 1988.
Flippo, Chet. *Graceland: The Living Legend of Elvis Presley.* San Francisco: Collins, 1993.
Frost, Robert. *Collected Poems, Prose, and Plays.* New York: Library of America, 1995.
Frost, Lesley. *New Hampshire's Child.* Albany, N.Y.: State University of New York Press, 1969.
Frost, Lesley Lee. *The Frost Family's Adventure in Poetry.* Columbia: University of Missouri Press, 1994.
Gillis, John R., ed. *Commemorations: The Politics of National Identity.* Princeton, N.J.: Princeton University Press, 1994.
Grant, Ulysses. S. *Memoirs and Selected Letters.* New York: Library of America, 1990.
Guralnick, Peter. *Last Train to Memphis: The Rise of Elvis Presley.* Boston: Little, Brown, 1994.
Hall, Patricia, and Charlie Seemann, eds. *Folklife and Museums.* Nashville, Tenn.: American Association for State and Local History, 1987.
Hammel, Lisa. "Pursuing the Past in Deerfield." *The New York Times.* October 2, 1988.
Harbaugh, William Henry. *The Life and Times of Theodore Roosevelt.* New York: Collier Books, 1966.
Harris, Neil. "The Battle for Grant's Tomb." *American Heritage.* August 1985.
Hayden, Dolores. *Seven American Utopias: The Architecture of Communitarian Socialism, 1790–1975.* Cambridge, Mass.: MIT Press, 1976.
Hine, Thomas. *Populuxe.* New York: Alfred A. Knopf, 1986.
Holzer, Harold. "Lincoln's Early Years." *The New York Times.* February 8, 1998.
Jackson, Charles O., ed. *Passing: The Vision of Death in America.* Westport, Conn.: Greenwood, 1977.
Kavanagh, Gaynor. *History Curatorship.* Washington, D.C.: Smithsonian Institution Press, 1990.
Kermode, Frank. *The Uses of Error.* Cambridge, Mass.: Harvard University Press, 1991.
Lathem, Edward Connery, and Lawrance Thompson. *Robert Frost: Farm-Poultryman.* Hanover, N.H.: Dartmouth Publications, 1963.
Lee, Antoinette J., ed. *Past Meets Future: Saving America's Historic Environments.* Washington, D.C.: Preservation Press, 1992.

Lewis, Thomas S. "'To Be, To Do, To Suffer:' The Memoirs of Ulysses S. Grant." The Edwin M. Moseley Faculty Research Lecture, Skidmore College, Saratoga Springs, N.Y., 1985.

Lindgren, James M. *Preserving Historic New England*. New York: Oxford University Press, 1995.

Mansfield, Howard. "Birth of A Station." *International Design*. September/October 1990.

———. "Britain's Phone Kiosks." *Places: A Quarterly Journal of Environmental Design* 6.2. Winter 1990.

———. "Gas, Food & Signage." *International Design*. March/April 1990.

———. "Going for the Gaudy." *The Washington Post*. November 25, 1988.

———. "A Modern Detective for Historic Houses." *The New York Times*. June 18, 1987.

———. "Recreating a Classic House Shingle by Shingle." *The New York Times*. August 25, 1988.

———. "The Ribbon Across the Chair." *Metropolis*. July/August 1986.

Melvoin, Richard I. *New England Outpost: War and Society in Colonial Deerfield*. New York: W. W. Norton, 1989.

Marling, Karal Ann. *Graceland: Going Home with Elvis*. Cambridge, Mass.: Harvard University Press, 1996.

McBryde, Isabel, ed. *Who Owns the Past?* Melbourne: Oxford University Press, 1985.

McCullough, David G. *Mornings on Horseback*. New York: Simon & Schuster, 1981.

McDaniel, George. *Hearth and Home: Preserving a People's Culture*. Philadelphia: Temple University Press, 1982.

McFeely, William S. *Grant: A Biography*. New York: W. W. Norton, 1981.

McGiffin, Robert F. *Furniture Care and Conservation*. Nashville, Tenn.: American Association for State and Local History, 1992.

Miller, Amy Bess. *Hancock Shaker Village/The City of Peace*. Hancock, Mass.: Hancock Shaker Village, 1984.

Mostafavi, Mohsen, and David Leatherbarrow. *On Weathering: The Life of Buildings in Time*. Cambridge, Mass.: MIT Press, 1993.

National Park Service. *Respectful Rehabilitation*. Washington, D.C.: Preservation Press, 1982.

Norkunas, Martha K. *The Politics of Public Memory*. Albany, N.Y.: State University of New York Press, 1993.

Peteron, Merrill D. *Lincoln in American Memory*. New York: Oxford University Press, 1994.

Pitkin, Thomas M. *The Captain Departs*. Carbondale: Southern Illinois University Press, 1973.

Roosevelt, Theodore. *Theodore Roosevelt, An Autobiography*. New York: Macmillan, 1913.

Samdok Bulletin. "Contemporary Museum Research in Sweden." September 1995. Samdoksekretariatet Nordiska Museet, Box 27820, S-115 93 Stockholm, Sweden.

Sandwith, Hermione, and Sheila Stainton. *The National Trust Manual of Housekeeping*. New York: Viking, revised, 1991.

Schlereth, Thomas J. *Artifacts and the American Past*. Nashville, Tenn.: American Association for State and Local History, 1980.

Seale, William. *Recreating the Historic House Interior*. Nashville, Tenn.: American Association for State and Local History, 1979.

Sprigg, June. *Shaker Design*. New York: Whitney Museum of American Art, in association with W. W. Norton., 1986.

———, and David Larkin. *Shaker Life, Work, and Art.* Boston: Houghton-Mifflin, 1987.

Stavenow-Hidemark, Elisabet. *Home Thoughts from Abroad. An Evaluation of the Samdok Homes Pool.* Samdoksekretarietet: Nordiska Museet, Box 27820, S-115 93 Stockholm, Sweden.

Strangstad, Lynette. *A Graveyard Preservation Primer.* Nashville, Tenn.: American Association for State and Local History, 1988.

Stillinger, Elizabeth. *Historic Deerfield.* New York: Dutton Studio Books, 1992.

Thompson, Lawrance. *Robert Frost's Affection for New Hampshire.* Derry, N.H.: Robert Frost Trustees, 1967.

Ward, Gerald W. R., and William N. Hosley, Jr. *The Great River.* Hartford: Wadsworth Atheneum, 1985.

Wilson, Edmund. *Patriotic Gore.* New York: Oxford University Press, 1962.

Wright, Patrick. *On Living in an Old Country: The National Past in Contemporary Britain.* London: Verso, 1985.

The Birds Keep Their Secrets

Aeronautics. "The Wright Biplane, Model 'B.'" September 1911.

Biddle, Wayne. *Barons of the Sky.* New York: Simon & Schuster, 1991.

Crouch, Tom. *The Bishop's Boys: A Life of Wilbur and Orville Wright.* New York: W. W. Norton, 1989.

Geibert, Ron, and Tucker Malishenko, eds. *Early Flight: 1900–1911.* Dayton, Ohio: Landfall Press, 1984.

Hughes, Thomas P. *American Genesis.* New York: Viking, 1989.

———. *Elmer Sperry, Inventor and Engineer.* Baltimore: Johns Hopkins University Press, 1971.

Leslie, Stuart W. *Boss Kettering.* New York: Columbia University Press, 1983.

Mansfield, Howard. "What Makes It Wright?" *Air & Space Smithsonian.* June/July 1994.

———. *Skylark: The Life, Lies, and Inventions of Harry Atwood.* Hanover, N.H.: University Press of New England, 1999.

McFarland, Marvin W. *The Papers of Wilbur and Orville Wright.* Vol. I. New York: McGraw-Hill, 1953.

Napoleao, Aluizio. *Santos-Dumont and the Conquest of the Air.* Rio De Janeiro: National Printing Office, 1945.

Neely, William. *Pilots: The Romance of the Air.* New York: Simon & Schuster, 1991.

Thomas, Hugh. *The Spanish Civil War.* New York: Harper & Row, 1961.

Santos-Dumont, Alberto. *My Airships.* New York: Century Company, 1904.

White, Lynn. *Medieval Technology and Social Change.* Oxford: Clarendon Press, 1962.

Wykeham, Peter. *Santos-Dumont: A Study in Obsession.* New York: Harcourt, Brace & World, 1962.

Young, David, and Neal Callahan. *Fill the Heavens with Commerce.* Chicago Review Press, 1981.

Flow

Adams, Russell B. *King Camp Gillette: The Man and His Wonderful Invention.* Boston: Little, Brown, 1978.

Canedy, Dana. "Where Nothing Lasts Forever." *The New York Times*. April 24, 1998.

Conrad, Peter. *Imagining America*. New York: Oxford University Press, 1980.

Dominguez, Joseph R. *Your Money or Your Life*. New York: Penguin Books, 1993.

Ewen, Stuart. *All Consuming Images*. New York: Basic Books, 1988.

Faggen, Robert, ed. *Striving Towards Being: The Letters of Thomas Merton and Czeslaw Milosz*. New York: Farrar, Straus & Giroux, 1997.

Gillette, King C., and Franklin Fargo. "What To Do With Your Old Razor Blades." *Liberty*. January 15, 1927.

Jackson, J. B. *A Sense of Place, A Sense of Time*. New Haven, Conn.: Yale University Press, 1994.

Mansfield, Howard. *Cosmopolis: Yesterday's Cities of the Future*. New Brunswick, N.J.: Rutgers, 1990.

———. "The Razor King." *American Heritage of Invention and Technology*. Spring 1992

Musil, Robert. *The Man Without Qualities*. New York: Alfred A. Knopf, 1995.

Schor, Juliet B. "Work, Spend, Work, Spend: Is This Any Way To Live?" *The Washington Post*. January 19, 1992.

Sears, John F. *Sacred Places, American Tourist Attractions in the Nineteenth Century*. New York: Oxford University Press, 1989.

Sullivan, Mark. *Our Times*. Vol 1. New York: Charles Scribner's Sons, 1927.

Pulos, Arthur J. *American Design Ethic: A History of Industrial Design to 1940*. Cambridge, Mass.: MIT Press, 1983.

———. *The American Design Adventure, 1940–1975*. Cambridge, Mass.: MIT Press, 1988.

Wegener, Frederick. *Edith Wharton: The Uncollected Critical Writings*. Princeton, N.J.: Princeton University Press, 1996.

A Moment's Bright Flash

Benes, Peter, ed. *New England Meeting House and Church: 1630–1850*. The Dublin Seminar for New England Folklife. Annual Proceedings 1979. Boston University, 1979.

———, and Phillip D. Zimmerman. *New England Meeting House and Church: 1630–1850*. A Loan Exhibition at The Currier Gallery of Art, Manchester, N.H. Boston University, 1979.

Boyer, Paul. *By the Bomb's Early Light*. New York: Pantheon Books, 1985.

Dietrich, Bill. "Nevada Test Site." *The Seattle Times*. Webedition, July 1995.

Donnelly, Marian C. *The New England Meetinghouses of the 17th Century*. Middletown, Con.: Wesleyan University Press, 1968.

The Economist. "Still Ticking at Ground Zero." February 14, 1998.

Fermi, Rachel, and Esther Samra. *Picturing the Bomb: Photos from the Secret World of the Manhattan Project*. New York: Abrams, 1995.

Gallagher, Carole. *American Ground Zero: The Secret Nuclear War*. Cambridge, Mass.: MIT Press, 1993.

Griswold, Wesley S. "Atomic Ruins Reveal Survival Secrets." *Popular Science*. July 1955.

Hancock History Committee. *The Second Hundred Years of Hancock, New Hampshire*. Town of Hancock, N.H., 1979.

Harris, John, ed. "The Second Meetinghouse in Dublin. Extracts from the Second Town Clerk's Book (1807–1828)." Dublin, N.H., Historical Society.

Heywood, William Sweetzer. *History of Westminster, Mass. 1728–1893*. Lowell, Mass.: Vox Populi Press, 1893.

Hill, Gladwin. "Atom Blast Rocks a 'Capsule Town' and Tank Troops." *The New York Times*. May 6, 1955.

———. "Stand-ins Set for Atomic Test." *The New York Times*. April 25, 1955.

———. "'Town' Does Well in Atomic Blast." *The New York Times*. May 7, 1955.

Kasson, John F. *Civilizing the Machine*. New York: Penguin Books, 1977.

Laughner, Patrice. "Common Threads Lives Again!" *Common Threads: The Newsletter of Harrisville, N.H.* December 1997.

Mansfield, Howard. *The City Remembered, The City Celebrated: A Syracuse Sketchbook*. Unpublished ms., 1981.

———. "Memory, Silence & Souvenirs: Saving The Places We Love." Lecture. Colby-Sawyer College, New London, N.H., August 12, 1997.

———. "New Ipswich: A Cautionary Tale." *Monadnock Perspectives* 9, 1, 1988.

———. "Our New Buildings Have Disturbing Things to Say." *The (Oakland) Tribune*. January 28, 1985.

———. "The Paving of Peterborough, The Greening of Keene." *Monadnock Perspectives* 9, 4, 1988.

———. "Putting Walden Woods Back on the Map." *Places: A Quarterly Journal of Environmental Design* 7, 3. Summer 1991.

———. "Small Towns, Large Questions." *Yankee*. March 1998.

———. "The Selling of Small-Town America." *The New York Times*. March 6, 1983.

———. "Sense of Place: What Makes a Village." Lecture. Nantucket Atheneum, Nantucket, Mass., April 24, 1997.

———. "Signs of the Times." *The Boston Globe*. March 21, 1997.

———. "Six Appeal." *International Design*. May/June 1991.

———. "That Village You Love Needs Your Help Now." *Concord Monitor*. February 14, 1997.

———. "Tomorrow's City Is New But Not Improved." *Los Angeles Times*. May 7, 1988.

The New York Times. "Lesson from Nevada." May 7, 1955.

———. "Quake Harm In Assisi is Considered Irreparable." September 28, 1997.

Popular Science. "'Blastproof Building Sets Atomic-Age Style." October 1955.

Preston, John. "The Turnpike Road—Fortune or Folly." Paper prepared for the New Ipswich, N.H., Historical Society.

Reynolds, David S. *Walt Whitman's America*. New York: Alfred A. Knopf, 1995.

Robin, Joseph Jay, and Charles Brown, eds. *Walt Whitman of the New York Aurora*. University Park: Pennslyvania State University Press, 1950.

Ruell, David L. "The 'Round' Meetinghouse of New Hampshire and Vermont." *Historical New Hampshire* 36. Summer/Fall 1981.

Scammell, Derek S., ed. *Nevada Test Site News & Views*. April 1993.

Scully, Daniel V. "Designs on the Future: Autoweek Design Forum." *Autoweek*. January 10, 1994.

Shopshin, William C. *Restoring Old Buildings for Contemporary Uses*. New York: Whitney Library of Design, 1986.

Sinnott, Edmund W. *Meetinghouse and Church in Early New England*. New York: McGraw-Hill, 1963.

Smarz, Laurie J. "The Third Meetinghouse." Hatfield, Mass., Historical Society, December 9, 1982.

Symmes, Richard W., and E. Robert Hornsby. "Elmwood Junction, New Hampshire." *B & M Bulletin*. Fall 1974.

Taylor, Alan. *Liberty Men and The Great Proprietors: The Revolutionary Settlement on the Maine Frontier, 1760–1820*. Chapel Hill: University of North Carolina Press, 1990.

Time. "Rehearsal for Disaster." May 16, 1955.

Webster, Donovan. *Aftermath: The Remnants of War*. New York: Pantheon, 1996.

Wendel, C. H. *American Gas Engines Since 1872*. Sarasota, Fla.: Crestline, 1983.

Winslow, Ola Elizabeth. *Meetinghouse Hill*. New York: Macmillan, 1952.

Young, James Harvey. *The Toadstool Millionaires*. Princeton, N.J.: Princeton University Press, 1961.

Zweig, Paul. *Walt Whitman: The Making of the Poet*. New York: Basic Books, 1984.

Old Home Day, Every Day

Adkins, Nelson F. "Samuel Woodworth." *Dictionary of American Biography*. New York: Charles Scribner's Sons, 1936.

Anderson, Thomas F. "'Old-Home Week' in New England." *New England Magazine*. August 1906.

Brault, Gerard J. *The French-Canadian Heritage in New England*. Hanover, N.H.: University Press of New England, 1986.

Brown, Dona. *Inventing New England*. Washington, D.C.: Smithsonian Institution Press, 1995.

Calhoun, Jack. "Calhoun's Comments." *Lakeside*. New Hampshire Lakes Association, June 1997.

Coad, O.S. "The Plays of Samuel Woodworth." *The Sewanee Review* 27. April 1919.

Concord (N.H.) Monitor. April 1–30, 1899.

Corning, Charles R. "Governor Rollins." *The Granite Monthly*. September 1899.

The Critic. "Samuel Woodworth." January 24, 1829.

Duyckinck, G.L. "Samuel Woodworth." *Cyclopedia of American Literature*. 1855.

Fremont, N.H., Old Home Service. August 15 and 22, 1948.

French, George, ed. *New England: What It Is, and What It Is to Be*. Boston Chamber of Commerce, 1911.

The Granite Monthly. "An Important Historical Event: Newport's 150th Anniversary." August-September 1911.

———. "Old Croydon and Its 'Old Home Day.'" October 1910.

———. "150th Year Celebration, Pittsfield, N.H." November 1921.

———. "Old Home Week." June 1929.

Hilfer, Anthony Channell. *The Revolt from the Village, 1915–1930*. Chapel Hill: University of North Carolina Press, 1969.

Irving, Washington. *The Sketch-Book*. Boston: Allyn and Bacon, 1928.

Mitchell, John Hanson. *Walking Towards Walden*. New York: Addison-Wesley, 1995.

Morris, George P. "The Oak." *The New-York Mirror*. January 7, 1837.

New Hampshire Historical Society. New Hampshire Old Home Week Association reports, scrapbooks, and files. Concord, N.H.

New Hampshire Old Home Week Association. *Old Home Week in New Hampshire*, 1899.

———. *Old Home Week In New Hampshire, 1900*.

———. *Old Home Week In New Hampshire, 1901*.

———. *Old Home Week In New Hampshire, 1902*.

———. *Old Home Week, 1923*.

——. *Old Home Week, 1942.*
——. *Fiftieth Annual Old Home Week in N.H., 1948.*
Quinn, Arthur Hobson. *A History of the American Drama from the Beginning to the Civil War.* New York: Harper & Brothers, 1923.
Rollins, Frank W. *Old Home Week Addresses.* Concord, N.H.: Rumford Press, 1900.
——. "New Hampshire's Opportunity." *New England Magazine.* July 1897.
——. "The Renaissance of New England." *The Independent.* January 10, 1901.
San Francisco Chronicle. "Good-by to Bard." July 11, 1937.
Stilgoe, John R. *Common Landscape of America, 1580 to 1845.* New Haven, Conn.: Yale University Press, 1982.
——. "The Wildering of Rural New New England 1850–1950." *Proceedings of the New England-St. Lawrence Valley Geographical Society* 10. October 1980.
Stocking, Kathleen. *Letters from the Leelanau.* Ann Arbor: University of Michigan Press, 1990.
Taft, Kendall B. *Minor Knickerbockers.* New York: American Book, 1947.
Turner, Frederick. *Spirit of Place: The Making of an American Literary Landscape.* San Francisco: Sierra Club Books, 1989.
Wilson, Harold Fisher. *The Hill Country of Northern New England.* New York: Columbia University Press, 1936
Woodworth, Frederick A., ed. *The Poetical Works of Samuel Woodworth.* 2 vols. New York: Charles Scribner, 1861.
Woodworth, Samuel. "Memoirs of a Sensitive Man About Town." *New-York Mirror.* 1833–1834.
——. *The Poems, Odes, Songs, and Other Metrical Effusions.* New York: Abraham Asten and Matthias Lopez, 1818.

The Lost Language of Villages

Dubos, Rene. *The Wooing of the Earth.* Scribners, 1980.
Dunning, Joan. *Secrets of the Nest.* Boston: Houghton Mifflin, 1994.
Mansfield, Howard. "To Make A Village." *The Boston Globe Magazine.* July 14, 1996.
Reps, John. *Town Planning in Frontier America.* Princeton, N.J.: Princeton University Press, 1969.

Solace on the Block

Bailey, Emma. *Sold to the Lady in the Green Hat.* New York: Dodd, Mead, 1962.
Learmount, Brian. *A History of the Auction.* London: Barnard & Learmount, 1985.
Mansfield, Howard. "Pound 'Em! Pluck 'Em!" *Yankee.* May 1994.

Repose

Benedikt, Michael. *For an Architecture of Reality.* New York: Lumen Books, 1987.
Brooke, James. "A Move to Rid Parks of Snowmobiles." *The New York Times.* February 7, 1999.
Citizens Resisting Expansion of Military Use of Our Airspace. "Air Force Bombing Flights Over Taos." http://laplaza.org/~totem/mof.html. April 1, 1998.

Curtiss, Glenn H., and Augustus Post. *The Curtiss Aviation Book.* New York: Frederick A. Stokes, 1912.

Doherty, Tony. "Answer That Phone!" Tony Doherty file. Glenn Curtiss Museum, 8419 Route 54, Hammondsport, N.Y.

Frankel, Adam S., and Chris Clark. "Marine Mammal Research Program: Results from Over a Year of Acoustic Transmissions." May 14, 1997. The ATOC Homepage. http://atocdb.ucsd.edu/

Jones, Howard Mumford, and Walter B. Rideout. *Letters of Sherwood Anderson.* Boston: Little, Brown, 1953.

Matthrews, Mark. "Snowmobiles Disturbing the Peace in National Parks." *The Washington Post.* March 1, 1997.

Meadows, Donella. "Vroom-Vroom Here, Vroom-Vroom There." *The Keene Sentinel.* March 23, 1998.

Montgomery, Sy. "From Sea to Noisy Sea." *Animals.* March/April 1997.

Picard, Max. *The World of Silence.* Chicago: Henry Regnery, 1952.

U.S. Department of the Interior/National Park Service. *Report on Effects of Aircraft Overflights on the National Park System.* July 1995.

Von Durckheim, Karlfried Graf. *The Japanese Cult of Tranquility.* New York: Samuel Weiser, 1974.

The Whale-Watching Web. "US Navy Sonar System Threaten Marine Mammals." www.physics.helsinki.fi/whale/action/Ifa02.html. April 1, 1998.

Woodward, Calvin. "So Much for Silence." *The Keene Sentinel.* April 8, 1997.

Buzzland

Csikszentmihalyi, M., and E. Rochberg-Halton. *The Meaning of Things.* Cambridge: Cambridge University Press, 1981.

Hart, Moss. *Act One, An Autobiography.* New York: Random House, 1959.

Liebling, A. J. *The Press.* New York: Ballantine Books, 1961.

Mending

Borowitz, Eugene B. *Renewing the Covenant.* Philadelphia: Jewish Publication Society, 1991.

Dan, Joseph. *Gershom Scholem and the Mystical Dimension of Jewish History.* New York: New York University Press, 1988.

——. *Jewish Mysticism and Jewish Ethics.* Seattle: University of Washington Press, 1986.

Fackenheim, Emil C. *To Mend the World.* New York: Schocken Books, 1982.

Scholem, Gershom. *Major Trends in Jewish Mysticism.* New York: Schocken Books, 1946.

——. *On the Kabbalah and Its Symbolism.* New York: Schocken Books, 1965.

——. *Sabbatai Sevi: The Mystical Messiah, 1626–1676.* Princeton, N.J.: Princeton University Press, 1973.

An Arkload of Noahs

Bailey, Lloyd R. *Noah: The Person and the Story in History and Tradition.* Columbia, S.C.: University of South Carolina Press, 1989.

Bush, Donald J. *The Streamlined Decade.* New York: George Braziller, 1975.

Crouse, Chuck. "B & M 6000: A New Era in New England Railroading." *B & M Bulletin.* June 1985.

Mansfield, Howard. "Agent of Change." *International Design.* November/December 1988.

——. "The Unfinished Tapestry." *Yankee.* March 1998.

Meikle, Jeffrey. *Twentieth Century Limited.* Philadelphia: Temple University Press, 1979.

Morrell, Robert S., and R. Stoning, Jr. *Winds of Imagination.* New York: Newcomen Society of the United States, 1990.

Papanek, Victor. *The Green Imperative.* New York: Thames & Hudson, 1995.

——. *Design for Human Scale.* New York: Van Nostrand Reinhold, 1983.

——. *Design for the Real World.* 1971. Reprinted, New York: Van Nostrand Reinhold, 1984.

Steiner, Ralph, and Caroline Steiner, eds. *In Spite of Everything, Yes.* Albuquerque: University of New Mexico Press, 1986.

Acknowledgments

For their interviews, I thank: Peter Acker, Maryann Arrien, Emma Bailey, Terry Barlow, Jack Calhoun, Randy Cook, Doug Cooper, Abbott Lowell Cummings, Doug and Ruth Driscoll, Ray Hamilton, David Howard, Kristine Larsen, Paul Levasseur, Stephen Mack, Col. Ken Martin, Ralph McCutcheon, Donlyn Meyer, Robert Morrell, Sr., Robert Morse, Waine Morse, Dave Mullin, Don Pensa, Daniel V. Scully, Stephen W. Slyvia, Robert M. Stevens, William Sullivan, Linda Weidman, Harold Yeaton, and Charles Young.

For allowing to me to join up with them at Antietam, special thanks to Mike Sebor and the Sixth New Hampshire Volunteer Infantry Historical Association: Robert Corrette, Robert Duffy, Alan Gross, Roger Joly, Michael Ryder, Nancy Sebor, James Sutherland, and Walter Sy.

For research help: Ellen Derby, Kirk House, Robert M. Oksner, Steve Sherman, and the organizers of Restoration '93, December 6–8, Boston.

I thank two philosophy professors for their discussions of Heraclitus and Plutarch: Dr. Beth Preston (tenured), and Roger Eastman (happily retired). Visits with David Adams of Adams and Roy in Portsmouth, N.H., to discuss preservation were refreshing. David H. Watters' thoughts about the Robert Frost farm were helpful.

I thank Eric Aldrich and Dwayne Denehy for their tour of Elmwood Junction. For assembling a masterful survey of the New England meetinghouse, I thank Robert B. Stephenson, coordinator of the conference on Meetinghouses, Steeples, Tower Clocks & Weathervanes, June 14, 1996.

For their comments at an early reading of the manuscript, I thank Dan Chartrand, Mary and Tasha Garland, Paul and Robbie Hertneky, Robert and Judith Oksner, and Elizabeth Marshall Thomas.

I received quite a few thoughtful letters about *In the Memory House*. A few of these comments helped set me on the course for *The Same Ax, Twice* —in particular, those of Hanna Stephenson and L. Phillips Runyon III.

For the gift of optimism, I thank Leona Dona and Patryc Wiggins.

Once again I owe much to my agent Christina Ward, and to my wife and editor Sy Montgomery.

I thank these people for their help. The errors are mine, which is the glory of it.

ABOUT THE AUTHOR

Writing about preservation, architecture, and American history, Howard Mansfield has contributed to *The New York Times, American Heritage, The Washington Post, Historic Preservation, Yankee,* and other publications. Mansfield has explored issues of preservation in three of his previous books, including *In the Memory House,* of which *The Hungry Mind Review* said, "Now and then an idea suddenly bursts into flame, as if by spontaneous combustion. One instance is the recent explosion of American books about the idea of place. . . . But the best of them, the deepest, the widest-ranging, the most provocative and eloquent is Howard Mansfield's *In the Memory House.*"

He is on the advisory board of the Monadnock Institute of Nature, Place and Culture, and chair of the Hancock Town Library Trustees, and an occasional guest on radio and TV shows commenting on issues of historic preservation.

He and his wife, the writer Sy Montgomery, live in a one-hundred-year-old house that they have left mostly alone.

Library of Congress Cataloging-in-Publication Data

Mansfield, Howard.
    The same ax, twice: restoration and renewal in a throwaway age / by Howard Mansfield.
        p.   cm.
    Includes bibliographical references.
    ISBN 1–58465–028–1 (alk. paper)
    1. Historic preservation—United States.   2. United States—History—Philosophy.   1. Title.
E159 .M37   2000
973—dc21   99–56170